ISLAM

DISMANTLED

The Mental Illness of
Prophet Muhammad

By

Sujit Das

With a Preface by Ali Sina

In the interests of keeping cost as low as possible for the readers and to
raise public awareness of the true nature of Muhammad's prophethood and
support, the Author decided to sell this book on a non-profit basis.

Publisher: Felibri.com
felibri@gmail.com
Publication date: January 2012
Distributed by Ingram Book Group

Islam Dismantled / by Sujit Das.
Includes index.
ISBN 978-1-926800-06-6
1. Muhammad, Prophet, d. 632--Psychology.
2. Islam—Controversial literature. I. Title.

*****

Picture on the cover: The flight of Muhammad and Abu Bakr to Medina. Color lithograph by A.C. Michael. (Original in a private collection)

*****

Dedicated to the victims of Islamic jihad worldwide

Your sufferings are not forgotten

*****

One of the most interesting and harmful delusions to which men and nations can be subjected is that of imagining themselves special instruments of the Divine will.

Bertrand Russell

There are no misunderstandings in nature; they are only to be found in the realms that man calls 'understanding'.

Carl Jung

Islam Dismantled

CHAPTER 3: MUHAMMAD'S STRANGE MINDSET   67

Preface
By Ali Sina

We know about no other founder of a major religion as much as we know about the prophet of Islam. The tales about Moses, Jesus, Buddha, Krishna and Zoroaster are shrouded in myths, but the stories about Muhammad are detailed. There are hundreds of thousands of anecdotes about everything he said and did, how he ate, how he dressed, how he spoke, walked, cleaned his teeth and his private parts, what made him angry and how he reacted to criticism, how he dealt with his detractors, and countless other narratives that allow us to have a fairly accurate image of his personality and character.

In his book, *The 100: A Ranking of the Most Influential Persons in History*, Michael Hart places Muhammad at the very top. Yet, despite being the most influential person in history and the fact that there is so much detail about his life available, he has remained a mystery to virtually everyone, both the believers and unbelievers.

Opinions about Muhammad vary. There are those who believe he was the noblest person who ever walked on Earth and those who think he was a sadist murderer. It is hard to find any other personage in history that is so highly esteemed by one group of people and scorned by another. What is the truth? Was Muhammad a prophet or a liar? How can opinions about one man vary so diametrically? There are people who don't believe in Jesus, Buddha or Krishna, and yet they don't revile them. What makes Muhammad different? Why his detractors consider him a villain?

There is no doubt that Muhammad was convinced of his status as a prophet. You can't fool so many people if you are in doubt yourself. Therefore, it can't be said that he was lying. Yet, it can be easily demonstrated that Muhammad was making up his religion to suit his needs while at the same time he was convinced of what he was saying. There are many anecdotes about Muhammad that show he believed in his prophetic mission. At the same time there is ample evidence that what he said was not true. How that can that be possible? How can a person lie and believe in his own lies?

To answer this question we have to study the psychology of our subject. No study of Muhammad is complete without taking into account his mental makeup. It is by understanding his mind that we can understand him and then the whole picture becomes clear to us.

Muhammad had a unique sense of entitlement. He raided villages and towns, massacred thousands of unarmed people, chopped and burned their trees, looted their properties, raped their women, enslaved their children, tortured them in the most inhumane ways, and yet, he was convinced to be the best of the creation, an excellent example (Q.33:21), exalted above other prophets in degrees (Q.2:253), the preferred one (Q.17:55), a mercy to the worlds (Q.21:107), and the one who has risen to a praised estate (Q.17:79), which he said none but he would receive and that is to act as God's counselor on the Day of Judgment. In one hadith he is reported saying that if it were not for him God would not have created the universe.

There is a huge gap between Muhammad's claims about himself and his conduct. There is hardly any other person whose claims and deeds are so diametrically opposed to each other. His followers focus on his claims. They believe in his words. His detractors focus on his deeds. There lies the discrepancy.

How can one be so divorced from reality to believe the universe is created for him and that he is the best the world has ever produced while engaged in the most despicable crimes of theft, rape, assassination, pedophilia and genocide?

In this book, Sujit Das unravels this mystery. He does not just tell the story, but he unveils the story behind the story. He analyzes the prophet of Islam from a perspective that few have. Das delves into the psychological impulses that controlled Muhammad and made him the phenomenon that he became.

Sahih Muslim (4: 2127) reports a hadith narrated by 'Aisha. She said, one night when the Prophet was spending the night in her apartment, he got up in the middle of night when he thought she was asleep, took hold of his mantle slowly and put on the shoes slowly, and opened the door and went out and then closed it lightly. "I covered my head," continues Aisha, "put on my veil and tightened my waist wrapper, and then went out following his steps till he reached Baqi' (the cemetery). He stood there and he stood for a long time. He then lifted his hands three times, and then returned and I also returned. He hastened his steps and I also hastened my steps. He ran and I too ran. He came (to the house) and I also came (to the house). I, however, preceded him and I entered (the house), and as I lay down in the bed, he (the Holy Prophet) entered the (house), and said: Why is it, O Aisha, that you are out of breath? I said: There is nothing. He said: Tell me or the Subtle and the Aware would inform me. I said: Messenger of Allah, may my father and mother be ransom for you, and then I told him (the whole story). He said: Was it the darkness (of your shadow) that I saw in front of me? I said: Yes. He struck me on the chest which caused me pain, and then said: Did you think that Allah and His Apostle would deal unjustly with you?" Then Muhammad told Aisha that Gabriel had commanded him to go to the inhabitants of Baqi' (to those lying in the graves) and beg pardon for them.

Hadiths like this abound, which confirm Muhammad was sincere in his belief. The story makes little sense. Why would the Almighty command his prophet to go to the cemetery in the middle of the night to supplicate Him to pardon the dead? If He wants to pardon them why would He need someone to lobby for it? But the fact that Muhammad wakes up in such odd hours and goes to the cemetery surreptitiously, tells us that he probably saw a ghost that he thought was Gabriel and the experience must have appeared real to him.

This story is irrational. It is not reasonable to believe that God would make such a silly request from his prophet. "Go to the cemetery and pray to Me (the God) so I forgive the dead," makes no sense. Yet, Muhammad must have been convinced of it to do it. This enigma can be solved only if we study his psychology. This story and many others like it tell us that the prophet of Islam had vivid hallucinations that to him seemed real.

This book does not use technical jargons. Das writes in plain language that can be understood by everyone. His analysis is crucial to understand Muhammad. He presents ample evidence to show that the prophet of Islam suffered from malignant narcissism and neurotic disorder. He had hallucinations that he thought were real, like when he claimed that he had ascended to heaven and visited the dead prophets.

Das argues that much of the behaviors of Muslims, including terrorism, hooliganism and their paranoia are deeply rooted in their prophet's psychology. Muslims do what Muhammad did. They want to be like him.

*Ali Sina is the founder of Faith Freedom International, the grassroots movement of ex-Muslims. He is also the author of **Understanding Muhammad: A Psychobiography of Allah's Prophet**, the book that inspired many Muslims to awake and question their cherished faith.*

A Note to the Readers

"Truth can never be told so as to be understood and not be believed."
William Blake (1757 - 1827)

Muhammad, the self-proclaimed Prophet of Islam, is known as the "Apostle of Peace" by the Muslims. However, the truth is just opposite. Muhammad was an extremely cruel man whose entire prophetic life was based on victimizing innocents and indulging in mindless violence, carnage and massacre. He was a man who destroyed peace wherever he went, and in its place brought terror, bloodshed and death.

Islam stands or falls on the credibility of Muhammad on which we do not have single evidence but unfathomable doubts because his conduct was immoral. But he successfully twisted the sense of morality of his followers, distorted their sense of "humanness" and linked "doing good" and "a service to God" to all ungodly things. Briefly, he had given a sacred aura to crime and terrorism.

Was Muhammad truthful and sincere when he claimed the title of Prophet? Or, was he a vulgar imposter who posed as a Prophet with his eyes upon a throne from the beginning? Where can we find some concrete evidence that Qur'anic revelations were not Muhammad's delusions or his conscious fabrications? Where is the "divine" verification for the "divine" revelations? If we put the Qur'an in chronological order and correlate it with the context of Muhammad's life as was reported in Sira, Sunna and Hadith; we find Allah mirrored Muhammad's character. Allah was too dumb to be God and too immoral to be divine.

In this treatise I have no intention of testing God. I just want to test Muhammad's claim to the title of messenger of God because I cannot blindly accept his claim. Throughout the recorded history of humankind, many imposters have posed as "god-man" with well-packaged gimmickry and fooled us. Muhammad may be a true Prophet or he may be an imposter. We must test him to see which he is. Anyone who claims to be a Prophet must be prepared to have his prophecy tested.

This treatise is a critical investigation, where I have probed deep into the strange fantasy world of Muhammad not only in search of an answer but also to unfold many mysteries of Islam and Muslims. First, I had looked at Muhammad through the spectacle of blind faith and then through the spectacle of science, logic and modern development of psychological and mental disorder studies. This document contains the findings of my investigation.

This document is heavy reading. I ask for readers' patience on this.

Sujit Das

Mumbai (India)
01.01.2012

About the Author

I live at Mumbai, the commercial city of India. Because of the distinctive nature of my job, I travel a lot, mostly abroad.

After the destruction of the twin towers of WTC, my interest grew in Islam. During those initial days I was confused. Muslims all over the world point their fingers at Western society and comment on how degenerate Westerners have no sense of family and that as a consequence, crime, immorality and violence are rampant all over the West. But the truth is completely different. The highest incidences of violent crimes such as murder, rape, child molestation, dismemberment and armed robbery happen in Islamic countries. In Non-Islamic countries, wherever terrorist and subversive activities take place, one is sure to find the presence of Muslims. Slowly I took it a serious hobby to make an in-depth study of Islam. My initial questions were,

1. What exactly is it that makes Muslims so viciously engaged in violent crimes against the rest of humanity?
2. Why are all terrorist activities that target innocent non-Muslim victims always abetted by Muslim terrorists?
3. What is it that makes the Muslim mind so subject to criminality and the display of such violent tendencies right from his/her childhood days?

Shortly I concluded that Islam cannot be a divine religion, rather it is a "mind control devise". Prophet Muhammad, the founder of Islam, was not a Prophet of God, rather a charlatan and Qur'an is not a holy book but a terrorist manual. However I continued my study on Islam and tried to examine the Qur'an to have a better understanding of its author. After studying Qur'an and Shahi Hadith collections, I came to the conclusion that the Prophet was suffering from a mental illness and he was delusional. So I dipped into psychology books to understand the nature of his mental illness. After spending a couple of years with the books of psychology and psychotherapy I realized that Muhammad was suffering from Malignant Narcissism and Neurotic Disorder.

I have absolutely no hate for the Muslims. In fact many of my close friends are Muslims. How can I hate the Muslims, they are the first victims of Islam. Every Muslim is an abductee from the civilization in which he once belonged and put into a mental slavery. Same diagnosis is applicable to the Arabs also. Though they did not have to adopt foreign customs and language, which made the transition to Islam less disruptive, they too were cut off from their original pagan culture.

I hate the ideology which enslaves the Muslims and make them terrorists. My stanch enemy is Islam and not the Muslims. I want to dismantle this doctrine of hate and murder. My intention is not only to confront Islamic jihad but at the same time to rescue the Muslims from the evil grip of Islam. I want to see the Muslims returning back within the fold of humanity by rejecting Islam.

Introduction

"Muslims need to write an honest biography of the Prophet that does not shun the truth, least of all cover it up with the dishonest subterfuge of condescending the Western scholars".

Ibn Warraq (2000, p. 21)

Towards the beginning of last century, there was a rising interest among the Western scholars to investigate the origins of Islam and its founder, the Prophet Muhammad. These scholars had used highest standard of historical scholarship available at that time. Their main aim was to collect authentic information about Muhammad and the rise of early Islam by carefully separating the facts from fictions. In some ways the research on Muhammad was inspired by a similar type of investigation of Christianity made famous by Albert Schweitzer's work *The Quest of the Historical Jesus*.

All the religions except Islam have their origins covered in mystery. Islam, as Renan (Warraq, 2000, p. 15) used the famous phrase, *"[Islam] was born in the full light of history"*, stands firm and clear in front of us. Unlike semi-mythical religious figures, e.g., Moses, Christ, Adi Shankara, Buddha or Mahavira Jain; the founder of Islam is as well known to us as that of any other historical personality. Several thousand short stories about Muhammad were collected in the Shahi Hadith.

In view of the above; though it appears to be comparatively easier to write an analytical history of Islam and its founder, actually it is not so easy, as Spencer (2006, p. 19) commented, *"Most Western non-Muslims know virtually nothing about the Prophet of Islam"*. But the question is, how many practicing Muslims know their Prophet well? Has an honest biography of Muhammad yet been written? There are enough pious and totally unobjective traditions of Muhammad preserved by the Muslim religious community, but what is lacking in these sources is honesty. Even today, numerous works in Arabic and other Muslim majority languages appear each year. These books try to portray Muhammad as a holy man, a seer, visionary and miracle worker; which are far away from truth. The reason, no Muslim can write an honest biography of their Prophet, is that the biography of Muhammad is a subject that is taboo, and as Rodinson (1981, p. 24) commented, *"... is permitted only when written as apologetic and edifying literature"*. Hence, objective historical research on Muhammad has long been severely handicapped both by the resistance of the Muslim societies to Western analysis of their sacred traditions and by the apologetic approaches of many Western scholars who had compromised their investigation for fear of offending Muslim sensibilities. Therefore, most of the books today tell us about Muhammad of faith not the Muhammad of history.

However in recent times, thanks to all the Muslim, ex-Muslim and non-Muslim writers; a lot of scholarly work had been produced *"which could offend certain readers"*. These freethinkers and scholars have endangered their lives by revealing to the public information about Muhammad and Islam that public had never heard before. For this reason; Theo Van Gogh was shot and stabbed to death in Netherlands and his associate Ayaan Hirsi Ali had to live with bodyguards and armored cars (Ali,

2007, p. xii), Taslima Nasrin has been living in exile since 1994, Faraj Foda was shot dead in front of his office in Cairo, Nasr Hamid Abu Zayd fled out of Egypt to escape the death penalty, and Sayyid Mahmoud al-Qimni was forced to recant all his writings. Unfortunately, before the outside world would get a chance to read their works, these writers were silenced through murder, terrorization, and death-threat, and their writings were banned in the Muslim world (Ahmed, 2006, p. ix). But who can stop the truth from spreading?

With the help of these scholars, who had broken the myth of Muhammad and exposed the Muhammad of history, we can trace Muhammad's fluctuations of thought year by year, his actions, his achievements, family life, abnormal sexual behavior, strength and weaknesses. If we compare our findings with that of modern development of psychological studies, the image of Muhammad that surfaces, is far away from any holy religious figure but that of a person who was suffering from severe mental illness. And if we probe further deep into the mystery of Allah and carefully make a distinction between superstition and science, we have hardly any doubt left that it was his mental illness and hallucinatory experiences which were solely responsible for creating Allah, Qur'an and Islam altogether.

Chapter1: The Flashback of a False Prophet

1.1: Muhammad's Strange Prophetic Claim

The religion of Islam was developed from the prophetic claim, preaching and life of Muhammad early in the seventh century of the Christian era. During that time, the old Arabian paganism was in a process of slow disintegration, and Judaism and Christianity were widely gaining popularity. Several self-proclaimed Prophets had arisen with various degrees of success in convincing people. In the beginning Muhammad was such a self-proclaimed Prophet, but with time he successfully synchronized certain basic elements of Judaism and Christianity with the pagan practices and added some nationalistic Arab pride and it has become a world religion today.

From the authentic Islamic sources it appears that Muhammad thought of himself as in the succession of the Old Testament men of faith who was sent on a divine mission by the one and only God, Allah. Throughout the Qur'an he pretended that his mission is the sequel of the previous Semitic Prophets. Like Noah, Jonah, and Elijah, he preached a religious message in the name of this Supreme Lord; like Moses he issued legislation in His name; and like Abraham, he was not only a maintainer of righteousness but also the founder of a community of the righteous. But unlike Christianity, his religious endeavor was an utter failure unless he was able to draw the sword and use it successfully to impose his religion on others.

Muhammad declared himself a Prophet of Allah when he was about forty years old. Bukhari's Hadith (1.1.3) recorded Muhammad's first experience with the angel Gabriel that was less heavenly and more demonic. Once in the cave of Hira the angel Gabriel came to him with some written messages from Allah and asked him to read. Muhammad replied, *"I do not know how to read"*. Three times Muhammad expressed his inability to read, but Gabriel forcefully gave him the message of Allah – the famous first revelations of the Qur'an of the Surah ninety-six.

In the name of thy Lord Who created (Q: 96.1),

Created man from a clot (Q: 96.2).

Read: And thy Lord is the Most Bounteous (Q: 96.3)

Who taught (to write) with the pen (Q: 96.4)

Taught man that which he knew not (Q: 96.5)

The fact that Allah's messages started descending upon Muhammad in a violent way is entirely sufficient for a rational person to have doubt on the truthfulness of the Qur'anic revelations. Surprisingly, Muhammad himself was the first person to doubt the genuineness of the revelations. Bewildered and terrorized, he hurried back to his wife; "*What's wrong with me?*" he asks his wife. Just as kids hide under the covers when they are afraid of monsters in the dark, Muhammad told his wife to wrap him in a blanket. He did not want to see the cause of terror again, and thought that he was either going mad or possessed by an evil spirit.

After this first revelation, Allah was silent for about three years. Muhammad was so sad that he wanted to commit suicide. Several times he intended to throw himself from the top of high mountains but every time he went up the top in order to throw himself down, Gabriel would appear before him and said, "*O Muhammad! You are indeed Allah's Apostle in truth*". This is how Muhammad began to believe that he was a messenger of God – a messenger of such a demonic God whose influence caused him to attempt suicide.

How many Muslims are aware of Muhammad's suicide attempts? Few Islamic leaders will teach this to their fellow Muslims because it casts a stain upon Muhammad; it brings doubt to his trustworthiness and the credibility of his assumed "heavenly" experience. Some Muslims deny the sources of the story while others, knowledgeable about the sources, respond by saying that the shock of the experience caused him to attempt suicide.

Allah confirms in the Qur'an (33.40) that Muhammad was the seal of the Prophets. According to Islamic sources (Muslim: 30.5790; Sunnan Abu Dawud: 32.4071; Bukhari: 1.4.189), Muhammad had a big mole as big as a pigeon's egg on his back between the shoulders which he claimed as the proof of his prophethood. There is no religious scripture which confirms that a mole between the shoulders is a sign of prophethood. What he showed as a proof of Allah's seal was a physical defect which anyone can have. There is no divinity in this. It is simply beyond the capacity of a logical thinker how this is supposed to be one of the proofs that convince people of Muhammad's prophethood!

Muhammad gave no concrete proof of his heavenly appointment. Did he lie shamelessly to fool the Arab pagans? Was he under delusion? The validity of Islam depends absolutely on the reliability of Muhammad. If there is no solid reason to conclude that Muhammad was the true messenger of God, we may reasonably suppose that Islam is false. If we can prove that Muhammad was untrustworthy, Islam self-destructs. The scholars, who are most familiar with Arabic sources and have clear understanding of the life and time of Muhammad, e.g., Margoliouth, Hurgronje, Lammens, Arthur Jeffery, Clair-Tisdall, Andrew Rippin, Ibn Warraq and Caetani, are the most decisive against Muhammad's prophetic claim. The more we read their valuable research works, the more we find it difficult to disagree with them. Muhammad declared that lying is acceptable if it is used to propagate the cause of Islam. This particular statement should make us wonder how often Muhammad took advantage of this principle while claiming his title of a Prophet and preaching his message.

If we take Qur'an as the primary foundation of Muhammad's prophethood, the doubt is still not dispelled at all. We need to ascertain how firm ground does it provide. There are serious doubts about the trustworthiness of Qur'an also. Like Muhammad's prophetic claim, Qur'an itself is self-declarative – there is no external proof. This book describes itself by various generic terms, comments, explains, distinguishes, puts itself in contrast with other religious books and claims to be holy. The Qur'anic claims are great, but what is miserable is that, this supposed to be holy book fails to prove either Muhammad's prophethood or its divine origin. Ultimately, it becomes a circular reasoning. Qur'an is God's word because Muhammad said so, and Muhammad was God's Prophet because Qur'an says so. But circular reasoning is a logical fallacy. We are not happy with this.

1.2: The Embarrassment of Satanic Verses

Traditional Islamic sources admit that Muhammad was at one time inspired by Satan to put some verses into the Qur'an. When Muhammad first began preaching in Mecca, he thought that the Meccans would accept his religion. But the Meccans were not receptive to him which made Muhammad angry, and he started taunting them for years by insulting their religion and Gods. Meccans refused all dealings with him and his followers. Eventually to appease the Meccans, Muhammad recited the following Qur'anic verses,

> *Have you then considered the al-Lat and al-Uzza and Manat, the third, the last ... these are the exalted Gharaniq (a high flying bird) whose intercession is approved.* (Q: 53.19-20)

Al-Lat, al-Uzza and Manat were some of the local idols worshipped in Mecca. Previously Muhammad had spoken against them in his monotheist preaching but now he recited that their "*intercession is approved*". This made the Meccans very pleased and the boycott was lifted shortly. However, soon Muhammad realized that by acknowledging the local idols al-Lat, al-Uzza and Manat he had made a terrible blunder. He had undermined his own position that of the sole intermediary between Allah and the people, and by doing so he made his new religion indistinguishable from pagan beliefs and hence redundant. So he retracted and said the two verses acknowledging pagan idols were satanic verses, i.e., the verses inspired by Lucifer, the Biblical Satan. This was Muhammad's most embarrassing moment. Islam crumbled in the wake of the Prophet's satanic indulgence. He desperately tried to make amends for the satanic verses and recited the following verse.

> *Surely Allah does not forgive that anything should be associated with Him, and He forgives what is besides this to whom He pleases; and whoever associates anything with Allah, he indeed strays off into a remote error.*(Q: 4.116)

Subsequently, the relevant verses were also modified with the final form what is now in the modern Qur'an.

> *Have ye thought upon Al-Lat and Al-'Uzza.* (Q: 53.19)

> *And another, the third (goddess), Manat?* (Q: 53.20)

> *What! for you the male sex, and for Him, the female?* (Q: 53.21)

> *Behold, such would be indeed a division most unfair!* (Q: 53.22)

Many of his followers left him on this account realizing that Muhammad was either making up the Qur'an or he was delusional (Sina, 2008, p. 16). Muhammad had to run away from Mecca in shame. The shame of defeat was so much that Muhammad and Abu Bakr had to flee through window. On their way out of town, both had to hide in a cave for fear the Meccans would find them (Winn, 2004, p. 587). Tabari and Ishaq wrote,

> *When the Messenger decided upon departure, he went to Bakr and the two of them left by a window in the back of Abu's house and went to a cave in Thawr, a mountain below Mecca.* (Ishaq: 223)

> *The Messenger came back to Mecca and found that its people were more determined to oppose him and to abandon his religion, except for a few weak people who believed in him.* (Tabari: VI.118)

However, after this blunder Muhammad was more careful not to make the mistake again. He just hammered a nail into his own prophetic coffin. Muslims are very uncomfortable with the satanic verses episode, and this had been the subject of endless and bitter controversy (Walker, 2002, p. 111). But there is no reason to reject this incident. It was recorded by devout Muslims; like, al-Wikidi, al-Baydawi, al-Zamakshari, Tabari, Ibn Ishaq, Ibn Hisham, Ibn Sa'd and Bukhari. It is most unlikely that such a story would have been fabricated by all of them. While this event is well documented in Islamic sources, current day Islamic leaders rarely tell Muslims or the general public about it. We can make three logical conclusions from this satanic verses incident. First; a Qur'anic verse can be modified or deleted at a later date. Second; it casts a shadow over the veracity on Muhammad's entire claim to be a Prophet, and finally; Satan proved that Qur'an is not a miracle. Qur'an challenges, *"produce a Surah of the like thereof, and call your witness beside Allah if ye are truthful"* (Q: 2.23); Satan took the challenge and did it. Did Muhammad carefully planned a ploy to win the hearts of the Meccans, or was it his subconscious mind that had suggested to him a sure formula which provided a practical road to unanimity? We will look for an answer in subsequent chapters.

1.3: The Traditional Sources

In the West, the critics of Muhammad are quick to claim that he was either possessed by demons or he was a conscious fraud, or he was under severe delusion. We have no concrete evidence to support one claim and discard other but at least we all agree to the point that there was certainly something wrong with Muhammad. The Western scholars judge the Prophet by the standards of human morality and conscience. But Muslims' thinking is different. They have accepted Muhammad as a "superior being" and "the mercy of God among mankind" (Sina, 2008, p. 6). Therefore further criticism is unnecessary.

Though Muslims dismiss all attacks on their faith as anti-Islamic polemic and a calculated and deliberate misrepresentation of their religion from Christian prejudice and Zionist-instigated ill-will, the irony is that, even if we reject and leave aside all these Western scholars and depend only on authentic traditional sources for information, we still cannot find anything which suggests that Muhammad was a superior being or the mercy of God. Instead, we have thousands of accounts that do portray him a psychopath criminal. But, are the traditional sources reliable?

1.3.1: The Reliability of Traditional Sources

Our knowledge and understanding of early Islam and its founder mainly rests on the writings we call Sira, al-Maghazi, Qur'an, Qur'anic exegesis (Tafsir), Tabari's history, and Shahi Hadith collections.

Sira means "biography"; likewise *Sirat Rasul Allah* is the biography of the messenger of Allah written by Ibn Ishaq (704 - 767(?)). This is the earliest life of Muhammad of which we have any trace. Ishaq was one of the main authorities on the life and times of the Prophet. He had a very high reputation (e.g., al-Zuhri spoke of him as *"the most knowledgeable man in Maghazi"*). Ishaq's biography provides the sole account of Muhammad's life and the formation of Islam written within 200 years of his death. This work is very important for the researchers not only because it is the earliest biography but also for the reason that Ishaq was a free thinker and he was free from any influences of later idealizing or myth-making tendencies. While the character, message, and deeds portrayed within its pages are the direct opposite of Christ's and his disciples, the Sira's chronological presentation is similar in style to the Christian Gospels. His work contains much information of a character that is devastatingly unfavorable to the Prophet.

Al-Maghazi is the early Muslim military expeditions or raiding parties in which Muhammad took part in the Medinan period. But this term seems to have been more or less often used synonymously with term Sira.

The history of al-Tabari (Abu Ja'far Muhammad Ibn Jarir al-Tabari) is a mine of information for historical and critical research by Western scholars. This Persian historian was a devout Sunni Muslim, a commentator of the Qur'an and widely traveled. It is believed that he memorized the Qur'an at the age of seven, was a qualified religious leader at eight, and left home for further study at the age of twelve. He had not only devoted much time to history but in mathematics and medicine also. In his history, he did not hesitate to express his independent judgment. He derived much of his material from the oral traditions and literary sources, e.g., the works of al-Wiqidi, Ibn Sa'd, Abu Miknaf and of course Ibn Ishaq.

Qur'an's claim to divine origin rests on the ahadith (plural of Hadith). The books of traditions are the records of what Muhammad did, what he enjoined, what was done in his presence and what he did not forbid. Hadith collections also include the authoritative sayings and doings of his companions. Muhammad was aware that people were taking note of all his casually uttered words and that stories of what he did were being passed around. He was aware of the dangers and warned against the practice because some of his words may get included in the Qur'an by mistake (Brahmachari, 1999, p. 131). But the trend once started could not be stopped and was accelerated after his death (Walker, 2002, p. 172). Hadith contains material from pre-Islamic times also. Much was added to it after Muhammad's death with fresh material with the growth of Islamic empire.

It is true that much of the Hadith collections was fabricated before Imam Bukhari (his full name was Muhammad Ibn Ismail Ibn Ibrahim Ibn al-Mughirah Ibn Bardizbah al-Bukhari) made his compilation; e.g., Ibn Abi-I-Awja (executed 772 for apostasy) confessed before his death that he had fabricated more than 4,000 ahadith, in which he forbade Muslims what was in fact permitted and vice versa and he made Muslims to break the fast when they should have been fasting (Warraq, 2003, p. 45). There are instances where many ahadith were invented to serve the political purposes of the Umayyad, the Abbasids and later dynasties of Caliphs and handing down of the traditions went downwards to the level of a business enterprise as a means of livelihood (Goldziher, 1971, p. 169). Also a large amount of non-Islamic material was drawn into by the compilers which even included sayings of Buddhist wisdom, Roman stories and verses from the Zoroastrians, Jewish and Christian scriptures and even Greek philosophy (Gibb, 1969, p. 51). Shortly the number of ahadith already in circulation and still being invented became unimaginable, as one Muslim authority wrote (Nicholson, 1969, p. 145), *"in nothing do we see pious man more given to falsehood than in the traditions"*. So it was urgently necessary to compile an authentic collection. The best-known and most authoritative compilation is by Bukhari. Bukhari had examined a total of 6,00,000 traditions. He preserved some 7,000 (including repetitions), which means he rejected some 593,000 as inauthentic (Crone, 1987, p. 33). Excluding the repetitions, there remained only about 2760 in total. Second only to Bukhari's collection is the work of Muslim Ibn al-Hajaj, which contains three thousand traditions. These compilations are believed to be Shahi Hadith (authentic traditions).

Regretfully, the above five oldest and most trusted Islamic sources do not portray Muhammad a superior being or any kind of mercy of God among mankind. The sources reveal that he was a thief, a liar, an assassin, a pedophile, a shameless womanizer, a promiscuous husband, a rapist, a mass-murderer, a desert pirate, a warmonger, a spineless coward and a calculating and ruthless tyrant. It is certainly not the character profile of the founder of a true religion.

Moreover, there is no reason to believe that the Bukhari's collections were later corrupted by religious rivalries. Other traditional books were written by pious Muslims, the copies are preserved and certainly it would not be the characteristic of believers to portray their Prophet as a villain. After all Muhammad had promised them paradise in exchange of their acceptance of Islam. How can they malign their beloved Prophet?

Similarly the trustworthiness of Christian sources cannot be doubted either. By the time Muhammad received his first revelation early in the seventh century; Christianity was already an established religion and had been in law of the exclusive faith of the Roman kingdom, the superpower of the Mediterranean for some two centuries. Christianity also had been planted from Ethiopia to Ireland and Morocco to Georgia and in Mesopotamia, i.e., modern Iraq (Fletcher, 2003, pp. 4, 6). The multiplicity and diversity of the Christian texts stands as a proof of an intellectual life of Christendom within the Roman world. In fact this was a new era when this faith was slowly coming out of the religious orthodoxy. As the grip of the Orthodox Church was relaxed, there was a wave of theological deviants and the contemporaneous Christians evaluated Muhammad and his sect as yet another such group which had gone astray. It was unthinkable to them that Islam might be "a new religion" in the strict sense of the term.

The Muslim invaders remained on friendly terms with the Christian populations of the land they conquered. Qur'an (29.45) requires Muslims should respect the Ahl al-Kitab, the people of the book, that is to say the Christians and Jews. Hence we have hardly any doubt on the authenticity of early Christian sources. It was too late for the Christians to realize the true nature of Islam.

1.4: Discrediting Muhammad using Traditional Sources

The original book of Ibn Ishaq is lost to history, and all we know of it is what is quoted from it by the later writers, mainly Ibn Hisham and Tabari. These quotations are fortunately quite reliable. Ibn Hisham edited and abridged Ishaq's work about sixty-five years later. In his edition, Hisham (Guillaume, 1955, p. 691) wrote,

I am omitting things which Ishaq recorded in this book. I have omitted things which are disgraceful to discuss and matters which would distress certain people.

This particular comment speaks volumes. Today we need to know, what are the *"disgraceful to discuss"* topics Hisham omitted from Ishaq's original work and what are the *"matters which would distress certain people"*. We understand Hisham was actually compromising with the truth to save his life, which depended upon not offending the cleric-kings during his time. But he was honest enough to admit that he had compromised with the truth. As Margoliouth (cited Warraq, 2000, p. 340) commented, *"The character attributed to Muhammad in the biography of Ibn Ishaq is exceedingly unfavorable ... for whatever Muhammad does he is prepared to plead the express authorization of the deity. It is however, impossible to find any doctrine which he is not prepared to abandon in order to secure a political end. At different points in his career he abandons the unity of God and his claim to the title of a Prophet. This is a disagreeable picture for the founder of a religion, and it cannot be pleaded that it is a picture drawn by an enemy."*

However, a few modern historians have attempted to recover the lost portion of Ishaq's work by applying the Biblical criteria of "Form and Redaction criticism" (Form criticism is an analysis of literature, particularly the Bible, to discover earlier oral traditions, e.g., stories, legends and myths. Redaction criticism is concerned with when and by what process did a particular section of the Bible reach its final literary form) to the basis historical assemblage of Ishaq.

The pagan Meccans were wise enough not to believe Muhammad's gigantic claim because they had seen many such imposters. There are more than a dozen verses which confirm that Muhammad and the "voice" he had heard were ridiculed by the pagans. They thought that Muhammad was fabricating verses, or in the parlance of those days, he was demon-possessed. The contemporaries of Muhammad called him *majnoon* (lunatic, crazy, possessed by jinn) (Sina, 2008, p. 6) or a soothsayer *kahin*. This is very explicit in the ten Qur'anic verses 15.6, 23.70, 34.8, 34.46, 37.36, 44.14, 52.29, 68.2, 68.51 and 81.22. In a few instances, there are verses 21.5, 36.69, 37.36 and 52.30 where an alternative explanation was given that Muhammad was an ambitious but fanciful poet who had merely invented it all.

To defend himself Muhammad added several references to Biblical Prophets likewise accused of ghost-possession, e.g., earlier Prophets in general (Q: 51.52), Noah (Q: 23.25), Moses (Q: 26.26, 27; 51.39). Let it be on record that the Bible nowhere mentions such an allegation against Noah, Moses or most other Prophets.

The one exception is Hosea, a Prophet apparently unknown to Muhammad, "*They call the man of the spirit a madman*" (Hosea: 9.7). Undoubtedly, Muhammad, whose knowledge of the Bible was only sketchy, was merely projecting his own plight onto Noah and Moses. Muhammad's silly arguments stood on a very slippery ground; something like this – "I am a Prophet but am not acknowledged by my narrow-minded contemporaries, just as the ancient genuine Prophets were not given due recognition either at first instance. Hence I am also a genuine Prophet". Muhammad lost many of his followers on this account.

Bukhari (9.87.111) recorded that Muhammad's prophethood was confirmed by a cousin of Khadija, a Christian convert from Judaism, named, Waraqa Bin Naufal. But Waraqa died mysteriously after few days of confirming his prophethood. The fact that Waraqa was a Christian had been a source of embarrassment to Muslims. Hence they often deny it. Some overenthusiastic Muslim sources say that by recognizing the Prophet Waraqa converted to Islam. However, some modern scholars contend that Waraqa actually rejected Muhammad and the text of Ibn Hisham's version of the Sira was later corrupted (Spencer, 2006, p. 53). There is no account in voluminous Hadith that Waraqa converted to Islam and the details of his mysterious death. From the Hadith collections we can find minutest details of Muhammad's activities and the events of early Muslim communities. The first conversion of a Christian priest would have been a momentous event. Waraqa was the most revered holy man in Mecca. Why the cause of his death was not recorded in the Hadith? Though it would appear shocking, I guess that Waraqa was murdered by Muhammad. This is a possibility which we cannot ignore. After Muhammad and Khadija had used him, he became a liability; someone who could and would profess that his claims were untrue. Once Waraqa was dead, Muhammad felt free to concoct any lies and attribute them to him and the deception continued unabated.

Strangely, even there is a mention in Bukhari (4.56.814) that Muhammad was once challenged by a Christian convert who reverted back to Christianity by seeing that Muhammad was actually faking the Qur'anic revelations and openly declared, "*Muhammad knows nothing but what I have written for him*". There was a similar observation by one of the Muhammad's scribes; Abdullah Ibn Abi Sarh, who used to write down Allah's revelations. When Abdullah suggested some changes to Muhammad's dictation, Muhammad readily agreed with him. This led Abdullah to suspect Muhammad's claim of reception of messages from God, apostatized and left Medina for Mecca. He then proclaimed that he (Abdullah) too could easily write the Qur'anic verses by being inspired by Allah (Caner & Caner, 2002, p. 45).

When Muhammad advised a small group of his followers to flee Mecca, the Christian king of Abyssinia received them and gave them protection. In biographies of Muhammad there are many references of a Christian monk named Bahira who is said to have recognized in him the signs of a Prophet. In 638, when Jerusalem was surrendered to Muslims, Sophronius (Patriarch of Jerusalem), who had negotiated the surrender of the city to the Muslims, explained the invasion of Palestine as divine punishment for the sins of the Christians. The notion was that the Muslims were the instruments of the God's wrath (Fletcher, 2003, p. 16). The idea that Islam might be "a new religion" was unthinkable to the Christians. But slowly they recognized Muhammad as a man of blood and his followers as irredeemably violent.

Throughout the medieval period, all of the characteristics of Muhammad that confirmed his authority in the eyes of Muslims were reversed by Christian authors and turned into defects. When Christians recognized Islam as a rival religion to Christianity they simply refused the notion of a new Prophet after Christ (Ernst, 2005, p. 14). The traditional belief that Muhammad was illiterate, which to Muslims was a proof of divine origin of Qur'an, indicated to the Christians that he must have been a fraud. When challenged by the Meccans to produce miracles, Muhammad said that Qur'an was his only miracle. While Muslims viewed this as a proof of the spirituality of his mission, Christian antagonists considered this lack of miracles as clear evidence that Muhammad was a fake.

In 850, a monk called Perfectus went shopping in the capital of Muslim state of al-Andalus. Here he was stopped by a group of Arabs who asked him whether Jesus or Muhammad was the greater Prophet. There was a trick in the question because it was a capital offence in the Islamic empire to insult Muhammad, and Perfectus knew it. So at first he responded cautiously. He gave an exact account of the Christian faith respecting the divinity of Christ. But suddenly he snapped and burst into a passionate stream of abuse, calling Muhammad a charlatan, a sexual pervert and the antichrist himself and a false Prophet spoken of in the Gospel (Foxe, 1827, pp. 76-7). He was thrown into the prison but later released because the judge realized that he was provoked by the Muslims. However after few days of his release, the Muslim pranks provoked him once more and Perfectus cracked a second time and insulted Muhammad in such crude terms that he was again taken and later on executed. Few days later, another Christian monk, named Ishaq appeared before the same judge and attacked Muhammad and his religion with many crude and disgusting words. His insulting words to Muhammad and Islam were so strong that the Judge, thinking him drunk or deranged, slapped him to bring him to his senses. But Ishaq persisted in his abuse, and the Judge ordered his execution too. A few days after Ishaq's execution, six monks from the same monastery arrived and delivered yet another venomous attack on Muhammad; they were executed too (Armstrong, 2006, pp. 22-3). That summer, about fifty monks died this way.

Those Christian monks had all the rights to call Muhammad a fake. They were wise people and they had studied Muhammad and his religion thoroughly. The two biggest Christian criticisms of Muhammad were undoubtedly in relation to his military activities, marriages and sexual perversions. For Christians, the celibacy and nonviolent approach of Jesus Christ were generally seen as indispensable characteristics of true spirituality. The cruelty of Muhammad and his sexual perversion were taken as clear proof that Muhammad could not be on the same exalted level as Jesus. The early Christian critics of Muhammad generally described him as motivated by a combination of political ambition and sensual lust. But the success of Islam raised a disturbing theological question: How had God allowed this impious faith to prosper? Could it be that God had deserted His own people?

The earliest reference to Muhammad in Christian literature is found in the writings of seventh century. The Armenian *Chronicle of Sebeos* (history attributed to Sebeos) says that Muhammad was an "Ishmaelite" who claimed prophethood. In the coming years many Biblical scholars realized that though Islam and Christianity have many similarities; like, praying, fasting, pilgrimage, giving alms, etc., actually Islam is against Christianity. During the middle ages of Christian Europe, Christians had very strong negative feelings against Muslims, e.g., Bede, a monk and Biblical scholar described Qur'an as "*a parody of sacred Scripture of Christianity [Bible]*" and Muhammad as a pseudo-Prophet, who and his followers have made war on

Christians and seized their holy places (Fletcher, 2003, p. 19). In a work of Biblical commentary in 716, Bede described Muslims as *"enemies of the Church"*.

Another prolific writer of theology was John of Damascus. He hailed from an ethnic Arab family whose three generations had served the Muslim rulers. He was one of the earliest Christian writers to concern himself at any length and in a systematic way with Islam. He was the first scholar to explain the Biblical deviation of the Ishmaelites. He went on to criticize Muhammad as a false Prophet who cribbed part of his teaching from the Old and New Testaments and also from the sayings of a heretic Christian monk, Bahira. According to John, Muhammad wrote down *"some ridiculous compositions in a book of his"* (Chase, 1958, p. 153), which he claimed had been sent down to him from heaven. Around 745, John composed a play *Dialogue between a Saracen and a Christian* which envisages a situation in which a Muslim puts awkward questions to a Christian on such matters as the nature of Christ, creation, free will and many others. The Christian parries these questions so skillfully that at the end of the play *"the Saracen went his way surprised and bewildered, having nothing more to say"* (Seale, 1978 p. 70). John also quoted at length but selectively from Qur'an and mocked the faith of the Ishmaelites.

During late eighth or early ninth century, a short work was composed probably in southern Spain by an anonymous writer, known as *Ystoria de Mahomet* where Muhammad was called as *"a son of Darkness"* who stole some Christian teaching and claimed to be a Prophet. He put together an absurd farrago of doctrine delivered to him by a vulture claiming to be the angel Gabriel. He was a slave to lust and incited his followers to war, which he justified by laws for which he falsely claimed divine inspiration. He foretold his resurrection after his death but in the event his body was fittingly devoured by dogs (Wolf, 1990, pp. 97-9). This anonymous author, like the John of Damascus, was very knowledgeable of Islam. He was well-versed with the Qur'an and often gave fairly recondite references from this book.

In a Christian work named *Doctrina Jacobi Nuper Baptizati* (the teaching of Jacob the newly-baptized) a tract of anti-Jewish literature written in dialogue form composed probably in Palestine round about the time of the surrender of Jerusalem. At one point the following words were attributed to one of the speakers, Abraham, a Palestinian Jew (Fletcher, 2003, pp. 16-7),

A false Prophet has appeared among the Saracens... They say that the Prophet has appeared coming with the Saracens, and is proclaiming the advent of the anointed one who is to come. I, Abraham referred to the matter to an old man very well-versed with the scriptures. I asked him: 'What is your view; master and teacher, of the Prophet who has appeared with the Saracens?' He replied groaning mightily: 'He is an imposter. Do the Prophets come with sword and chariot? Truly these happenings today are works of disorder... But you go off, Master Abraham, and find out about the Prophet who has appeared.' So I, Abraham, made enquiries, and was told by those who had met him: 'There is no truth to be found in the so-called Prophet, only bloodshed; for he says he has the keys of Paradise, which is incredible'.

Muhammad's prophetic life can be divided into two distinctive periods, the Meccan period and Medinan period. During the first period i.e., Meccan period, he was a simple preacher and warner. But his preaching was clearly, from the worldly point of view, an utter failure, and as a result of thirteen years of propaganda he had won no more than a handful of converts. But the scene completely changed at Medina where he gained in power and his message lost the beauty. Here he was what one might simply call a robber chief. After conquering Mecca, he entered as a political leader rather than a religious leader, and was recognized by Meccans as such. So he was changing his color as situation dictated. Throughout his prophetic mission, he dealt with Jews and Christians keeping strict political aims in mind. At the initial stage, Islam was an absurd truth claim like a practical joke but afterwards it became serious. So while estimating the significance of Muhammad, we should not judge him solely as a mystic or religious reformer, though he may have the elements of both; rather as a ruthless politician and opportunist pressed with peculiar political problems amongst barbarous people and at a critical moment of history.

Therefore the picture that emerges of the Prophet in these traditional accounts is not at all favorable to Muhammad. Muslims cannot complain that this representation of their beloved Prophet was drawn by an enemy. The early Arabs did not believe in his prophetic claim and Muhammad was taken aback when those intellectuals pointed to the weaknesses of the Qur'an. They fell heavily on Muhammad and demanded answers and explanations to the irrationalities they spotted in the Qur'an, but Muhammad stood there wordless and powerless like a fool. By seeing the irrationalities, there was large scale apostasy. Many early Muslims lacked any deep religious sense; they were opportunists and wanted only worldly successes. Many confessed their belief but had no inclination towards Islam and its dogma and ritual. It was not faith in Allah, but the greed and unbridled carnality that led the army of Islam from victory to victory. The Bedouins, who knew nothing but the poverty-stricken life of the desert, were prime targets for anyone who offered an escape from their misery, even if it meant death to attain it. Therefore, they accepted Muhammad's nonsense as heavenly revelations. If things went wrong, the Bedouins were ready to drop the new faith as quickly as they had adopted it. It is estimated that at the death of Muhammad the number who really converted to Muhammad's doctrine did not exceed a thousand (Warraq, 2003, p. 41). Present day cult leaders perform much better than Muhammad.

Many people rejoiced hearing the news of Muhammad's death. In the city of Hadramaut (Yemen) Twenty-six women marked the occasion of Prophet's demise by staining their hands with henna, a practice associated with festivities, and played on the tambourine (a shallow, handheld drum made of a circular wooden frame with a calfskin or plastic drumhead stretched across the top), thinking that Muhammad's demise signaled a return to their former spiritual traditions. Historians called them *The Harlots of Hadramaut*. This embarrassing incident is recorded in Ibn Habib al-Baghdadi's book, *Kitab al-Muhabbar*. Two Muslim leaders reported the event to Caliph Abu Bakr. Following his order, those twenty-six women were punished in a gruesome manner and that by having their hands chopped off (Ahmed, 2006, pp. 182-3). This incident linked woman and song with blasphemous behavior.

The Qur'an itself confirms that there were Arab skeptics in Mecca who did not accept the "fables" recounted by Muhammad. Those skeptics certainly had every right to do so. They even accused him of plagiarizing the pagan Arab poets. Some verses were attributed to al-Qays (Imra'ul Qays) a famous pre-Islamic Arabian poet (Warraq, 2003, p. 41). Muhammad stole several poems of this poet and added them to his Qur'an. It was the custom of the orators and the poets to hang up the composition of their literary work upon the Ka'ba. One day, Fatima, the daughter of Muhammad was repeating two passages from Sabaa Mu'allaqat. Suddenly she met the daughter of Imra'ul Qays, who cried out (Warraq, 1998, pp. 235-6), "*O that's what your father had taken from one of my father's poems and calls it something that has come down to him out of heaven*". Even today this story is told amongst the Arabs. The Qur'anic plagiarism is so prominent that Muslims cannot deny this. But how can they explain this incident? Did the poems of Imra'ul Qays were also divinely inspired like Qur'an?

1.5: Discrediting Muhammad using the Modern-day Sources

The prime target of the Western censor has been the founder of Islam himself. Michael Hart in his book, *The 100: A Ranking of the Most Influential Persons in History* places Muhammad at the very top of the list (cited Sina, 2008, p. 5), but he did not mention if the influence was positive or negative, as Walker (2002, p. 312) lamented, "*[there is] no great figure in history, who is so poorly appreciated and no great religious leader so maligned in Western writings as Muhammad*".

Ernst (2005, p. 11) concluded, "*It is safe to say that no religion has such a negative image in Western eyes as Islam*". It is useless to engage in competition between religious stereotypes, but one can certainly see Gandhi and his advocacy of nonviolence as a positive image of Hinduism, and Dalai Lama with his amazing positive and widespread recognition as a representative of Buddhism, and likewise, Mother Teresa or Pope of Christianity. In this respect, Islam certainly lacks any such influential figure though Muslims are the majority population in some fifty countries. Muslims from all over the world are feared as terrorists in the Western world which is neither a propaganda nor misunderstanding; it is simply the truth. And, as Shaikh (1995, p. 4) commented, "*The greatness of the leader depends upon the quality of his follower*", surely this poor image of Muslims does not reflect well on Muhammad.

In 1843, a work on the life of Muhammad, based on historical analysis, was published by Gustav Weil. He put forward the idea that Muhammad was suffering from epilepsy. Aloys Sprenger, a German physician, supported Weil. According to Sprenger, he was also a psychopath (Schimmel, 1985, p. 248). Another author, Franz Buhl, described that in his Medinan phase, Muhammad revealed the ugly side of his character – cruelty, dishonesty, untrustworthiness; someone whose leading principle was "*the end justifies the means*" (Warraq, 1995, pp. 86, 89). Another two prominent scholars, Margoliouth and Macdonald, believed (cited Walker, 2002, p. 315) that Muhammad's seizures were artificially produced; those acts were merely a device by which he secured sanction for his revelations.

Muir's work on Muhammad was based on original Muslim sources, and published between 1856 and '61. Muir was specialized in debating Muslim clerics and entertained the suggestion that Muhammad was inspired by the devil. He also adopted the more scientific criticism (originally advanced by the Sprenger) that Muhammad's prophetic experiences were due to epilepsy (Ernst, 2005, p. 22). In his work, Muir had passed a judgment on Muhammad's character that was repeated over and over again by subsequent scholars. According to him, Muhammad though religiously motivated during Meccan period, showed his "*feet of clay*" during

Medinan period where he was corrupted by power and worldly ambitions (Warraq, 1995, p. 87). The inconsistencies in Muhammad's character was specifically pointed out by Muir, "*He justified himself by 'revelations' releasing himself in some cases from social proprieties and the commonest obligations of self restraint*".

It is of course shocking that Muhammad transformed to a bandit chieftain, who was unwilling to earn an honest living after he gained power at Medina, as Caetani (cited Warraq, 1995, p. 88) observed, "*If Muhammad deviated from the path of his early years, that should cause no surprise; he was a man as much as, and in like manner as, his contemporaries, he was a member of a still half-savage society deprived of any true culture, and guided solely by instincts and natural gifts which were decked out by badly understood and half-digested religious doctrines of Judaism and Christianity*".

Perhaps, Margoliouth did the most brilliant study of the life of Muhammad that has yet appeared. According to Margoliouth, Muhammad was a patriot, keenly alive to the opportunities of his time. Islam was created as a method to unite the Arabs and make them a strong military force. In this process the religious appeal played an important part but there was also a complete absence of moral scruple. On the success of Muhammad, Margoliouth commented that Muhammad's success was not due to the objective truth of the Qur'an but to his skill as an organizer and military leader. Muhammad was thoroughly familiar with the shortcomings of the Arabs and utilized them to the utmost advantage, and he was able to seize opportunities and distrusted loyalty when not backed by interest.

Hume referred to Muhammad as a "*pretended Prophet*" and commented, "*[The Qur'an is a] wild and absurd performance*". Hobbes wrote (cited Hitchens, 2007, p. 17), "*... to set up his new religion, [Muhammad] pretended to have conferences with the Holy Ghost in form of a dove*". Also, Gibbon (1941, p. 240) concluded that Muhammad's claim that he was the apostle of God was "*a necessary fiction*". Will Durant believed that Muhammad was a conscious fraud and concluded (1950, p. 176), "*Muhammad felt that no moral code would win obedience adequate to the order and vigor of a society **unless men believed the code to have come from God***". Carlyle wrote, "*His Qur'an has become a stupid piece of prolix absurdity; we do not believe like him that God wrote that*" (Warraq, 1995, pp. 10, 24). Becker, yet another prominent critic, commented (1909, p. 29) that the companions of Muhammad had very little interest in religion and most of them were utterly ignorant about the fundamental tenets of the religion preached by him. For those early Muslims, as Becker commented, "*... the new religion was nothing more than a party cry of unifying power, though there is no reason to suppose that it was not a real moral force in the life of Muhammad and his immediate contemporaries*". Elsewhere Becker (cited Warraq, 2000, p. 554) concluded, "*... bursting of the Arabs beyond their native peninsula was, like earlier irruptions in which the religious element was totally lacking due to economic necessities*".

Anwar Shaikh completely discredited Muhammad. According to him (1995, p. 24), Muhammad had a strong dominance urge. He was not a Prophet but the builder of an Arab empire and this was an integral part of his supposed to be prophethood. Islam was built around the sanctity and significance of his own person which he had achieved by various means. Islam is an Arab national movement and Muhammad was possibly the greatest national leader born anywhere on earth. Also, Qur'an is highly contradictory. Thus instead of leading, it misleads the people. Prophethood has nothing to do with guidance; it is simply a political doctrine. Shaikh (1995, pp. 6, 12) commented, *"God's messenger is God's servant by name only. In practice he is God's superior... Islam is less a religion and more an Arab national movement"*.

Rodinson, the latest biographer of Muhammad, believed that Muhammad really did experience sensory phenomena translated into words and phrases which he interpreted as messages from God, and subsequently he developed an idea of receiving those messages in a particular way. These experiences were Muhammad's hallucinations. Muhammad was sincere but sincerity is not a proof. At Medina this inspired visionary transformed into an imposter. Rodinson (1980, pp. 218-9) commented, *"[Muhammad was] driven by necessity to produce a convenient revelation at the appropriate moment and at no other, in the way the mediums have been known to resort to fraud in similar cases"*.

Before last century, there was hardly any Hindu evaluation, neither of the Prophet and his Qur'an nor even of Islamic doctrine in general. The first detailed criticism of Islam, the Prophet and in particular of the Qur'an was done by Swami Dayananda Saraswati, the founder of the Vedic reform movement *Arya Samaj*, in 1875. Dayananda was a freethinker. In his literary work, he mainly focused on the Qur'anic contradictions, irrational beliefs and inhumane injunctions in the Islamic scriptures. Dayananda (cited Smith, 2009) wrote,

Having thus given a cursory view of the Qur'an I lay it before the sensible persons, with the purpose that they should know what kind of book the Qur'an is. If they ask me, I have no hesitation to say that it cannot be the work either of God or of a learned man, nor it can be a book of knowledge.

The Qur'an is the result of ignorance, the source of animalization of human being, a fruitful cause of destroying peace, an incentive to war, a propagator of hostility amongst men and a promoter of suffering in society.

Dayananda had equally criticized the negative sides of Hinduism; e.g., caste system, untouchability, widow marriage, etc. Later, *Arya Samaj* criticism of the Prophet typically focused on his dictatorial and immoral personal behavior, like *Rangila Rasul* (literally, the playboy Prophet) written by Rajpal which highlighted Muhammad's abnormal sexual preferences. Rajpal was later stabbed to death by a Muslim fanatic. Christian critics, no matter how fiercely criticize Muhammad, usually appreciate at least Prophet's belief in monotheism which never impressed these Hindu authors.

Swami Vivekananda, a well-known Hindu monk and social reformer, was another original thinker who had questioned the nature of Muhammad's leadership with the nature of his prophethood. According to him, Muhammad had to be ruthless in imposing adherence to his belief in his own divine mission because this belief could not stand on its own, based as it was on a delusion. He offered one hypothesis of what had happened to Muhammad so as to make him believe in his own selection as God's sole living spokesman. Muhammad, as Vivekananda (1947, p. 184) believed, used to practice *Yoga* – an ancient form of Hindu-Buddhist meditation. But he was unaware of the dangers of experimenting with *Yoga* without competent guidance. As a result his brain was deranged.

Gisbertus Voetius, a seventeenth century Dutch Calvinist theologian cherished the same view of Vivekananda. Voetius believed that Muhammad suffered from mental disturbance which was a result of his improper meditative experiments. The Hindu *Yoga* manuals emphatically warn against wrongly practicing the techniques of *Hatha Yoga*. The practices of *Yoga* produce excellent result if used properly and under efficient guidance and certain precautions. But if the protective measures are neglected then it may cause brain damage. As example; *Pranayama* (breath control or control of the vital energies), if practiced improperly, can impair the nerve systems, and the very foundation of a healthy body and sound mind is shaken causing much harm to the person (Iyengar, 1976, p. 434). This may cause hallucination. The learner, in a state of hallucination, may experience some mystic phenomena, which he may think as "certain states of consciousness" or some kind of "enlightenment". But in reality these are serious delusions – both auditory and visual. The most typical among these is megalomania; witness the self-importance of the religious gurus and messiahs in the modern cult scene. Similarly, *Kundalini Yoga* is also very ill-reputed. If practiced in proper manner, the person can attain such a state when he can even manipulate the "force" or "energy" of the universe in his favor. In *Kundalini Yoga*, the person deliberately induces a psychotic state on himself, but for an unstable person this may easily lead to real psychosis. Hindu Yogis and Masters had warned the learners repeatedly on this topic.

In a speech given at London on November 17, 1896, Vivekananda said, *"One religion may ordain something very hideous. For instance, the Mohammedan (Islam) religion allows Mohammedans to kill all who are not of their religion. It is clearly stated in the Koran, 'Kill the infidels if they do not become Mohammedans'. They must be put to fire and sword. Now if we tell a Mohammedan that this is wrong, he will naturally ask, 'How do you know that? How do you know it is not good? My book says it is'"*. In another speech given in the Universalist Church, Pasadena, California, on January 28, 1890, he said, *"In this line the Mohammedans were the best off; every step forward was made with the word the Koran in the one hand and the sword in the other. Take the Koran, or you must die; there is no alternative"*.

The famous historian of international reputation, author, researcher and an expert of Islamic history of India, Sir Jadunath Sarkar (1870 - 1958) mainly focused on the intolerant attitude of Islam. According to him (1972, pp. 163, 164, 169),

> *The murder of infidels is counted a merit in a Muslim. It is not necessary for him to grow a rich growth in spirituality. All he needs to do is to slay a certain class of his fellow-beings [infidels] or plunder their lands and wealth and this act itself will raise his soul to heaven.* **A religion, where followers are taught to regard robbery and murder as religious duty, is incompatible with the progress of mankind or with the peace of the world.**

> *The toleration of any sect outside the fold of orthodox Islam is no better than compounding with sin and the worst form of sin [according to Islam] is polytheism, the belief that the one true God has partners in the form of other deities. Such a belief is the rankest ingratitude to Him who gives us our daily bread.*

According to Sarkar, the political and religious condition under which the Hindus were forced to live in a Muslim state raised a great barrier between them. The political supremacy of the Muslims was absolute, and the Hindus could not even aspire to it under Islamic rule. Sarkar (cited Syed, 2004, pp. 320-1) wrote,

The poison lay in the very core of Islamic theocracy. Under it there can be only one faith, one people and one all overriding authority. The state is a religious trust administered solely by His people (the Faithful) acting in obedience to the commander of the faithful, who was in theory and very often in practice too, the supreme general of the army of militant Islam.

There could be no place for nonbelievers. Even Jews and Christians could not be full citizens of it, though they somewhat approached the Muslims by reason of their being 'the people of the book' or believers in the Bible, which the Prophet of Islam accepted as revealed.

The Quran (IX.29) calls upon the Muslims 'to fight those who do not profess the true faith, till they pay Jyzia with the hand in humility'. This was a poll-tax payable by Hindus for permission to live in their ancestral homes under a Muslim sovereign.

Sharat Chandra Chattopadhyay, the great humanist and the legendary Bengali novelist, believed that Hindu-Muslim unity is impossible because of two reasons. First, Muslims lack culture from birth whereas the Hindus born with culture. Second, Muslims' full solidarity is for Arabia. Though they live in India, they do not feel any responsibility for India. Gandhi dreamt for Hindu-Muslim unity, but failed miserably. Muslims will never identify themselves with India. Chattopadhyay (Sarat Rachanabali, Vol. 3, p. 475) wrote,

In fact if the Muslims say, 'We want unity with the Hindus', it cannot be anything but a deception. One would say that the Muslims invaded India just to plunder, not to set up a kingdom. But they were not satisfied with loot only; they demolished Hindu temples, broke the idols and raped Hindu women. In fact they never spared to do the maximum harm and insult to other people's religion and humanity"

When the Muslims will come down from their high horse of religion, probably then they will realize a human being cannot be proud with the fundamentalism of his religion, and this is nothing but unparallel barbarism. But the Muslims are yet to go a long way before they realize it. ***But their eyes will never open unless the whole world together teaches the Muslims a good lesson.***

Ambedkar (1940, part 3, ch. 7) had the same opinion as Chattopadhyay, as he wrote, *"From a spiritual point of view, Hindus and Muslims are not merely two classes or two sects such as Protestants and Catholics or Shaivas and Vaishnavas. They are two distinct species. For them Divinity is divided and with the division of Divinity their humanity is divided, and with the division of humanity they must remain divided".*

Another well-respected historian, P. N Oak, compared the butchery of innocent Hindus by the Muslim raiders with Hitler's persecution of the Jews (1996, p. 12). According to Oak (1996, p. 389), ***"[The history of Islam is] a millennium long*** *devil dance of murder, massacre, rape and plunder, trickery, treachery, tyranny and torture across the world by Islam from the day of its inception".* Islam owed its progress and establishment almost entirely to the sword and deception. If there were no sword and deception, the law of Muhammad would not have established.

In recent years, another two prominent Hindu scholars, Ram Swarup and Sita Ram Goel have further developed Swami Vivekananda's position on the subject of Muhammad's prophethood. According to them, the pagan Arabs had every right to reject Muhammad's claim. They recognized him as a fake and that his prophetic claim was nothing but a deluded consciousness, which then propagated on a war footing. The history will not forgive them for one mistake – the mistake of being defeated. Actually they failed to understand the deceitful ways of Muhammad and could not match his mailed fist in the final round. It was neither the first nor the last time that a democratic society succumbed in the face of determined gangsterism. We have seen how Stalin, Hitler and Mao tse-tung succeeded in our own times.

Ram Swarup appropriately commented that Muslims need sword to sell their God because their God failed in spirituality. He (1992) wrote, *"The need of the time is to examine the whole concept and assumptions of revelatory religions, such as of a particular community being 'chosen' as the swordsmen or salesmen of god. When a divine message commands, kill the idolaters wherever you find them, we must give a close look not only to the message but also to the messenger and his source of inspiration".* About Muhammad's distorted morality and Muslims' mentality, Ram Swarup (1984, ch. 1, Introduction) wrote,

> *To rob a whole people is piety, but to remove a paltry something from a looted treasure is moral depravity of a magnitude that deserves eternal fire. Men driven by ordinary temptations indulge only in petty crimes and small lapses, but committing real enormities needs the aid of an ideology, a revelation, a God-ordained mission.*

> *The believers are conditioned to look at the whole thing through the eyes of faith. An infidel in his fundamental 'misguidance' may find the Prophet rather sensual and cruel, and certainly many of the things he did, do not conform to ordinary ideas of morality. But the believers look at the whole thing differently. To them morality derives from the Prophet's actions; the moral is whatever he did. Morality does not determine the Prophet's actions, but his actions determine and define morality. Muhammad's acts were not ordinary acts; they were Allah's own acts.*

A book, published during June 1990, *Hindu Temples: What Happened to Them (A Preliminary Survey),* was a collection of articles written by Arun Shourie, Harsh Narain, Jay Dubashi, Ram Swarup and Sita Ram Goel. It is perhaps the first attempt on the part of some prominent scholars to dig from the graveyard of history the identity of some two thousand temples of India destroyed by the Muslim invaders and rulers. The book is not an exercise in rewriting history, but is an effort to present the facts and give a clear view of the truth hitherto unknown. Not only were the temples destroyed but even their materials were used in constructing mosques at those places. This was done obviously to hurt the sentiments of the Hindus. The volume two of the same book was published during March 1993, which contained many further proofs exclusively to Islamic evidence, historical as well theological.

Arun Shourie pointed out many unscientific verses in the Qur'an and criticized its author for his ignorance. Instead of accepting the mistakes about unscientific Qur'anic cosmology, the Islamists try to cover it by silly explanations which further make them a laughing stock. These silly explanations to protect Qur'an from a divine downfall do not bring prestige either to Qur'an or Muhammad. Shourie (2002, p. 468) wrote, *"Instead of studying the heaven and earth, we are taught how perverse and distorted interpretations can be put on everything. And how what is being done amounts to calumny upon the Holy Book because what is being proposed is nothing but adding clauses to the Word of God. **The duty incumbent upon a Muslim is to make science accept Islam"**. Shourie also widely criticized Islam for the ill-treatment of women, deep hatred for the infidels, the cruel Sharia law and the authorities of Mullahs in issuing fatwa. Elsewhere, Shourie quoted many militant and unethical verses of the Qur'an and concluded that **Qur'an should be banned** (2008, p. 435). Rushdie's book *The Satanic Verses* was banned because *"it would hurt the feelings of certain group of people"*, then under the same reason, Qur'an should be banned because it offends the feelings of the whole non-Muslim world.

In India, whenever a book is published critical to Muhammad, Qur'an or Islam; Muslims demand to ban the book. They usually take shelter under Sections 153A and 295A of the Indian Penal Code (I.P.C) and Section 95 of the Criminal Procedure Code for preventing every public discussion of their creed in general and of their Prophet in particular. In addition, the clerics issue death sentences against people who have said anything against their religion. But, two heroic sons of India, Himangshu Kishore Chakraborty and Chandmal Chopra, both from Calcutta, turned the table against the Indian Muslims.

On July 20, 1984, Chakraborty wrote to the Secretary, Department of Home Government of West Bengal, demanding the ban of the Qur'an. He wrote again on August 14, 1984, but received no response. Chakraborty thereafter met Chopra, who also wrote to the Department of Home Government on March 16, 1985, but his letter was not answered. Chopra therefore filed a Writ Petition at the Calcutta High Court on March 29, 1985 stating that publication of the Qur'an attracts Sections 153A and 295A of the I.P.C and Section 95 of the Criminal Procedure Code because it *"incites violence, disturbs public tranquility, promotes, on ground of religion, feelings of enmity, hatred and ill-will between different religious communities, and insults other religions or religious beliefs of other communities in India"* (Goel, 1987, ch. 1). The details of these lawsuits are recorded in the book *Calcutta Qur'an Petition* written by Sita Ram Goel.

There are many thoughtful comments from the great thinkers, philosophers, statesmen and historians which speak volumes. These scholars have closely studied the Islamic scriptures, and many of them also had interacted with the Muslims and closely observed them or have been directly affected by Islam. As example; Alexis de Tocqueville (French thinker/historian) commented (cited Spencer, 2005, p. 25), *"I studied the Quran a great deal. I came away from that study with the conviction that by and large there have been few religions in the world as deadly to men as that of Muhammad. So far as I can see, it is the principal cause of the decadence so visible today in the Muslim world."* And, the quote that perhaps best summarizes Islam comes from John Quincy Adams (cited Blunt & Blunt, 1830, p. 269), *"The essence of his [Muhammad's] doctrine was violence and lust: to exalt the brutal over the spiritual part of human nature. While the merciless and dissolute dogmas of the false prophet shall furnish motives to human action, there can never be peace upon earth and goodwill towards men"*.

If religion is by definition irrational and prone to violence, Harris posits Islam as the most exemplary in this regard. As he wrote (cited Amarasingam, 2010, p. 41), *"Islam, more than any other religion human beings have devised, has all the makings of a thoroughgoing cult of death"*. Elsewhere Harris commented (cited Cappi, 2007, p. 46), *"As a matter of doctrine, the Muslim conception of tolerance is one in which non-Muslims have been politically and economically subdued, converted, or put to the sword"*.

Unlike the Western scholars, in India, criticism of Islam is relatively less. Several books criticizing Islam and its role in Indian history have been banned only because the politicians do not want to lose the Muslim vote-bank. In 1982, the National Council of Educational Research and Training of India issued a directive for the rewriting of school texts. Among many other things it stipulated that, *"characterization of the medieval period as a time of conflict between Hindus and Muslims is forbidden"* (cited Knap, 2009, p. 200). Therefore, negationism (denial of history) has become India's "official" educational policy. To appease the Muslims, the Government of India will not tell Indian children about the Hindu-Kush genocide. The Hindu-Kush is about a 1000 mile long and 200 miles wide mountain range that stretches between central Afghanistan and northern Pakistan. History tells us that the conquest of Afghanistan near 1000 A.D was followed by the slaughter of the entire Hindu populace in the area. That is why the region is called Hindu-Kush, means Hindu-slaughter, where the Hindu slaves from the Indian subcontinent were slaughtered in harsh Afghan mountains to the extent that their blood formed streams that flowed through hillside (Knap, 2009, p. 32). The pre-Islamic name of Hindu-Kush mountain range was *Pariyatra Parvata* (Savarkar, 1985, p. 206). The policy of negationism is the cause behind the ignorance of Hindus about the real magnitude of the Hindu genocide by Muslim invaders. In spite of this the debate on Islam is going in full force both on the Internet and in the printed form.

In sum; what historians throughout the world are unable to find, even in this twenty-first century, is a name more hateful than Muhammad, a religious book more intolerable and unholy than Qur'an, a God more demonic than Allah and a belief more dangerous than Islam. As Muir commented (1992, p. 522), *"The sword of Mohammad and the Koran are the most stubborn enemies of civilization, liberty and truth which the world has yet known"*.

In the history of all religions and cults, the most successful lecherous man who used God for his personal gain is Muhammad – a liar, thief, murderer and rapist till his last breath. Today more than one billion people believe in Muhammad without knowing his true character. Some of them, who understand, continue to be Muslims because they have redefined their morality and ethics to fit within the teachings of Islam, which are floridly lacking in morality. They, therefore, redefine what is good and evil in order to fit their lives into what is preached by Islam, instead of examining Islam to see if it fits within the good life. As Ataturk, the founder of Modern Turkey commented (cited Peter, 2010, p. 362), *"This is Islam, an absurd theology of an immoral Bedouin, a rotting corpse which poisons our lives."*

From the very beginning of Muhammad's mission, neither Muhammad nor Islam had any shortage of critics. From the point of view of historical truth, only the scholar has the right to criticize, but from ethical or social point view the right of criticism belongs to everyone. Even the most sympathetic scholars seem to have genuine problem with writing about Muhammad as a Prophet under divine guidance and the Qur'an as the authentic word of a God. Muhammad performed so poorly as a Prophet of Allah that he even discredited himself by his own word and actions as we are going to see next.

1.6: Discrediting Muhammad by His Own Words and Conduct

Muhammad's life was full of contradictions. There is a vast difference between "Muhammad of faith" and "Muhammad of fact". Often he did not practice what he preached. Qur'an originally treated Muhammad as a humble messenger of Allah but gradually this relationship developed into duality, and finally, Muhammad appeared as God's superior. This was the time when the whole divine drama of Muhammad was exposed and the lecherous Prophet of Islam hammered a nail in his own coffin. In context of the satanic verses, Tabari and Ibn Sa'd recorded these disgraceful words of Muhammad,

> *I have fabricated things against God and have imputed to Him words which He has not spoken.* (Tabari: VI.111).

> *I ascribed to Allah, what He had not said.* (Ibn Sa'd, Kitab Al-Tabaqat Al-Kabir, vol. 1)

This single confession of Muhammad is enough to disqualify him of his prophetic claim. Muhammad said that he was deceived by Satan and a revelation from Allah confirmed it. But how can we be sure that the second revelation was also not from Satan? The guaranty of "genuineness" of one revelation cannot be another revelation. If Muhammad could be deceived by Satan once, how could he know on all the other occasions that he had not been deceived? How can we ignore the possibility that Gabriel was actually the Satan himself in disguise and hence the whole Qur'an is satanic? Allah challenged in the Qur'an,

> *And if ye are in doubt concerning that which We reveal unto Our slave (Muhammad), then produce a Surah of the like thereof, and call your witness beside Allah if ye are truthful.* (Q: 2.23)

Satan took Allah's challenge and easily produced "*a Surah like this*". Muslims believe that Qur'an is miraculous in beauty and no one can make anything to compare to it because it is divine. Satan produced the verses and Muhammad spoke those words from Satan, but everyone including Muhammad himself thought that those verses were part of the Qur'an. Surely those satanic verses sound exactly like those of the Qur'an. If not, then surely Muhammad, his followers and the Quraysh would never have accepted them. The second point is related to Qur'anic verses 15.39-40. According to these two verses, Satan can deceive and mislead only those who are not sincere to Allah. Therefore, if Satan were able to deceive Muhammad and distort the revelations of Allah, it follows that Muhammad could not have been a sincere slave of Allah.

There is another way of looking at the above divine mystification. Qur'an says,

Perfected is the Word of thy Lord in truth and justice. There is naught that can change His words. He is the Hearer, the Knower. (Q: 6.115).

Qur'an also confirms that the Bible, or in the Islamic language, Taurat, Zabur and Anjeel are the words of God. Thus, they cannot be tampered with, and one can rely upon the truthfulness of the stories that have been narrated therein. Therefore, based on the Qur'anic sanction, we can rely upon the truthfulness of the Bible. Bible (Deuteronomy: 18.20) says,

But the Prophet who speaks a word presumptuously in My [God] name which I have not commanded him to speak . . . that Prophet shall die.

From the above statement we can conclude that either Muhammad was a false Prophet or Qur'an was false. In any case the loser is Muhammad. The satanic verses incident confirms that Qur'an was corrupted. But then Qur'an (6.115) also says that no one can change God's words. **So Qur'an itself confirms that Qur'an is falsified.** There is another point to note. Muhammad really had a very painful death. He died as a result of eating poison-mixed food that he did not know about (Bukhari: 5.59.713, 719, 731). If he were a real Prophet, Allah would have warned him in advance by a timely revelation.

According to Qur'an, Muhammad was only a man sent to warn the Meccans and a messenger to convey a divine message to them.

Say: I do not have the power to acquire benefits or to avert harm from myself, except by the Will of Allah. Had I possessed knowledge of the unseen, I would have availed myself of much that is good, and no harm would have touched me. But I am only a Warner and a bearer of glad tidings for a nation who believe. (Q: 7.188).

Say: 'I am only a human like you...' (Q: 18.110)

Qur'an also says, *"... Allah is the Absolute, Owner of praise"* (Q: 2.267). But another verse just goes in opposite direction, where Muhammad completely reverses his role. As a result, Allah becomes Muhammad's sycophant. Allah declared in His Qur'an,

Lo! Allah and His angels pray peace to Prophet. O ye who believe also ***shower praises on him and salute him with a worthy salutation.*** (Q: 33.56).

This is the height of Qur'anic stupidity. Why Allah needs to pray peace to His messenger? If Allah is the only God then He is praying to whom? If Allah is the only Owner of praises, then why Qur'an also instructs Muslims to salute Muhammad? In all other religions, it is man who worships God, but in Islam, it is God who worships man (Muhammad). Then, who is the real God of Muslims – Allah or Muhammad? Who is inferior – the God or the man? Muslim's five times prayer is actually meant for whom – Allah or Muhammad?

Allah specifically told Muslims not to worship anyone except Allah.

Surely I am Allah, there is no god but I, therefore serve Me and keep up prayer for My remembrance. (Q: 20.14).

But during Muhammad's lifetime, his followers used to worship him like a living God and Muhammad did not object to it. Bukhari recorded,

Narrated Ibn 'Abbas; Abu Bakr said, 'To proceed, if you used to worship Muhammad, then Muhammad is dead, but if anyone of you used to worship Allah, then Allah is alive and shall never die'. (Bukhari: 5.59.733).

Since Allah is the Absolute, Owner of praise; associating someone else with Allah is the most dreadful sin in Islam. In the strict Qur'anic terminology this is known as "Shirk". Qur'an says,

Allah does not forgive (the sin of inventing an) association with Him, but He forgives other sins to whomsoever He will. He who associates with Allah has invented a great sin (Q: 4.48).

Allah forgives not that anyone should be associated with Him (Allah); less than that He forgives to whomsoever He will. Whoso associates with Allah anything, has gone astray into manifest error. (Q: 4.116).

But Muhammad had committed this sin. "Shahada", the basic confession for every Muslim, associates the name of Muhammad with that of Allah in the same sentence – *"La ilaha illa Allah wa-Muhammad rasul Allah"*. This is how praising Muhammad is an integral part of the daily prayers of the Muslims. This is a serious blasphemy. Since the earth is divided into several time zones, and every moment somewhere on the earth, there are some Muslims praying to Allah facing Mecca, this unpardonable sin is being committed by the Muslims in turn ever since the birth of Islam. What an irony! Muhammad committed this offensive sin for the first time, and since then Muslims are doing it again and again, but till date, no one amongst them ever noticed it. We wonder why Allah is still silent.

Muhammad repeatedly advised Muslims not to disobey Allah's instructions, but in many instances, he did not follow what he preached.

Any daytime sexual activity during the fasting days is forbidden (Q: 2.187). But Muhammad slept with Umm Salama during her period, kissed her while fasting and used to take bath from the same pot after having sex under a woolen sheet (Bukhari: 1.6.319). Also he used to kiss and embrace (his wives) during fasting (Bukhari: 3.31.149). Sucking was the favorite sexual activity of Muhammad. He used to kiss and suck Aisha's tongue while they were fasting (Sunnan Abu Dawud: 13.2380).

Muhammad also violated Allah's rule on dower (mehr) and the time of waiting (idda) in marrying a divorced/widowed woman. In Sharia law (Islamic law), the payment of mehr is compulsory in marriages, and widows to wait four months and

ten days for re-marriage. Qur'an says,
> Give women their dowries freely, but if they are pleased to offer you any of it, consume it good and smooth. (Q: 4.4).

> And those of you who die and leave wives behind such wives shall wait by themselves for four months and ten (nights). When they have reached the end of their waiting period, there shall be no offence for you in whatever they choose for themselves kindly. Allah is Aware of what you do. (Q: 2.234).

After attacking Khaybar, Muhammad took as a captive a beautiful teenage-girl, named Safiyyah, and married her without paying any dowry (Bukhari: 5.59.523, 524). To hide his treachery, Muhammad claimed that marrying Safiyyah was in itself a respect for her; her dowry was her manumission (freeing somebody from slavery) from being a sex-slave to Muhammad (Muslim: 8.3326). Nowhere in the Qur'an Allah has made it legal to use manumission of a slave-woman to be used as her dowry. Muhammad simply invented this rule according to his convenience.

Before falling into the hands of this perverted man, Safiyyah was the legal wife of a Jewish Chief. Muhammad had killed her husband after subjecting him to brutal torture. When Muhammad had satisfied his lust for blood, on the same night he took Safiyyah into his tent to have sex with her. He was supposed to have waited for four months and ten days before he could even touch her but he did not do that. He was so lustful that he never bothered to obey Allah's instruction, and took the new captive girl on the same day she became a widow by Muhammad himself. Bukhari (4.52.143) says that Muhammad married Safiyyah because she was beautiful and gave a grand feast at the wedding, and then he had forceful sex with her.

Allah put a restriction on the number of wives, which Muhammad did not obey.

> If you fear that you cannot act justly towards the orphans, then marry such women as seem good to you; two, three, four of them. (Q: 4.3).

Some Islamic sources confirm that he married at least twenty-two times. After his shameful marriage with Zaynab, the wife of his adopted son, Zayd, Allah gave a restriction that he could not collect any more wives.

> It is not lawful for thee (to marry more) women after this, nor to change them for (other) wives, even though their beauty attract thee, except any thy right hand should possess (as handmaidens). (Q: 33.52).

But Muhammad married at least thirteen times after this.

Muhammad also violated the Qur'anic law on the punishment of sex offenders. Pre-marital sex and extra-marital sex are two most serious offences. Allah instructed in His Qur'an,

> You shall lash the fornicatress and the fornicator each with a hundred lashes. In the religion of Allah, let no tenderness for them seize you if you believe in Allah and the Last Day; and let their punishment be witnessed by a party of believers. (Q: 24.2).

But Muhammad did not apply this Qur'anic rule when his friend admitted having committed a punishable offence (sexual) because the man prayed with him (Bukhari: 8.82.812). Just for praying to Allah his punishment was forgiven. But how could Muhammad override Allah by violating the relevant Qur'anic verse?

A man and a woman who are not close relatives (i.e., those who are not in the prohibited class for marriage purposes) cannot, under any circumstances, be alone together. This moral guardianship is endorsed in the Qur'an,

Say to the believing men that they should lower their gaze and guard their modesty: that will make for greater purity for them: And Allah is well acquainted with all that they do. (Q: 24.30).

Muhammad violated the above Qur'anic code of conduct. He had an adulterous relation with his first cousin-sister, Umm Hani bint Abu Talib, who was a married woman. He used to sleep in her house if no one was around. Once Muhammad was sleeping at Ka'ba, but at nightfall, he stealthily went to Umm Hani's house and spent the night with her. When the people did not find him at Ka'ba, they went looking for him and when he was discovered in the house of Umm Hani, he was embarrassed, so was Umm Hani. This was the night of Muhammad's famous journey to Jerusalem and paradise from Umm Hani's house (more precisely, from her bed). When this adulterous affair was leaked out, Muhammad had to leave Mecca and settle in Medina. Afterwards, when he conquered Mecca, he went to Umm Hani's house and openly stayed there overnight. Also, following Hadith demonstrates Muhammad's sexual attitude towards single women, divorced or widowed, rich or poor, which clearly violates the Qur'an.

A young princess, Jauniyaa (a princess) was brought to Muhammad to have sex with him but she was reluctant to give herself to him; Muhammad was angry and raised his hand to beat her... (Bukhari: 7.63.182)

Why hundred lashes were not given to him every time he crossed the limit?

Muhammad violated the Qur'anic rule on sex with menstruating women. According to Qur'an; menstruation is an injury and Muslims are prohibited to have sex during a woman's period. After the period is over, man can have sex in any manner, at any time and at any place.

They ask you about menstruation. Say: 'It is an injury. Stay away from women during their menstrual periods and do not approach them until they are cleansed. When they have cleansed themselves, then come to them from where Allah has commanded you. (Q: 2.222).

But Muhammad did not spare his wives when they were in heavy menstruation. He used to order Aisha to put on an Izar (dress worn below the waist) and fondled her in bath even when she was in her periods (menses) (Bukhari: 1.6.298). Often he would put his cheek and chest in between the naked thighs of a menstruating Aisha (Sunnan Abu Dawud: 1.270). Though caressing and foreplay do not necessarily constitute actual coition, we should not forget that these lustful activities are just the beginning of further sexual gratification.

Qur'an (2.187, 197) prohibits having sex with women when in ihram (purity state spent inside a mosque) or when performing Hajj. But Muhammad had violated this injunction. Once when he went to Mecca to perform Hajj and a proposal of marriage was offered to him, he quickly accepted the offer and married the woman even though he was in sacred state wearing ihram (Sunnan Abu Dawud: 2.10.1840).

From the above examples it is very clear that Muhammad did not have much regard for the Qur'an or even to his own words when it came to marrying women and having forceful sex with them.

Fasting is an important religious practice for Muslims which was actually a pagan tradition. Muhammad reintroduced fasting during the month of Ramadan, but exempted himself because he found it difficult to abstain from food and water from dawn to dusk. He ate whenever he pleased. Ibn Sa'd wrote (cited Sina, 2008, p. 99), *"The Messenger of Allah used to say 'We the Prophets are required to eat our morning food later than others and hurry in breaking our fast in the evening'."*

These are just a few examples of how Muhammad did anything he liked, placed himself above Allah's law, broke moral and ethical codes whenever it suited him, and then made his Allah reveal a verse to confirm that whatever he had done was all right. Aisha, the child bride of Muhammad had noticed it and perhaps sarcastically or innocently told him,

> *Narrated Aisha: ... I said (to the Prophet),' I feel that your Lord hastens in fulfilling your wishes and desires'.* (Bukhari: 6.60.311).

It is expected that a Prophet, who claimed to be God's messenger on earth, should demonstrate the wisdom and infallibility of the divine law through his own action. But since Muhammad had not done it deliberately, it implies that he was neither a representative of God nor the model of action, for being above Allah's law. Also, if Allah gives his Prophet dispensation from His own law, then Allah's law is no more than a joke because if His chosen Prophet himself cannot carry it out, then how can Allah expect the ordinary believers to obey His commandments?

Qur'an is a mockery of divine law and Muhammad's own action proves it. Qur'an was Muhammad's own composition, and thus, he could treat himself as he wished and Allah was only a supposition to serve his purpose. Therefore, if Qur'an is truly God's words, then by disobeying God, Muhammad surely goes to hell and Muslims are also destined to hell; and if Qur'an is false, then Muhammad's prophethood stands on what ground? In any case Muhammad is the loser.

Muhammad seemed to have not much faith on Allah during wars. In none of the wars he waged, he did put his life in danger. He encouraged martyrdom amongst his followers, but the precautions he used to take for himself were most unprophetlike. He often stood behind the fighting Muslims wearing two coats of chain-link mail (flexible armour of interlinked rings), one on top of another. The double armouring would make him too heavy and his movements used to be difficult. He could not even stand in this condition, let alone walking. While in this awkward position, he used to shout towards the front and encourage his men to show bravery and not to fear death, promising them high-bosomed virgins, etc., in paradise. Sometimes he used to grab a handful of sand and throw it in the air in the direction of the enemy cursing them in the name of Allah (Sina, 2008, pp. 99, 100). This is the best he had ever contributed in a war with the nonbelievers. But while collecting the booty or captured women for sex, he was well ahead of everyone. He convinced the believers that use of booty from the spoils of war are lawful and good and he used to collect one-fifth of the booty in Allah's name.

And know that whatever ye take as spoils of war, lo! a fifth thereof is for Allah, and for the messenger... (Q: 8.41)

It has been narrated on the authority of Abdullah b. 'Umar that the Messenger of Allah used to give (from the spoils of war) to small troops seat on expeditions .... and Khums (one-fifth of the total spoils) was to be reserved (for Allah and His Apostle) in all cases. (Muslim: 19.4337)

Allah divided the booty stolen from the first caravan after he made spoils permissible. He gave four-fifths to those He had allowed to take it and one-fifth to His Apostle. (Ishaq: 288)

Muhammad was like a parasitic vampire. What Muhammad wanted to mean by saying, "*booty is for Allah and His Apostle*"? Did Muhammad throw booty in the direction of the Ka'ba and ask Allah to grab whatever He wanted, and Allah came out hurriedly with a gunny to collect His share and again hurriedly go inside the Ka'ba and wait eagerly for the next arrival of booty? Or, was this a trick and Muhammad got benefited out of this trick?

All faithful Muslims offer their prayers five times a day to acknowledge and adore Allah facing in the same direction. In Islam, this direction is called as "Qibla", i.e., the direction of worshipping God. Bukhari (6.60.20) says that every nation has its Qibla. The sacredness of this direction is confirmed in the Qur'an.

And every one has a direction to which he should turn, (Q: 2.148)

And from whatsoever place you come forth, turn your face towards the Sacred Mosque. (Q: 2.149)

And from whatsoever place you come forth, turn your face towards the Sacred Mosque; and wherever you are turn your faces towards it. (Q: 2.150).

However, once Muhammad declared Jerusalem, the most sacred Jewish city, as the Qibla for the Arab Muslims. He did it purely from political purpose, though he had to violate the Qur'an. He thought the Jews would accept him as Prophet. But the Jews refused which turned Muhammad against them. So after treating Jerusalem as Qibla for about sixteen months he changed it for Ka'ba, a sanctuary of Mecca his own hometown. If Qibla is so sacred, why he had changed it to Jerusalem and again back to Mecca? Is there any doubt that the change of Qibla from Ka'ba to Jerusalem and again back to Ka'ba was not God's will but a selfish desire of Muhammad? Following ahadith prove that he did not believe in the sacredness of Qibla.

Narrated `Abdullah bin `Umar: People say, "Whenever you sit for answering the call of nature, you should not face the Qibla or Baitul–Maqdis (Jerusalem)." I told them, 'Once I went up the roof of our house and I saw

Allah's Apostle answering the call of nature while sitting on two bricks facing Baitul–Maqdis (Jerusalem)'. (Bukhari: 1.4.147).

Narrated Abu Aiyub Al–Ansari: Allah's Apostle said, "If anyone of you goes to an open space for answering the call of nature he should neither face nor turn his back towards the Qibla. (Bukhari: 1.4.146).

Narrated `Abdullah bin `Umar: I went up to the roof ... and saw Allah's Apostle answering the call of nature facing Sham (Syria, Jordan, Palestine and Lebanon regarded as one country) with his back towards the Qibla. (Bukhari: 1.4.150)

Narrated `Abdullah bin `Umar: Once I went up the roof of our house and saw Allah's Apostle answering the call of nature while sitting over two bricks facing Baitul–Maqdis (Jerusalem). (Bukhari: 1.4.151)

From the above narrations, it is very clear that Muhammad had no respect either for Ka'ba or Jerusalem. He had instructed his followers to respect Qibla by not facing or turning back towards this holy direction while answering the call of nature, but he never bothered to follow it.

All the above points lead to one logical conclusion – the "Allah" of Islam is not real. Muhammad was a charlatan and Allah was his "puppet" who had spoken whatever Muhammad wished. Muhammad's own action proves that Allah is a myth – conscious or subconscious fabrication of an imposter.

Muhammad saw the Arabs as either good fighters in his cause, enemy infidels, or useless hypocrites. Whenever Muhammad disliked anyone, he often used to call him a hypocrite. Hypocrisy is the worst form of unbelief, and it carries a terrible punishment under the Islamic law. Bukhari wrote,

The Prophet said, 'The signs of a hypocrite are three: −1. Whenever he speaks, he tells a lie. −2. Whenever he promises, he always breaks it (his promise). −3. If you trust him, he proves to be dishonest'. (Bukhari: 1.2.32).

The irony is that, according to his own definition, Muhammad himself was the biggest hypocrite as we are going to see now.

Telling lie to kill the enemies and to advance the cause of Islam is allowed in Islam. This is called "al-taqiyya" (holy deception). In the spirit of taqiyya, Muslims can tell a lie the way we breathe. They even lie to each other. Taqiyya was originally a Shiaa practice. The Shiaas used to protect their faith from Sunnis by practicing taqiyya (Miller, 1997, p. 433; Lewis, 2003, p. 25). However, now the whole Muslim world practices it. In Islam, deception and faith mutually support one another. Muhammad even allowed his followers to abuse him verbally to win the trust of the enemies (cited Sina, 2008, p. 57). Also, on several occasions he broke his promise for a political advantage.

Allah willing, if ever I [Muhammad] take an oath to do something, and later on I find that it is more beneficial to do something different, I will do the thing which is better, and give expiation for my oath. (Bukhari: 4.53.361).

After the death of Khadija and Abu Talib, Muhammad thought that it might be unsafe for him to stay at Mecca. Luck favored him; in the summer of 621, he gained the trust of twelve visitors from the oasis settlement of Medina. They accepted Islam and promised Muhammad to propagate his message at Medina. Next summer another seventy-five people from Medina accepted Islam, and assured Muhammad to defend him. Al- Bara, a Medinan convert told Muhammad, *"By Him who sent you with the truth, we will protect you. We give our allegiance and we are man of war possessing arms which have been passed on from father to son"* (Khan, 2009, p. 20). If the people of Medina had not given shelter to Muhammad, certainly his divine mission wound have been a total failure and his name would have sunk into oblivion like those of so many other Prophets of the same period. But what he gave them in return? He raised a band of hooligans from the converts (known as Ansars) and started attacking the rich Meccan caravans. Abu Afak, a 120 year old man, lamented that his people became followers of Muhammad who had caused them to surrender their intelligence and become hostile to one another. Muhammad got him assassinated. A Jewish mother, Asma bint Marwan, was so outraged that she composed a poem cursing the men of Medina for letting a stranger divide them and for allowing him to assassinate Abu Afak. Muhammad got her assassinated too.

In March 628, Muhammad signed an agreement with the Meccans which demanded a cessation of hostility from both sides for a ten year period. In Islamic history, this is known as "the treaty of Hudaybiya". But it took very little time for Muhammad to breach this treaty. Within just two years time of signing the treaty of Hudaybiya, his army became strong enough to defeat the Quraysh. In January 630, he marched towards Mecca with an army of ten thousand fighting men.

Simply speaking, the people of Medina trusted Muhammad but he proved to be disloyal. The Quraysh trusted Muhammad but again he proved to be treacherous. These are just two examples of his dishonesty. Enough had been recorded about the treachery of Muhammad. The history of Islam is full of treachery and deceit. As Sina (2008, p. 101) lamented, *"From incest to polygamy, from rape to pedophilia, from assassination to genocide, the Prophet of Allah did them all and encouraged his followers to do the same"*.

Therefore, according to Muhammad's own definition, he was the biggest hypocrite of Islam. He was an imposter in a divine robe to deceive people.

1.7: The Message of Prophet Muhammad

Every established religion has a certain core message. But before I talk about Allah's message to humankind through Muhammad, let me examine what are the messages of other world religions.

Jainism is the only religion which has the principle of *Kathora Ahimsa* (strict nonviolence) as its central doctrine. Hinduism talks about *Sarva dharma sambhava* (equal respect for all religions). Hinduism is also known as *Sanatana Dharma* and the five principal virtues prescribed by all schools of *Sanatana Dharma* are, nonviolence, truthfulness, non-stealing, chastity and non-covetousness. Buddhism speaks about toleration, kindness, humbleness, peace and *Pancha Sila* (the five rules of morality – killing any living being, stealing, adultery, lying, drinking intoxicating drinks). Sikhism advises us to restrain from *Punj Chor* (five cardinal vices – ego, lust, greed, attachment, anger) which should be fought with the weapons of wisdom and knowledge.

Christianity teaches us love, brotherhood and forgiveness. All the teachings of Christianity are based on four essentials: humbleness or faith and trust in God, communication with God through prayer and self-denial, observance of the law which is written in Scripture and in the hearts of those who love the truth, and the offering of sacrifice to God and partaking of the sacrificial offering. The Jews believe that God appointed them to be His chosen people in order to set an example of holiness and ethical behavior to the world and peace is seen as something that comes from God, which would only be fully realized when there is justice and harmony not just between peoples but within individual communities.

But the instructions of Allah and Muhammad's worldview were totally different from the other religions. Muhammad's bizarre beliefs, incredible teachings, self-elevation and immense hate are well reflected in his Qur'an. In sum; a religion like Islam is a curse upon humankind. The Prophet of Islam did not come to the world to bring something good like other religious teachers. He came to this world to preach hatred, brutality and slaughter.

> *The Prophet said, 'Hear me. By Him who holds Muhammad's life in his hand, **I will bring you slaughter***'. (Ishaq: 130; Tabari: VI.101)

> *Then, when the sacred months have passed, slay the idolaters wherever ye find them, and take them (captive), and besiege them, and prepare for them each ambush. But if they repent and establish worship and pay the poor-due, then leave their way free. Lo! Allah is Forgiving, Merciful.* (Q: 9.5).

Muhammad's only message to the world was **"I will bring you slaughter"**, and he had performed well as he had promised – efficiently and ruthlessly.

Muhammad masterfully exploited the concept of prophethood with Qur'an as the only proof of his absolute authority. Theoretically, through Qur'anic revelations, Allah wants to guide the humans to save them from hell, and in return for the favor, He demands absolute submission that the humans should only worship Him and live by His laws without ever questioning their purpose, validity and relevance. But there is a "catch" in this argument. Only a belief in Allah is not sufficient, they have to believe Muhammad as the only messenger of Allah. According to Qur'an,

> *Say: Obey Allah, and obey the Messenger* (Q: 24.54)

> *And obey Allah and the Messenger, that you may be shown mercy.* (Q: 3.132).

> *If you love Allah, and follow me (Muhammad), God will love you, and forgive you your sins.* (Q: 3.31)

> *And We did not send any messenger but that he should be obeyed by Allah's permission.* (Q: 4.65)

Since Allah cannot be seen or contacted by anyone other than Muhammad, the words of Muhammad begin to rank as the words of Allah and as time passes Allah recedes into the background. Muhammad, who (apparently) claimed to be Allah's most humble servant, now rises as the dominant force in the strange God-Prophet relationship. At this time, Muhammad holds the keys of paradise. Therefore, a person must believe in Muhammad to qualify for paradise and the person who believes in Allah alone, cannot rank as a believer. He is an infidel and must go to hell, no matter how righteous he may be. This is the true nature and purpose of Muhammad's claim of prophethood. He wanted to elevate himself, as Sina (2008, p. 16) commented, "*After 23 years of preaching, the core message of Muhammad remained the same. **Islam's main message is that Muhammad is a messenger and that people must obey him. Beyond that, there is no other message.** Failure to recognize him as such entails punishment, both in this world and the next. Monotheism, which is now the main argument of Islam, was not originally part of the message of Muhammad*". As Voltaire (cited Walker, 2002, p. 313) concluded, "*There is nothing new in the religion of Islam except the claim that Muhammad is the Prophet of Allah. All else is borrowed*".

Theoretically Muslims "surrender to Allah", but in practice they "surrender to Muhammad". Here lies the purpose of Islam's deceitful divine message – "People must obey Muhammad". And for those who fail to obey Muhammad, there is his stern warning – "I will bring you slaughter". The main theme of Islam is only this; spiritual and moral upbringing of the soul is of no importance.

The end result of Muhammad's evil message is disastrous to both Muslims and non-Muslims. Muhammad had permanently divided the humankind into two groups – the Muslims are Allah's party and the non-Muslims are Satan's party. Allah hates non-Muslims and wants their death and destruction. Since the true Muslims must follow this poisonous teaching of Islam, a two-nation theory arises immediately, as Shaikh (1998, p. 161) lamented, "***The only relationship between a Muslim and a non-Muslim is that of ill-will, hatred and animosity***". Today an Islamic nation does not require any particular reason to attack a non-Muslim nation. According to Qur'an, all religions except Islam are false. Therefore, Allah is the enemy of all the non-Muslims. It is by itself a heinous crime not to acknowledge Muhammad as the last Prophet of Allah.

Let us read following two verses.

O ye who believe! Choose not your fathers nor your brethren for friends if they take pleasure in disbelief rather than faith. Whoso of you taketh them for friends, such are wrong-doers. (Q: 9.23).

Say: If it be that your fathers, your sons, your brothers, your mates, or your kindred; the wealth that ye have gained; the commerce in which ye fear a decline: or the dwellings in which ye delight - are dearer to you than Allah, or His Messenger, or the striving in His cause; - then wait until Allah brings about His decision: and Allah guides not the rebellious. (Q: 9.24).

Muhammad's demand to be recognized as a Prophet was so strong that in the above two verses Allah tells the believers to treat their own parents, children and relatives as enemies if they do not believe in Islam. Preaching intolerance, lack of concern and thanklessness towards one's own parents immediately disqualify Muhammad as a Prophet and proves without doubt that he was a fake and brought no divine message from God.

1.8: Muhammad's Miracles

According to the Islamic sources, Muhammad performed many miracles. He visited a temple in Jerusalem which did not exist and then ascended to heaven (Q: 17.1), multiplied bread and dates (Bukhari: 5.59.428; 4.56.780), produced water for an army for ablution from a small pot (Bukhari: 1.4.170, 1.4.194, 1.7.340, 4.56.779; Muslim: 30.5656-9), brought rain for seven days until the valleys flooded (Bukhari: 8.73.115), visited the towns of jinns and converted some jinns to Islam (Muslim: 26.5559), stuck a huge solid rock and it became like sand (Bukhari: 5.59.427), fought and subdued a big demon (Bukhari: 1.9.450), etc. When the companions departed from Muhammad on a dark night, they were led by two lights (Allah's magic light) lighting the way in front of them till they reached their houses (Bukhari: 1.9.454, 4.56.833). The list of Muhammad's miracles is never-ending.

The moon-splitting miracle (Bukhari: 4.56.831, 4.56.832, 5.58.208, 5.58.209, 6.60.388-91) is amazing. When Muhammad invited Meccans to accept Islam, the Meccans requested him for a miracle. Hence Muhammad split the moon into two. A piece of the moon went towards the mountain. Afterwards this part remained over the mountain, and the other part went beyond the mountain. The two parts of the moon remained apart during the whole lifetime of Muhammad.

The cave miracle is another wonder of Allah which is related to the concerning in hiding in the cave of Thawr. The miracle is that none of these things were there when the Prophet and his companion entered the cave, and that thereafter, the spider hurried to weave its cobwebs, the two pigeons to build their nest and to lay their eggs, and the tree to grow its branches around the door. Ibn Hisham and Haykal had excluded the story. In the same connection, the following verses were revealed.

If you [the people] do not help Muhammad, then know that God Will. For God helped him when the unbelievers drove him out, and he and his companion hid in the cave. At that time, the Prophet said to his companion, 'Grieve not for God is with us.' It was then that God sent down his peace upon him and assisted him with hosts invisible that the word of God might be supreme and that of the unbelievers might be repudiated. God is almighty and all-wise. (Q: 9.40)

Remember how the Unbelievers plotted against thee, to keep thee in bonds, or slay thee, or get thee out (of thy home). They plot and plan, and Allah too plans; but the best of planners is Allah. (Q: 8.30).

Then there is a sword miracle also. Once when Muhammad was sleeping under a tree, someone took hold of his sword to attack him. Muhammad woke up and found him standing upon his head with the sword in his hand. The attacker asked, *"Who can protect you from me?"* Muhammad said, *"Allah"*. The attacker remained standstill and the sword refused to obey him (Muslim: 30.5665).

In various traditional sources (cited Shaikh, 1999, pp. 13-14; Schimmel, 1985, pp. 150-51; Andrae, 1955, p. 35; Dasti, 1985, p. 2; Mahmud, 1978, p. 39) there are many amazing claims about Muhammad.

1.   Muhammad was created from a divine light. Allah first created the light of Muhammad, out of which He then proceeded to create everything which constitutes this world.
2.   When Muhammad was born, the house was filled with light, the stars in the sky bowed to such an extent as if they are about to fall on the earth, the angels started singing, the idols everywhere fell on their faces, and fire-worshippers in Persia and India noticed that their temple-hearth which had been lit for a thousand years, turned ice-cold, a lake of Persia was flooded which caused the palace of Khosroes (the king of Persia) to crack.
3.   Muhammad was born circumcised and detached from the umbilical cord and there was no pollution on his body at the time of birth.
4.   Muhammad was a Prophet when the body and soul of Adam were still in the making.

The only purpose of the above astonishing claims was to prove that Muhammad was a chosen Prophet of Allah before his birth and he was born guided. In fact the Muslim scholars claim that his prophethood was established even before Adam was created. It is said that Allah made an agreement with all the future Prophets, and under Allah's agreement all the future Prophets accepted and acknowledged Prophet Muhammad as the final Prophet and told their followers to believe in him. When Amina (Muhammad's mother) was pregnant, she heard a voice tell her, "*You are pregnant with the Lord of this people, and when he is born, say 'I put him in the care of the One from the evil of every envier', then call him Muhammad*". Sometimes Amina would see a strong light shining from her belly by which she could make out the castles of Syria (Aslan, 2006, p. 19). When looked through the spectacle of blind faith, the miracle claims are great. But blind faith or blind belief is something felt by the mind. It distinguishes the ideas of judgment from the fictions of the imagination (Hume, 1992, p. 42). Let us see, how they look like through the spectacle of science, reason and logic.

1.8.1: Refuting the Claims of Muhammad's Miracles

Some of the miracles; e.g., *al-asra al-miraj* (two parts of the night journey), were Muhammad's hallucinations. This will be discussed in details in next chapter. Many other miracles were attributed to Muhammad so as to make him look saintly, which were all fabrications of his sycophant followers. In addition, there are many miracles which were claimed by Muhammad himself which no one but he could verify, and many contemporary Muslims doubted them because some of those miracles are too ridiculous, hardly more than childish jokes, and Muhammad proved himself a laughing stock. Qur'an confirms that the pagan Meccans repeatedly asked Muhammad to perform a miracle so that they could believe him.

They say: 'We will not believe in you until you make a spring gush from the earth for us, or, until you own a garden of palms and vines and cause rivers to gush forth with abundant water in them; or, until you cause the sky to fall upon us in pieces, as you have claimed, or, as a surety bring Allah with the angels in front; or, until you possess an ornate house of gold, or ascend into the heavens;

and we will not believe in your ascension until you have brought down for us a book which we can read. (Q: 17.90-93).

Therefore, Allah performed a mountain miracle for Muhammad. According to an old tradition (Walker, 2002, p. 220), when the Meccans demanded Muhammad to prove his divine mission by making a mountain move, he replied that only Allah has the power to do that. However, by repeated demands from Meccans, Muhammad thought of giving it a try. Turning to the direction of Mount Safa, Muhammad commanded it to come to him, but with much humiliation, the Mount Safa did not come. Then Muhammad exclaimed, *"Allah is compassionate! Had it come it would have caused an earthquake or fallen upon us to our destruction. I will therefore go to the mountain instead, and thank God for his mercy!!!"* Surprisingly, when Muslims read this story with the spectacle of faith, they see a miracle in it. However, this incident gave birth to the popular saying – "If the mountain will not come to Muhammad, then Muhammad will go to the mountain", which means, you have to do things for yourself instead of expecting the world to give you what you want, or, God does not act according to man's will.

Then again some Meccans asked Muhammad to send Gabriel or some other angel to them so that they could believe Muhammad – *"O Muhammad, if an angel had been sent with thee to speak to men about thee and to be seen with thee".* (Ishaq: 181). By seeing Muhammad in a mess, Allah came for his rescue and replied in a revelation (Q: 6.9) that in order to send an angel, he would have had to make him appear as a man and that would leave the nonbelievers in an utterly confused state (Spencer, 2006, p. 75). Allah also consoled Muhammad telling him that before him many other Prophets were mocked.

They say: Why is not an angel sent down to him?" If we did send down an angel, the matter would be settled at once, and no respite would be granted them. (Q: 6.8)

Other Messengers have been mocked before you. But those who scoffed at them were encompassed by that they had mocked. (Q: 6.10)

And they say: "What sort of a messenger is this, who eats food, and walks through the streets? Why has not an angel been sent down to him to give admonition with him? (Q: 25.7)

If We had made him an angel, We would have given him the resemblance of a man, and would have as such confused them with that in which they are already confused. (Q: 6.9)

Messengers before thee, indeed, were mocked, but that whereat they mocked surrounded those who scoffed at them. (Q: 21.41)

The Meccans again wanted to know why there was no miracle if Allah was so powerful. Muhammad was comparing himself to Moses and Jesus. Both of them were visited by angels and did miracles. Why Muhammad could not? The Meccans disputed his claims and mocked him mercilessly saying his religion was a forgery, a counterfeit. Qur'an says,

Or they say: He (Muhammad) hath invented it. Say: Then bring ten Surahs, the like thereof, invented, and call on everyone ye can beside Allah, if ye are truthful! (Q: 11.13).

Or (Why) has not a treasure been bestowed on him, or why has he (not) a garden for enjoyment? The wicked say: Ye follow none other than a man bewitched. (Q: 25.8)

Throughout the pages of the Qur'an, at least twenty times, his clan accused him of being the only Prophet who could not do a miracle. Muhammad's inefficiency in producing even a single miracle is well recorded by his biographer Muhammad Husayn Haykal. In this biography, *The Life of Muhammad* published originally in 1933, Haykal (1976, chapter 5) wrote that Abu Lahab and Abu Sufyan, two noblemen of Quraysh, repeatedly asked him to perform some miracles.

Why don't you change Mount Safa and Mount Marwah into gold? Why don't you cause the book of which you speak so much to fall down from heaven already written? Why don't you cause Gabriel to appear to all of us and speak to us as he spoke to you? Why don't you resurrect the dead and remove these mountains which bound and enclose the city of Makkah? Why don't you cause a water fountain to spring whose water is sweeter than that of Zamzam, knowing how badly your town needs the additional water supply?

They challenged him to do as much as Moses or Jesus had done. In ridicule, they asked, "*Why does not your God inform you of the market prices of the future in order to help you and us in the trade of tomorrow?*" (Mahmoud, 2008, p. 37). They also asked him when the final hour (end of the world) will come. All these questions and demands were answered once and for all by a revelation. Allah commanded Muhammad,

They ask thee about the (final) Hour - when will be its appointed time? Say: "The knowledge thereof is with my Lord (alone): None but He can reveal as to when it will occur. Heavy were its burden through the heavens and the earth. Only, all of a sudden will it come to you." They ask thee as if thou Wert eager in search thereof: Say: "The knowledge thereof is with Allah (alone), but most men know not." (Q: 7.187)

Say: I do not control any benefit or harm for my own soul except as Allah please; and had I known the unseen I would have had much of good and no evil would have touched me; I am nothing but a warner and the giver of good news to a people who believe. (Q: 7.188).

Muhammad never wanted to be a miracle worker simply because he could not perform miracle. He accepted that every Prophet before him was given miracles because of which people believed them (Bukhari: 6.61.504). The pagan Meccans could not be blamed for troubling Muhammad for demanding at least one miracle. From other parts of Arabia, there were many charlatans who claimed to be God's messenger. They had at their disposal magic tricks which they presented as proof of their divine mission. One of them was Musaylima who had a sizable following from his own tribe. He used to run up and down the country showing a flask with a narrow neck in which he had inserted an egg which he had learnt from a Persian juggler. This was his miracle. He also recited rhymed sentences that he passed off as verses of a second Qur'an (Warraq, 2000, pp. 145-6). There was another miracle claimant Awkia Bin Zohir al-Ia'adi who used to go to a lower place in Mecca, climb a ladder and tell people that God spoke to him in that place (Ahmed, 2006, p. 7). This proves how much it was necessary for a man to make some tricks as miracles to promote himself to the rank of a Prophet.

The claims in traditional Islamic sources that Muhammad was a chosen Prophet of Allah before his birth and he was born guided were fake publicities. Muhammad was fathered by an idolater and his mother was a pagan woman. Muhammad received his first revelation when he was meditating in a desert cave called Hira at the age of forty. Till that time he knew nothing about Qur'an. If he were born guided, as believed by many, why he wasted forty years of life and thus knowingly neglected Allah's command?

In fact, Muhammad was not much religious before he claimed the title of a Prophet. Before he immigrated to Medina, he did not even know that Jews and Christians have serious theological differences (Armstrong, 2006, p. 15). Obviously, Muhammad had a religion till the age of forty and this could not be anything but the faith of his forefathers. If he were born guided, how Allah allowed it? After all Allah is supposed to be all-knowing.

Jabir b. Samura reported Allah's Messenger as saying, 'I recognize the stone in Mecca which used to pay me salutations before my advent as a Prophet and I recognize that even now'. (Muslim: 30.5654)

From the above Hadith, it is obvious that Muhammad used to visit the Ka'ba, before his prophethood, when 360 statues were worshipped by different Arab tribes. So, if for worshipping the statues, the nonbelievers are roasting in hell, Muhammad is also roasting in hell with them. Similarly; the angels started singing and the idols everywhere fell on their faces, fires of all fire-worshipers in Persia and India became cold, a lake flooded which caused a palace to crack at the birth of Muhammad, etc., were absurd claims. No historian had ever recorded the songs sung by angels or idols fall or fire became cold. If something extraordinary had happened, history books must have told us. Furthermore if Muhammad was really such a great miracle worker, why he could not perform a single miracle in front of the Meccans?

Muslims' claim that Muhammad was born detached from the umbilical cord cannot be true. Umbilical cord is the only source of supplying nourishment and an unborn baby cannot stay alive in the womb without being attached to it. If this fable was true, Muhammad would have lived without food and water after birth, but he did need food and water like everybody else. The story of pregnant Amina is equally nonsense. If she had really witnessed any such divine occurrence, she would have taken much care of Muhammad by herself, instead of giving him to a nurse Halima.

In sum; there was not a single miracle to prove Muhammad's claim of prophethood. There were no healings, walking on water, parting seas, raising folks from the dead or feeding multitudes. There are no fulfilled prophecies, like the exacting and detailed predictions that Biblical Prophets routinely made to demonstrate their divine authority. But the most troubling part about our absolute reliance on Muhammad's testimony that he and his Qur'an were divinely inspired is that Muhammad's character was as deficient, and his life was as despicable, as anyone who has ever lived.

These miracles attributed to Muhammad are later additions. The traditions concerning Muhammad were written down in Baghdad more than a hundred years following his death. Till that time, they were oral traditions which rested entirely in the memory of those who have handed them down. Many myths were invented and added to these oral traditions in an attempt to make Muhammad appear Messianic. The Muslim scholars who had fabricated those miracles had well-defined agendas and a practical and selfish reason to do so. When Islam appeared as a religious rivalry to Christianity, they tried their best to make Muhammad look as godly as Jesus; otherwise they would be out of business.

As a result, since the Gospels proclaimed that Christ was the light of the world, Muslims contrived Allah first created the light of Muhammad, out of which Allah created everything which constitutes the world. They even claim that Muhammad's body emitted luminous waves rendering him visible in thickest darkness. One night this miraculous light enabled Aisha to find a needle. Also, Muhammad produced no shadow (Warraq, 2000, p. 171). The story of pregnant Amina is remarkably similar to the Christian story of Mary, who, when pregnant with Jesus, heard the angel of the Lord declare, *"You will be with child and will give birth to a son, and you are to give him the name Jesus. He will be great and will be called the Son of the Most High"*. (Luke: 1.31-32). The story of Bahira (a Christian monk who is said to have recognized in Muhammad the signs of a Prophet) was borrowed from Jewish scriptures. It resembles the Jewish story of Samuel (1 Samuel: 16.1-13). Believing in fictitious and historically worthless tales is worse than unknowing the truth.

There was another reason, those miracles were fabricated. Since everything associated with Muhammad was demonic rather than divine and Qur'an could not stand by its own merit, Muslim scholars choose to deceive others by fraudulent means to keep the falsehood of Islam "alive" and steady going. The bread and butter of the Muslim scholars and clerics come from the business of Islam. At least those lies, though ridiculous and childish, provided their Prophet with some impression of credibility which was sufficient to attract the feebleminded people.

The Muslim scholars pass the story on to next generation and thereafter. Soon it takes on a life of its own and becomes more colorful with time and enters the realm of folklore, myth, and legend. Ultimately it is accepted by the mainstream Muslims as authentic. Today, the legend of Muhammad appears like a ridiculous collection of absurd fables and in the worst style. According to Kennedy (2008, p. 22), these fables are so contradictory and inconsistent that we cannot be certain for anything; even the very existence of Muhammad was questioned.

According to Qur'an, the only miracle associated with Muhammad was the revelation of the Qur'anic Surahs themselves. But the satanic verses incident even refuted this Qur'anic claim as already discussed earlier. Qur'an is the only religious book which is expected to be read and recited in Arabic only. It is not necessary to understand the meaning of a single word. In Qur'an, there are large numbers of contradictions and inaccuracies, and grammatical, historical, scientific, numerical and ethical errors. This book is haphazardly written. There is no chronology, no chapters of definite subject matters. Often the verses are unrelated to other and a whole chapter is a mixture of many subjects at random. It is utter stupidity to believe that this book is from God.

If Muhammad was involved in a miracle, or could do one, all he would have had to do to silence his critics was to explain the ones that had taken place, or simply summon his God's power to perform one. But no! He failed miserably.

1.9: Conclusion

No religion in the world has been as harshly criticized as Islam. Attacks pointing out the irrationality of Islam started from Muhammad's day and they are still continuing. Walker (2002, pp. 311-2) laments that there is not only a lack of understanding between Islam and the West but also a lack of a desire to understand. But Walker does not tell us this "*lack of understanding*" or "*a lack of a desire to understand*" is on whose part. Are Muslims misunderstanding the Western critics or it is the critics who are at fault. If the critics say that Islam is an alien, aggressive and fanatical faith, should we accuse them for their lack of understanding? Or, should we appreciate these critics for their "correct" understanding?

If we want to study Christianity, we cannot do it without learning about Christ. Similarly we cannot think about studying Buddhism by ignoring Lord Buddha, and Jainism without Mahavira Jain. Likewise, if we want to understand Islam, we have to read about Muhammad.

The greatness of the leader depends upon the quality of the followers. A poisonous tree produces poisonous fruits only. A psychopath murderer cannot teach "nonviolence" like Gandhi. Our experience shows, a Christian or Buddhist or Hindu, with deep and sincere religious devotion, can become one Mother Teresa, Dalai Lama or Gandhi. But in Islam, we see leaders like, Ayatollah Khomeini, Osama Bin Laden, Ahmadinejad, Mullah Omar, etc. We cannot say Dalai Lama, Mother Teresa, or Gandhi was more religious and more sincere than Osama Bin Laden, Ahmadinejad or Mullah Omar. The argument is about something else – what are the teachings (and demands) of that religious group and the founder of that group? Let us compare few words of Muhammad, Allah and Qur'an with that of other religious leaders/ doctrines.

And slay them wherever ye find them, and drive them out of the places whence they drove you out, (Q: 2.191)

Then said Jesus, Father, forgive them; for they know not what they do. (Luke: 23.34)

Do not injure another. Love everyone as your own self, because the whole universe is one. In injuring another, I am injuring myself; in loving another, I love myself. (The Vedanta Philosophy of Hinduism)

I will instill terror into the hearts of the unbelievers. (Q: 8.12)

Protect religion from hatred. (Hindu epic Mahabharata: Vanaparva 213.29)

Warfare is ordained for you, though it is hateful unto you; but it may happen that ye hate a thing which is good for you, and it may happen that ye love a thing which is bad for you. Allah knoweth, ye know not. (Q: 2.216)

If anyone strikes you on the right cheek, turn to him the other also. (Matthew: 5.39)

For he who insults you (Muhammad), will be cut off. (Q: 108.3)

Love your enemies and pray for those who persecute you. (Matthew: 5.44)

Then, when the sacred months have passed, slay the idolaters wherever ye find them, and take them (captive), and besiege them, and prepare for them each ambush. (Q: 9.5)

Let your mind be filled with love. Your pain shall be sent far away, and peace shall come to your home. (Siri Guru Granth Sahib)

Lust, anger, and greed are the three gates of hell leading to the downfall (or bondage) of the individual. Therefore, one must (learn to) give up these three." (Bhagvada-Gita: 16.21)

Make ready for them all thou canst of (armed) force and of horses tethered, that thereby ye may dismay the enemy of Allah and your enemy, and others beside them whom ye know not. (Q: 8.60)

A person who has given up all desires for sense gratification, who lives free from desires, who has given up all sense of proprietorship and is devoid of false ego - he alone can attain real peace. (Bhagvada-Gita: 2.71)

If anyone desires a religion other than Islam (submission to Allah), never will it be accepted of him; and in the Hereafter, He will be in the ranks of those who have lost. (Q: 3.85)

And know that whatever ye take as spoils of war, lo! a fifth thereof is for Allah, and for the messenger... (Q: 8.41)

You shall find peace, doing seva (selfless service) (Siri Guru Granth Sahib)

The Supreme Lord said: Fearlessness, purity of the inner psyche, perseverance in the yog of Self-knowledge, charity, sense-restraint, sacrifice, study of the scriptures, austerity, honesty; nonviolence, truthfulness, absence of anger, renunciation, calmness, abstinence from malicious talk, compassion for all creatures, freedom from greed, gentleness, modesty, absence of fickleness, splendor, forgiveness, fortitude, cleanliness, absence of malice, and absence of pride - -- these are the (twenty-six) qualities of those endowed with Divine virtues. (Bhagvada-Gita: 16.1-3)

So when you meet in battle those who disbelieve, then smite the necks until when you have overcome them, then make (them) prisoners, and afterwards either set them free as a favor or let them ransom (themselves) until the war terminates. (Q: 47.4)

In the midst of this world, do seva, and you shall be given a place of honor in the Court of the Lord. (Siri Guru Granth Sahib)

How many a township have We destroyed! As a raid by night, or while they slept at noon, Our terror came unto them. (Q: 7.4).

You have a right to perform your prescribed duty, but you are not entitled to the fruits of action. Never consider yourself the cause of the results of your activities, and never be attached to not doing your duty. (Bhagvada-Gita: 2.47)

Does there still exist a "*lack of understanding*" or "*a lack of a desire to understand*"? Today, instead of talking about Islamic terrorism, should we be more concerned about Buddhist terrorism or Jain terrorism? Taslima Nasrin's and Solomon Rushdie's books were banned because "*it would hurt the feelings of certain group of people*"; is there a "*lack of understanding*" if we say Qur'an should be banned because it offends the feelings of the whole non-Muslim world?

Practically everything associated with Muhammad was decidedly unprophetlike. Whereas all other religious leaders preached love and brotherhood, talked about life, freedom & purification of soul and spiritual upbringing; Muhammad focused on hate, violence, and punishment. In his religion, war was elevated as a supreme religious duty. He approved plunder, incest, pedophilia, thievery, lying, assassination, genocide, and rape in the name of God. Paradise is no way better than a brothel and hell is a torture chamber. Muhammad was so spiritually deprived that he could not see anything beyond earthly pleasures even after death; leave aside any moral upbringing. It is really surprising that today more than a billion Muslims put their blind trust on this seventh century criminal, whose life was an example of what not to do, rather than how to behave.

His God is an ungodly God. This God is so ridiculous that He is ready to bribe man with the paradisiacal luxuries, and if man does not fall for it, He frightens him with the most sadistic torture of hell. Yet this stupid God, Allah, calls himself independent, absolute and disinterested. Such a God is nothing but a clever myth invented by Muhammad. With this invention, Muhammad declared Allah as the real Master, and himself as his humble servant. This way he fooled the people by personalizing his authority in the name of God and imposed his dictatorship on them. In theory, Muslims are following Allah's guidance, but in practice, they are offering their blind obedience to Muhammad. With all the Qur'anic revelations, Allah slowly moved away into the background, leaving the front seat to Muhammad.

The authority of the Qur'an is unquestionable and it leads to hell. Allah is very specific on this matter.

O believers! Do not ask questions about things that if revealed to you, may cause you trouble. But if you ask a question about something when the Qur'an is being revealed, it will be made known to you. Allah has forgiven you what you

did to date, Allah is Forgiving, Forbearing. (Q: 5.101).
Some people before you did ask such questions and later lost their faith because of those very things. (Q: 5.102)

Narrated by Ash-sha'bi ... I heard the Prophet say, 'Allah has hated you for asking too many questions (in disputed religious matters).' (Bukhari: 2.24.555)

Why Muslims are not allowed to ask questions about the Qur'anic revelations? How God can hate us for asking many questions? The answer is simple. If Muslims start asking questions, the imposture of Muhammad will be exposed causing the fall of Islam. Therefore by revealing those two verses in the guise of Allah, Muhammad had banished reasoning from the kingdom of Islamic faith, making fanaticism the foundation of his doctrine. As Sina (2008, p. 6) lamented, ***"Muslims are genuinely incapable of questioning Islam. They dismiss every doubt and consider things that are incomprehensible as 'test' of God. To pass that test and to prove their faith, all they have to do is to believe in every nonsense and absurdity unquestioningly"***.

Truth and logic are two biggest enemies of Islam. Toland (cited Gunny, 1996, p. 168) wrote, *"He [Muhammad] clearly saw that the spirit of inquiry would not favor him. This is how Islam maintained itself"*. Muhammad recommended blind faith without question and absolute obedience because of his inability to teach the faith intelligibly. This is how the Prophet of Islam succeeded and his religion survived for more than fourteen centuries. He had done whatever he liked in the name of Allah because all his actions counted as the divine will. He claimed that he had no choice but to act accordingly. Thus, whatever may happen to the others, Muhammad always remained blameless.

Muhammad's strong dominance urge motivated him to rise above his fellow-beings. He sought distinction by imposing his will on others. A book like Qur'an was essential for him to achieve his goal. The psychologists say that the most effective way of securing dominance is by arousing someone's fear. The second one is favor. Whatever man does, he does out of fear or to gain favor. Muhammad had very skillfully exploited man's psychological mechanism, which consists of fear and favor. In Islam the very idea of paradise and hell is based on this. Qur'an repeatedly told Muslims to fear God.

While other religions like; Christianity, Hinduism, Judaism, Buddhism, Jainism took a straight path; Islam proliferated in a wrong direction because the defining core belief of Islam is wrong. It is nothing but the paranoid delusion and hallucination of an ordinary early-medieval unlettered Arab businessman. Putting such vain self-delusion on a par with the profound insights of a Shankaracharya, a Christ, a Buddha, a Confucius, a Mahavira Jain, a Laozi, a Socrates, a Plato, or a Gandhi, is plainly absurd. The words like *"lack of understanding"* and *"a lack of a desire to understand"* are simply eyewash. The simple truth is that everything is fake in Islam. The God is a fake, the Prophet is a fake and God's message is also a fake. The Western critics of Islam know this very well.

Chapter 2: Muhammad's Neurotic Disorder and Hallucinatory Confusions

"Nothing is too wonderful to be true".

Michael Faraday (1791 - 1867)

"[But] we also know how cruel the truth is, and we wonder whether delusion is not more consoling".

Henri Poincare (1854 - 1912)

2.1: The Mystery of Cave Hira

Due to some reasons, Muhammad loved the seclusion of a cave in Hira. Tabari (VI.67) recorded that loneliness became dear to Muhammad, and he used to seclude himself in the cave where he would engage in the *Tahannuth* (pagan religious rites performed in Ramadan that included fasting) worship for a number of nights before returning to Khadija and getting provisions for a like period.

Muhammad's this type of behavior was not normal. After all he was a family man with a rich wife. He could get the desired seclusion in his home to practice his religious rituals. If God is everywhere, then why the privacy of a cave was essential? He was not much religious until he was visited by the angel Gabriel. Were these religious rituals actually lame excuses? Was he depressed?

Cave Hira is no more than 3.5 meter by 1.5 meter in length and width (Sina, 2008, p. 154). This is the size of a small toilet. What Muhammad used to do in this small space? Since he liked loneliness, then it is obvious that he used to close the small entrance of the cave. Few days and night deep and pointless thinking (fantasy daydreaming), not having proper food and water, lack of oxygen inside the cave, mental fatigue – does this entire thing caused a hallucination? Was it his initial stage of madness? This is a possibility we cannot ignore.

2.2: The Strange Subconscious Mind

"There are in the mind processes and purposes of which one knows nothing at all, has known nothing for a long time, and has even perhaps never known anything".

Sigmund Freud

Muhammad was sincere in his claim of prophethood. He had a genuine and deep religious conviction which proved his sincerity. Toynbee (1935, p. 468) wrote, *"Muhammad actually thought that he was sacrificing his worldly prospects. He cannot have suspected that he was on the road to making his worldly fortune"*. But, sincerity is not a proof. Some people may sincerely believe in the existence of ghosts, whereas others may sincerely disbelieve in it. If someone's sincerity can be taken as an authentic proof, then whose sincerity is to be taken into account?

Muhammad was not the first person who claimed to have received messages from God. Throughout the recorded history of mankind, there are literally hundreds of thousands of people who declared themselves as a spokesman of God. Even today, in the mental hospitals and in the cult scene, we can find many mentally disordered and strange people who, likewise, believe to be regular recipients of messages from some unknown divine sources. They are "honest" in their claim and "sincere" in their declaration. Often those people manage to make others believe in their claims too. Many of them set themselves up as cult leaders, revered by a group of followers as their direct "telephone line" to God or the spirit world.

The human mindset is strange. If we dip into psychology textbooks, we will find hundreds perfectly bona fide cases of people who in a state of hallucination hear things and see visions. Often, they do not agree that these are hallucinations, and claim quite genuinely that they have never seen or heard all these before. However, an objective study of their cases shows that these are simply fresh associations produced by the unconscious working on things, which have been seen or heard once but forgotten. It can be proven that there was a time (often not a very remote) when these things were familiar and conscious, even if they are no longer today. As Sagan (1997, p. 131) wrote, *"Snatches of song or foreign languages, images, events that we witnessed, stories that we overheard in childhood can be accurately recalled decades later without any conscious memory of how they get into our heads"*.

Before we proceed further, it is intended to discuss a bit on conscious and subconscious mind. We know something about our conscious mind as we can make certain presumptions about our consciousness. Consciousness is the fact of the awareness of our thinking, feeling, and doing. These conscious acts are sometimes termed as conscious mind. The conscious mind represents only ten per cent of the total capacity of the human brain. It sleeps when the person sleeps; it is more straightforward and logical, and is focused in terms of activity on the left hand side of the brain for the majority of people. Similarly, certain acts are performed without conscious awareness. They arise from the subconscious mind. The subconscious mind represents ninety per cent of the total capacity of the human brain. It is focused on the right hand side of the brain.

Subconscious mind is the sum total of our past experiences. What we feel, think, or do forms the basis of our experience. These experiences are stored in the form of subtle impressions in our subconscious mind. Some scientists say that the subconsciousmind stores all possible experiences of a lifetime (Shrikhande, 2009, p. 191). The subconscious mind is awake when we are asleep. These impressions often interact or commingle with one another and give a strange outcome. On coming with contact with certain external factors the necessary conditions are fulfilled, and these subtle impressions surface in their manifest form. Often this resultant impression is so strange that the person himself cannot recognize it, and then he thinks that it is generated from an external source. As Tomkins (1995, p. 55) said, *"There are many ways of 'knowing' anything"*. These "memories" are called false memories and they are so strong that they often replace reality. In fact, it is the task of psychoanalytic treatment to make conscious everything that is pathologically subconscious, i.e., to recollect the "missing" memory, and if necessary, to replace the false memory with it.

The genius of the subconscious mind had fascinated the poets, philosophers and psychologists alike. Kant describes subconscious mind as *"immeasurable ... field of obscure ideas"* (Jung, 1933, p. 1). The ancient intellectuals had fully accepted the existence of a subconscious mind though they had nological explanation for this (Tallis, 2002, p. 5). However, the present day psychologists have realized that the strange performances of subconscious mind are not at all supernatural or divine as it was thought to be, but purely natural and earthly. It was Sigmund Freud who for the first time denied any supernatural basis of subconscious mind and hence his work was pretty original (Talvitie, 2006, p. 34). Freud's idea on subconscious differed to a great extent from those of his contemporaries (Zarctsky, 2004, pp. 15-40). Freud also created a consistent system through which the human actions could be interpreted in terms of subconscious aims and memories, and with this help, the psychic disorders can be treated. In a brief, Freud put forward the idea that psychic disorders are related to subconscious mind and this plays an important part in the development of neurosis.

2.2.1: Subconscious Mind and Neurosis

Carl Jung, the famous student of Freud and an equally-gifted psychoanalyst, had established many concepts in psychoanalysis and psychiatry which are now fundamental in the study of the mind. Jung (1933, p. 1) agrees with Freud that it is the subconscious that plays the major part in the development of neurosis. Jung's hypothesis on subconscious mind and neurosis is very important for dream-analysis because dream-analysis stands of falls with the acceptance or rejection of it. The dream-analysis of Muhammad is an important part of this chapter.

There are various causes of neurosis. Anxiety, depression and post-traumatic stress are the main causes, and in rare cases; stroke, schizophrenia and epilepsy can also cause neurosis. Technically speaking; neurosis is actually an outdated diagnosis that is no longer used medically. The disorders that were once classified as a neurosis are now more accurately categorized as neurotic disorders. Patients who are suffering from neurotic disorder have behavioral problems. There is an unusual shift in mood, energy, activity levels, and the instability while carrying out day-to-day routine tasks. A neurotic is such an odd person who can never have things as he would like them in the present, and for the same reason he can never enjoy the past. Such a person never learns the art of life.

Depression is one of the major causes of neurotic disorder. Statistics show rise in the frequency of cases of mental depression for men at the age of forty and for women the neurotic difficulties occur somewhat earlier – between thirty-five and forty (Jung, 1933, p. 104). This is the time a significant change in the human psyche takes place. We should not forget that around the age of forty Muhammad claimed to have commenced receiving Allah's revelation and started a new chapter of his life.

Muhammad was obsessed with rituals. This indicates that he was suffering from obsessional neurosis. According to Freud, obsessional neurosis is the direct outcome of subconscious mental processes. In this disorder, the patient is bound to obey some rules though he does not know where it came from, what it meant or to what motives it owed its power (Strachey & Gay, 1966, p. 344). This strange "force" is so strong that the patient may struggle against it, or decide to transgress it, or rage against it – none of this makes any difference to him carrying it out. The rule is to be obeyed, and the patient asks himself vainly why. This compulsive force originates from subconscious mind and has a strong influence to the conscious mind. Muhammad had explained every minute detail on how to wash one's face, nose, ears and hands. He had also instructed how many times a Muslim should pray and how and which direction it is to be performed. For Muhammad these were very significant. Bukhari recorded,

> *Narrated `Abdullah bin `Amr: ... We were just passing wet hands over our feet (and not washing them properly) so the Prophet addressed us in a loud voice and said twice or thrice:* **'Save your heels from the fire'**. (Bukhari: 1.3.57).

A patient suffering from obsessional neurosis can spend hours even whole day and night to conform to the imposing rules. Muhammad never maintained a proper personal hygiene. He was filthy and lice-ridden (Muslim: 49.4699; Bukhari: 4.52.47), but it never bothered him. He was more worried about washing feet to save the heels from hellfire. For the patient, obsessional ideas and obsessional impulses are, of course, themselves conscious but anything more than the performance of obsessional actions escapes conscious perception. The whims would not have become symptoms if they had not forced their way into consciousness.

This is the incredible strength of subconscious mind. Dostoevsky embraced the mystery of subconscious in his novels (Talvitie, 2006, p. 32) and in Homer's poems the subconscious appears as an internal mechanism that receives the wishes of God (Claxton, 2004, p. 61). As Freud (Strachey & Gay, 1966, pp. 344-5) explains, "*[The compulsive force] gives the patient himself the impression of being all-powerful guests from an alien world, immortal beings intruding into the turmoil of mortal life – these symptoms offer the plainest indication of there being a special region of the mind shut off from the rest*". As Fromm (1978, p. 18) observed, "*... in view of the nature of the unconscious mind, the influence of the unconscious upon us is a basic religious phenomenon*".

This is perfectly normal. When the neurotic patient cannot find any logical explanation; often thoughts of God, divinity, spirituality, paradise, hell, certain end of the world, divine mission, etc., comes in his mind. By mistake he may take it as a sign of some kind of "spiritual enlightenment". Such a person is often found to have such an unexpected amount of strong will and quiet resolve, bordering on stubborn obstinacy that his whole soul becomes absorbed in his aspirations and he seems more possessed by his ideas than possessing them. On top of this, if the person is illiterate and superstitious, there are more chances that he would fool himself more easily. This very self-assurance of "being enlightened" may make the person a saint (Mother Teresa) or a monster (Muhammad and many similar cult leaders).

Such was the case with Muhammad. His subconscious mind played a trick on him causing much mental disturbance. Being illiterate and superstitious, he could not find a logical explanation. Muhammad's first experience with Gabriel was strangely very similar to the experience of one of his close friends, Hassan Bin Thabit. Hassan was a poet of Medina, who later became Muhammad's personal Poet Laureate. Hassan came to write poetry under the influence of afemale jinni. Macdonald (cited Zwemer, 1908, pp. 126-7) wrote, "*She [the female Jinni] met him [Hassan] in one of the streets of Medina,* **leapt upon him, pressed him down and** *compelled him to utter three verses of poetry. Thereafter he was a poet, and his verses came to him ... from the direct inspiration of the Jinn. He refers himself to his 'brothers of the Jinn' who weave for him artistic words, and tells how weighty lines have been sent down to him from heaven".*

There is an extraordinary parallel between the terms used in the story of Hassan's encounter with the female jinni and the accounts of Muhammad's first confrontation with Gabriel. The expressions Hassan used are exactly those used of the sending down, i.e., revelations of the Qur'an. Did Muhammad's sick mind play a trick on him, recapture Hassan's story and subconsciously pass it off as his own?

Muhammad himself, his wife Khadija and the early followers mistook his hallucinations as spiritual experiences. We cannot blame those seventh century Arabs for their mistakes; it was the parlance of the day. But today, in these days of science, we can certainly find out the true nature of Muhammad's enlightenment. Freud was a hardcore atheist who had grown up without any religious indoctrination (Gay, 1987, p. 37; Riviere *et al*, 1960, p. xiii). This is one of the reasons; Freud's view on subconscious certainly did not incorporate any hidden religious agenda, and he based his theory totally on the philosophy of science. Unfortunately, this was not the case for those early followers of Muhammad.

Psychoanalysts often discuss about the applicability of dream-analysis in the treatment of neurotic disorder. The dream gives a true picture of a subjective state, while the conscious mind denies that this state exists. The dream comes in as the expression of an involuntary psychic process not controlled by the conscious outlook. Hence a dream is not influenced by the patient's views as to how things should be, but it simply tells how the matter stands. A patient, whose neurotic disorder unfits him for normal life, can be successfully treated only when the actual cause of his disorder is discovered which is possible through dream-analysis.

2.3: A Logical Explanation of Muhammad's Mystic Experience

"You talk to God, you're religious. God talks to you, you're psychotic".
Doris Egan (1955 –)

Undoubtedly, Muhammad's first experience with Gabriel in the cave was either a conscious fabrication or a hallucination. The Hadith which had documented this divine confrontation inside a cave logically cannot be true. Any sensible reader will find a flaw in Muhammad's claim. Bukhari recorded,

Narrated Aisha: The truth descended upon him while he was in the cave of Hira. The angel came to him and asked him to read. The Prophet replied, "I do not know how to read. The Prophet added, "The angel caught me (forcefully) and pressed me so hard that I could not bear it any more. He then released me and again asked me to read and I replied, 'I do not know how to read.' Thereupon he caught me again and pressed me a second time till I could not bear it any more. He then released me and again asked me to read but again I replied, 'I do not know how to read (or what shall I read)?' Thereupon he caught me for the third time and pressed me, and then released me and said, 'Read in the name of your Lord, who has created (all that exists) has created man from a clot. Read! And your Lord is the Most Generous." (Q: 96.1, 96.2, 96.3). *Then Allah's Apostle returned with the Inspiration and with his heart beating severely.* (Bukhari: 1.1.3).

Now the most distressing questions are;

1. The angel did not introduce himself as Gabriel. Then how did Muhammad know that it was really Gabriel?
2. Why the Gabriel did not know that Muhammad was illiterate? Why Allah did not tell him? Did Allah forget; is it possible for God to forget?
3. How Gabriel could be aggressive towards Muhammad repeatedly, the dearest messenger of Allah? It is recorded in the Qur'an (33.56) that Muhammad was so close to Allah that, even Allah showered praises on Muhammad and the angels saluted him.

None had witnessed the above incident. Later on several times Gabriel visited Muhammad, but nobody else had ever seen this super natural creature. In fact, Muhammad could not give a single proof of the existence of his Allah and Gabriel. If Gabriel existed, at least someone would have seen him or heard him. A real experience can be shared by others, not a hallucinatory experience. But luck favored Muhammad; at least some people around him could not see the fallacy of his story. This is how Muhammad started his divine business of Islam.

This vision in the cave Hira is interpreted differently by various critics. Some believe, it was Satan himself who visited Muhammad in the guise of Gabriel. But leaving aside a superstition-based argument, it might be a command that originated from Muhammad's own subconscious, as Walker (2002, p. 97) puts forward his argument; possibly, Muhammad's own subconscious commanded him to read and study the books of Jews and Christians, whose scribes were given pens to write down the truth of God's dispensation in their scriptures, which the Arabs lacked.

There is another point which is worth mentioning. The first revelation which he received in the cave was a representation of an ancient Semitic tradition of revelation (Shaikh, 1995, p. 6). Moses mediated between God and man and narrated the story of a burning bush which though burnt suffered no consumption at all (Exodus: 3.2). It was the genius of Moses who realized that it was God of Abraham, Isaac and Jacob under whose glory such a mysterious event was taking place. Moses did not forget to tell his people that he did not want to be their leader but was acting under duress. Moses told God that he was not willing to be the divine viceroy owing to his stammer and lack of eloquence (Exodus: 4.10). However, he agreed to carry the yoke of authority because his attitude angered the Lord. Thus Moses had no choice but to become God's viceroy and announced that God had sent him to his people. This way first he found a God for the people, and then appointed himself as God's messenger to enforce certain commands in the name of his God.

Now let us re-examine Muhammad's mystic experience and summarize all the facts. In all possibilities; a command originated from his subconscious mind "to read and study", which mixed up with the amazing story of Hassan and took the model of the Semitic tradition of revelation of Moses. These impressions interacted and commingled with one another, took a strange shape, and surfaced in its manifest form as a vivid hallucination. This resultant impression was so strong that even

Muhammad himself could not recognize it. He thought that it was generated from an external supernatural source, Allah.

Hallucinations may occur to normal people in perfectly ordinary circumstances. Various factors like; prolonged fasting, sleeplessness, tumors, sensory deprivation, epileptic seizures, mental fatigue, strong wishful thinking or migraine headaches are the major causes of hallucination. The mechanism within the brain that helps us to distinguish conscious perceptions from internal (often memory-based) perceptions misfires. As a result, hallucinations occur during periods of consciousness and often felt as real experiences. They can appear in the form of visions, voices or sounds, tactile feelings (known as haptic hallucinations), smells, or tastes. They are sought out in many cultures and considered a sign of spiritual enlightenment. There are countless instances in the world's religions where Patriarchs, Prophets, or Saviors repair themselves in deserts or mountains, and assisted by hunger and sensory deprivation, encounters Gods or demons which are unrelated to outside events. Psychedelic-induced (with hallucinogenic drugs – the yesteryears Hippie culture) religious experiences were a hallmark of the Western youth culture of the 1960s. This experience is often described respectfully by the words such as "transcendent", "numinous", "sacred", "holy" and "out of the world" (Sagan, 1997, p. 105).

There are various signs and symptoms of such complex hallucinations. The most common is rigid muscles – muscle stiffness (rigidity) often occurs in the limbs and neck. Sometimes the stiffness can be so severe that it restricts the size of the movements and causes extreme pain and suffocation (Admin, 2010). In addition, there might be "thought blocking" (a break in the train of thoughts) and "word salad" (an extreme form of incomprehensible speech when one word has no relation to the next) (Compton & Kotwicki, 2007, p. 65). This perfectly explains why his first divine experience was so painful. Muhammad said that the angel caught him (forcefully) and pressed him repeatedly so hard that he could not bear it any more. Actually, Muhammad felt difficulty in breathing which he understood in his hallucination as being chocked by Gabriel. This caused "thought blocking" – the initial confusion between Gabriel and Muhammad that left him terribly shaken. A true God cannot be the author of horrible experience and confusion.

2.4: Traditional Islamic Sources on Muhammad's Hallucination

"If a delusion is not to be got rid of by reference to reality, no doubt it did not originate from reality either".

Sigmund Freud

Traditional Islamic sources give us enough evidence that Muhammad regularly hallucinated.

1. Once during the childhood of Muhammad two men in white clothes came to him with a golden basin full of snow. They took him and split open his body, took his heart and split it open and took out from it a black clot which they threw away. Then they washed his heart and his body with that snow until they made them pure (Ishaq: 72).

2. Magic was worked on Muhammad by a Jew and he was bewitched so

that he began to imagine doing things which in fact, he had not done. (Bukhari: 7.71.661, 6.60.658; Muslim: 26.5428).

3. Omar asked Muhammad, *"Tell me; what is the most amazing saying which your familiar spirit communicated to you?"* Muhammad replied, *"He came to me a month before Islam and said: Have you considered the Jinn and the hopelessness and despair of their religion?"* (Ishaq: 93).

4. One day two persons came to Muhammad in his dream. One of them asked the other, *"What is the ailment of this man?"* *"He has been bewitched. He is under the spell of magic."* *"Who cast the magic spell?"* *"A Jew."* *"What material did he use?"* *"A comb, the hair knotted on it, and the outer skin of the pollen of the male date-palm."* (Bukhari: 4.54.490, 7.71.658).

5. Magic was worked on Muhammad so that he used to think that he had sexual relations with his wives while he actually had not. That is the hardest kind of magic as it has such an effect. (Bukhari: 7.71.660).

6. The stem of a date-palm tree used to cry like a pregnant she-camel, when a pulpit was placed upon it for Muhammad to give a sermon till the time he got down from the pulpit and placed his hand over it (Bukhari: 2.13.41).

7. When Muhammad used to eat, he had seen the foods glorifying Allah (Bukhari: 4.56.779).

8. Muhammad saw Gabriel with six hundred wings. Gabriel can also take the form of a human being (Bukhari: 6.60.380, 4.56.827).

9. Once a tree informed Muhammad that the jinns heard the Qur'an (Bukhari: 5.58.199).

10. When Muhammad was in Mecca, the roof of his house was opened and Gabriel descended, opened his chest, and washed it with zamzam water. Then he brought a golden tray full of wisdom and faith and having poured its contents into his chest he closed it (Bukhari: 1.8.345).

11. Once when Muhammad was offering prayer, Satan came in front of him and tried to interrupt his prayer, but Allah gave Muhammad an upper hand; he choked him. Muhammad thought of tying the Satan to one of the pillars of the mosque until Muslims get up in the morning and see the Satan. But Allah made the Satan return with his head down (humiliated). (Bukhari: 2.22.301).

12. Muhammad had even seen the future. On the Day of Resurrection, the sun will come near (to the people) to such an extent that the sweat will reach up to the middle of the ears, so, when all the people are in that state, they will ask Adam for help, and then Moses, and when everyone is failed, they will come to Muhammad. (Bukhari: 2.24.553).

13. Muhammad could hear the voices of the dead persons in their grave. Once he went through the graveyards of Medina and heard the voices of two humans who were being tortured in their graves. By hearing the conversation between two dead people he said, *"They are being punished, but they are not being punished because of a major sin, yet their sins are great. One of them used not to save himself from (being soiled with) the urine, and the other used to go about with calumnies"*. Then he asked for a green palm tree leaf and split it into two pieces and placed one piece on each grave, saying, *"I hope that their punishment may be abated as long as these pieces of the leaf are not dried"*. (Bukhari: 8.73.81).

14. Dead bodies could listen to Muhammad's words, but they could not answer (Ishaq: 306; Bukhari: 5.59.314-7).
15. Muhammad heard the sound of torture of the Jews in their graves. (Muslim: 40.6861)
16. When Muhammad looked at Allah, he saw Allah as a light (Muslim: 1.341, 342).
17. Muhammad saw the signs of Allah in a green screen covering the horizon. (Bukhari: 6.60.381).
18. Muhammad saw the display of paradise and hell on the wall of a mosque facing the Ka'ba. (Bukhari: 1.12.716).
19. Muhammad could see in front and behind of him. (Muslim: 4.853, 854, 855, 856).
20. Once Gabriel brought a kettle from which Muhammad ate and gained the power of sexual intercourse equal to forty men (Ibn Sa'd: Volume 1).
21. Muhammad heard Bilal's footsteps in paradise in front of him (Bukhari: 2.21.250).
22. Muhammad saw a man dragging his intestine in paradise (Muslim: 40.6838)

According to Ali Dasti (cited Islam-Watch, 2007), while wandering around the lonely spots near Mecca, Muhammad used to hear voices.

In the days before the appointment, whenever Mohammad walked beyond the houses of Mecca to relieve nature's demands, and as soon as the houses disappeared behind the bends in the path, a voice saying 'Peace upon you, O Apostle of God!' rang out from every rock and tree that he passed. But when the Apostle looked to one side or the other, he did not see anybody. There were only rocks and trees around him.

Muhammad's hallucinations were both auditory and visual. Probably he was also suffering from schizophrenia. The Arabs used to think that magic had worked upon him. It does not reflect well on Muhammad. If magic could work upon him, it means Allah had failed to protect His messenger. Neither the stem of a palm tree can cry like a she-camel nor can food glorify anyone while being eaten. A creature with six hundred wings is tough to imagine. Such a creature is less divine and more comical. It is impossible to open a heart without surgery. Dead people cannot talk, rocks are of course inanimate, and trees do not have vocal cords. The story is so repugnant to reason that many later theologians disbelieved it and maintained that the voices were voices of angels. All these tales were believed by the seventh century Arabs, but today we know for certain that Muhammad was hallucinating.

On certain occasions Muhammad entertained suicidal thoughts. Once when revelations stopped, Muhammad proceeded to climb a mountain and throw himself down and die. But Gabriel stopped him halfway up to the mountain and proclaimed, "*O Muhammad! You are the Messenger of Allah, and I am Gabriel*". He looked upwards and saw Gabriel in the form of a man putting his legs on the horizon. Gabriel called him again. Muhammad stopped in his place as if he was hypnotized. He tried to shift his eyes away from him, but towards whatever region of the sky he looked, he saw Gabriel as before. If we want to make some sense out of this divine confusion, we have to conclude that the image what Muhammad saw was actually in his own head (Sina, 2008, p. 110). So in whatever direction he turned his head Gabriel appeared in that direction.

Once while walking, Muhammad heard a voice from the sky. When he looked up, he saw Gabriel sitting on a chair between the sky and earth (Bukhari: 6.60.448). But we can find a flaw in this story. Muhammad had seen that Gabriel had 600 wings. Logically, a creature which has wings does not need a chair to sit to float between sky and earth. Furthermore, if the Gabriel can really sit in between sky and earth, why nobody saw him? Hallucinations are deceptive lies, and the worst part of lying is that the liar tends to forget what he had said before.

Muhammad sincerely took all these hallucinations as signs of divinity. By seeing his sincerity, many of the feebleminded followers believed him. But many intelligent Meccans recognized that he was mentally ill. Timely, Allah certified his hallucinations as divine inspiration as in the following two Qur'anic verses.

Certainly he saw of the greatest signs of his Lord. (Q: 53.18).

And your comrade is not mad. Surely he beheld Him on the clear horizon. (Q: 81.22, 23).

Muhammad was not an original thinker. He simply did not know how to have a logical and organized thinking. Bits and pieces he had learnt here and there about Christianity and Judaism, and based on this, his handicapped brain worked overtime and produced those hallucinations. But, once Allah stamped them in the Qur'an, the hallucinations became heavenly. Allah's authority is so strong that no Muslim is capable of questioning them ever since the birth of Islam. For them the belief comes before the understanding. As Dasti (cited Warraq, 1995, p. 4) lamented, "*Belief can blunt human reason and common sense*". All they have to do is to believe. Logic and understanding have no value at all. It never occurred to their brains that the voice might have been the voice of Muhammad's own disturbed mind.

2.5: Muhammad's Famous Night Journey

Muhammad's famous night journey (*al-Isra* and *al-Mi'raj*) with Gabriel to Jerusalem and then to heavens was a dream-hallucination. Buraq, a white animal, half mule, half donkey, with a human head and with wings (some enthusiastic Muslim sources even add the tail of a peacock) carried Muhammad on her back. Muhammad and Gabriel went their way until they arrived at the temple at Jerusalem where he found Abraham, Moses, and Jesus, along with a company of Prophets and acted as their imam in prayer. After prayer, Buraq took him to each of the heavens till the seventh heaven and he received royal treatment in each of the heavens.

Muslims go out of their way to give some credibility to this stupid story. The stupidest part of the story is that when Muhammad allegedly visited the temple in Jerusalem, there was no temple in Jerusalem. About six centuries before al-Buraq took flight, the Romans had already destroyed it. By 70 A.D not a single stone was left on another. According to Bible, the Temple of Solomon was built around tenth century BC. The Dome of the Rock was raised on the foundations of the Roman

Temple of Jupiter in 691 and the al-Aqsa mosque was constructed over a Roman basilica on the southern end of the Temple Mount in 710 by the Umayyads (Sina, 2008, p. 120). So if there was no temple then which temple did he visit, unless we conclude that the whole incident was a hallucinatory experience?

And then, what about the divine animal Buraq – the half mule, half donkey white animal with a human head? This divine transportation system of Allah had wings on its sides with which it propelled its feet, putting down each forefoot at the limit of its sight. Buraq does not resemble to any animal known to humankind – half mule, half donkey with a human head – what a poor and idiotic expression. Such a creature, if ever existed, would resemble more to Muhammad himself than anything else. In Islamic scriptures there is no shortage of stupidity. If he had a creative brain, he would have seen something better in his hallucination.

However, Muhammad had seen angels in the heavens. The Egyptian Muslim scholar and historian, Haykal (1976, Chapter 8) describes Muhammad's heavenly experience as follows,

The first heaven was of pure silver and the stars suspended from its vault by chains of gold; in each one an angel lay awake to prevent the demons from climbing into the holy dwelling places and the spirits from listening indiscreetly to celestial secrets.

This is the height of Islamic stupidity. All these nonsense used to fascinate the seventh century illiterate Arabs, but today, anyone with a little knowledge in astronomy will laugh at these bizarre tales. Ishaq wrote,

After the completion of my business in Jerusalem, a ladder was brought to me finer than any I have ever seen. An angel was in charge of it and under his command were 12,000 angels each of them having 12,000 angels under his command. (Ishaq: 184)

It is hard to imagine that 144,000,000 angels are holding a ladder. Haykal continued with Muhammad's divine experience at different levels in the heaven,

There [in the first heaven] Muhammad greeted Adam. And in the six other heavens the Prophet met Noah, Aaron, Moses, Abraham, David, Solomon, Idris (Enoch), Yahya (John the Baptist) and Jesus.

He saw the Angel of Death, Azrail, so huge that his eyes were separated by 70,000 marching days. He commanded 100,000 battalions and passed his time in writing in an immense book the names of those dying or being born.

He saw the Angel of Tears, who wept for the sins of the world; the Angel of Vengeance with brazened face, covered with warts, who presides over the elements of fire and sits on a throne of flames; and another immense angel made up half of snow and half of fire surrounded by a heavenly choir continually crying: 'O God, Thou hast united snow and fire, united all Thy servants in obedience to Thy Laws'.

The divine stupidity of *al Mi'raj* is again at its peak. The angel of death, angel of tears and angel of vengeance were the products of Muhammad's hallucination. Is it possible to imagine a creature made up half of snow and half of fire? Such distorted thoughts lead to stress to a healthy mind. In the seventh heaven, he saw such a strange creature which cannot be even envisioned. Haykal continues,

In the seventh heaven where the souls of the just resided was an angel larger than the entire world, with 70,000 heads; each head had 70,000 mouths, each mouth had 70,000 tongues and each tongue spoke in 70,000 different idioms singing endlessly the praises of the Most High.

It is not only difficult but also stressful to visualize a creature like this. How did he know that the angel was larger than the world? How did he count the creature's number of heads, mouths, tongues, etc., when he was believed to be illiterate? Why Allah created such a horrible beast? Why Allah allowed the beast to enter paradise, while it was supposed to be in hell? After seeing the absurdities of Muhammad's night journey, many of his followers left Islam. To save Muhammad from further humiliation, Allah revealed,

Behold! We told thee that thy Lord doth encompass mankind round about: We granted the vision which We showed thee, but as a trial for men … We put terror (and warning) into them, but it only increases their inordinate transgression! (Q: 17.60).

This verse is too silly. Muhammad claimed to have visited a temple which was destroyed long before him and claimed to have seen angels, gibberish creatures at heaven but could not produce any proof, but Allah wanted the Muslims to believe him without question because it was a test to them. Helpless Muhammad took Allah as witness.

He said: My Lord knows what is spoken in the heaven and the earth, and He is the Hearing, the Knowing. (Q: 21.4).

But the Arabs ridiculed him saying that his night journey was either a dream, or a fabricated story.

Nay, say they, (these are but) muddled dreams; nay, he hath but invented it … (Q: 21.5)

Similar to his vision in the cave, the *al-Mi'raj* had an extraordinary parallel with another account *The Secrets of Enoch*, which, composed by an unknown Jewish sectarian group, predates Muhammad by four centuries. Enoch, a three hundred and sixty-five years old man, was taken by two angels and made to pass through the seven heavens, one by one. According to Charles (1999, pp. 4-11, 13-24, 37-39), while Enoch was fast asleep, two angels came to him, called him by his name and said, "*Have courage, Enoch, do not fear; The Eternal God sent us to thee. Thou shalt today ascend with us into heaven*". They took him on their wings and bore him up to the first heaven and placed him on the clouds. In various layers of the heaven, Enoch saw two hundred angels who fly with the wings (some of them had six wings) and rule the stars, angels guard the treasure houses, seven bands of very bright and very glorious angels in sixth heaven sweet and loud singing and all songs of praise, etc. There is a possibility that the *al-Mi'raj* dream-hallucination was a subconscious representation of this ancient story of Enoch which Muhammad might have heard somewhere. However, to put an end to all the arguments regarding Muhammad's night journey, let us quote from Ibn Ishaq.

Umm, Abu Talib's daughter, said: "He [Muhammad] slept in my home that night after he prayed the final night prayer. A little before dawn he woke us, saying, 'O Umm, I went to Jerusalem.' He got up to go out, and I grabbed hold of his robe and laid bare his belly. I pleaded, 'O Muhammad, don't tell the people about this for they will know you are lying and will mock you.' He said, 'By Allah, I will tell them.' I told a Negress [female Negro] slave of mine, 'Follow him and listen' (Ishaq: 184)

Therefore, Umm, the daughter of Abu Talib, confirmed that Muhammad's famous night journey actually happened in his dream which Muhammad mistook as a real experience. It means, the incident was actually a dream-hallucination. Many of the Meccans also believed the same. Qur'an confirms it.

He said: My Lord knows what is spoken in the heaven and the earth, and He is the Hearing, the Knowing. Nay! say they: medleys of dreams; nay! he has forged it; nay! he is a poet; so let him bring to us a sign as the former (prophets) were sent (with). (Q: 21.4, 5).

Next, I wish to interpret this dream-hallucination.

2.5.1: A Logical Explanation through Dream Interpretation

Dream is a mild hallucination. It transforms the thoughts into sensory images, mostly of a visual sort. Freud calls it "hallucinatory satisfaction" and "hallucinated fulfillment of wish". Though there are some minor differences between Freud and Jung's analysis, both agreed that interpreting a dream can be justified entirely from a scientific standpoint. Since the subconscious mind plays an important part in neurosis and dreams are the direct expression of subconscious psychic activity, the practicability of dream-analysis is beyond any question.

A healthy mind can very easily distinguish between dream and reality; but the neurotic patients, who cannot identify dreams and take it as a real experience, need serious medical attention. For them, the dream is a genuine material, not a distorted substitute for something else. A dream does not simply give them expression to a thought but represent the wish-fulfillment as a hallucinatory experience often with a distortion. Muhammad could not differentiate dream from reality, hence calling him a neurotic patient is not an exaggeration at all. Bukhari (8.77.610) wrote,

*Narrated Ibn 'Abbas' ... **Allah's Apostle actually saw with his own eyes the vision of all the things, which were shown to him on the Night Journey to Jerusalem. It was not a dream.***

According to Freud, dream has a sense and it can give meaningful clues if it is translated "backwards" and the distortion is undone. If we analyze this dream-hallucination of Muhammad, we can uncover many facts and create a mental map of this seventh century mental patient.

In 1900, Freud published a major work on the interpretation of dreams where he concluded that the study of the dreams is not only the best preparation for the study of the neurosis but dreams are themselves a neurotic system. He used two terms for dream-interpretation, namely, *Manifest dream-content* (what the dream apparently tells us) and *Latent dream-thoughts* (the unconscious thoughts that occur to the dreamer), and concluded (Strachey & Gay, 1966, p. 139), *"Dream as a whole is the distorted substitute for something else, something unconscious, and that of the task of interpreting a dream is to discover this unconscious material."*

Now, with the help of Freud's theory we can throw a large amount of light on Muhammad's strange night journey hallucination. His dream-hallucination has both the above distinctive characteristics as described below.

Manifest dream-content: Buraq; Muhammad met Abraham, Moses, and Jesus, along with a company of Prophets, and acted as their imam in prayer; visiting a temple which did not exist; silver and gold in Allah's paradise; various angels, etc.

Latent dream-thoughts: wish-fulfillment, ambition fulfillment, erotic wishes, anger, self-glorification, frustration.

When Muhammad's prophetic claim was under serious doubt after the satanic verses incident, he had a strong desire to reinforce it. As Freud (Strachey & Gay, 1966, p. 264) wrote, *"Dream-work consists essentially in the transformation of thoughts into a hallucinatory experience. How this can happen is sufficiently mysterious"*. Muhammad wanted to replace the Ka'ba with a more credible shrine, desperately needed a new Qibla (direction of prayer) and a new object to exploit. He simply dreamed off the satisfaction of his secret needs. Allah had at His power to have taken Muhammad from his bed (or Umm's bed) straight up to the heavens, but to impress the importance of Jerusalem upon Muslims; Muhammad was first taken to Jerusalem. In doing so, Allah made the al-Aqsa mosque of Jerusalem "a new object to exploit". Once the religious importance of al-Aqsa mosque was established, Muslims turned their Qibla towards Jerusalem. However, after 16 /17 months, Allah commanded in His wisdom for the Muslims to face Ka'ba again.

The second troubling question is; why suddenly Allah decided to invite Muhammad to His garden in the seventh sky? The reason was that Muhammad desperately needed a miracle. The *al-Mi'raj* served that purpose. All he wanted was to elevate himself at the cost of God. He had an insatiable craving for praise. His secret desires were projected as a hallucination. Qur'an says,

> Glorified be He Who carried His servant by night from the Inviolable Place of Worship to the Far distant place of worship the neighborhood whereof We have blessed, that We might show him of Our tokens! Lo! He, only He, is the Hearer, the Seer. (Q: 17.1)

The first few words of this verse need to be read between the lines. *"Glorified be He"* – it is absurd to think that God wanted to glorify Himself. Rather, it was Muhammad who was elevating himself in the name of God. If God is glorified by allowing Muhammad to enter paradise, undoubtedly, Muhammad was overvalued. The ego satisfaction comes from comparing ourselves to our opponent and feeling that we are better in some way. Muhammad used Allah for an ego boost. Freud (Strachey & Gay, 1966, p. 175) wrote, *"... the dreamer's own ego appears in every dream and plays the chief part in it."*

Another latent dream thought was ambition. Muhammad wanted to rise above all other Biblical Prophets. All of them had routinely made exacting and detailed predictions to demonstrate their divine authority. But Muhammad was not capable of producing a single miracle, and he knew this inadequacy very well. Hence, in his hallucination, he was greeted by all the Prophets; e.g., Adam, Noah, Aaron, Moses, Abraham, David, Solomon and Jesus. By doing so, this ambitious neurotic patient joined the rank of a Prophet without having a single miracle in his account. Then he led all the Prophets in prayer. It proved his superiority over other Prophets; he was glorified amongst all. Of course Muhammad was superior to all Prophets, otherwise why Allah sent Buraq – a special transport system for him? Ishaq shows, what an important person Muhammad was!

When I came up to mount him (Buraq), he shied. Gabriel placed his hand on its mane and said, 'Are you not ashamed, O Buraq, to behave in this way? By Allah, none more honorable before Allah than Muhammad has ever ridden you before. The animal was so ashamed that he broke out into a sweat, and stood so that I could mount him. (Ishaq: 182).

Now, we will talk about Muhammad's erotic wishes – another latent dream-thought. Ishaq wrote.

He took me into Paradise, and there I saw a damsel with dark red lips. I asked her to whom she belonged, for she pleased me much when I saw her. She said, Zaid [Muhammad's adopted son]. The Apostle gave Zaid the good news about her. (Ishaq: 186)

This damsel with ruby lips was Zaynab, the wife of his adopted son, Zayd, whom Muhammad married later by trickery. In Muhammad's hallucination, Zaynab traveled from earth to paradise and then back to the land of her future husband. Nobody knows how she could be present in paradise before her death and without being tried by Allah on the Day of Judgment, which, according to Muslim belief, is yet to come.

In his dream, Muhammad saw the angel of death and the angel of tears. The latent dream-thoughts are revenge, anger, frustration and unhappiness (caused by frustration). Anger because he was ridiculed by the opponents, and frustration because his newfound religion was not shaping well. Hence, in spite of Allah being all-merciful, he did not see the angel of smile, angel of happiness, angel of love, angel of mercy, angel of kindness, angel of optimism and the angel of humanity. All these angels did not come to Muhammad because he was a creature of hate and revenge. His dreams were censored in his subconscious.

Another point demonstrates the fallacy of his *al-Mi'raj*. Though Muhammad took a visionary travel to the paradise, nowhere can we find any statement that he was awestruck neither by the previous Prophets whom he bragged to have visited in different skies nor by facing Allah himself. Were the demonic creatures, angels and Buraq more awe-inspiring than visiting legendary Prophets in the grandeur of the seven heavens and talking with Allah? The legendary Prophets and Allah did not have any awe-inspiring effect on him because the "picture" was already there in his subconscious mind. He just dreamed off the pre-fabricated picture according to his need.

All dreams are obstructed by dream-distortions which make the dream seems strange and unintelligible to us. For the children, there is hardly any distortion; for adults, the distortion is less; while for the neurotic patients, obviously it is much more. Often there are omissions, modifications, fresh groupings of the material; which are the activities of dream-censorship and instruments of dream-distortion. These two factors give the dream the strangeness on account of which the dreamer himself is not inclined to recognize it as his own production and makes "surprising discoveries" which confuse others.

The *al-Mi'raj* fascinates the Muslims so much that they try to redecorate the various dream-distortions of their Prophet to give some credibility to it. The unique physical appearance of Buraq – the half mule, half donkey with a human head – tells that it was a dream-distortion. Why Buraq did not resemble to an elephant? It is because Muhammad did not know how an elephant looks like. During those days there was no elephant in Arabia. Elephants are entirely vegetarian and most of Saudi Arabia is covered in desert with hardly any vegetation for these huge animals to survive. Muhammad loved donkey-riding and the name of his legendary donkey was Yafur (Warraq, 2000, p. 241). So Buraq was at least half donkey. Why a human head? It is because a creature with a human head is more intelligent than a creature with an animal head. Allah's divine creature must be smart. I am not sure why the other half looked like a mule, or more scientifically, what was the unknown content for this "distorted substitute", i.e., the half mule. Allah knows best!

According to Muhammad, the first heaven was of pure silver and the stars were suspended by chains of gold. Angels lay awake to guard it and to prevent the spirits from listening indiscreetly to celestial secrets. If heaven is an absolute spiritual place, why it was decorated with pure silver and gold – the earthly things which need to be guarded? Let me undo the distortion and remove the censorship. It is not unusual for a beggar to dream of a grand feast, or a cobbler to become a king, or a political novice to become the President of his state, or a greedy person like Muhammad to dream pure silver and chains of gold, etc. When a person is unhappy in real life, his secret wishes are often censored and rise up in his dream. The distortion is greater when the wishes that are to be satisfied by hallucination worsen.

Much stringent examination is needed to undo the distortion of other manifested elements; e.g., the angel larger than the world with seventy thousand mouths. We often hear of fabulous beasts in ancient mythology and folklore, which were no doubt "creative" imaginations. Though we call this as creative, actually this type of imagination is quite incapable of "inventing" anything. It only combines components that are strange to one another and makes a composite figure (Strachey & Gay, 1966, p. 211); as example; A is dressed like B, acts like C, thinks like D, and looks like E etc. This is what we call a composite structure. Buraq itself was a composite structure of a mule, donkey and a human. When the final product "condenses", it takes totally a new shape which presents an alien appearance to the dreamer himself and much more so to anyone who is unacquainted with him personally.

2.6: Pre-conclusion: Divine Interpretation of Muhammad's Hallucinations

"Ignorance is ignorance; no right to believe anything can be derived from it."
Sigmund Freud
"The greater the ignorance the greater the dogmatism."
Sir William Osler (1849 - 1919)

Muslims fail to recognize Muhammad's hallucinations as figments of the distorted imagination of his sick mind and always look for some divine explanation to analyze them. This is primitive mentality. The psychic world of the Muslims and their state of consciousness has much similarity with the state of mind of a primitive man. The mentality of an archaic man (the word "archaic" means primal - original), retained by modern social people, is a serious subject matter of psychology.

Those archaic men had strange personalities. They used to flatly deny the most evident underlying connections, and instead of accounting for things as accidents or on reasonable grounds, should simply cling upon supernatural ideas, as example; witchcraft, spirit, sorcery, voodoo and the power of the tribal medicine men. For them the real explanation was always supernatural. But the fact is that those primitive men were no more logical or illogical than we are. Only difference is that their presuppositions were not the same as ours. It is a rational presupposition of ours that everything has a natural and perceptible cause. Similarly, the faith of the Muslims is based on certain presuppositions. Muslims simply assume (as if they "know" from their birth) that Muhammad was a Prophet and Qur'an contains purely God's instructions. These two presuppositions are so strongly embedded in their minds that they completely obliterate the facts and accounts for no aspect of the authenticity of Muhammad's prophethood. As Jung (1933, p. 119) commented, *"There are no misunderstandings in nature; they are only to be found in the realms that man calls 'understanding'."*

This is the only reason Muslims fail to identify Muhammad's so-called divine experiences as hallucinations. If a person changes his concept of reality in such a way as to admit that all psychic happenings are real and no other concept is valid, then he will never find any contradiction in his views. Such a person with "voluntary blindness", no matter whatever his conscious development or education or social status, is still an archaic man at the deeper levels of his mind. On every opportunity, he will take every painful effort to falsify reality and uphold Muhammad's neurotic disorder as spiritual.

2.7: Conclusion

"How often have I said to you that when you have eliminated the impossible, whatever remains, however improbable; must be the truth?"
Sherlock Holmes in Sir Arthur Conan Doyle's "The Sign of Four"

Muhammad's first experience with Gabriel was a "Command hallucination". In this type of hallucination, the command is clear and powerful from a mysterious voice that no one else can hear. People feel that they are being told what to do by an imposing or mythic figure. They are sometimes ordered to assassinate a prominent personality, sacrifice a human being or a child, or harm themselves by the wish of God, or devil, or demons, or angels, or aliens (Sagan, 1997, p. 131). These voices compel the patient to obey them by making him helpless at the mercy of it. If he is reluctant to comply, dire penalties are threatened. Voices usually do not introduce themselves, e.g., "This is God speaking", is never heard. This leaves the patient wondering – Who would issue such a command? Who could speak inside my head? He assumes that it is God or Jesus or Satan or the Head of a covert spy agency, or criminals, or the leader of a gang.

Command hallucinations may devastate a person turning him to a cold-blooded, conscienceless killer. As example; Jeffrey Macdonald, who murdered his wife and two children in 1970, claimed that the "acid heads" had committed the crime. Macdonald was the subject of the book and movie *Fatal Vision* (McGinniss, 1989). Kenneth Bianchi, who raped, tortured and killed a dozen women, was mistakenly believed to have a multiple personality and crimes had been committed by "Steve" (O'Brien, 1985). Ted Bundy, a serial killer who killed several dozen of young women, claimed that a "malignant entity" had taken over his consciousness (Hare, 1993, p. 4). Very similar to Muhammad's hallucination, all these are some kind of delusional psychic experiences. Stout (2005, p. 54) concludes that, when the human brain is impaired in this way, "The voices told me to do it" is not a joke but a horrifying reality and such a person can act on his delusional idea much against his conscience and will.

Intellectual ideas always attract us because we are capable of thinking. But when an idea is the expression of so-called psychic experience which bears fruit in religious beliefs, it represents forces that are beyond logical justifications and moral sanctions. Jung (1933, p. 42) commented, *"They [the forces] are always stronger than man and his brain. Man believes indeed that he moulds these ideas, but in reality, they mould him and make him their unwitting mouthpiece"*. For Muhammad (only for him) his hallucinations were real experiences. When he said that he was divinely commanded to preach in the name of Allah, he was telling the "truth" (only for him). He believed in his cause; his "honesty" in his prophetic claim and divine mission was based on this illusive "truth" which gave him such a strong willpower. This deceitful "sincerity" of Muhammad misled many Arabs to believe in him and to join his creed. This is how Islam started with a falsehood.

A quote from Freud (Strachey & Gay, 1966, p. 104) will help us to understand Muhammad's sincerity and such misleading truthfulness, *"Doctors have observed cases in which a mental disease has started with a dream and in which a delusion originating in the dream has persisted; Historical figures are reported to have embarked on momentous enterprises in response to dreams"*. If there is any truth in Islam, it is this deceptive truth amidst a vast ocean of falsehood.

When the Qur'anic verse 17.1 was revealed, the falsehood of *al-Mi'raj* dream-hallucination became sacred. In the history of religions, the lunacy of Muhammad's night's journey is one of the most absurd lies ever uttered in the name of religion. Muhammad was a neurotic patient who needed psychoanalytic treatment. A lunatic cannot bring anything real; he can only bring delusion, deception and confusion. These are the gifts of Muhammad to the Muslims.

Muhammad had shown all the symptoms of his lunacy. When a psychoanalyst treats a patient to restore him to health, his first concern is to relieve him of all the symptoms of his illness. Often the patient meets the analyst with a violent and tenacious resistance throughout the process of his treatment. On many occasions, the patient himself does not realize that he is putting up a struggle in the interest of his illness against the person who is helping him. A well-experienced psychoanalyst understands this fact, and he knows that if he falls back, the treatment is destined to fail. A person who came to a dentist because of an unbearable toothache will, nevertheless, try to hold the dentist back when he approaches the sick tooth with a pair of forceps.

Following few words from Freud needs particular attention because next I am going to analyze some Qur'anic verses through its understanding.

The patient's resistance is of very many sorts, extremely subtle and often hard to detect; and it exhibits protean changes in the forms in which it manifests itself ... at one moment, he [the patient] declares that nothing occurs to him, at the next that so many things are crowding in on him that he cannot get hold of anything ... he then admits that there is something he really cannot say... he says something has occurred to him, but it concerns another person and not himself. (Strachey & Gay, 1966, pp. 355-6).

Though the early Arabs turned away from Muhammad knowing that he was a lunatic, they were kindhearted and were even ready to pay for medical assistance to cure his lunacy (Haykal, 1976, ch. 5). But instead of listening to them, Muhammad started putting up resistance in the interest of his illness and against those people who wanted to help him. Allah revealed,

When the Unbelievers see thee, they treat thee not except with ridicule. "Is this, (they say), the one who talks of your gods?" and they blaspheme at the mention of (Allah) Most Gracious! (Q: 21.36)

The above verse confirms that Muhammad was hurt by the ridicule which made him upset. This is *"extremely subtle and often hard to detect"* resistance. As time passed, his struggle in the favor of his illness *"exhibited protean changes in the forms in which it manifests itself"* and the following verse was revealed,

Behold! We told thee that thy Lord doth encompass mankind round about: We granted the vision which We showed thee, but as a trial for men ... We put terror (and warning) into them, but it only increases their inordinate transgression! (Q: 17.60).

Now, let us examine the above verse from a Freudian perspective.

"A trial for men" – Muhammad is projecting his morbid dream-hallucination upon his critics. According to Allah the night journey was a trial whose authenticity depends on the acceptance of the people. Believing in Muhammad's prophetic claim is something which *"concerns another person and not himself"*.

"We put terror (and warning) into them" – Muhammad is putting up strong psychological resistance to uphold his delusion by instilling fear in opponent's mind, as Freud concluded elsewhere (Riviere *et al*, 1960, p. 50), *"... the need for illness got the upper hand in them over the desire for recovery"*.

This "divine" lunatic, who was supposed to be in a chain in an insane asylum, started his "divine" mission with "divine" deception and "divine" dishonesty. He was totally absorbed in himself. As time passed, he introduced the fear factor in his mission. At any cost the show must go on. He struggled hard to protect his delusions through terror and this verse was revealed,

> For them is torment in the life of the world, and verily the doom of the Hereafter is more painful, and they have no defender from Allah. (Q: 13.34).

When the reality is reversed or replaced by delusion, it is the hare that shoots the sportsman, elephants climb bamboo trees, a lunatic succeeds as a Prophet and millions of angels bring a ladder for him to ascend the heaven to keep an appointment with God, and God glorifies the Prophet but does not give him the power to perform a single miracle. Seeing is not always believing – this is what every dreamer understands, but if a lunatic in a divine robe cannot, problem begins for everyone.

Chapter 3: Muhammad's Strange Mindset

In religious front, we often hear the phrase "divine experience". As we have seen in previous chapter, often these divine experiences and visions are delusions or hallucinations, and in reality, they have no meaning. Many so-called Prophets have various degrees of success in deceiving common people but their claims generally die with them. Though Muhammad was one of them, his claim did not die with him. He successfully established a religion which is still going strong and causing much devastation even after fourteen centuries of his death.

Archer (1924, preface) commented, *"Muhammad the mystic is a greater figure than we have dreamed"*. According to him there may be some pathological elements in Muhammad's life and the essential thing in Muhammad's experience was that he was a mystic. He described (1924, summary), *"Muhammad was a mystic in the technical sense, and that, too, not merely in mental attitude, but in habitual practice"*. In this chapter, the mysticism of Muhammad is going to be unraveled. To unfold the mystery, we need to examine how the various components of his strange mind had interacted with each other. But before we do so, a basic discussion on psychology is required. I wish to start from the very beginning.

3.1: An Introduction to Freud's Id, Ego, and Superego Concepts

Before Aristotle, the science of psychology and the philosophy of mind were indistinguishable. However, during the long stretch of time between Aristotle and Immanuel Kant, a new approach to philosophy appeared – a philosophy based on science. As Kant wrote, *"Perceptions without conceptions are blind"* (cited Durant, 2006, p. 352). Before Aristotle, the philosophers just pondered about theories and based their theories on observation; but these scientific philosophers wanted to know more about the "biography" of mind, i.e., psychobiography and how it functions. For a long time this new scientific study was in its infancy till the time of Sigmund Freud, who was one of the first men to explore deep into the science and philosophy of the mind, and in doing so revolutionized both philosophy and psychology. From this time science actually started replacing religion.

Freud's and Jung's understandings of how the mind works and the structures of the mind replaced the idea of the soul and its functions. For Freud, the mind was central to human development and function, and his later theory (during 1920) of its three components – the id, ego and superego shapes who we are and how we act (Stevenson & Haberman, 2004, p. 161). Freud believed that these three components are distinct but they interact with each other closely. They are the parts that make up a person's personality. We are controlled by these three parts of the mind, and they control our varying levels of consciousness, as well as our desires and worldview. Though some psychologists have questioned the validity of Freud's theory of the workings of the mind, the theory does remain one of the most influential till today.

The hypothesis of narcissism was first proposed in 1909. Before Freud, some notable psychoanalytic studies were conducted by Havelock Ellis, Paul Nacke and

Margaret Mahler. Freud first used the term "narcissistic" in 1910 and thereafter narcissism soon took a central place in his thinking. In 1914 he published a paper exclusively devoted to narcissism called *On Narcissism: An Introduction*. Though Freud's initial work served as a basis for the definition of a Narcissist, he only scratched the surface of the narcissistic personality (Wesner, 2007, p. 5). Otto Rank published the first psychoanalytical paper in 1911 specifically concerned with narcissism, linking it to vanity and self-admiration. In 1923, Martin Buber published an essay *Ich und Du* (I and Thou), in which he pointed out that our narcissism often leads us to relate to others as objects instead of as equals. Later on, various other psychologists including Melanie Klein, Heinz Kohut and Otto Kernberg added more to Freud's theory.

During the 1970s and after, James F. Masterson further developed Freud's theory of the three components of the mind. Masterson is internationally renowned for his clinical work, research, and the writings on personality disorder. Masterson used the terms real self (or, true self), false self and superego. In recent years, volumes of material had been written on this subject by established psychologists, e.g., Christopher Lasch's 1979 best selling book *The Culture of Narcissism*, Sam Vaknin's *Malignant Self Love: Narcissism Revisited*, Sandy Hotchkiss's *Why It is always about You: The Seven Deadly Sins of Narcissism,* and a combined work by Twenge and Campbell by the name *The Narcissism Epidemic* just to mention a few. In this chapter and subsequent chapters we will do extensive study on these three basic components and compare the findings with that of Muhammad and his Allah as reported in Qur'an, Sunna and Hadith collections.

The true self (id) is not influenced by the external world. The false self (ego) is evolved to deal with the true self, and superego authorizes false self to do so. The false self seeks pleasure and comfort, and tries to avoid things that are unpleasant by analyzing the situation and by deciding whether to proceed with the action or remain idle (Kline, 1972, pp. 126-7). For a person with perfect mental health, the actions (and inactions) and the interactions between real self, false self and superego do not cause any harm either to him or people around him. But when these three components are not in balance, the person suffers from mental disorder.

Muhammad did not have any spiritual power. We have already discredited him by every possible logical manner and showed with clear proof that he was not a messenger of any kind of God. He was perfectly human with all human weaknesses and worldly desires. Did the three components of his mind worked against each other and therefore caused a personality disorder for him? Before we search for an answer, we should study the psychopathology of Muhammad.

3.2: The Psychopathology of Muhammad

In every society and amongst all races, we can find individuals, who because of something in their mental set up or their personal history, find it difficult or even impossible to adjust to the roles which society expects them to perform. In some cases their behavior brings them into violent conflict with their environment. Some of these individuals are very successful in their professional lives but miserable in their family and social lives. They sincerely believe that they are exceptional and hence they are not bound by the norms and rules of the society. This "denial of reality" is such a "feeling" which they cannot even explain, and because of this, they utter words and gestures which are quite outside the normal behavioral patterns of ordinary people. One of the most common features amongst these people is "megalomania", which is a non-clinical word defined (Fowler, 2010, p. 278) as,

1. A psychopathological condition characterized by delusional fantasies of wealth, power, or omnipotence.
2. An obsession with grandiose or extravagant things or actions.

According to traditional Islamic sources Muhammad was a megalomaniac. In Islam only belief in Allah is not enough to enter paradise and Muslims must believe the prophethood of Muhammad also. If Muhammad was only a spokesman of God, why Muslims have to praise Muhammad in their daily prayers? Though in Islam Allah is portrayed as all-powerful, this is in theory only. In practice, Muhammad is the central figure in Islam and Allah is just a piece of decoration. Allah is obliged to throw a person in hell even if he is sincerely devoted to Him but does not believe in Muhammad. So we can see how helpless the God of Islam is. Does such a pathetic God exist? Following quotes show that Muhammad lived in a grandiose fantasy world and was a denier of reality. He re-interpreted reality to fit his fantasies.

Allah's Apostle said, 'Whoever obeys me will enter Paradise, and whoever disobeys me will not enter it.' (Bukhari: 9.92.384)

Allah's Apostle said, 'Whoever obeys me, obeys Allah, and whoever disobeys me, disobeys Allah, and whoever obeys the ruler I appoint, obeys me, and whoever disobeys him, disobeys me.' (Bukhari: 9.89.251)

Allah's Apostle; the Lord of the Muslims, Leader of the Allah Fearing, Messenger of the Lord of the Worlds, the Peerless and Unequalled. (Ishaq: 233)

Allah addressed the believers and said, 'In Allah's Apostle you have a fine example for anyone who hopes to be in the place where Allah is.' (Ishaq: 467)

I heard Allah's Apostle saying, 'He who obeys me, obeys Allah, and he who disobeys me, disobeys Allah'. (Bukhari: 4.52.203)

Those who speak negatively of Allah and His Apostle shall be cursed. (Q: 33.57)

Though Muhammad placed himself as a humble servant of Allah, we cannot see any humbleness in the above words, and surprisingly, his God tolerated his arrogance. And after a certain period elapsed, Allah became less important than Muhammad and Muhammad emerged as "the living God". With this appearance, the person of Muhammad stood out above all in front rank and Allah was given a secondary position in His capacity as the auxiliary of the Prophet. Allah is no longer the Supreme Being and now He is inferior to Muhammad. Muhammad wrote in his Qur'an,

Lo! Allah and His angels pray peace to Prophet (Muhammad).O ye who believe also shower praises on him and salute him with a worthy salutation. (Q: 33.56)

*... and **when they (nonbelievers) come to thee, they salute thee, not as Allah salutes thee, (but in crooked ways)** ... Enough for them is Hell: In it will they burn, and evil is that destination! (Q: 58.8)*

The above two verses are enough to prove that the Allah was a myth and Muhammad was a rude imposter. He not only ridiculed and belittled his God, but at the same time also represented the entire divine system as a big joke. His behavior was a standard megalomaniac behavior. A person who thinks that he is superior to God and thus God salutes him is a denier of reality. Muhammad was so full of himself that he got carried away. Throughout Qur'an, Allah has no authority alone and He is so pitifully helpless without His messenger that if we completely erase the name of Allah from hundreds of verses throughout the Qur'an, and Muslims are asked to believe in, to submit to, and to obey Allah and His Apostle, practically nothing would change.

Before we proceed further, we should understand what the terms "Personality Disorder" and specifically "Narcissistic Personality Disorder" exactly mean. Then we should see how much these characteristics fit into his strange personality profile.

3.3: Understanding "Personality Disorder"

"I believe that the world should revolve around me!"

A popular song

Each individual in this world has a unique personality made up of traits that come from both our genetic make up and our life experiences, yet we tend to behave in fairly predictable ways. It is a vital part of what makes us who we are and how we interact with others. However, if a person's pattern of behavior, mood, social interaction, or impulsiveness causes distress to him, or to other people in his life, he is diagnosed as having a personality disorder. It is the ultimate misidentification. The personality of such a person is too rigid to the point that he is unable to change it in reaction to changing circumstances. He mistakes his habits for his identity. Though the person feels that his behavioral patterns are normal or right, people with personality disorders tend to have a narrow view of the world and find it difficult to participate in social activities. To diagnose a personality disorder, the patient's problematic behaviors must appear in two or more of the following areas,

1.   Perception and interpretation of the self and other people.
2.   Intensity and duration of feelings and their appropriateness to situations.
3.   Relationships with others.
4.   Ability to control impulses.

Personality disorders are considered to have their onset in late adolescence or early adulthood. A diagnosis of personality disorder to children is very rare because children's personalities are still in the process of formation which may change considerably by the time they are in their late teens. One of the ten major personality disorders is Narcissistic Personality Disorder (NPD).

3.4: Understanding "Narcissistic Personality Disorder"

"*Mirror, mirror on the wall,*
Who in the land is fairest of all?"

"*You, my queen, [you] are fairest of all.*
Famous is thy beauty majesty",

(*...but behold, a lovely maid I see*
Rags cannot hide her gentle grace
Alas, she is fairer than thee.)

From "Snow White", a fairy tale by Walt Disney

NPD is defined more distinctively as a pattern of grandiosity (exaggerated claims to talents, importance, or specialness) in the patient's private fantasies or outward behavior, a need for constant admiration from others, and a complete lack of empathy for others.

The myth from which narcissism gets its name is in Greek mythology. According to Greek folklore, Narcissus was a hero who was renowned for his beauty. Once he fell in love with a reflection in a pool, not realizing it was his own, and perished there, not being able to leave the beauty of his own reflection in the water. He was so mesmerized by his own unattainable reflection that he exclaimed "*then let me look at you and feed my wretched frenzy on your image*" (Vazire *et al*, 2008, p. 1440). Havelock Ellis was the first student of psychology to incorporate the Narcissus myth into the body of psychological literature.

DSM (Diagnostic and Statistical Manual of Mental Disorders) specifies nine diagnostic criteria for NPD. For the clinicians to make the diagnosis of a Narcissist, an individual must fit five or more of the following descriptions (Livesley, 1995, p. 205; Benjamin, 1996, p. 143),

1. He has a grandiose sense of self-importance (exaggerates activities and demands to be considered superior without real evidence of achievement).
2. He lives in a dream world of exceptional success, power, beauty, genius, or "perfect" love.
3. He thinks of himself as "special" or privileged, and that he can only be understood by other special or high-status people.
4. He demands excessive amounts of praise or admiration from others.
5. He feels entitled to admiration, compliance, or favorable treatment from others.
6. He is exploitative towards others and takes advantage of them.
7. He lacks empathy and does not recognize or identify with others' feelings.
8. He is frequently envious of others or thinks that they are envious of him.

9. He has an "attitude" or frequently acts in haughty or arrogant ways.

Major components of Narcissistic self

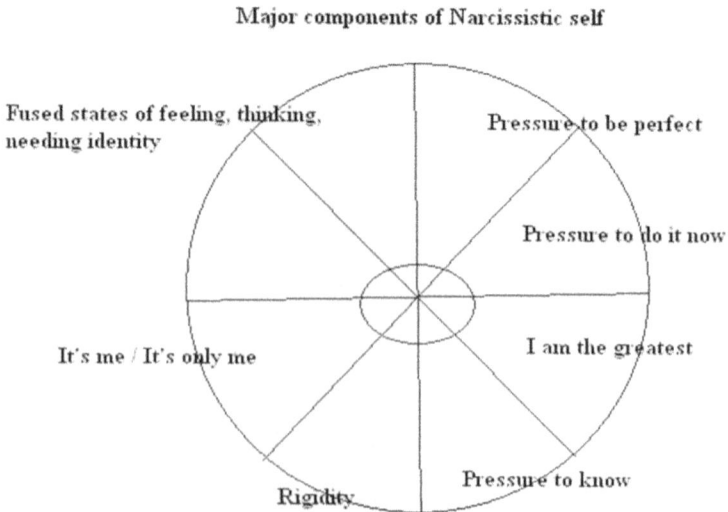

Fused states of feeling, thinking, needing identity

Pressure to be perfect

Pressure to do it now

It's me / It's only me

I am the greatest

Rigidity

Pressure to know

The above diagram can best be understood if compared with the abnormal mindset of the wicked queen of snow white. This queen is not asking the mirror because she is curious. She is asking because her identity is wrapped up in her unchallenged beauty and superiority. Rather than just accept she is a typical woman subject to short-lived beauty, gray hair, wrinkles, weight gain, etc, and that she must compete fair and square with her competitors on the great catwalk of life; instead she insists on being *numero uno*, forever. She is not actually number one, but she is definitely number one in thinking that she is number one. Secondly, in the event the mirror drops the bomb and breaks the bad news to her that indeed she has been replaced as Grand Champion, she needs to know who the lucky lady is, so that the opponent can be eliminated from the scene, thus replacing the balance of her own private universe.

The Narcissist's personality is based on a defensive false self that he must keep inflated at any cost in order not to feel the underlying rage and depression associated with an inadequate, fragmented sense of self (Masterson, 1990, p. 90). This "inflated false self" is like a balloon. If there is a leak in the balloon, i.e., the inflated false self cannot be preserved, he feels very miserable and insecure because it punctures the narcissistic grandiosity and reflects the discrepancy between NPD expectations or fantasies and the reality what he wants to deny at all costs (Beck & Freeman, 1990, p. 239). About 1% of the general population and 2 to 16% of the clinical population have NPD. Seventy-five per cent Narcissists are male.

As long as this false self is adequately inflated, it provides him "energy" to float high, oblivious to frustration and depression. This is the reason a Narcissist seems to immune to life's changes (both positive and negative) much to the admiration or envy of those around him. In fact the common impression given by a

Narcissist is that depression is simply not a part of his life. But this is an illusion. Successful Narcissists (successful in the sense that his perception of the world and his place in it manages to prevent him from questioning his importance) appear to be very creative. But actually they are not capable of creating anything new; they just "assemble" or "copy-paste". Hence, all his "creativities" are haphazard which contributes nothing valuable to the society he lives. Narcissism is always a losing game. His only creation is his false self.

Narcissists are strongly determined. Often he is quite talented to develop a life style through deception and manipulation that will resonate to his grandiose projections of himself and fuel his narcissistic needs. In this air-tight cocoon of narcissistic enjoyment he relaxes, and life seems to be pretty good. He feels very comfortable and secure, and as long as nothing punctures this closed circle, he will not be aware of any serious personality problems. The emperor must not be told that he does not have cloths.

Narcissists are pathological liars, which means either they are unaware of their lies or feel completely justified and at ease in lying to others. They are masters of deception. First they tell a lie and then they genuinely believe in their own lies (Vaknin, 1999, p. 24). This way they are capable of even deceiving themselves. They are extremely offended if contradicted or even criticized. They often see the difficulties that they have with others as external and independent of their behavior or input (Beck & Freeman, 1990, pp. 5, 6). They enjoy "putting something over" on other people, obtaining their feelings of superiority by lying to, victimizing and manipulating them.

In short; a Narcissist has two different personalities or two selves – the true self which is the real one, and the false self which is the fabricated and projected one. These two selves are at serious conflict with each other. Many celebrities, politicians, movie stars (in general, the prominent personalities and public figures) and show-off men have two personalities – the "real" one which they reserve for their family and relatives and the "forged" or "false" or "concocted" one which they exhibit in public. This is perfectly healthy behavior as long as the real self and the false self are not in clash with each other. These prominent personalities and public figures are not necessarily suffering from any mental disorder. But for a Narcissist, as Masterson (1990, p. 174) wrote, *"The Narcissist resembles a psychological turtle with a hard, impenetrable shell inside of which is an equally soft, fearful center; the impaired real self."* As Kernberg (1985, p. 2) wrote, *"[The Narcissists are] having a cohesive, albeit highly pathological, grandiose self which hide the inner identity diffusion and aimlessness."*

A Narcissist has no genuineness. The more successful is his false self, the more he becomes divorced from his true self and married to his false self. His true self is so much dominated by the false self that the true self is actually paralyzed. His life is constantly on the display – the display of the false self, a monodrama in an open theater where everyone has an access. For a sane person, the false self and the true self are at friendly terms with each other and never try to subdue each other which a Narcissist is deprived of. The false self is not overprotective to the true self; it is simply defensive to the true self. The false self is so suspicious that it exercises censorship on his dreams also (Riviere *et al*, 1960, p. 8). For a Narcissist, his true self is the worst enemy of his false self. The biggest fear of a Narcissist is that his true self may get accidentally activated.

3.4.1: The Seven Deadly Sins of Narcissism

Hotchkiss (2003, part 1) identified a characterization what she called the seven deadly sins of narcissism. This characterization is a clear, well set out, very readable examination of the nature, effects, provenance and prevalence of narcissism and a concise summary of the symptoms of narcissism.

Shamelessness– Shame is the primary painful feeling for not being good enough, or while experiencing humiliation. It is a basic emotion that begins early in life. Shame can keep a normal individual from developing close relationships with others and from enjoying life itself.

The Narcissist has the opposite problem. Shame is the feeling that lurks beneath all unhealthy narcissism. He appears to be abnormally shameless because he cannot process the shame in a healthy way; he simply accuses others when he is at fault. Actually he feels shame, but he is capable of bypassing the shame or simply dumps the burden of shame onto others. So it appears that the shame does not touch him or he is immune to it.

Magical thinking – Narcissists see themselves as perfect using distortion and illusion known as magical thinking which often has a placebo effect. Some very common narcissistic magical thinking are – I am immune and completely safe, nothing can happen to me, I am the best, the world revolves around me and I am at the center, the world is created for me, without me the humanity is a failure, I am not answerable to anyone, sin cannot touch me, etc.

There was a Narcissist who constantly compared himself to Christ, because he was Jewish and born in late December (Twenge & Campbell, 2010, pp. 212-3). If magical thinking really worked, it would be possible at any time for a group of us to get together for few seconds and visualize world peace, a stable global economy, no child molesters, no murderers, and no violent crimes of any type, no pollution, no famine, no homelessness, no poverty and no disease. We could prevent, even undo, tsunamis, tornadoes, hurricanes and nuclear disasters. We could resurrect the dead. In this case we would be God. Though a lot of healthy people spend some time in magical thinking, they do not deny the hard reality. This is where the Narcissist fails. He does not even score higher on objective IQ tests (Twenge & Campbell, 2010, p. 28). For him, his magical thinking replaces reality.

Arrogance – Humbleness is the opposite of narcissism. Arrogance is the divorcement from reality – a life of deception and lies. Arrogant people are often skilled liars and deceivers who wear their deception without the suspicion of others. Arrogance cannot handle critical situations and might simply resolve to violence. An arrogant Narcissist is interested only with self, not with the welfare of others. In spiritual arrogance the Narcissist has an unhealthy inflated opinion of the self. He lives in self-importance, succumbs to flattery and praises of men and builds his self-glory in monument out of human viewpoint. He cannot respect others because he has too much respect for himself. When he feels deflated, he re-inflates his false self by arrogantly diminishing, debasing, or degrading somebody else. He has contempt for those he views as inferior. The real downside of arrogance is negativity. Arrogance in a Narcissist leader invariably leads to megalomania and it results in collapse of ethics. Though he is simply too proud to be humbled, below the surface there is often a thin veil of insecurity.

Envy – Narcissists are constantly envious of other people. They may secure a sense of superiority in the face of another person's ability by using disrespect to belittle him. This is their unique way of interacting with the world. They envy others their success, or brilliance, or happiness, or good fortune. If a Narcissist comes across someone who appears to know more or have more than he does, he will attempt to devalue that person. Sometimes he may even choose to destroy the "object" (for a Narcissist others are merely objects) that gives him so much grief by provoking in him feelings of inadequacy and frustration. By this way the Narcissist elevates himself. The alternate favorite way out is the *Schizoid Solution* (complete avoidance from meaningful social and emotional contact with others). When the Narcissist finds that it is too painful for him to see the success and the happiness of others and he cannot do anything to devalue them, he prefers loneliness. He simply withdraws himself from the society or engages in such jobs where he can avoid mixing with the people he envies. So he creates a bubble universe, something like a dream world where he is the king.

Entitlement – The Narcissists hold unreasonable expectations of particularly favorable treatment and automatic compliance because they consider themselves uniquely special. Any failure to comply will be considered an attack on their superiority, and the perpetrator is considered to be an "awkward" or "difficult" person. **The Narcissist simply assumes – "I deserve"**. Defiance of their will is a narcissistic injury that can trigger narcissistic rage. Often Narcissists will only interact with people they feel are their equals. A sense of unhealthy entitlement is a substantial barrier to forgiveness. For them forgiveness is hard to do because they "lose face". Forgiveness is too costly in terms of pride, so they do not want to face the costs of forgiving others. They have to remain "honorable" in their own eyes. For this reason they are often very cruel. If necessary, they will create hypothetical offence situations to inflict pain on others. Over time, such unforgiving tendencies may prevent the healing of wounded relationships and lead to social alienation.

Exploitation – It can take many forms but always involves the unjustified use of others without regards for their feelings, interests or preferences. Often the other is in a submissive position where resistance would be not easy, or even impossible. When we replace worn out objects we do not grieve for them. Similarly Narcissists do not grieve for those they discard. There is a complete lack of empathy and humanity. The Narcissists have emotional maturity of a five year old child and they are satisfied with their distorted personal ethics. **The standard line for a Narcissist for several thousand years is – "You owe me".**
The Narcissists are often very charming and can make people around them feel special and desired. They do that in order to leverage what they want out of them: validation, respect, and favors they are not entitled to. When people question this behavior or challenge the Narcissist, he devalues them and casts them aside, only to find soon new "friends" to exploit. The Narcissist is best at his exploitation when he wears a religious mask. The religious Narcissist takes advantage of tragedy and grief of other people to secure future narcissistic supply.

Narcissistic abuse may sometimes go unnoticed by others even by the victims themselves. This is called *ambient abuse*. This is the most dangerous type of abuse, because it is more difficult to pinpoint and identify. In the long term the ambient abuse erodes the victim's sense of self-worth and self-esteem. Slowly the victim loses faith in his ability to manage and to cope with the world and its demands. His self-confidence is destroyed, and a kind of mental paralysis encroaches him.

Bad Boundaries – Everyone has a right to protect and defend himself. Personal boundaries are guidelines, rules or limits that a person creates to identify for him what are reasonable, safe and permissible ways for other people to behave around him, and how he will respond when someone steps outside those limits. The ability to set up personal boundaries is recognized as an essential component of a healthy relationship. It is the same old "yours, mine and ours" concept which determines – what belongs to you, what belongs to me and what we share.

When a reasonable boundary is set, it defines the limit of personal (physical, emotional and mental) or professional behavior. A normal person understands his own boundary and the boundaries of others with whom he interacts. The boundaries are not negotiable, and others can neither determine it from the outside nor should have a say in setting them or in upholding them. Only the person decides when they have been breached, what constitutes a transgression, what is excusable and what not. In the mind of a Narcissist, there is no boundary between self and other; he is simply not aware of it. He fails to understand that others are separate and are not extensions of him, and cannot define where individuality ends and the world begins. Others either exist to meet his needs or may as well not exist at all. Those who provide narcissistic supply to the Narcissist will be treated as if they are part of the Narcissist and be expected to live up to those expectations.

3.5: Understanding "Malignant Narcissism"

Malignant narcissism is a syndrome consisting of a cross breed of NPD, the antisocial personality disorder (also often referred to as psychopathy or sociopathy), as well as paranoid traits (a dysfunctional thought process heavily influenced by anxiety or fear, often to the point of irrationality and delusion). It differs from NPD in that the malignant Narcissists derive much higher levels of psychological gratification from accomplishments over time. This way their mental disorder worsens with time. Also, they suffer from many other mental disorders. This is called co-morbidity. Because the malignant Narcissist becomes more involved in this psychological gratification, he is prone to develop the antisocial, the paranoid, and the schizoid personality disorders. The term "malignant" is added to the term Narcissist to indicate that individuals with this disorder tend to worsen in their impulse controls and desires over time.

Malignant narcissism is believed to be the worst of all the personality disorders. This psychological problem sometimes can be partially treated with medications and therapy but this can help to reduce aggravating symptoms only. Though NPD is found in the current version of the *Diagnostic and Statistical Manual of Mental Disorders*, malignant narcissism is not. Hence it should be considered a theoretical or experimental diagnostic category, not as an official diagnosis; rather a syndrome.

Individuals with malignant narcissism would be diagnosed under NPD.

Erich Fromm first coined the term malignant narcissism in his 1964 book *The Heart of Man*, describing it as a *"severe mental sickness"* representing *"the quintessence of evil"* (Monte, 1995, p. 595). He characterized the condition as *"the most severe pathology"* and *"the root of the most vicious destructiveness and inhumanity"*. For a malignant Narcissist the outside world *"has ceased to be real"* because he has made himself the substitute for reality – his own *"god and the world."* He is great not for something he has achieved but for some presumed quality he has. As a result, he does not *"need to be related to anybody or anything"* (Fromm, 1964, pp. 65-8, 77). In doing so, he removes himself even more from reality and becomes more and more isolated in a fantasy realm of grandiosity.

Kernberg understood malignant narcissism as the worst form of narcissism, and in 1984 he first proposed malignant narcissism as a psychiatric diagnosis and used the terms "malignant narcissism" and "psychopathic behavior" interchangeably. He pointed out that the antisocial personality was fundamentally narcissistic and without morality. Malignant narcissism includes a sadistic element, creating, in essence, a sadistic psychopath. Kernberg called "malignant" those Narcissists whose grandiosity is built around aggression and destruction of those who offer love. These are sadistic antisocial types with a deeply paranoid orientation toward life who so idealize their own aggressive power that they have killed off the sane and loving parts of themselves that might have enabled them to develop attachments and tolerate dependence (Hotchkiss, 2003, p. 168). Malignant Narcissists only wish to destroy, symbolically castrate, and dehumanize others. Their paranoia becomes so intense in old age that they are virtually unapproachable even by the people who are very closely related to him. They ultimately not only destroy themselves but also everyone around them, like "necrophiles" (sexual attraction towards corpses). It is always better to deal with these people by being careful about their dehumanizing capabilities. They are even capable to fool the therapists treating them. Followings are the special characteristics of malignant narcissism.

Aggressiveness

1. Glibness / superficial charm.
2. Grandiose sense of self-worth.
3. Pathological lying,
4. Cunning, manipulative, deceitful,
5. Criminal versatility.
6. Lack of remorse or guilt, callous / lack of empathy, absence of conscience
7. Characteristic demonstrations of joyful cruelty and sadism.
8. Failure to accept responsibility for own actions.
9. Blame-game
10. Promiscuous sexual behavior, many short-term marital relationships.
11. A psychological need for power.

Socially deviant lifestyle

1. Parasitic lifestyle.

2. Impulsivity (Inclined to act on urge rather than thought).
3. Family and social irresponsibility.
4. Juvenile delinquency, pedophilia.

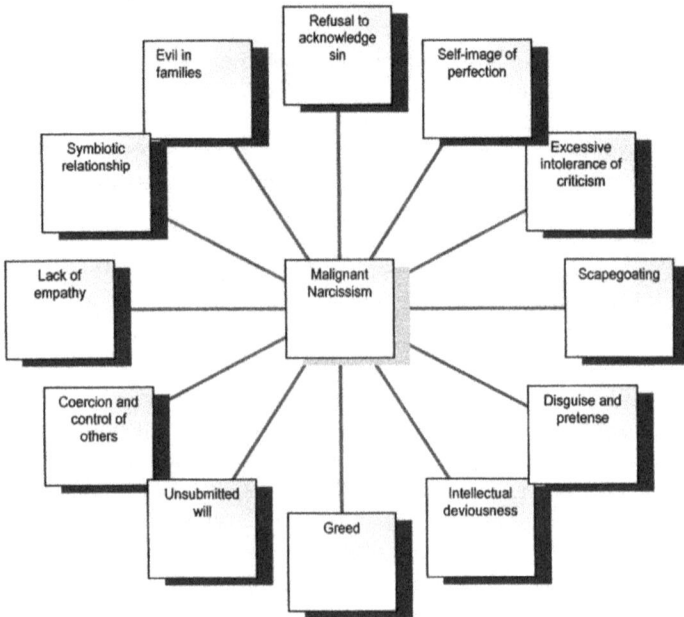

The above traits are common amongst individuals with psychological disorders. However the psychopaths and malignant Narcissists must display a strong tendency towards these characteristics. Whereas the psychopath displays more antisocial features, the malignant Narcissist desires "unlimited power" and "everything". He cannot delay gratification. He does not want to be equal to God but he wants even God to be inferior to him. He often moves above and beyond his contemporaries by making full use of his capabilities. The malignant Narcissists hardly make positive contributions to the society; their contributions are often negative and harmful.

Malignant narcissism is a deadly illness. They deserve our genuine compassion. However, it is an extremely dangerous situation when a malignant Narcissist is in a position of power where he can create endless suffering and destruction. They have a sadistic "willingness to kill" just to protect their own self-serving delusions. This makes them particularly dangerous, as they will literally stop at nothing to hold onto the position of power in which they find themselves. War and an atmosphere of violence is the situation in which they feel most themselves. Malignant Narcissists are ruthless murderers (whether it be physically or psychically) who are criminally insane. Many psychiatrists feel the destructive behavior of a malignant Narcissist is an attempt to maintain his false self in the same way an alcoholic is desperate to construct his life to perpetuate his drinking, no matter whatever is the cost (Zayn & Dibble, 2007, p. 87). They can literally turn a man into a corpse without giving a second thought about the consequences. It is a tragic and destructive life.

As we are going to see subsequently, all the aforementioned characteristics of malignant narcissism were prominently present in Muhammad, and with further critical analysis of the extent of his cruelty, abnormal sexual indulgence, paranoia and extreme greed; it is possible to prove that the beloved Prophet of the Muslims was actually a malignant Narcissist.

3.5.1: The Defensive False Self of a Narcissist

"It terrifies me to think of saying 'This is me; this is my skin'. So I cop out on myself by being some other person, living with some other person's fantasy. It becomes my fantasy. I know it's not my real self. It's fake. But I'm fake. If I let my real self come out, I will be all alone and I cannot handle that".

A Narcissist's confession (Masterson, 1990, p. 19)

The defensive false self of a Narcissist is characterized by self-importance, grandiosity, and omnipotence. The false self is bogus and fragile because it is based on a grandiose fantasy rather than on reality, and it is defensive because its purpose is not to cope or adapt to reality, but to reinforce grandiosity in order not to feel depressed (Masterson, 1990, p. 93). Because of this, the Narcissist is always alert and at war with his own true self to prevent it from emerging.

A Narcissist cannot be happy unless he is the best. They often seem to be the people who have everything – talent, wealth, power. They also have a strong sense of knowing what they want and how to get it. They are intelligent and often manipulative. Many are very successful at work but a close observation of these people reveals that underneath of this "well-constructed mask" of grandiose style behavior, they are actually insecure, miserable people (Masterson, 1990, p. 91). The Narcissist is at the mercy of his inner demons (Zayn & Dibble, 2007, p. 67). His life is empty at its core and he often fails to realize that beneath this narcissistic glitter there is an impaired real self. In fact a time comes when the Narcissist becomes a slave to his false self like a person becomes addicted to drugs. Finally the impaired true self becomes like an apparition.

Vaknin (1999, p. 9) wrote, *"A Narcissist is an actor enacting a monodrama, yet forced to remain behind the scene. The scenes take the center stage instead"*. This is where the false self is in action. For example, a reporter on a crime scene may feel as if he is really a participant and he starts reacting that way. The Narcissist does not cater at all to his true self because he does not love his true self. He is at love with the reflection of his true self, i.e., the false self. He is always pressurized to keep moving to keep reinforcing his sense of grandeur. He may be a workaholic to satisfy his false self and hence "nothing to do" is a threat to him. Hence holidays are very stressful for a Narcissist because holidays focus on things not directly related to him (Zayn & Dibble, 2007, p. 77). He sees no red or amber lights ahead to make him stop or slow down. He moves at full speed toward his goal. Whether it is a lucrative business arrangement or a prospective romantic partner or spouse, the Narcissist lunges ahead with extreme self entitlement, feelings of superiority and an iron will that cannot be deterred. Ultimately he adopts the old saying – "not to move forward is to drop behind". This often makes him an extremely restless person.

Another distinctive characteristic of the false self is that it develops a strong defense mechanism to protect itself from the intolerable feeling of shame about personal shortcomings and inferiority complex (Hotchkiss, 2003, p. 14). Narcissists want to avoid these two things at any cost. So when we encounter arrogance in a Narcissist, it is not really the pride that we are seeing but a deep and irrational fear of being worthless. His superiority complex is in fact an extension of his inferiority complex. The feeling of supremacy often serves to mask a cancerous complex of inferiority.

Vaknin (1999, p. 157) wrote, "*The Narcissist has a fake, substitute ego. This is why his energy is drained. He spends most of it on maintaining, preserving and protecting the wrapped unrealistic images of his (false) self and of his (fake) world. The Narcissist is a person exhausted by his own absence*". What is the cause of his exhaustion? Twenge & Campbell (2010, p. 276) observed, "*... there has been a giant transfer of time, attention and resources from reality to fantasy.*" Zayn & Dibble (2007, pp. 67, 87) concluded,

> *The entire entity of a Narcissist is based on a lie. He created a false self as a means of acceptance and approval and was forced to cultivate that lie in order to maintain his existence.*

> *The Narcissist lives a tragic and destructive life, trying to balance on the sharp and rocky peak of his false self. Much of the Narcissist's psychic energy is directed towards maintaining this balance within himself and his environment and the resulting stress and frustration accumulates.*

Narcissists strongly oppose any force that threatens to knock them from their precarious positions. That is why they are very envious of others. Value is always relative, not absolute. The false self of a Narcissist thinks this way – if someone else's stock goes up, my stock automatically goes down. When the false self feels deflated, it can reinforce itself by diminishing, humiliating or degrading someone else. If his balloon gets punctured by the ill winds of life, it can only be repaired by proving that someone else is more inferior to him.

3.5.2: The Narcissistic Supply

A Narcissist is strongly motivated by the continuous need for "supplies" to feed the grandiose conception of himself. In this sense; the word "supplies" means those specific activities and relationships that reinforce his grandiosity. He feeds off other people, who hurls back him an image (the inflated false self) that he projects to them. This is their sole function in this world – to reflect, to respect, to applaud and to detest – in a word, to assure that the false self of the Narcissist exists (Vaknin, 1999, p. 9). Other people exist in a Narcissist's life to please him. For him, the people are like "useful tools" and "opportunities", and therefore they should be used and exploited. The purpose of their very existence is to mirror the Narcissist's image of himself – unique, special and important. Otherwise they have no right to tax his time, energy or emotions – this is what a Narcissist feels.

The narcissistic supply can be anything that feeds his fragile false ego. He always goes around "hunting and collecting" the way the expressions on people's faces change when they notice him. He places himself at the center of attention, or even as a figure of controversy. He lives in a world which is black (being unknown and deprived of attention, i.e., deprivation of narcissistic supplies) and white (being famous and celebrated, i.e., rich narcissistic supplies). For a Narcissist the world looks like a place where the only food is meat and all the humans are cattle. That is why, at the most primitive level, Narcissists think they "have to" act the way they do in order to survive.

A Narcissist continuously rates people round him for potential supply sources. First he conducts a binary test – can this or that person provide him with narcissistic supply? For him, those who fail this test simply do not exist. "*They are two dimensional cartoon figures*", as Vaknin (1999, p. 38) commented, "*Their feelings, needs and fears are of no interest or importance*". Those persons who filtered through are regarded as "human" and the Narcissist would nurture and cultivate those people. Needless to say that he loses interest in them once he judges that they have lost their capacity to supply him what he needs. He is not at all concerned or interested either in the person or in the circumstances, and he has no time or energy for anything, except the next narcissistic fix, no matter what the price and who is trampled upon (Vaknin, 1999, p. 39). It is impossible for him to commit himself emotionally to another human being because in doing so, the underlying emptiness, rage and depression of his impaired true self will be exposed. He is fully self-absorbed and self-centered; there is no place for sentiment. An emotional involvement means directing his feeling and interest to another but as far as he is concerned; there is no "other" in his life.

Narcissists are never satisfied and crave for more power. The more power they have, the more freely they can diminish others to keep themselves inflated. They "misuse" the power to secure more narcissistic supplies and often cause unjustified harm to others without provocation.

3.5.3: The Causes of Narcissism

The root causes for the development of an inflated false self is comparatively a new topic in psychological studies which is not thoroughly understood yet. There is still considerable speculation on how the narcissistic personality develops. It seems the Narcissist suffers a developmental arrest prior to the emergence of real self in early childhood but how and why this arrest occurs is not always clear. Another theory regards NPD as a young child's defense against psychological pain. These two perspectives have been identified with two major figures in psychoanalytic thought, Heinz Kohut and Otto Kernberg respectively. Both these theories go back to Freud's pioneering work *On Narcissism: An Introduction*. According to Freud, narcissistic disorders originate in very early childhood development, and this early origin is thought to explain why they are so difficult to treat in later life.

Both the researchers traced the roots of NPD to disturbances in the patient's family of origin, specifically to the problems in the parent-child relationship before the child turned three (Masterson, 1981, pp. 16, 24). But they disagree in their accounts of the nature of these problems. According to Kohut, the child grows out of primary narcissism acquiring a more realistic sense of self and a set of personal ideals and values but if the parents fail to provide appropriate opportunities for idealization (e.g., mother's decreasing availability to meet his every need), the child remains "stuck" at a developmental stage in which its sense of self remains grandiose and unrealistic while at the same time he remains dependent on approval from others for self-esteem.

In contrast, Kernberg views NPD as rooted in the child's defense against a cold and unempathic parent, usually the mother. Masterson (1990, p. 102) agreed with Kernberg, and observed that the mothers of the Narcissists are emotionally cold and exploitative narcissistic personalities themselves who ignore their child's separation and individual needs in order to mould him to fit their own uncompromising standards and serve their own emotional needs. Emotionally hungry and angry at the depriving parents, the child withdraws into a part of the self that the parents value; whether looks, intellectual ability, or some other skill or talent. This part of the self becomes hyper-inflated and grandiose. Any perceived weaknesses are "split off" into a hidden part of the self. Splitting gives rise to a lifelong tendency to swing between extremes of grandiosity and feelings of emptiness and worthlessness.

Zayn & Dibble (2007, pp. 6, 7) have a rather simplistic hypothesis. According to them, during an important stage of the personality development of a child, a significant individual enters his life who needs him to be something other than what he is. The child then feels as if he has to be different in order to be loved or accepted by that individual. It devastates the emerging "self" of the child. Unable to be the person he actually is and still gain acceptance, the child adapts by splitting his personality into a real and a false self. He learns to hide the real self because it is seen in a negative way and tries to compensate for his "shortcomings" by creating a "special" self – a person who will be loved and admired by all. When the child grows up, he becomes what the environment "needs him to be" and in turn he makes those around him into what he "needs them to be".

However, in all accounts, the child emerges into adult life with a history of unsatisfactory relationships with others. Today all the famous psychologists agree that unempathic parenting is one of the major causes of NPD (Costello, 1996, p. 148). The Narcissist feels unprepared for adulthood because he has been raised with an unrealistic view of life. For him reality is replaced by delusion. The child grows up with a grandiose view of the self and a conflict-ridden psychological dependence on others. Ultimately he shows the symptoms of a full-blown narcissism.

3.5.4: The Narcissistic Rage

A major characteristic of a Narcissist is his rage originating from his distorted inner world. This is not like any other type of anger; it is unpredictable, highly over-reactive and without a valid reason. Kohut coined the term "narcissistic rage"; and according to him (1977, p. 243), the narcissistic rage develops out of a profound sense of disappointment and loss of self-objects. It is an empty depression based on the "depleted self". In fact much of the Kohut's writing deals with the analysis of narcissistic rage and its socio-political impact (surprisingly, his analysis perfectly explains the rise of Hitler in Germany). Kernberg describes the narcissistic rage as revengeful and compulsive, and it is a driving need to "pay back" another for some insult that threatens the Narcissist's well-defended persona (Donaldson-Pressman & Pressman, 1997, p. 144). Even a small disagreement may trigger a rage. It is also non-selective. Anyone who is nearby of a raging Narcissist is at risk for insult and attack regardless of his guilt or innocence.

Many researchers have made significant contributions to the field of knowledge on narcissistic rage. As a summary, we can assume that there are two main reasons of this abnormal outburst of anger. First, when the Narcissist sees glimpses of his true self, he feels threatened. So he initially devalues the person(s), and if it does not work, he uses rage to regain control. Secondly, when a conflict needs to be resolved he cannot fight fairly because he follows no ethical guidelines. So he wants to win the game with a sudden outburst of anger. He wants to "convince" the targets that it is "their fault". The hostility continues even after the victims admit to faults that are not their own, or forced to devalue their own past achievements, and even try to make amends or beg mercy.

There is another destructive aspect of narcissistic rage. It is the duration. The rage is not just a flash fire that quickly burns out. It is not easily quenched because the anger is not rationally connected to others; it continues to seethe and burn until the Narcissist's internal stability is regained (Zayn & Dibble, 2007, p. 86). He has a persistent feeling of ill-will and resentment, and his anger will brood for years over what others consider being insignificant matters. Even when others may try to make amends, he still sees the person who triggered his rage as someone who has the potential to threaten his carefully fashioned false self.

3.6: Correlating Muhammad and Malignant Narcissism

There are literally thousands of short stories available about Muhammad in the authentic sources, and unlike other semi-mythical religious figures, he is as well known to us as that of any other prominent historical figure. By comparing all the information we have about Muhammad to modern development of psychological studies on NPD, it is possible to make an objective study to evaluate the character and psychological make up of Muhammad. And with this investigation, the Prophet Muhammad stands naked in front of us, the divinity vanishes into thin air and we can identify him as a malignant Narcissist in a divine robe. We can clearly see his inflated false self and the monodrama he enacted yet skillfully remained behind the scene. We can make out that the aforementioned seven deadly sins were significantly present in him.

Now, I should explain, step by step, why Muhammad thought of himself as "special" or "privileged" and demanded excessive praise, why he lacked empathy and enjoyed "putting something over others", how he became a slave to his false self, and how he failed to realize that beneath this narcissistic glitter there was an impaired real self. Next, I wish to answer the question; was he unaware of his lies or felt completely justified while lying to others about his prophetic mission?

Lastly, I intend to discover the impaired true self of Muhammad.

3.6.1: The Narcissistic Delusion of Muhammad

Muhammad was a massive denier of reality. He often retreated into a fantasy world to avoid feelings of low self-esteem. If we apply Freud's theory of id, ego and superego to understand his strange mental setup, we can clearly identify the three important "players" of his mind.

Id (true self, real self) – Muhammad: the weak, orphaned, neglected and unloved, coward, insignificant, illiterate and poor merchantman of Mecca who never got a meaningful employment in his life, and lived a parasitic life with the wealth of his wife.

Ego (false self) – Prophet Muhammad: the Apostle of Allah, the best of creation, the preferred one, an excellent example to humankind, exalted above other Prophets in degrees and mercy to the world. Allah first created the light of Muhammad, out of which, everything which constitutes this world, were created. He is on a divine mission to conquer the world for Allah.

Superego – Allah: The God, who had chosen Muhammad as His last Prophet and took special care for every whimsical demand of his beloved Prophet. Allah is the most merciful and most powerful God. He is the Lord of the worlds and best of all the Creators.

On the day Muhammad had a vivid hallucination in the cave Hira (i.e., received his first revelation), his false self realized the self-importance. This was the time, he clearly separated the concepts of real self and false self, and in this process a confusion arose. Since he was also a neurotic patient, this delusion/confusion was deep-rooted in his mind. As Freud (Strachey & Gay, 1966, p. 103) concludes that a delusion, for instance, meets one squarely and with definite outlines; e.g., suddenly a neurotic patient says straight out with all sincerity – "I am the Emperor of the World" and starts putting forward many "cleverest" arguments in support of his delusional beliefs which any child can see are nonsensical.

Such a person is a riddle hard to understand, but if we put him under Freudian analysis, the confusions disappear. According to Freud (Strachey & Gay, 1961, p. 39), some delusions are derived from human wishes and they are psychiatric delusions. In psychiatric delusions, the wish-fulfillment is the most prominent factor in its motivation and in doing so the patient completely disregards its relations to reality. It is so deep-rooted that there is no scope for verification in the patient's mind. He just allows himself to be carried away by his delusion, and at any cost he will never let his belief be torn from him. Psychiatric delusions often take their rise from the patient's childhood and once we understand the root causes, we can also understand how much energy it took to form them. In the case of Muhammad, it initiated when he was hardly five year old but erupted when he was about forty.

However, under his psychiatric delusion, Muhammad felt entitled to regular admiration, compliance, or favorable treatment from others. From this day, his false self started dominating his true self and it continued until his true self was actually paralyzed. In sum, he had constructed an air-tight cocoon of narcissistic enjoyment where he could relax, feel good and feel secure – all because he had invented a lie that he was the chosen Prophet of Allah. He mistook his hallucination for real and thus believed in his own lie. However, his psychopathic behavior was not noticed by others till the time he got a strong foothold in Medina.

After the first revelation when Allah was silent for a long time, Muhammad was depressed. He realized that his inflated false self could not be preserved and the narcissistic grandiosity "balloon" would be punctured, which may ultimately activate his true self. He felt so miserable and insecure that he even wanted to commit suicide.

In the beginning of his prophetic mission, Muhammad was not sure who should be his God. When he received the first revelation, overnight he changed his rank from a merchant-man to a Prophet without even knowing from whom he received the divine instruction. The "voice" he had heard in the cave did not tell him about the identity of his God because it was a command hallucination. In spite of that, he started warning the Meccans with dire consequences if they did not accept him as a Prophet while he himself was in such a delusion.

Initially Muhammad tried various brands of God, but he was frustrated with the response from his audience and changed his mind several times. Surprisingly, the real Allah did not come forward to remove his confusion. Later on he realized that all the pagans, despite their numerous idols, were wholly devoted to their moon God, Allah, because they believed that Allah had the ability to inflict punishment as well as rewards. This is the only reason Muhammad choose the pagan Allah as his God. Therefore, those who try to single out Allah and glorify him above the other Meccan idols should remember that Muhammad could just as easily have picked Manaf, al-Lat, al-Uzza, or any of the others. Allah did not find Muhammad but it was Muhammad who looked for a suitable "Allah" to preach in His name. The deception of this seventh century malignant Narcissist started from here.

3.6.2: Identifying the Defensive Inflated False Self of Muhammad

The defensive inflated false self of Muhammad was the role he played under the title of a Prophet for the entire period of his prophetic mission. His true self was subdued and his inflated false self played the monodrama with a Prophet's cap on his head. Muhammad was quite aware that a direct self-promotion would be seen as repulsive and hence would be rejected. A Prophet cannot stand alone unless he has a God to certify him. In other words, the false self of a Narcissist cannot survive without the authorization of a superego. Throughout Muhammad's prophetic mission, Allah had no other job but to defend his beloved Prophet.

To preserve his false self and to exaggerate his own importance, Muhammad had made some extraordinary claims about himself. Apart from thinking that he was the "*seal of the Prophets*" (Q: 33.40); this megalomaniac regarded himself as "*Khayru-l-Khalq*" (the best of creation), an "*excellent example*" (Q: 33.21), and gave us a hint that he was "*exalted above other Prophets in degrees*" (Q: 2.253). He also claimed to be "*the preferred one*" (Q: 17.55), sent as a "*Mercy to the Worlds*" (Q: 21.107), and will be "*raised to a praised estate*" (Q: 17.79). Also, in ahadith he had made many strange claims – I am from Allah and believers are from me, the very first thing Allah ever created was my soul, first of all things the Lord created my mind, Allah created me noble and gave me noble character (cited Adil, 2002, p. 29). Allah very generously declared, "*Were it not for you, I would not have created the universe.*" (Tabaqat, Volume - 1).

Narcissists are mentally sick and their claims are strange. They also lack in judgment (Vaknin, 1999, p. 19), and massive deniers of reality (Masterson, 1990, p. 93; Vaknin, 1999, p. 23). This is what we understand from the extraordinary claims of Muhammad. People say outlandishly positive things about themselves (e.g., I am smarter than Stephen Hawking) when it is obvious that they are covering up for a perceived deficiency (e.g., he dropped out of high school). Only a malignant

Narcissist can be so cut off from reality as to claim that God had created universe because of him. Undoubtedly, Muhammad was talking about a nonexistent past, a nostalgia based on narcissistic delusion. According to Vaknin (1999, p. 86), when there is lack of narcissistic supplies, the Narcissists hark back to a past that *"never existed except in the thwarted grandiosity of the Narcissist. The longer the lack of narcissistic supply, the more this past is glorified, re-written, missed and mourned. This serves to enhance all the other negative feelings."*

This is the real cause of his self-glorification by faking an invented past. When he claimed that Allah first created his mind and soul, or, universe was created for him, or, someone washed his heart with snow when he was a child; he was in fact starving from narcissistic supplies. His lies are easy to catch because his claims were self-contradictory. In the beginning of his mission he did not even know who his God was. Now we know how easily Muhammad could swing back and forth between the two extremes – reality and fantasy. The whole religion of Islam stands on Muhammad's truth claim; but how to determine, in his truth claim how much fantasy and how much truth is there? Twenge & Campbell (2010, p. 276) conclude, *"There is a giant transfer of time, attention and resources from reality to fantasy ... corroded interpersonal relationships... a switch from deep to shallow relationships, a destruction of social trust, and an increase in entitlement and selfishness."*

Muhammad was a pathological liar, and the past he inflated was full of false memories and fantasies which were actually falsifications of his false self. Vaknin (1999, p. 157) commented, *"The Narcissist is bound to develop false memories, conjure up false fantasies, anticipate the unrealistic and work his intellect to justify them"*. A healthy person preserves some senses of continuity and consistency – both in his thought and in his actions that serves as a point of reference. It links his past and present actions and future plans. These senses of continuity and consistency are regulated by memory, eagerness, imagination and understanding. For a Narcissist, the senses are relegated to the false self. Hence an aura of dishonesty is attached to all of them. Since the false self has a false perception, it weaves enchanted and grandiose fables as substitutes. This is how Muhammad evaluated himself and the world around him. Vaknin (cited Sina, 2008, p. 82) suggested that the Narcissists, while masters of self-deception or even malignant con-artistry, are usually fully aware of the difference between true and false, real and make-believe, the invented and the existing, right and wrong, etc. But they can convince themselves of those lies as if they were absolute truth by making suitable changes in the story.

When faced with limits or criticism, the Narcissists are apt to turn nasty and defensive because the balloon of narcissistic grandiosity may get punctured by criticism. Therefore they overreact to criticism by becoming angry or humiliated. Allah prohibited criticism in Qur'an with the verses 5.101,102 and Muhammad demanded an unquestionable obedience from the Muslims. He knew that if Qur'anic criticism was allowed then it would lead to a situation where his false self would be exposed. A false self cannot survive without delusion, deception and lie; simply because it is false. Muhammad could not stand as a Prophet simply because he was a bogus. The deception is at the very core of Islam.

The images of the true self are derived mostly from reality and to a small extent from fantasy, i.e., what one wishes as well as what one really is. The false self, on the other hand, is derived mostly from immature fantasies (Masterson, 1990, p. 23). Muhammad's prophethood was his fantasy. The motive of Muhammad's false self was not to deal with the reality but to work against it. The false self, however well set up, always lacks something (Winnicott, 1960, p. 152). This is exactly what Muhammad had feared. He lacked the capability to silence his critics in a fair debate because his prophetic claim was based on the quicksand of grand delusion. All he wanted was to relax in his air-tight cocoon of narcissistic enjoyment where he could feel secure. But despite of all his efforts to project himself as a Prophet, there were many instances when he behaved in such manners that were *"disgraceful to discuss"*. Ibn Ishaq truthfully recorded them in his *Sirat Rasul Allah*, but Ibn Hisham removed them in his version to save Muhammad from humiliation.

Muhammad needed a large number of followers to secure narcissistic supply sources. Allah was a useful apparatus of Muhammad to achieve this, i.e., to keep his false self alive and steady going. If Allah had not revealed the verses in perfect time and in perfect manner, Muhammad's false self could have collapsed. The fake prophetic false self of Muhammad required creating a scarecrow to pose as a true God and to speak out in divine voice so that Muhammad's position as a Prophet could be established. Neither Qur'an nor Allah had any other purpose beyond than this. Once Muhammad died Allah became silent forever. When the Narcissist is dead, with him dies the hunger of the false self for narcissistic supplies. But Islam did not die with Muhammad; it survived because Muhammad left a book containing his poisonous instructions in the name of God. Muslims, when pick up this book of instructions and put their trust on it, indirectly come within the narcissistic grip of Muhammad. We will discuss more on this in the forthcoming chapter on Qur'an.

3.6.3: The Development of Muhammad's Narcissism

The circumstances of Muhammad's childhood confirm that his family had fallen on harder times. Muhammad's father Abdullah died before his son's birth leaving very little for the family, and Amina, mother of Muhammad, died when he was only six (Geiler & Saleeb, 2002, p. 70). Amina lacked interest in her child and wanted to give her to a nurse. But it was difficult for her to get a nurse because she was a poor widow and hence the pay was miserable. When infant Muhammad was shown to some women who were looking for infants to nurse, one of them was reported to have said, *"An orphan! And with no money! And what can his mother do?"* (Rodinson, 1980, p. 45). Ultimately Halima took away the child with much unwillingness because she did not get a child from a wealthy family, and her family desperately needed the extra income even though it was not much. There was a possibility that Halima or her family did not treat the infant well due to this.

However, at the age of five, Halima returned Muhammad to his mother Amina, but again she was reluctant to take her child back. One year after reunion, Amina died. So Muhammad was neglected not only by his foster mother but by his real mother also. Being orphan in those days was a curse. In Qur'an Muhammad recalls those cursed days of his lonesome orphanhood.

The Last shall be better for you than the First. Your Lord will give you, and you will be satisfied. Did He not find you an orphan and give you shelter? Did He not find you a wanderer so He guided you? Did He not find you poor and suffice you? Do not oppress the orphan. (Q: 93.4-8)

Those were clearly Muhammad's words put to Allah's mouth. Allah, like a puppet sitting on a ventriloquist's knee, is expressing His frustration on behalf of Muhammad. Here the Narcissist is playing a monodrama in an open theater where everyone has an access; Muhammad remained behind the scene, while Allah took the center stage and echoed Muhammad's words of frustration.

But why there was so much neglect? Was it only poverty? Often the parents of a Narcissist are Narcissists themselves. If the mother is a Narcissist, she may be unusually distressed with changes in her body in her pregnancy. When the child arrives, the Narcissist mother may be depressed as the newborn has some demands from her. This leaves little opportunity for her to satisfy her grandiose fantasies. Often she looks for a way out; she does not hesitate to take advantage of someone else's offer to shoulder some or the entire burden. If there is no way out, she shows extreme carelessness (of course, unless others are watching) to the child (Hotchkiss, 2003, p. 49). Authentic Islamic sources do not tell much about Amina, hence we are not very sure if she was a Narcissist herself but her behavior strongly suggests it. However, certainly, a discrepancy between Muhammad's chronological age and the level of his psychological functioning formed at his adolescent days which widened with time till his death.

Those Qur'anic verses show how much the memory of his neglected childhood had pained Muhammad. The psychological scars, left in his mind, never healed. Muhammad made his dead mother responsible for all the sufferings caused to him. When he conquered Mecca, about fifty years after Amina's death, he visited his mother's grave and told his companions (cited Sina, 2008, p. 11), *"This is the grave of my mother; the Lord has permitted me to visit it. And I sought leave to pray for her, but it was not granted. So I called my mother to remembrance, and the tender memory of her overcame me, and I wept"*.

Because of faulty parenting and traumatic childhood experiences, Muhammad suffered a developmental arrest prior to the full emergence of his true self. The first few years of a child are a very crucial stage, which may make or break the child. Clinical experience shows that childhood trauma and abuse are almost impossible to erase. Modern brain research tends to support this sad view but offers some hope. Vaknin (1999, p. 217) wrote, *"Traumas are inevitable. They are an inseparable part of life. But in early childhood – especially in infancy (ages zero to four) they acquire an ominous aura, an evil, irreversible meaning. No matter how innocuous the event and the surrounding circumstances, the child's vivid imagination is likely to embed it in the framework of a highly idiosyncratic horror story"*.

During this period, the child struggles hard with an important developmental task – the formation of a healthy, autonomous self. The caregivers and parents are required to be tolerant, sympathetic and clear on boundaries of what is good and bad, for which they first need to have a realistic sense both of themselves and of the child. They should also be able to control their own aggressive impulses; otherwise, a healthy mental development of the child is threatened.

If Amina was a Narcissist, she created a fertile ground for the creation of a future Narcissist. Muhammad remained trapped in the narcissistic position like an extension of his mother just as she was of him. His sense of self became grandiose and unrealistic, and at the same time he remained dependent on approval from others for self-esteem. Though Muhammad gave the impression of a well-balanced man in his adulthood, it is certain that he had a conflict-ridden psychological dependence on other people.

3.6.4: Why Allah did not allow Muhammad to pray for his mother?

The simple logic is, Muhammad could not forgive his mother even long after her death. God cannot be unjust, and God's unwillingness in this case is just absurd. Allah was a "finger-puppet" of Muhammad. Thus Allah said whatever Muhammad wanted Him to say. Underneath this dramatic divine rejection there remains the fact that it is impossible for a Narcissist to forgive someone particularly his mother. He has overly complicated relationship with his parents, mainly with his mother. As Zayn & Dibble (2007, p. 5) wrote, "*Sometimes the Narcissist shares stories about his childhood or reveals specific details about his mother, which demonstrate a possible strained mother/son relationship.*"

For a Narcissist his parents never die; they live on to torment him, to persecute and prosecute him, and to put him on constant trial (Vaknin, 1999, p. 172). Their criticism, mental torture, apathy, other forms of abuse and berating him – all these things live long after their physical death. This is the internal chaos that haunts the Narcissist. Even after several decades of his mother's death, Muhammad was still tormented because he had a bitter and complicated relationship with his mother. Therefore, it was not Allah who prevented Muhammad from praying for his mother, but it was Muhammad's own preference which he skillfully put on Allah. If Allah was really so angry with Muhammad's mother, why He allowed Muhammad to visit her grave? How disgusting it is to think that the God is still angry with a woman who is dead for over half a century.

The display of outburst of fake emotions had specific purpose to obtain certain result. By shedding few drops of crocodile tears, Muhammad sent a deceitful emotional message to mislead the people around him. Narcissist's parents are narcissistic supply sources. By ignoring his mother in front of others, though long after her death, Muhammad's false self just "reinvested" itself through the look of others. Once he devalued his mother, his own value was increased, but at the same time he proved that he was not cruel. By mimicking real emotions artfully, Muhammad made other people believe that he was more human than common. It was his "mask of sanity".

3.6.5: The Narcissistic Supply Sources of Muhammad

The narcissistic supply means quite specifically the activities and relationships that reinforced Muhammad's grandiosity. Muhammad demanded total obedience and required excessive admiration, adulation, attention and affirmation from his followers. He reinvested himself through the look of his followers.

He (Muhammad) cannot be questioned concerning what He does and they shall be questioned (for theirs). (Q: 21.23)

In order that ye may believe in Allah and His Messenger, that ye may assist and honour Him, and celebrate His praise morning and evening. (Q: 48.9)

The Prophet said, 'None of you will have faith till he loves me more than his father, his children and all mankind'. (Bukhari: 1.2.14)

In the above quotes, Muslims are being exhorted to not only help and obey Muhammad without question but also to love, revere and glorify him day and night! Muhammad wrote the verse 48.9 and put it in Allah's mouth to make himself a cult-figure – an object of praise, worship and glorification! More precisely, the malignant Narcissist was hunting for narcissistic supply sources.

A Narcissist is forced to use other people in order to feel that he exists. This is called "reinforcing feedback" (Masterson, 1990, p. 92). His sense of self-worth and self-esteem derive entirely from audience feedback because he has no self-esteem or self-worth (no such ego functions). In the absence of observers he shrivels to non-existence and feels dead. Hence the Narcissist's preying habit in his constant pursuit of narcissistic supply. It is an addictive behavior. Since at any cost the Narcissists have to protect their false images, they are often restless (Masterson, 1990, p. 92). Muhammad was continuously under pressure to maintain his status of a Prophet. During the last ten years of his prophetic career he had launched not less than eighty-six raids to plunder his enemies and had taken part personally in twenty-seven (Guillaume, 1955, p. 659). Under his order, the Muslim army fought many major battles to establish Islam.

After thirteen years of preaching, Muhammad could not gather more than a handful converts. Since the early Muslims were mostly slaves who had hardly any social standing, he was desperate to convert some influential people. During the pilgrimage season, Muhammad used to irritate the chiefs of tribes visiting the Ka'ba and invited them to embrace Islam. This way, he became a menace to the pilgrims. The keepers of Ka'ba knew that if Muhammad started babbling his nonsense to the pilgrims, it would detrimentally impact the revenue streams. So his influential uncle Abu Lahab used to follow him and warn the visiting the chiefs in advance.

Abu Lahab said: 'Muhammad is trying to bewitch you'. With that the Quraysh got up and left before the Messenger could speak. (Ishaq: 118).

It clearly shows that Muhammad's eagerness to gain some influential converts to his faith was so intense that it appeared he had gone crazy. As Zayn & Dibble (2007, p. 7) commented, "*Usually, the 'objects', with which the Narcissist chooses to merge, have traits or characteristics that the Narcissist wishes himself to obtain. That is why he is drawn to people with strengths in certain areas. We are supposed to feel flattered when we realize that even though it seemed like chance that we are brought together, that **the Narcissist actually 'hand-picked' us due to particular positive characteristics and strengths that we possessed**". Influential converts, i.e., "objects" with special strengths mean more narcissistic supply.

At Medina, Muhammad showed his real face. When he came to Medina, he was penniless. He was given asylum but what Muhammad gave them in return? He assassinated his critics, subdued them by dividing the population and established his rein of terror in that city to gain control. A Narcissist does everything with one goal in mind: attracting more narcissistic supplies (Vaknin, 1999, p. 98). In this respect, the Narcissists behave like alcoholics. They do not know when to stop but ask for more, more and yet more. They are always hungry and look for new victims. Muhammad wanted converts not because he was interested in humans. He never loved a human in his life; he only wanted to be surrounded with the "right" people who would appreciate and advertise him as the chosen Prophet of Allah. It does not matter for a Narcissist, if these attributes are superficial and not accurate indicators of a person's real worth; he takes them seriously and continues believing in his supremacy. Muhammad wrote in the Qur'an,

Do not fear people, but fear Me. And, do not take a small price for My verses. Those who do not judge with what Allah has sent down are the unbelievers. (Q: 5.44).

This Path of Mine is straight. Follow it and do not follow other paths, for they will scatter you away from His Path. With such Allah charges you, in order that you be cautious. (Q: 6.153).

Narcissists always rate people around them. First they ask a simple question to themselves – can this or that person provide him with narcissistic supply? If the answer is yes, he is interested, and if the answer is no, the person simply does not exist. The Narcissist changes his color like a lizard. He may flatter, adore, admire and applaud the "target" in an embarrassingly exaggerated and profuse manner in one moment; but at the very next moment he may abuse, and humiliate the same target in every possible way by violent displays of abuse, rage attacks, or cold detachment if the target fails to comply with his narcissistic requirements.

Muhammad fits perfectly into this profile. At the birth of Islam, Muhammad tried to formulate his religion in the style of Moses. He was much influenced by the rabbinic literature and borrowed extensively from the holy scriptures of Judaism. Wansbrough (cited Warraq, 2002, p. 24) argued that Islam emerged only when it came under the influence of rabbinic Judaism. Earlier scholars like Torrey also recognized that there were genuine borrowings from Jewish literature. Some present day critics of Islam have the same view, as Khan (2009, p. 42) mentioned that Muhammad was highly influenced by the learned Jews Rabbis, and some Jews used to tell him ancient history as recounted in the Torah. Even Muhammad agreed that the holy book of Jews can influence his Qur'an. Tabari wrote,

In this year, the Prophet commanded Zayd bin Thabit to study the Book of the Jews, saying, 'I fear that they may change my Book.' (Tabari: VII.167)

When Muhammad relocated in Medina in 622, a large number of thriving, rich and influential Jews and Polytheistic tribes lived there. Economically these tribes were much stronger than the uncivilized Arabs. In the beginning, Muhammad continued praising the Jews and their faith. He intended to pass himself off as a Prophet of those wealthy Jews. For this; he flattered them, maintained good relations with them and adopted many Jewish customs; e.g., fasting of *ashura* (later changed to *Ramadan*), *Zakat* (contribution to charity), and prohibition on eating the pig meat. He also introduced ceremonial ablutions and purifications, established the *Sabbath* observance on Saturday (later changed to Friday), circumcision, etc (Khan, 2009, pp. 42-44). Also he called himself *Nabi*, the Jewish term for Prophet and even adopted Jerusalem as the Qibla for his prayers. Ibn Ishaq wrote,

In the pagan era the Jews were scripture folk and we were pagans. They used to say, 'Soon a Prophet will be sent whom we shall follow.' When Allah sent his Apostle from the Quraysh and we followed him they denied him. (Ishaq: 254)

3: Muhammad's Strange Mindset

Muhammad thought that by this way he would be able to convert those wealthy and influential people to his creed. Though some polytheistic tribes joined him in small numbers, the wealthy Jews paid little attention. Allah started revealing verses specially designed to lure them. Many verses confirmed the Jewish stories of Genesis (Q: 2.30-38), and Judaic stories of Moses and the children of Israel (Q: 2.240-61). Then Allah strongly urged the Jews and Christians (and the monotheistic Sabians) to believe in the Qur'an alongside following their own scriptures to gain Allah's mercy (Q: 2.62; 22.17) and to accept Muhammad as their Prophet (Q: 5.19, 20). A logical minded reader will not fail to note that a Narcissist is desperately seeking attention from his potential victims.

Those who believe (in the Qur'an), those who follow the Jewish (scriptures), and the Sabians and the Christians, - any who believe in Allah and the Last Day, and work righteousness, - on them shall be no fear, nor shall they grieve. (Q: 5.69)

People of the Book! After an interval during which there were no Messengers, Our Messenger (Muhammad) has come to clarify (your religion) to you, lest you should say: 'No bearer of glad tidings or a warner has come to us.' Indeed, there has come to you a bearer of glad tidings and a warner. Allah has power over all things. (Q: 5.19).

(Remember) when Moses said to his people. 'Remember, my people, the favors which Allah has bestowed upon you. He has raised up Prophets among you, made you kings, and given you that which He has not given to any one of the worlds. (Q: 5.20).

However, still the Jews did not pay him any attention. The malignant Narcissist was again in action and the following verses were revealed.

We gave to the Children of Israel the Book, judgment and prophethood. We provided them with good things and preferred them above the worlds (of their time). (Q: 45.16).

Then to Moses We gave the Book, complete for him who does good, and (to make) plain all things, and guidance, and mercy, so that they might believe in the ultimate meeting with their Lord. (Q: 6.154).

We have sent down the Torah in which there is guidance and light by which the submissive Prophets judged the Jews, as did the rabbis and those of their Lord, guarding what they were required to of the Book of Allah, and for which they were witness. (Q: 5.44).

Children of Israel, remember My favor which I bestowed upon you and that I preferred your (Prophets among you) above the worlds. (Q: 2.122).

Yet among the people of Moses there was a nation who preached the truth and acted justly. (Q: 7.159).

The problem with a Narcissist is that when he starts, he does not know where to stop. In the following ahadith Muhammad gave much superior status to Moses.

The Prophet said, 'People will be struck unconscious on the Day of Resurrection and I will be the first to regain consciousness, and behold! There I will see Moses holding one of the pillars of Allah's Throne. (Bukhari: 4.55.610)

The Prophet said, 'Don't give me superiority over Moses. On the day of Resurrection Moses will be standing and holding a side of Allah's Throne'. (Bukhari: 4.55.620).

All the nations were displayed in front of me [Muhammad], and I saw a large multitude of people covering the horizon. Somebody said, 'This is Moses and his followers'. (Bukhari: 4.55.622).

Muhammad knew that if he could gain the influential Jews as his followers, he would be more powerful. Power for a malignant Narcissist is an affirmation of his superiority. It is also a means of controlling others to ensure narcissistic supplies – anything that can feed his fragile false ego. The more power he has, the more freely he can diminish others to keep his false self inflated (Hotchkiss, 2003, p. 14). This was the actual cause of Muhammad's urge to get the Jews as his followers. Neither he was interested in the Jews nor he ever loved them. He only wanted to see that the image of a Prophet is being hurled back at him by the Jews. He wanted the Jews to reflect him, to confirm him, to admire him and to applaud him – in a word Muhammad wanted an assurance from the Jews that he exists as a Prophet. He simply wanted to see his reflection in the eyes of the Jews.

Still unsuccessful; Muhammad desperately took one step further in his pursuit of gaining the Jews in his creed. Now he claimed that he is the Messiah whose coming was foretold in the Torah. Allah declared,

And to those who shall follow the Messenger the Unlettered Prophet (Muhammad) whom they shall find written with them in the Torah and the Gospel... (Q: 7.157).

The worst part of lying is that the liar keeps on forgetting what he had told before. Therefore, to cover-up one lie, the imposter needs to tell several lies. If Muhammad's coming was foretold in the Torah, then it also contradicted another revelation. According to Allah, the prophethood is bestowed upon the children of Israel only (Q: 45.16), and more specifically upon the family of Issac and Jacob (Q: 29.27). But Muhammad was an Arab, not an Israelite and his family-line leading up to Ishmael is different from those of Issac and Jacob. The Jewish Rabbis caught the liar red-handed on this point. Jews also rejected Muhammad's claim that Qur'an was divine revelation because it was not revealed in sacred language, Hebrew or Syriac. For Jews, Arabic was a language of poets and drunkards. They pointed out many contradictions in Qur'an, like Allah wrongly accused Jews of saying that Ezra (Ozayr) was the son of God (Q: 9.30) (Khan, 2009, p. 44). They also pointed out multiple errors in Muhammad's versions of the events of the Torah and called him ignorant of Jewish scriptures which his revelation claimed to affirm.

Jewish rabbis used to annoy the Apostle with questions, introducing confusion. (Ishaq: 239)

Julas the Jew used to say, 'If Muhammad is right we are worse than donkeys. (Ishaq: 242)

I have heard that Julas the Jew used to make false professions of Islam. (Ishaq: 245)

These Hypocrites used to assemble in the mosque and listen to the stories of the Muslims and laugh and scoff at their religion. (Ishaq: 246)

In sum; the Jews completely rejected Islam calling the revelations as garbled, fallacious and at times unintelligible. At this moment a Narcissist argues this way – "My feeling and needs are all that matter and whatever I want I should get. If you cannot make yourself useful in meeting my need, you are of no value. If you defy my will, prepare to feel my wrath." (Hotchkiss, 2003, p. 20). For Muhammad; mutuality and reciprocity were entirely alien concepts. The very existence of the Jews is only meaningful if they are ready to agree, obey, flatter and submit to Muhammad – in short to anticipate and meet every narcissistic need of Muhammad, as Vaknin (1999, p. 183) wrote, *"The Narcissist simply discards people when he becomes convinced that they can no longer provide him with narcissistic supply. This is an evaluation, subjective and highly emotionally charged. It does not have to be grounded on reality".*

A Narcissist first overvalues the "targets" in order to gain their trust and if his ambition is not fulfilled, then he starts devaluing them (Vaknin, 1999, p. 73). When Muhammad could not do it by means of flattery, he would do it by means of cruelty. Allah's tone and Muhammad's gesture towards the Jews started changing. In narcissistic frustration, Muhammad put the following words in the mouth of Allah. Allah was clearly dissatisfied because the Jews had rejected Islam and now the Jews are subjected to the wrath from Allah.

You will please neither the Jews nor the Nazarenes unless you follow their creed. Say: 'The guidance of Allah is the guidance. 'And if after all the knowledge you have been given you yield to their desires, you shall not have, other than Allah, either a guide or a helper. (Q: 2.120).

Some of those who are Jews change words from their context and say: "We hear and disobey; hear thou as one who heareth not" and "Listen to us!" distorting with their tongues and slandering religion. If they had said: "We hear and we obey: hear thou, and look at us" it had been better for them, and more upright. But Allah hath cursed them for their disbelief. (Q: 4.46)

And when there comes to them a Book from Allah, confirming what is with them,- although from of old they had prayed for victory against those without Faith,- when there comes to them that which they (should) have recognized, they refuse to believe in it but the curse of Allah is on those without Faith. (Q: 2.89)

Jew hatred in Islam started with these verses. No God can so miserably express frustration over the Jews. It was Muhammad himself, who felt helpless at the point of rejection. Therefore, again he started playing a monodrama. Allah took the center stage while Muhammad took a backseat behind the scene. Once the Jews rejected Islam, Muhammad was frustrated, but Allah expressed the frustrations on behalf of Muhammad. Bukhari recorded,

> *Narrated Abu Huraira: While we were in the Mosque, the Prophet came out and said, "Let us go to the Jews." We went out till we reached Bait-ul-Midras. He said to them, "If you embrace Islam, you will be safe.* ***You should know that the earth belongs to Allah and His Apostle, and I want to expel you from this land.*** *So, if anyone amongst you owns some property, he is permitted to sell it, otherwise you should know that the earth belongs to Allah and His Apostle".* (Bukhari: 4.53.392)

Gradually, Qur'an and the Hadith collections became a mine of anti-Jewish passages. In recent years some scholars try to argue that Islamic anti-Semitism, i.e., hatred of the Jews is only a recent phenomenon learned from the Nazis during and after the 1940s, and Jews lived peacefully under Muslim rule for centuries (Bostom, 2008, p. 22). Both assertions are gross ignorance of the scholars. It was Muhammad who set the example for anti-Semitism. Ibn Ishaq's *Sirat Rasul Allah* is full with Muhammad's deep hatred for Jews, so is Tabari's history. The frustrated God of Islam continued with anti-Jewish revelations.

> *Humiliation and abasement were pitched upon them (the Jews) and they incurred the Anger of Allah; because they disbelieved His signs and slew His Prophets unjustly; because they disobeyed and were transgressors.* (Q: 2.61).

> *You will find that the most people in enmity to the believers are the Jews and idolaters.* (Q: 5.82).

> *Believers, take neither Jews nor Christians for your guides. They are guides of one another. Whosoever of you takes them for a guide shall become one of their numbers. Allah does not guide the wrong-doers.* (Q: 5.51).

> *Believers, many are the rabbis and monks who in falsehood defraud people of their possessions and bar people from the Path of Allah. Give glad tidings of a painful punishment to those who treasure gold and silver and do not spend it in the Way of Allah.* (Q: 9.34).

> *Believers, do not take as guides those who were given the Book before you who have made of your religion a jest and a pastime, nor the unbelievers. Have fear of Allah, if you are believers.* (Q: 5.57).

> *Do those of the Lord and the rabbis not forbid them to speak sinfully and to devour what is unlawful? Evil indeed is what they were doing...The Jews say: 'The Hand of Allah is chained. 'Their own hands are chained! And they are cursed for what they said!* (Q: 5.63, 64).

In a fury against the Jews; Allah again started contradicting himself. Torah, which Allah had recognized as a divine book containing his *"guidance and light"* (Q: 5.44), and a *"blessing and guidance for the righteous"* (Q: 6.154) has now become *"perverted by the Jews"* (Q: 2.75). The Jews, earlier recognized by Allah as *"privileged above all people"* (Q: 45.15) are now *"liars and illiterates"* (Q: 2.78), *"those who show the greatest hostility to the believers"* (Q: 5.82), and *"selfish and envious people"* (Q: 2.109) whose hearts are as *"hardened as rocks"* (Q: 2.74). Now the Jews *"knowingly conceal the truth"* (Q: 2.42), and pursue *"vague and wishful fancies"* (Q: 2.111).

Allah started sending new revelations cursing the Jews – *"the curse of Allah is on those without faith"* (Q: 2.89), and changed the direction of Qibla to Mecca from Jerusalem (Q: 2.144). Muhammad started calling himself a *Rasul* instead of *Nabi*, the day of *Sabbath* was changed from Saturday to Friday (Juma) and many other Jewish customs and practices were modified (Khan, 2009, p. 45). This is called "devaluation" of the target. As Zayn & Dibble (2007, pp. 7, 8) described, *"When anyone tries to interfere with the image he [the Narcissist] has so carefully created, he experiences an injured feeling. To protect himself from that feeling, the Narcissist uses different types of defense mechanism. One such mechanism is 'devaluation'. By emotionally injuring others he protects his false self. That is why he felt the need to insult you or make you feel badly about yourself"*. The devaluation is not only shocking and devastating but also unexpected.

Muhammad continued devaluing the Jews with a great zeal. Now he started belittling Moses forgetting that once he had given much superior status to Moses.

> *Jabir Bin 'Abdullah narrated that when Umar came to Allah's Messenger, he said, "We hear the narration from the Jews, which sounds pleasing to us, so should we not write some of them?" Whereupon he said, 'Do you want to be baffled as the Jews and the Christians were baffled? I have brought to you (guidance) bright and pure and if Moses were alive now there would have been no alternative left for him but to follow me.'* (Tirmidhi: 177)

> *If (Moses) were alive (now), and he found my prophethood, he would have definitely followed me.* (Darimi and Mishkat: 1.20).

The only way Muhammad could re-inflate his false self was by diminishing, debasing or degrading the Jews. Allah, the "string-puppet" of Muhammad now claimed that He had transformed Jews into apes and swine. By the way, this is an ideal example of magical thinking. A human cannot be transformed to apes or swine by simply cursing them.

> *Say: 'Shall I tell you who will receive a worse recompense from Allah than that? Those whom Allah has cursed and with whom He is angry, and made some of them apes and swine ...* (Q: 5.60)

> *O you who have been given the Book! Believe that which We have revealed, verifying what you have, before We alter faces then turn them on their backs, or curse them as We cursed the violators of the Sabbath, and the command of Allah shall be executed.* (Q: 4.47)

You have surely known of those amongst you who transgressed the Sabbath. We said to them: 'Be apes, despised! (Q: 2.65)

And when they had scornfully persisted in what they had been forbidden, We said to them: 'Be apes, despised'. (Q: 7.166)

Even after so much devaluation, the Jews remained indifferent. The Narcissist felt that his false world was crumbling. Probably, Muhammad saw glimpses of his true self (which he tried so desperately to dominate). He had praised, respected, admired and applauded the Jews in an embarrassingly exaggerated and profuse manner, even had accepted the divine status of Moses, but now the time is up; it is time for narcissistic rage. It is time to abuse and humiliate the Jews in every possible way and to show violent displays of ill-treatment and rage attacks because the Jews failed to comply with his narcissistic requirements. The goal was to get from the Jews what he wanted. A Narcissist does not especially care which method he uses, so long as he finds one that works.

"Hell hath no fury like the Narcissist denied". Muhammad felt an unbridled urge to destroy the Jews. Ultimately he turned his sword against the Jews without any provocation and declared,

Abu Huraira reported Allah's Messenger as saying: The last hour would not come unless the Muslims will fight against the Jews and the Muslims would kill them until the Jews would hide themselves behind a stone or a tree and a stone or a tree would say: Muslim, or the servant of Allah, there is a Jew behind me; come and kill him; but the tree Gharqad would not say, for it is the tree of the Jews. (Muslim: 41.6985)

A Narcissist's natural reaction to rejection is to rage and pull down the self-worth of others to make him feel superior to others, to soothe his internal pain and hostility, and to rebuild his self-worth. The narcissistic rage cannot be compared with the healthy anger of a normal person. A healthy person needs a provocation to become angry but the Narcissist does not. Zayn & Dibble (2007, p. 86) described, *"The narcissistic rage can be triggered when the Narcissist feels challenged, insulted or criticized – even when someone just disagrees with him. He experiences this challenge as a threat to his very identity: his false self, and the false reality he's so painstakingly created in all relationships"*.

This explains why Muhammad's anger and hatred for the Jews did not quench out so easily. In narcissistic injury, the pain is devastating. After so much rejection, now it is time for him to take revenge. Zayn & Dibble (2007, p. 85) concluded,

"The only goal of narcissistic rage is to obliterate the target".

The fates of the three Jewish tribes who lived in and around Yathrib (before the advent of Islam, Medina was known as Yathrib); the Banu Qainuka, the Banu Nadir and the Banu Quraiza were well recorded in various Islamic sources. Those three tribes were the original inhabitants. The Narcissist Prophet of Islam forced the Qainuka and Nadir tribe into exile and mass assassinated some 800 to 900 male members of the Quraiza tribe and reduced their children and women to slavery.

With the elimination of the Quraiza, Medina was cleansed of the Jews. The malignant Narcissist's attention now turned to the Jewish community in Khaybar, another powerful Jewish stronghold in Arabian Peninsula. During 627, Muhammad got the leader of the Jews of Khaybar, Abu Rafi assassinated. Then in May 628, he set upon an expedition against them with himself at the command of a strong army some 1,600 fighting men. Kinana, the young grandson of Abu Rafi, was the leader of the Jews. He was tortured for the information of the whereabouts of his treasure and then put to death. All the fighting-aged men were put to sword and their women and children were taken as captives (Bukhari: 2.14.68). Tabari and Ishaq recorded,

May Allah's anger be intense against those who have bloodied the face of His Prophet. (Tabari: VII.120)

So Muhammad began seizing their herds and their property bit by bit. He conquered home by home. (Tabari: VIII.116; Ishaq: 511)

After the Khaybar massacre, Muhammad turned to the Jews of Fadak (a city situated two/three days of travel from Medina). The people of Fadak refused to accept Islam but offered Muhammad half of their land. So, Muhammad took half the land and allowed them to live there. This half land was the sole property of the Prophet because the Muslims did not have to fight a battle with the Jews.

After the Messenger had finished with the Khaybar Jews, Allah cast terror into the hearts of the Jews in Fadak. (Tabari: VIII.129)

Narcissists cannot feel the pain of others. Mass killing is seen as a direct avenue to fame and attention (Twenge & Campbell, 2010, p. 200). Muhammad was a predator and just did not know what it meant to be human. Those helpless people of three Jewish tribes were like two dimensional caricatures for him. They were given no right to survive because they were of no use for Muhammad for his narcissistic fix. Vaknin (1999, p. 149) wrote, *"The Narcissist is always the most fanatical, the most extreme, the most dangerous. At stake is never the preservation of the group – but his very own survival. As with other Narcissistic supply sources, once the group is no longer instrumental – the Narcissist loses all interest in it, devalues it and ignores it. In extreme cases, he might even wish to destroy it (as a punishment or revenge for its incompetence at securing his Narcissistic supply)"*.

During the first five years of Muhammad's mission, about twenty out of 114 chapters of Qur'an were revealed. These chapters mention very little about Christ, Bible and Christianity in general. Only after Muhammad had sent away some of his followers to Christian Abyssinia in 615, new revelations started coming down from Allah confirming Biblical stories, e.g., the Surah Maryam that talks about Virgin Mary, John the Baptist and miraculous birth of Jesus; affirming the Christian faith (Khan, 2009, p. 61). As Vaknin (1999, p. 149) wrote, *"Narcissists switch groups and ideologies with the ease with which they change partners, spouses and value systems. Narcissists are Narcissists first and members of their group only in the second place"*. Muhammad was in action again and this trend continued until some early period of his mission in Medina. By seeing the Biblical stories in the Qur'an, some Christians were confused and they mistook Islam as another prospering sect of

Christianity. Some of them converted to Muhammad's sect. This way Muhammad was partially successful in deceiving them. Allah generously declared that the Christians would also escape hellfire,

> *Those who believe in Qur'an ... and the Christians ... shall have their reward with their Lord; on them shall be no fear, nor shall they grieve.* (Q: 2.62).

However, the mainstream Christians paid him little attention. Christ specifically spoke of the false Prophets yet to come, and warned that if people report such a one in the desert – *"do not go there"* (Matt: 24.26). By seeing the rejection, Muhammad felt that he had been treated unjustly. Shortly; the Christians, like the Jews, turned to be his major critics adding insult to injury. The malignant Narcissist, despite borrowing so intensely from the Christian faith to formulate his religion, now would not hesitate to condemn the Christians. He denied the divinity of Jesus and his resurrection. Allah denied that Christ died on the Cross. If the death of Jesus on the Cross for the sin of mankind is denied, the Christian faith loses much of its claimed greatness. This is how the Narcissist took his sick revenge. Since Christians did not accept Islam, Qur'an invoked Allah's curse on them.

> *And because of their saying: We slew the Messiah, Jesus son of Mary, Allah's messenger - they slew him not nor crucified him, but it appeared so unto them; and lo! those who disagree concerning it are in doubt thereof; they have no knowledge thereof save pursuit of a conjecture; they slew him not for certain. But Allah took him up unto Himself. Allah was ever Mighty, Wise.* (Q: 4.157-8).

> *And with those who say: "Lo! we are Christians," We made a covenant, but they forgot a part of that whereof they were admonished. Therefore We have stirred up enmity and hatred among them till the Day of Resurrection, when Allah will inform them of their handiwork.* (Q: 5.14).

> *Indeed those who say: 'Allah is the third of the Trinity' became unbelievers. There is but One God. If they do not desist in what they say, a painful punishment will afflict those of them that disbelieve.* (Q: 5.73).

From the above verses we can see how much Allah was ignorant about basic tenets of Christianity. Allah thought that the Christians believe in three Gods and on this ground He attacked them. This is nothing more than a gross misrepresentation and distortion of the historic Christian position, as anyone with even an elementary knowledge of the Bible and church history can attest. To continue with Allah's hatred for the Christians,

> *Lord, she said, 'how can I bear a child when no human being has touched me? He replied: 'Such is the Will of Allah. He creates whom He will. When He decrees a thing, He only says: Be and it is.* (Q: 3.47).

> *Say: O followers of the Book! Be not unduly immoderate in your religion, and do not follow the low desires of people who went astray before and led many astray and went astray from the right path.* (Q: 5.77).

O People of the Book! Commit no excesses in your religion: Nor say of Allah aught but the truth. Christ Jesus the son of Mary was (no more than) a messenger of Allah, and His Word, which He bestowed on Mary, and a spirit proceeding from Him: so believe in Allah and His messengers. Say not "Trinity": desist: it will be better for you: for Allah is one Allah. (Q: 4.171).

Allah prescribed eternal hellfire for the Christians with Jews and idolaters for not joining Islam.

Lo! Those who disbelieve, among the People of the Scripture and the idolaters, will abide in fire of hell. They are the worst of created beings. (Q: 98.6)

They surely disbelieve who say: Lo! Allah is the Messiah, son of Mary. The Messiah (himself) said: O Children of Israel, worship Allah, my Lord and your Lord. Lo! Whoso ascribeth partners unto Allah, for him Allah hath forbidden paradise. The abode of Allah is the Fire. For the evil-doers there will be no helpers. (Q: 5.72).

After condemning the main doctrine of Christianity, Muhammad turned to the Christian priests. These priests, according to Muhammad, were greedy and devourer of people's wealth by evil means because they prevented the Christians from joining Islam. In the following two verses, Allah is clearly very angry with them.

They have taken as lords beside Allah their rabbis and their monks and the Messiah son of Mary, when they were bidden to worship only One Allah. There is no Allah save Him. Be He glorified from all that they ascribe as partner (unto Him)! (Q: 9.31).

O ye who believe! Lo! many of the (Jewish) rabbis and the (Christian) monks devour the wealth of mankind wantonly and debar (men) from the way of Allah. They who hoard up gold and silver and spend it not in the way of Allah, unto them give tidings (O Muhammad) of a painful doom. (Q: 9.34).

Even after condemning the main doctrine of Christianity, attacking the priests and prescribing hellfire for the Christians, the Narcissist was not happy. His super inflated ego was not satisfied. In the following ahadith, Muhammad made some absurd claims similar to what he made about the Jews,

Narrated Abu Huraira, Allah's Apostle said "How will you be when the son of Mary (i.e. Jesus) descends amongst you and he will judge people by the Law of the Qur'an and not by the law of Gospel. (Bukhari: 4.55.658)

Narrated Abu Huraira, Allah's Apostle said, By Him in Whose Hands my soul is, surely (Jesus) the son of Mary will soon descend amongst you and will judge mankind justly (as a Just Ruler); he will break the Cross and kill the pigs and there will be no Jizya (taxation taken from Kafirs). Money will be in abundance so that nobody will accept it, and a single prostration to Allah (in prayer) will be better than the whole world and whatever is in it. (Bukhari: 4.55.657)

Now Muhammad decided to take arms against Christians. With divine sanction from Allah, Muhammad launched military campaigns against all the kings who had rejected his call for submission to Islam. Amongst them there were Arab Christian kings of Yamama, Oman and Bahrain, and powerful foreign Christian rulers like, Governor of Egypt and the Byzantine Emperor Heraclius. The Governor of Egypt offered Muhammad with two beautiful slave girls as friendly gifts.

In September 629, Muhammad sent a strong force of three thousand Muslim warriors to Muta, a Christian border district of Syria. The Christian King clashed with Muhammad with greater military force and Muslims suffered severe losses. In February, 630, Muhammad sent another Muslim army to fight the Christian tribes of Oman. Under sword, some tribes were subdued to embrace Islam while others were forced to surrender half of their land and property in order to keep their Christian faith. In October 630, Muhammad again sent a large army of thirty thousand horses and foot soldiers to fight Byzantine frontier in Syria. However this massive army of Muslims retreated when spies arrived with the intelligence that a large Greek army had assembled at the border to confront the Muslim army (Khan, 2009, p. 64). In 632, Muhammad was preparing for another expedition against the Christians, but he suddenly fell terminally ill.

Muhammad's hate for Christians and Jews continued well into his death bed. Just a few days before his death, this revengeful Narcissist cried out, "*Oh Lord, destroy the Jews and Christians. Let the Lord's anger be kindled against them. Let there remain throughout Arabia no other religion except Islam.*" The dying wish of the malignant Narcissist was carried out to conclusion by his immediate successors by expelling the Jews and Christians from Arabia. Towards the end of seventh century, Arab armies forcibly conquered the well-established and urbane Christian societies of Palestine, Syria, Egypt, North of Africa, Spain, and later Asia Minor and the Balkans. Tens of millions of Christians were either forcibly converted to Islam or slaughtered in a slow motion holocaust (Morse, 2010, p. 53). The idolaters were also condemned by Allah. Qur'an says,

O ye who believe! The idolaters only are unclean. So let them not come near the Inviolable Place of Worship after this their year. If ye fear poverty (from the loss of their merchandise) Allah shall preserve you of His bounty if He will. Lo! Allah is Knower, Wise. (Q: 9.28)

... woe unto the idolaters. (Q: 41.6)

... their works are vain and in the Fire they will abide. (Q: 9.17)

And an announcement from Allah and His Messenger to the people ... that Allah and His Messenger are free from liability to the idolaters; (Q: 9.3)

... turn away from the idolaters... (Q: 6.106)

Wed not idolatresses till they believe; for lo! a believing bondwoman is better than an idolatress though she please you; and give not your daughters in marriage to idolaters till they believe, for lo! A believing slave is better than an idolater though he please you. (Q: 2.221)

It is not for the Prophet, and those who believe, to pray for the forgiveness of idolaters even though they may be near of kin (to them) after it hath become clear that they are people of hellfire. (Q: 9.113)

Muhammad was self-absorbed. He really did not understand the concept of others, much less love for them. He did not even know what normal human interaction is; he just tried to make an impression. In a normal healthy person, we can see a substantially genuine interest in others in addition to his interest in himself to hold up their hands. But the Narcissist does not want others to know them; it is his deepest, darkest secret. As Masterson (1990, p. 98) wrote, *"He has absolutely no interest in others for themselves. Narcissists are completely foreign to most of us in this regard. They do not realize or accept the fact that the world contains other human beings who are emotionally involved with each other and with their own legitimate needs and interests which are just as important as the Narcissist's".* As Zayn & Dibble (2007, p. 80) wrote, *"The narcissists need to feel right at all times. When people disagree with them, they don't see those disagreements as other opinions; they see them as direct attacks against their integrity."*

But, are all Jews and Christians bad in the eyes of Muhammad? Yes, it is. This is how the Narcissist generalizes his enemies. A Narcissist does not react to people (or interact with them) as individuals. Rather, he generalizes and tends to treat people as symbols or "classes".

The Prophet declared, 'Kill any Jew who falls under your power'. (Tabari: VII.97)

For Muhammad, anyone who is a Jew is an enemy of Islam. This is how he generalized people. He believed in "all or nothing" – either idealize or devalue people to the extreme. To the Narcissist, things and people are either entirely bad (evil) or entirely good. For this reason, a Muslim will go to paradise even if he is the worst criminal, and the Jews, Christians and Idolaters will go to hell only because they do not submit to Islam even if they are saints and pious people.

Being in a position of authority secures the uninterrupted flow of narcissistic supply. Fed by the awe, fear, subordination, admiration, adoration and obedience of his victims – the Narcissist thrives in such circumstances. He aspires to acquire authority by any means available to him. The more he gets the more he starves for. His thirst is never satisfied. In a particular moment, even God cannot escape him. He devalues God and shows to others that even God is powerless to him.

On several occasions, Muhammad disobeyed Allah outrageously by neglecting the Qur'anic injunctions as we have seen before. By neglecting Allah's instruction, Muhammad's narcissistic supply stock increased at the expense of God. He proved that even God is miserably helpless to him. Not to forget, there was another reason for Muhammad for not to follow Qur'an. A Narcissist is a show-off man. He always wants to give an impression that he belongs to his group and believes in equality but at the same time he is well aware of his superior position and consciously maintains his stance as an outsider. By neglecting Allah's instruction Muhammad proved that those instructions were for common Muslims and not for a great man like him. This is how Allah indirectly became his dominant source of narcissistic supply. This is such a conspiracy which even God cannot escape. As Vaknin (1999, p. 148) wrote, *"God is subsumed in a larger picture, that of the Narcissist's destiny and mission.*

God is to serve this cosmic plan by making it possible. Indirectly, therefore, God is perceived by the Narcissist to be at his service". Value is never absolute; it is always relative. By devaluing Allah, Muhammad put himself in a higher position. From his point of view when Allah's stock goes down his stock equally goes up.

It is expected that a Prophet must uphold God over his own self and devote his life for the service of his God. But in Islam it is theoretical. In practice, Muhammad put himself in a position superior to Allah. Muslims fail to see that Muhammad had absolutely no respect or fear for Allah. Let me analyze the following ahadith.

> *Narrated Abu Sa`id bin Al—Mu'alla: While I was praying in the Mosque, Allah's Apostle called me but I did not respond to him. Later I said, "O Allah's Apostle! I was praying." He said, "Did not Allah say' "Give your response to Allah (by obeying Him) and to His Apostle when he calls you." (Q: 8.24) He then said to me, 'I will teach you a Sura which is the greatest Sura in the Qur'an, before you leave the Mosque'.* (Bukhari: 6.60.1)

> *Narrated Abu Sa`id bin Al—Mu'alla: While I was praying, Allah's Apostle passed me and called me, but I did not go to him until I had finished the prayer. Then I went to him, and he said, "What prevented you from coming to me? Did not Allah say: "O you who believe! Answer the call of Allah (by obeying Him) and His Apostle when He calls you?" He then said, 'I will inform you of the greatest Sura in the Qur'an before I leave (the mosque)'.* (Bukhari: 6.60.170)

What we can understand from the above ahadith is summarized below,

1. A Muslim was praying to Allah and thus neglected Muhammad's call and continued praying (quickly), and once his prayer was finished he came to Muhammad.
2. His behavior made Muhammad angry. He asked him for a reason for not responding sooner. The Muslim gave an honest reply that he was praying to Allah. Hence he could not reply to Muhammad.
3. On hearing this, Muhammad quoted this verse from Qur'an, *"O you, who believe! Answer Allah (by obeying Him) and (His) Messenger when he calls you to that which gives you life."* (Q: 8.24).
4. But the Muslim was busy in praying to Allah which frustrated Muhammad, though Allah said, *"Answer Allah (by obeying Him)..."*
5. It means what Muhammad was frustrated because the Muslim did not obey him, even if he was praying to Allah.

The logical conclusion is, Muhammad was mightier than Allah. So desperately he needed attention that he could not bear even the simplest signs of him being neglected, even if it would mean placing him higher than his God. A Narcissist does not even leave the God to live peacefully. Muhammad could not tolerate to see that his Allah was getting more attention than him from a common Muslim. Once he realized that his false God Allah was revered more than himself, he came out with Qur'anic revelations demanding more respect. For a Narcissist, even God is his victim for narcissistic supplies. The only difference between God and Muhammad is that God does not believe that He is Muhammad. Qur'an says,

*When they (nonbelievers) come to thee, **they salute thee, not as Allah salutes thee,** (but in crooked ways) ... Enough for them is Hell: In it will they burn, and evil is that destination!"* (Q: 58.8)

The Narcissist tries to change his victims to a steady source of narcissistic supply. The victims obey his commands, pay attention to him, share his belief, admire his personality, applaud his personal traits, satisfy his needs and ultimately expected to be ready to die for him. The Narcissist does not change but his victims change themselves. Muhammad wanted to be superior to God and he had achieved his goal. In his lifetime, Muhammad literally became a "living God". The Muslims used to worship him.

In the beginning, Muhammad neither envisioned that his newfound religion would be so successful to spread well outside Mecca or in greater sense, outside the confines of Arabia nor ever thought that his religion could have been suitable for anyone other than Arabs. He was motivated by the success of the contemporary small-scale self-proclaimed Prophets in Mecca. Initially he wanted to be one like them and live a parasitic life by fooling a number of people at and near Mecca. The early verses confirm that Qur'an was written for to attract the Meccans.

And this is a blessed Scripture which We have revealed, confirming that which (was revealed) before it, that thou may warn the Mother of Villages and those around her. Those who believe in the Hereafter believe herein, and they are careful of their worship. (Q: 6.92).

And thus We have inspired in thee a Lecture in Arabic, that thou may warn the mother-town and those around it, and may warn of a day of assembling whereof there is no doubt. A host will be in the garden, and a host of them in the flame. (Q: 42.7).

Or do they say: He has forged it? Nay! it is the truth from your Lord that you may warn a people to whom no warner has come before you, that they may follow the right direction. (Q: 32.3).

And thou was not beside the Mount when We did call; but (the knowledge of it is) a mercy from thy Lord that thou may warn a folk unto whom no warner came before thee, that haply they may give heed. (Q: 28.46).

It is not for the townsfolk of Al-Madinah and for those around them of the wandering Arabs so stay behind the messenger of Allah and prefer their lives to his life. (Q: 9.120).

And We have made (this Scripture) easy in thy language only that they may heed. (Q: 44.58).

Surely We have made it an Arabic Quran that you may understand. (Q: 43.3).

From the above verses we can see that Allah spoke to Muhammad in Arabic which was used only in one particular geographic location and spoken by a certain group of people and its significance is for people in and around Mecca. If Islam is a universal religion, then why could not Allah create one universal language for all of humankind so that all people could benefit from that equally? Arabic Qur'an is certainly beneficial for the Arabs only. It means Islam is not a universal religion. Tabari recorded Muhammad's words on behalf of Allah giving importance to Mecca as a holy place.

I shall have one of those houses singled out for my generosity and distinguish it from all others by my name and call it my House. I shall have it proclaim my greatness, and it is upon it that I have placed my majesty. (Tabari: I.301)

In reality, Muhammad had hardly any respect for Mecca. He never hesitated to lead dozens of armed raids against the Meccans for control of the Allah's House. Muhammad's Islam was all about control of power, politics and money. Malignant narcissism worsens with time. As he grew in power his need for narcissistic supplies continued to increase. Now he is determined to conquer not only Mecca but the central Arabia also.

I heard Allah's Apostle saying, 'From my followers there will be a crowd of 70,000 in number who will enter Paradise whose faces will glitter as the moon.' (Bukhari: 8.76.550)

Verily! 70,000 of my followers will enter Paradise altogether; so that the first and the last amongst them will enter at the same time. (Bukhari: 4.54.410)

Allah's Apostle said, '70,000 of my followers shall enter Paradise like the full moon'. (Ishaq: 306)

At this point of his divine mission, Muhammad's vision was no greater than the conquest of Mecca and central Arabia. He needed to brainwash 70,000 people to fight for him (and if necessary die for him) which he thought to be sufficient to conquer the central Arabia. That is why he said, 70,000 of his people would enter paradise and their faces would "*glitter as the moon*". We should not fail to see how the malignant Narcissist was manipulating the Arabs for his selfish needs. Also another point needs to be noted. By "followers" Muhammad meant the Arabs, because at that time, the only followers that he had, were the Arabs. It means, the non-Arab Muslims have absolutely no chance to enter paradise.

But, little did he know that his religious deception would live on, infecting billions, and sending millions to their death. After conquering what he desired, Muhammad moves on. Now his Allah declares that Islam is a universal religion – it means the whole world is to be conquered for Allah. More correctly, Muhammad's narcissistic thirst for praise, respect, devotion, authorization and attention could never be quenched. Like an alcohol addict, the more he got, the more he needed. Allah revealed the following verses.

Lo! It is naught else than a Reminder for all people. (Q: 38.87)

When it is naught else than a Reminder to creation. (Q: 68.52)

Arabs were the first victims upon whom Muhammad had designed, maliciously and intentionally, with evil intentions. The Narcissist manipulates because he has genuine problems. He knows that manipulating is a good way to get what he wants. The victim's compliance rewards him. His motto is simple – "No pain, only gain at the expense of others".

3.6.5.1: Why Muhammad became an Outlaw?

For a Narcissist, being notorious is second best to being famous and of course it is far preferable to being ignored. For him, there is nothing called "bad publicity" – what matters is to be in the public eye. He has hardly any choice and equally enjoys all types of attention and likes as much to be feared as to be loved. His only bad emotional stretches are during periods of lack of attention, publicity or exposure.

If necessary, the Narcissist will gamble away all his savings, just to become heavily indebted, so that he can get some attention to remain in public eyes. He does not mind being humiliated if this were to make him more unique. He can even take off his cloths in public to get some applause for it (Twenge & Campbell, 2010, p. 251). Some somatic female Narcissists dress seductively to gain attention. Some wealthy Narcissists often invite the local newspaper to "catch them" in charity acts. Some even pretend to "become ill" to show others that they are overstressed or they need special attention during their pretended illness. If a child falls ill in the family, there are chances that the Narcissist will be lying in bed with a heating pad or tissue box, because it is very stressful for him to lose the spotlight. Sometimes they play "martyr" (Zayn & Dibble, 2007, pp. 91-2). These are the narcissistic mind games which are cleverly disguised and they play all these games when the situation is going out of control. Some Narcissists even cry – but they cry exclusively for themselves and they do so noticeably and publicly – to attract attention.

In sum; without public attention, the Narcissist crumbles, like the zombies or the "living dead" one sees in horror movies. It is terrifying and the Narcissist is ready to do anything to avoid it. But the problem begins when all these mind games fail. This is the time he wants to be notorious and feared because it is the only choice left to him to secure his supply sources. If he can secure attention by being the big bad wolf, he swiftly transforms himself into one. He shows no hesitation in eliminating men whom he had ceased to trust, either with or without the pretence of a fair trial. As Zayn & Dibble (2007, p. 34) wrote, "*Narcissists thrive on attention, whether it is positive or negative. It reminds them that they exist and that others notice them. When Narcissists are ignored, their very existence is threatened. Negative attention equals positive attention [supply] for a Narcissist.*"

As he aged, Muhammad was in pursuit of an ever-increasing supply, an ever-larger dose of adoration, and an ever-bigger fix of attention. With this he gradually lost his moral constraints. The more authority he got, the more he thrived. When he could not get the Jews as converts to Islam, he warned them "*O Jews, fear Allah and submit.*" (Ishaq: 257). On several occasions Muhammad repeatedly instructed others to fear Allah.

Allah helped you at Badr when you were contemptible, so fear Allah. Fear Me, (Ishaq: 392).

Pronounce the Name of Allah, and fear Allah. (Q: 5.4)

What is the matter with you that you do not fear Allah? (Muslim: 71.13)

Fear Allah; Allah is Severe in Punishment. (Muslim: 59.6)

Fear Allah as much as you can; listen and obey. (Q: 64.16)

Obey Allah and His Messenger. (Muslim: 8.1, 8.20)

This particular instruction *"Obey Allah and His Messenger"* is repeated numerous times in the Islamic scriptures, as if Allah is in a constant panicky state that He might not be taken seriously by the Muslims. But why Allah needs to be feared? Who else benefited the most, except Muhammad, when Allah was feared? It was a mind game of Muhammad. Narcissists interpret fear as respect or love. Any kind of emotion proves his existence and reinforces his delusion of omnipotence (Zayn & Dibble, 2007, p. 108). The "fear" factor is a very important aspect of Islam. When Muslims are instructed to fear Allah they have to fear Muhammad also because Allah and Muhammad command together. With fear comes the obedience. This is how he had secured obedience from his followers. A bandit leader does not preach crime to his followers in a peaceful manner, rather he wants to be feared and obeyed by his followers to carry out his unlawful orders. He demands authority so that law of the jungle can be established in the civilized society. Qur'an says,

He cannot be questioned for His acts, but they will be questioned. (Q: 21.23)

He who fears will obey. (Q: 87.10)

This is how Islam, the brain-child of Muhammad, propagates. According to the Qur'anic verse 59.21 even the mountains fear Allah. Muslims are slaves of Allah. Slaves must fear their masters. Through fear comes respect. Muhammad gained respect whereas he was supposed to be condemned as a criminal. In his lifetime, he was literally worshipped as God. It was not out of respect, but fear. Qur'an says,

Being niggardly with respect to you; but when fear comes, you will see them looking to you, their eyes rolling like one swooning because of death; but when the fear is gone they smite you with sharp tongues, (Q: 33.19)

The dominance urge of Muhammad had only one goal – to establish superiority on both friends and foes. Shaikh (1999, p. 13) commented, *"No person (in known history) has ever possessed the magnitude of dominance-urge that Muhammad did. If we turn the entire humankind into a pyramid, right at the apex shall be found the Arabian Prophet."* There are hundreds of jihadi verses in the Qur'an. If Allah was so hateful to the infidels, then why He did not eliminate the infidels with some so-called "divine punishment", e.g., massive earthquake, plague, flood, bad harvest, etc? Actually all these hatred originated in the sick mind of a malignant Narcissist. If Muhammad could establish himself as a Prophet in Mecca, he would not have become a bandit. When he could not achieve by peaceful means, he became violent.

3.6.5.2: Muhammad's Excessive Cruelty and Hatred for non-Muslims

Much had been talked about the cruelty of Muhammad in the traditional Islamic sources. There is no crime known to the society that he had not committed in the name of God. He was in fact a terrorist, criminal and murderer whose entire life was based on victimizing innocents and indulging in mindless violence, carnage and massacre. He was a man who destroyed peace wherever he went, and in its place brought terror, carnage and death. He did not possess a shred of pity or kindness, or the slightest sense of justice. He was obviously motivated by nothing but abnormal hatred for the society and greed for wealth and sex. The three main motivations behind Muhammad's heinous actions were as follows,

1. His fanatic greed for all the wealth that had been created by the blood, sweat and toil of the Jews, Christians and idolaters.
2. His maniacal craving for power at any cost. If the Jews and Christians had accepted him as their Prophet at first call, surely they would not have been tortured and mass murdered.
3. His paranoid fear of all other religions. This malignant Narcissist felt that he was superior, omnipotent, omniscient, invincible, immune, above the law, and omnipresent (magical thinking). Anything that threatened his sick fantasy had to be eliminated.

The bloody stories of Muhammad's trail of violence, hatred, sexual exploitation and bloodshed that soon destroyed the once flourishing culture of Arabia were well-documented by his biographers – surprise raids on merchant caravans and tribal settlements, the use of plunder thus obtained for recruiting an ever growing army of greedy desperados, assassinations of opponents, blackmail, expulsion and massacre of the Jews of Medina, attack and enslavement of the Jews of Khaybar, rape of women and children, sale of those victims after rape, burning alive, cruelty to animals, trickery, treachery and bribery employed to their fullest extent to grow the numbers of his religion, Islam, which ironically was supposed to mean "Peace"! Moreover; whenever this "Apostle of Peace" and "*a mercy to all the worlds*" (Q: 21.107) had committed one of his criminal onslaughts, he always justified the crimes by quickly claiming a divine revelation which conveniently removed the blame from his bloodied hands.

Muhammad was very sincere and alert to give an impression that Allah gave him authority to be cruel to others. This malignant Narcissist does not persecute, ransack, terrorize and abuse others in a cold, calculating manner. He does it as if he has an authority to do such horrible things. He does it so rudely that it becomes a sign of his true character. A Narcissist does not "own" his actions. He deliberately confuses guilt with responsibility. A sane person should feel guilty for terrorizing others, but for Muhammad it was his divine "responsibility" to terrorize.

Warfare is ordained for you, though it is hateful unto you; but it may happen that you hate a thing which is good for you and it may happen that you love a thing which is bad for you. Allah knoweth, you knew not. (Q: 2.216).

The Prophet said: Allah made me victorious with terror. (Bukhari: 1.7.331).

Narrated Abu Huraira: Allah's Apostle sent us in a mission (i.e. an army-unit) and said: I have ordered you to burn so-and-so and so-and-so, and it is none but Allah Who punishes with fire, so, if you find them, kill them. (Bukhari: 4.52.259).

Narrated 'Aisha: Allah's Apostle never took revenge (over anybody) for his own sake but (he did) only when Allah's Legal Bindings were outraged in which case he would take revenge for Allah's Sake. (Bukhari: 4.56.760)

So you did not slay them, but it was Allah Who slew them, and you did not smite when you smote (the enemy), but it was Allah Who smote, and that He might confer upon the believers a good gift from Himself; surely Allah is Hearing, Knowing. (Q: 8.17)

How skillfully Muhammad put the responsibility on Allah for having started the fighting and in terrorizing others. He did not say that he terrorized others, but it was Allah who made him successful in terrorizing others. Muhammad made Allah the author of his vicious thoughts and pretended that it was not his goal to kill his opponents but it was the decision of Allah, who was commanding him. This way Muhammad did not take any responsibility because he did not "own" his actions. The most insidious and devilish implication of the above Qur'anic verses is that Allah is completely justifying Muhammad's murder of the innocent people in warfare. Over and above, Muhammad is conveniently implying that warfare is hateful to him, but he participated in it because it was ordained by Allah! He was just carrying out Allah's instruction. Anyone who wants to achieve victory by terrorizing others is simply called a terrorist. But Muhammad was not a terrorist by choice, but by compulsion. It was Allah, who wanted him to be a terrorist. Nobody could blame Muhammad for whatever misery he had caused to the unbelievers and their women and children.

*And that do not exalt yourselves against Allah, surely **I will bring to you a clear authority**.* (Q: 44.19)

Narrated As-Sab bin Jaththama: The Prophet passed by me at a place called Al-Abwa or Waddan, and was asked whether it was permissible to attack the pagan warriors at night with the probability of exposing their women and children to danger. The Prophet replied, "They (i.e. women and children) are from them (i.e. pagans). 'I also heard the Prophet saying, 'The institution of Hima is invalid except for Allah and His Apostle'. (Bukhari: 4.52.256)

In the following verse, Allah says that to kill or to create warfare in the sacred month is a very grave offence, but to justify his own violation of Allah's rules, Muhammad came up with the idea that since the people killed were unbelievers, it was perfectly justified!

They ask thee concerning fighting in the Prohibited Month. Say: "Fighting therein is a grave (offence); but graver is it in the sight of Allah to prevent access to the path of Allah, to deny Him, to prevent access to the Sacred

Mosque, and drive out its members". Tumult and oppression are worse than slaughter. Nor will they cease fighting you until they turn you back from your faith if they can. And if any of you turn back from their faith and die in unbelief, their works will bear no fruit in this life and in the hereafter; they will be companions of the fire and will abide therein. (Q: 2.217).

During Ramadan (March 623) Muhammad ganged up all the criminals from Medina and set out to raid the caravan with three hundred men. The Meccans got word of the raid and sent out an army to protect the caravan. The Muslims killed some seventy Meccans and took seventy prisoners (Bukhari: 4.52.276). In history, this is known as battle of Badr. All seventy of the prisoners were ransomed and any prisoner who did not fetch a ransom had his head chopped off. Muhammad was delighted at the sight of his murdered victims. This time Muhammad needed a revelation that would not only forgive him of all the guilt for murdering so many innocent people but also give him the divine right to get a huge share of the plundered booty. Accordingly quite a few revelations magically appeared.

It is not for any Prophet to have captives until he hath made slaughter in the land. You desire the lure of this world and Allah desires for you the hereafter and Allah is Mighty, Wise. (Q: 8.67)

Had it not been for an ordinance of Allah which had gone before, an awful doom had come upon you on account of what ye took. (Q: 8.68)

Now enjoy what you have won as lawful and good and keep your duty to Allah. Lo! Allah is forgiving, merciful. (Q: 8.69)

The above revelations were in reference to the prisoners that Muhammad held for ransom after the battle. Allah the "Merciful" is saying that they should all have been killed! In addition, Allah is conveniently commenting that whatever loot Muhammad had plundered is "*lawful and good*" because it was done in the service to Allah. Therefore; murder, rape, plunder and destruction are all perfectly fine with Allah as long as they are done in the name of Islam! Muhammad is also insidiously making himself seem very kind for having spared the lives of the prisoners, when in fact he only let them live so he could get more money from the ransom for them. In today's world this is called "terrorism" of the worst kind.

Muhammad's most dreadful act of cruelty came in April 627, when he killed the entire adult male members (some 800 to 900 of them) of Quraiza tribe. Their adulthood was determined by the growth of pubic hair. The women and children were captured as slaves, their homes and properties were confiscated and distributed amongst Muslims. This beheading "ceremony" with heavy swords started in the morning and continued whole day long and then by torchlight into the following night (Khan, 2009, p. 48). Muhammad kept one-fifth of the captured property of the Quraiza and the rest was distributed amongst other Muslims. Amongst the female captives, the young and pretty ones became his sex-slaves. Muhammad himself took a beautiful woman, Rayhana, as his own concubine and took her to bed on the same night he had killed her male relatives. No historical record has enlightened us as to her state of mind of being raped by the man responsible for the decapitation of her husband and other males of her family a few hours earlier. As usual, Muhammad did not "own" his actions. Allah revealed a verse to clear Muhammad from taking any blame for his actions,

> He brought those of the People of the Scripture who supported them down from their strongholds, and cast panic into their hearts. Some ye slew, and ye made captive some. And He caused you to inherit their land and their houses and their wealth, and land ye have not trodden. Allah is ever able to do all things". (Q: 33.26, 27).

Narcissists have defense mechanisms by which they can disown their own actions. This way they are immune to taking any blame. They are apparently unable to predict the inevitable outcomes of their actions. Conscience is predicated on empathy. One puts oneself in other people's shoes and feels the way they do. Without empathy, there cannot be conscience. A Narcissist can only recognize his reality and no one else's. As Vaknin (1999, p. 67) wrote, "A Narcissist's behavior is directed by forces that he cannot master. Most of the time he is not even conscious of why he is doing what he is doing. When he is – he can't tell the outcomes. Even when he can – he feels powerless to behave otherwise. The Narcissist is a pawn in the chase game played between the structures of his fragmented fluid personality. So, in a classical – juridical sense, the Narcissist is not to blame, he is not fully responsible or aware of what he is doing to others".

The Narcissist feels that no evil can be inflicted on humans because they are like "objects". With this mindset, it is very easy for him to become an antisocial or a psychopath killer because he is not prevented by his conscience. He simply does not understand the pain of others. Some researchers conclude that even if he is able to recognize emotions in others, he is also able to disconnect that recognition from his own emotions (Abbott, 2007, p. 942). Hence he does not share the pain he inflicts on others. There is high incidence of NPD among prison inmates. What prevents sane persons from immoral, cynical, callous behavior is that they have ethical imperatives embedded in them through socialization and empathy. Rational people can differentiate between right and wrong and this particular ability is internalized in them. They can choose right from wrong when they face a moral dilemma. They empathize with other human beings by "putting themselves in their shoes", and refrain from doing unto others what they do not wish to be done to them.

When a malignant Narcissist's lack of empathy and concern, deficient social skills, and disregard for social laws and morals erupt and blossom, he becomes a full-fledged antisocial (sociopath or psychopath). When he is in the leadership, he continues his cruel acts unabated. Muhammad ignored the wishes and needs of others, broke the law as he liked, and violated all rights – natural, social, ethical and legal. He held people in contempt and disdain, derided society and its codes, and punished the innocent peaceful citizen who did no harm to him, by acting criminally and by jeopardizing their safety, lives, or property. The most pathetic part of this story is; whatever Muhammad did, he did in the name of God.

Vaknin (1999, p. 191) wrote that a malignant Narcissist provokes violence, often not knowing why he is violent. Like a vampire, he simply cannot avoid bloodshed. When Allah instructed that a Prophet should not take captives "until he hath made slaughter in the land" (Q: 8.67), it was not a God but a malignant

Narcissist talking in the name of God. Because of his defense mechanism, Muhammad was powerless to himself and did not know what would be the outcome of his cruel acts. It is hard to distinguish malignant Narcissists from psychopaths.

A malignant Narcissist is like a vulture which is attracted to corpses, and he is so much addicted to it that he destroys anyone who is around him. He simply cannot imagine any other way to live. In a psychiatric diagnosis in 1984, Kernberg used the terms "malignant narcissism" and "psychopathic behavior" interchangeably, and concluded that a sadistic element is included in malignant narcissism which makes the malignant Narcissist a cruel psychopath. For a psychopath, killing others is a small matter indeed.

Killing disbelievers is a small matter to us. (Tabari: IX.69).

Allah said, 'A Prophet must slaughter before collecting captives. A slaughtered enemy is driven from the land. Muhammad, you craved the desires of this world, its goods and the ransom captives would bring. But Allah desires killing them to manifest the religion'. (Ishaq: 327)

Allah and Muhammad humiliated every coward and made our religion victorious. We were glorified and destroyed them all. By what our Apostle recites from the Book and by our swift horses, I liked the punishment the infidels received. Killing them was sweeter than drink. (Ishaq: 576)

Psychopaths and malignant Narcissists are social predators completely free of internal restraints. They are motivated by bloodlust often filled with dreams and wild ambitions (Stout, 2005, p. 2). Their hallmark is a stunning lack of conscience; their game is self-gratification at other person's expense (Hare, 1993, p. 1). We can find these people in every race, culture, society and walk of life. Conscience is a sense of obligation. Genuine conscience brings positive changes to the society and to the world in various ways. It is deep-rooted in emotional connectedness. But unfortunately, the Prophet of Islam was bereaved of such a godly gift. He had a shallow emotion; lack of conscience was a "huge" and "secret" advantage for him, and because of this he was unfettered by guilt or remorse.

Muhammad was cruel to animals also. It is one of the distinguishing vices of low minds. The concept that people who are intentionally and repeatedly cruel to the animals are at risk of violence against people has been part of our popular culture for centuries (Merz-Perez & Heide, 2004, p. x). Kindness for animals is intimately connected with goodness of character of a man, and we can boldly assert that he who is cruel to animals cannot be a good man.

*On the authority of Abu Ya'la Shaddad ibn Aus, that the Messenger of Allah said: Verily Allah has prescribed proficiency in all things. Thus, **if you kill, kill well; and if you slaughter, slaughter well**.* (Al-Nawawi, Hadith no. 17).

This was Muhammad's way of pleasing Allah – "*If you kill, kill well; and if you slaughter, slaughter well*". The final humiliation for any animal undergoing the Islamic "Halal" process is the slitting of the throat preferably hanging upside down, held aloft by the rear legs while the animal is still breathing. A cut to the major blood vessels in the neck allows continuous drainage of blood out of the animal while still alive with a beating heart. Big animals like camels take few minutes to die in this condition. This is the "humanness" of Allah and his messenger. Where are the animal right activists who emphasize the idea that the most basic interests of non-human animals should be afforded the same consideration as the similar interests of human beings?

Muhammad would slaughter a large number of camels during his various pilgrimages. As his wealth and power increased, the scale of his sacrifices also increased. On his sixth year pilgrimage, he sacrificed seventy camels at Hodeibia and next year, he sacrificed sixty camels (Swarup, 1984, section 5.12). On the farewell pilgrimage (tenth year), one hundred camels were gathered. Muhammad slaughtered sixty-three camels by his own hand, one for each year of his life and rest were slaughtered by Ali. A piece of flesh from each animal sacrificed were put in a pot, and when it was cooked, both of them (Muhammad and Ali) took some meat out of it and drank its soup. (Muslim: 7.2803).

Al-Bara' reported: He [Muhammad] said: 'Offer it as a sacrifice. He who slaughtered after prayer, his ritual of sacrifice became complete and he in fact observed the religious practice of the Muslims'. (Muslim: 22.4823)

Abu Tufail 'Amir b. Withila reported: Allah's Messenger said, 'Allah cursed him who sacrificed for anyone besides Allah'. (Muslim: 22.4876).

Muhammad's mind was full of hate and depression. Depression and rage ride in tandem. For a Narcissist, as depression intensifies and comes to the surface of awareness, so does anger (Masterson, 1990, p. 64). At first, many of them cannot pinpoint the reasons why they are angry and project their rage to the world as if the whole world is their enemy. They cannot justify themselves. This is the internal hell of a Narcissist, and he continuously pays for it.

Did Muhammad have a conscience? No; not at all. Muhammad had no feelings of guilt or remorse no matter whatever he had done. He had absolutely no struggle with shame, and the very concept of responsibility was unknown to him. He could not stop simply because he was addicted to the excitement of being notorious. He lied profusely and was capable of killing millions of people without giving a second thought to protect his lies; it thrilled him. He overvalued himself by committing mass murder. As Stout (2005, p. 5) wrote, *"Terrorism (done from a distance) is the ideal occupation for a person who is possessed of bloodlust and no conscience, because if you do it just right, you may be able to make a whole nation jump. And if that is not power, what is?"*

Our very "humanness" depends largely on our self-knowledge and realization of self-worth. It largely depends on our experience of ourselves. An individual after experiencing thoroughly with his own self can understand and fully appreciate the "humanness" of others. In this respect, the malignant Narcissist has very little or no experiences of his own self. Muhammad lived in an invented world of his own design. He was like a fictitious figure in a grandiose script where he was the leading actor with his Allah as a supporting actor. Therefore, he possessed no skills which may enable him to cope with other human beings. To react emotionally to a malignant Narcissist is like preaching Gandhian nonviolence to an Afghan Taliban fundamentalist. Since a Narcissist cannot share other's emotions, he cannot put himself in their shoes. One cannot truly love others if he is unable to truly love himself. Loving the true self is healthy, but loving the "reflection" of the true self has severe drawbacks. In personality disorder studies, often a term is used – *Emotional Involvement Prevention Mechanisms* (EIPMs). The EIPMs are intended to prevent the Narcissist from getting emotionally involved (Vaknin, 1999, p. 127). For a Narcissist, people are either functional and useful to his pursuit of narcissistic supply or not a living creature at all.

By inflecting pain to others Muhammad felt superior. Though he enjoyed their sufferings, he was not a sadist. There is a small difference between a malignant Narcissist's victimization and sadism. Muhammad's cruelty had a purpose. The Narcissist tortures and abuses as a means to punish and to reassert superiority and grandiosity, but the sadist does so purely for enjoyment, like animal torture, child molestation, forced sex, etc (Vaknin, 1999, p. 184). But in both cases, the abusers are ruthless, self-centered, strictly rigid and unable to empathize with their victims.

After conquering Khaybar; Muhammad put Kinana to death after extracting information about the whereabouts of his treasure, took possession of the fortresses, killed all the able-bodied men, and distributed women amongst Muslims (Bukhari: 2.14.68). The war cry of Muhammad's companions at that battle was "*O you have been given victory, kill! Kill!*" (Bostom, 2008, p. 278). Amongst the captured women there was Safiyyah, Kinana's seventeen years old beautiful wife and two cousins of hers. Muhammad took possession of Safiyyah and took her to a tent for sexual pleasure on the same day he had killed her husband and many other male relatives. Two years before Safiyyah's father was killed along with many male relatives of her when Muhammad – the mercy of God among mankind – butchered another important Jews' tribe, the Quraiza.

How could Muhammad show this type of monstrous brutality against Safiyyah? In a single day Safiyyah was the wife of a Jewish tribal chief, a widow, a captive and wife of Muhammad. No one should think that Muhammad fell in love with Safiyyah's beauty and therefore decided to marry her right away. He wanted to show his superiority over the Jews. The Narcissist thinks this way – "I inflict pain, therefore I am superior" (Vaknin, 1999, p. 183). It was his strong urge to punish the Jews for not accepting Islam. He compensated his defeat by inflecting pain on them. The Narcissist himself is helpless to his narcissistic rage. After it explodes, the Narcissist does not know where to stop and how much punishment is enough for his victims. For a Narcissist, there is no moral dimension.

The brutal murder of Umm Qirfah is worth mentioning. She was murdered for no reason except that she was known as the wisest woman in Arabia (Ahmed, 2006, p. 22). Tabari (VIII.96) recorded, one of Muhammad's commanders tied her legs with rope and then tied her between two camels until they split her into two. Umm Qirfah was one hundred years old when she was subjected to such a cruel death.

Muhammad was an "intra-species predator" with an abnormal lack of empathy combined with strongly amoral conduct, masked by an ability to appear outwardly normal. For a malignant Narcissist; the world, the closest relationship and even his own body can become the enemy in the eyes of his false self (Masterson, 1990, p. 61). Narcissists smell blood where others smell beautiful emotions. Often the hate is so intense that he immensely hates himself but cannot show it to others. He avoids "emotional handles" – photographs, music identified with a certain period in his life, places, people, mementoes and emotional situations. He is scared that at any unguarded moment his true self may get accidentally discovered. This is one of the reasons, Muhammad prohibited drawing his portrait. He was so paranoid that he even feared to look at his own picture.

From deep inside, the Narcissist is fully capable of differentiating between right and wrong (Zayn & Dibble, 2007, p. 102). He is in his senses; he can make moral choices, and is perfectly capable of anticipating the results of his actions and their influences on others. But he remains indifferent because his false self simply cannot react in a healthy manner to a changing situation. He feels compelled to continue to pursue precisely the same path (Vaknin, 1999, pp. 44, 89). Muhammad could make moral choices but he was not capable to limit his behavior accordingly. Qur'an says,

When you speak, be just, even if it affects your own kinsmen. (Q: 6.152).

The good deed and the evil deed are not alike. Repel the evil deed with one which is better... (Q: 41.34)

...be good to parents and to kindred and to orphans and the needy, and speak kindly to mankind ... (Q: 2.83).

Give unto orphans their wealth. Exchange not the good for the bad (in your management thereof) nor absorb their wealth into your own wealth. (Q: 4.2)

Therefore, the orphan oppress not. (Q: 93.9).

The questions of morality, i.e., concepts such as good and evil, right and wrong, virtue and vice, justice, etc, did not bother Muhammad. He knew that looting and killing of innocents are evil deeds, but he did it. He knew that the orphans should not be oppressed, but how many orphans did he sell to the slave market after he devastated the Jewish tribes? He knew that one should speak kindly to a fellow human, but where were those moral standards when he declared, "*I will bring you slaughter*"? In his entire career, did he ever promote any ethical values; e.g., trust, honesty, good behavior, fairness, and kindness? As Stout (2005, p. 9) wrote, "*It is not that this group fails to grasp the difference between good and bad; it is that the distinction fails to limit their behavior. The intellectual difference between right and wrong does not bring on the emotional sirens and flashing blue lights, or the fear of God, that it does for the rest of us*". As Checkley (1976, p. 90) wrote, "*Beauty and ugliness except in a very superficial sense, goodness, evil, love, horror and humor have no actual meaning, no power to move him*".

The Narcissist often notices that something is wrong and people around him are not happy (Vaknin, 1999, p. 96). But emotionally he is so empty that he cannot find an answer. Because of this, sometimes an internal struggle starts. This time often the superego emerges for rescuing the false self of the Narcissist. With the confirmation from his superego, the Narcissist tries repeatedly to convince himself that everyone else is wrong, defiant, incapable and lacking in judgment, and he is not on the wrong side, and the other party is in fact the abuser and the future will correct the "misconception" and "misjudgment" about him. In sum; the superego convinces the Narcissist that he is victimized, not a victimizer.

Allah was Muhammad's superego. Superego (which I will discuss in details in a later chapter) is the inner voice of a Narcissist. It gives him authorization. Beyond this, superego is just a paper tiger, a filthy scarecrow impotent and powerless. Superego is not the same as false self, but it is the master of the false self. Both of them have well distinguished "imaginary" existence (only in the sick mind of a Narcissist). Though they often work in favor of each other, on rare occasions they can function against each other also. Hence superego is not strictly same as alter-ego, though most of the time it works as alter-ego.

3.6.5.3: Muhammad's Paranoia and Self-doubts

A malignant Narcissist is not only vile, cruel and malicious; he is also full of paranoia and self doubts (Lachkar, 2008, p. 30). He sees enemies and conspiracies everywhere. He often casts himself as the heroic victim (martyr) of some negative forces. The thinking is that a great man should have great enemies, or, every great Prophet must have an equally strong ungodly opponent, otherwise the Narcissist is devalued and with this devaluation his stock of narcissistic supplies is exhausted.

Likewise did We make for every Messenger an enemy, - evil ones among men and Jinns, inspiring each other with flowery discourses by way of deception. If thy Lord had so planned, they would not have done it: so leave them and their inventions alone. (Q: 6.112).

A person in authority, who wants to maintain his position by frightening others, cannot rest peacefully. Muhammad was not capable of trusting anyone. This way, he had developed paranoia. Ibn Ishaq recorded,

[Aisha recalls] "Muhammad never failed to come by our house every day at the two ends of the day. ...Once he came during the heat of the day so we knew that it was because of something special. When he came in dad [Abu Bakr] rose from his bed, and the Messenger sat down. Muhammad said, 'Send out those who are with you.' My father said, 'Prophet, these are my daughters [one of which is now your wife]; they can do you no harm, may my father and mother be your ransom.' (Ishaq: 223).

This is abnormal. Muhammad did not even trust those two small children and Abu Bakr had to swear by his parent's names to remove his paranoid fear. As Zayn & Dibble (2007, pp. 46, 92) concluded, "*To a Narcissist, the friends and even the family members of his partners, pose a threat of exposing his real self. He really is oblivious to the feelings of others*". Vaknin (1999, p. 116) commented, "*He attacks those he thinks take him for granted, or those who fail to recognize his superiority, those who render him "average "and "normal". And they, alas, include just about everyone he knows*".
Following verses reflect Muhammad's panic.

Remember how the unbelievers [Meccans] plotted against you (O Muhammad), to keep you in bonds, or slay you, or get you out (of your home). They plotted, and Allah too had arranged a plot; but Allah is the best schemer. (Q: 8.30).

And they (the disbelievers) schemed, and Allah schemed (against them); and Allah is the best of schemers. (Q: 3.54)

While revealing these verses, Allah forgot that he was supposed to be the all-powerful and all-knowing. Why Allah needs to arrange a plot if he is all-knowing? It is just an insult to God to say that He is the best plotter or a world-class schemer. Actually these were Muhammad's own words put in Allah's mouth. Muhammad was preoccupied with baseless doubts about the trustworthiness of the Meccans. Here Muhammad is again playing a monodrama, Allah took the center stage and Muhammad remained behind the scenes. A God does not need to be *"the best schemer"* but Muhammad does for his narcissistic manipulation. He felt a certain amount of pressure to maintain his self-created world, and did it through deceptive scheming, plotting and cheating. As Zayn & Dibble (2007, p. 92) concluded, *"A Narcissist always seems to be thinking and planning. His mind never rests. It takes a lot of work to maintain control of his world and all the relationship involved. There never seems to be real happiness or peace for the Narcissist".*

A man who sees enemies everywhere has to be the best schemer (or cheater!). The scheming Prophet had found the perfect God to take away his burden. Ishaq recorded Muhammad's words put in Allah's mouth,

I am the best of plotters. I deceived them with My guile so that I delivered you from them. (Ishaq: 323).

In Islam the word "guile" is used in the same way the Bible defines Satan – *"insidious and cunning, a crafty or artful deception, duplicity"* (cited Winn, 2004, p. 361). Zayn & Dibble continued, *"He uses his sense of power to control those around him and to change situations in his favor. He lies awake at night creating possible scenarios for situations that may never come into existence and prides himself of all the back-up plans he invents for 'just in case'. Instead of viewing those situations as unnecessary worry when things don't play out the way he imagined, the Narcissist feels proud that, at least, he had been prepared".*

A real God cannot suffer from paranoia. Allah is not an "all-knowing" God. There is at least one thing which this ignorant God does not know, i.e., "What is real?" The fact is that those verses were not revealed by any God or supernatural, rather they originated from the delusional mind of the fake Prophet of Islam. Low self esteem and strong hatred can give rise to paranoia and the process of Qur'anic revelation to Muhammad was a classic case of paranoid delusion. Science had already spoken out the truth about the true nature of his prophethood.

3.6.5.4: The Paradise and the Hell

"Hum ko maaloom hai janat ki haqeeqat lekin,
Dil ke behelane ko Ghalib ye khayaal accha hai."

(Of course I [Ghalib] know there is no such thing as paradise, but to fool yourself, Ghalib, you need such pleasant thoughts.)

Mirza Ghalib (1796 - 1869)

117

3: Muhammad's Strange Mindset

"An awkward, unscientific lie is often as ineffectual as the truth."

Mark Twain (1835 - 1910)

In Islam, the very concept of both paradise and hell is immoral and disgusting, more satanic than divine. This view of paradise is so vulgar, demeaning, sexist, and immoral, and hell's torments are so hateful that any logical minded person will find it repulsive. A God shall never resort to sex, violence and torture to gain followers. To criticize Islam and Muhammad, this particular topic is often taken up by both non-Muslim and ex-Muslim scholars.

According to Qur'an; in paradise, there are gardens and vineyards, and high-bosomed virgins with a truly overflowing cup (Q: 78.31-33), the virgins are bashful, dark-eyed and as chaste as the sheltered eggs of ostriches (Q: 37.40-48), virgins are self-sealing loving companions (Q: 56.35-37), Muslims will wed these virgins (Q: 44.51-55), the virgins shall recline on couches ranged in rows (Q: 52.17-20) and the virgins are untouched by man or jinns and they as are fair as corals and rubies, sheltered in their tents and within reach will hang fruits (Q: 55.53-58, 70-77).

Allah's promise of seventy-two virgins fascinates every Muslim. The grand prize seventy-two virgins is a big motivation for the Islamic suicide bombers for going to a mission. Tirmidhi recorded,

> *Narrated Al-Miqdam ibn Ma'dikarib: Allah's Messenger said,' The martyr receives six good things from Allah... [one of this is] he is married to seventy-two wives of the maidens with large dark eyes; and is made intercessor for seventy of his relatives'.* (Tirmidhi: 1067).

After promising paradise, Muhammad realized that a man cannot have so much sexual power to have sex with seventy-two virgins. So he gave a vivid description of the sexual organs of the heavenly virgins and promised the Muslims prolonged erection of their sexual organs. Not only this – the believers can father a son also!

> *Abu Sa'id al-Khudri, reported that Allah's Messenger said, 'When a believer will wish a son in the Paradise, its conception and its birth will happen in one single hour as he wishes'.* (Sunaan Ibn Majah: 5.4338)

> *Anas 'Umama reported that Allah's Messenger said ... Allah, the Mighty and glorious will marry him with seventy-two wives, two will be from virgins (haurine) with big eyes and seventy, will be his inheritance from the people of the Hell-Fire. Everyone of them will have a pleasant vagina and he (the man) will have sexual organ that does not bend down (during sexual intercourse).* (Sunaan Ibn Majah: 5.4337).

Allah's paradise has a free sex-market where there is no limit of the number of sexual partners. Women and young boys are on display as if in a fruit market where believers can choose the desired ripeness.

> *Ali narrated that the Apostle of Allah said, 'There is in paradise an open market wherein there will be no buying or selling, but will consist of men and women. When a man desires a beauty, at once he will have intercourse with*

them as desired'. (Al-Ghazali's Ihya Ulum al-Din, Vol. 4, no. 34).

However, after promising plenty virgins, Muhammad suddenly realized that some of his followers were homosexuals and hence virgins were of no use for them. Homosexuality was and is widely practiced in Arabia. Many famous poets of Arabia have glorified homosexuality in their literature. To please the homosexual Muslims, Allah promised them young boys. Qur'an says; the handsome boys are like scattered pearls (Q: 76.19), well-guarded (Q: 52.24) and of perpetual freshness (Q: 56.17). Whenever the Muslim clerics are asked to explain the purpose of boys in paradise, they say that they are servants of the faithful. But why a servant has to be ever-young, beautiful like pearls, dressed in brocades and bracelets. He can surely be old, ugly and poorly dressed. It should not matter as long as he serves his master sincerely and maintains personal hygiene. These pearl-like boys are supplied by Allah to provide "special" service to the homosexual Muslims.

For vulgar people, sex is not enjoyable without alcohol (readers, no offence please!). So Allah promised plenty wine in His paradise. Wine was an extremely precious commodity in the dry deserts of Arabia where it was rare to find vineyards. According to Qur'an; the gardens have river of wine (Q: 47.15), pure wine, securely sealed; whose very dregs are musk (Q: 83.25, 26), Muslims will recline on jeweled couches and will be served by those pearl-like boys with bowls and ewers and a cup of purest wine (Q: 56.12-39), served with goblet filled at a gushing fountain, white and delicious. The wine will neither dull their senses nor befuddle them (Q: 37.40-48), and by drinking Allah's wine, the faces of the Muslims will have the mark of glow of joy (Q: 83.24).

Sex is not enjoyable in empty stomach either. Also, one needs lots of nutrition in order to have the energy to perform with so many virgins and young boys. Hardly any vegetation is seen in the deserts. Most of Muhammad's companions had never tested any fruit in their life except dates and dry pomegranates So Allah included inexhaustible supply of milk, honey and every variety of fruits in his "paradise-package". Qur'an confirms that Muslims would feast on fruits and be honored in the gardens of delight (Q: 37.40-48), everlasting fruits (Q: 13.35; 43.68-73), two kinds of every fruit (Q: 55.52), near and easy to reach (Q: 55.54), all kinds of trees and delights (Q: 55.47-49), choicest fruits (Q: 56.20, 21), while feasting with silver vessels and crystal goblets, Muslims will feel neither the scorching heat nor the biting cold and trees will spread their shade around them, and fruits will hang in clusters over them (Q: 76.13-21), and rivers of milk whose taste never changes and rivers of honey pure and clear (Q: 47.15).

The problem with a Narcissist is that when he lies, he does not know where to stop and he lies so often that it becomes a second nature to him (Vaknin, 1999, p. 260). So the best of Allah is more amazing. In Allah's paradise, one does not have to go to the toilet (Muslim: 39.6798). All-merciful Allah had provided a much better system for getting rid of body waste. Muslims will simply sweat it out. Not only this, their sweat will be that of musk and they will glorify and praise Allah as easily as breathing.

After promising fruits, wine, milk and honey and plentiful sex; Allah's next luxury for Muslims is pure drinking water. One of the major problems in the desert of Arabia was shortage of pure water. Muhammad knew very well that to the Arabs fresh water was an item of luxury. Hence paradise is watered by incorruptible running streams in which they will abide forever (Q: 13.35; 3.136, 198; 22.23; 47.15), fountains of clear flowing water in the gardens (Q: 15.45), and every garden has two running fountains in continuous abundance (Q: 55.50-51, 66-67).

Muslims will have plenty of worldly things to pursue in heaven, e.g., decked with pearls and bracelets of gold, and garments of silk (Q: 22.23), garments of fine green silk and rich brocade and adorned with bracelets of silver (Q: 76.21), wives will be given goblets of gold (Q: 43.70-71), recline on green cushions and fine carpets (Q: 55.76), inner linings will be of rich brocade (Q: 55.54), and dressed in rich silks and fine brocade (Q: 44.53). Also, Bukhari (4.52.48; 4.55.546) confirms that there is ample space in paradise; it has one hundred grades and the first meal of paradise is caudate lobe of fish-liver.

If we have to believe the Qur'an, then Allah's paradise is a celestial brothel. Muhammad knew very well that he was leading a group of lecherous Muslim warriors who were not much motivated by religion. Their only motivation was sex with captured women, collection of slaves and booty. To make these Muslims happy, Muhammad concocted the above verses as Allah's revelation. The erotic description of paradise that glitters with the fulfilment of all sorts of worldly desires and sexual enjoyment was nothing but a sinister ploy of a Narcissist to gain converts in his religion. Bukhari wrote,

> *The Prophet said, 'Nobody who dies and finds Paradise would wish to come back to this life even if he were given the whole world and whatever is in it, except the martyr who, on seeing the superiority of martyrdom, would like to come back to get killed again in Allah's Cause.'* (Bukhari: 4.52.53)

Narcissists are master manipulators. They are thoroughly dishonest with others and their constant dishonesty and lies are both disturbing and unbelievable. They lie so profusely that the abyss between the fact and (narcissistic) fiction becomes too gaping to ignore. Stout (2005, p. 43) commented, "*He lies artfully and constantly, with absolutely no sense of guilt that might give him away in body language or facial expression.*" Muhammad convinced his followers that a Muslim is God's soldier whose life is bought by Allah in return for paradise. Therefore jihad is obligatory for every Muslim. Let us analyze few Qur'anic verses.

> *God has bought from the believers their selves and their possessions against the gift of Paradise; they fight in the way of God; they kill, and are killed; that is a promise binding on God...* (Q: 9.111)

> *Lo! Those who believe and do good works, theirs are the Gardens of Paradise for welcome.* (Q: 18.107)

> *... Who will inherit Paradise. There they will abide.* (Q: 23.11).

> *So pray unto thy Lord, and sacrifice.* (Q: 108.2)

If we sum up the above four verses, our understanding goes like this – Allah has purchased the souls of Muslims to kill and get killed in Islamic jihad and for other good works (blind faith in Muhammad, raping the nonbeliever's women and enslaving their children, plundering, etc). In exchange they are promised by Allah for a grand welcome in paradise where they will dwell forever. Hope the readers can realize that not a God but a malignant Narcissist wrote those verses. A quote from Zayn & Dibble (2007, p. 92) will further clarify the topic, "*Narcissists expect sacrifices to be made in order to maintain their false selves. They feel that most people, since they are neither special nor extraordinary, should gladly lay down their menial lives in order to preserve the life of the important narcissists*".

Muslims seek paradise – not in life, but in death. Therefore, they gladly lay down their lives following the Qur'anic instructions. Muhammad sought paradise – not in death, but in life. Therefore, he lived like a tyrant, lavishly on other's toil. Muhammad promised his followers paradise in Allah's name, and his brainless followers gave him the world in exchange.

Narrated by 'Abdullah bin Abi Aufa, Allah's Apostle said, 'Know that Paradise is under the shade of swords'. (Bukhari: 4.52.73)

Narrated by Jubair bin Haiya, 'Our Prophet has informed us that our Lord says: 'Whoever amongst us is killed as a martyr shall go to Paradise to lead such a luxurious life as he has never seen, and whoever survives shall become your master'. (Bukhari: 4.53.386).

Allah's erotic paradise is the largest and the sweetest carrot that is ever dangled before the Muslims to motivate them to fight in the cause of Allah. When a suicide bomber kills himself in his mission and takes lives of several innocent others, does he ever give it a thought – who benefits from his sacrifice? He cannot, simply because his thoughts are adjusted. He sacrifices his life without understanding that he had been victimized by Qur'anic manipulation of his Narcissist Prophet.

Before the battle of Uhud, a Muslim asked, 'Messenger, where shall I be if I am killed?' He replied: 'In Paradise.' The man fought until he was killed. (Muslim: 20.4678)

Narrated by Abu Jamra; the delegation of the tribe of 'Abdul Qais came to the Prophet and said, O Allah's Apostle! We cannot come to you except in the sacred month and there is the infidel tribe of Mudar intervening between you and us. So please order us to do something (religious deeds) so that we may inform our people whom we have left behind (at home), and that we may enter Paradise (by acting on them). (Bukhari: 1.2.50)

He [Muhammad] had promised us a reward in Paradise for faithful service. We pledged ourselves to war in complete obedience to Muhammad no matter how evil the circumstances. (Ishaq: 208)

Narrated Jabir bin 'Abdullah: On the day of the battle of Uhud, a man came to the Prophet and said, "Can you tell me where I will be if I should get martyred?" Prophet replied, "In Paradise." The man threw away some dates he was carrying in his hand, and fought till he was martyred. (Bukhari: 5.59.377)

Muhammad was not a humble servant of Allah; he had risen as the dominant force in the strange God-Prophet relationship. Therefore, a Muslim must believe in Muhammad to qualify for paradise. He, who believes in Allah alone, cannot rank as a believer; he is an infidel and must go to hell, no matter how righteous he may be. Thus, it is Muhammad who holds the key of paradise. All that we must do to go to paradise is to have a little faith in Muhammad's prophethood. Our good conducts, ethics and morality are not at all important.

The lure of Islamic paradise turned early Muslims into moth eager to cremate themselves in the flame of the Allah's cause, i.e., holy jihad. Muhammad knew this side of human weakness very well. His paradise has arrangements for fun for everyone. If Muhammad wanted to lure a person who was addicted to animal sex, then he would have added animal sex in his paradise-package too. Let us compare the vivid description of Allah's paradise with the burning sands of Arabia; without water, vegetation, pastures, rivers and gardens. And regarding sex; though Arabia did have plentiful women for the Arabs to practice polygamy, the sexual facilities are not certainly comparable with the virgins of Allah's paradise.

The whole existence of a Narcissist is a derivative of his false self, a deceitful invention and its reflection (Vaknin, 1999, p. 111). Allah is so desperate that He bribes man with the paradisiacal luxuries, and if man does not fall for it, He frightens him with the most sadistic torture of hell. Yet, Allah calls Himself independent, absolute and disinterested! Little thoughts are required to understand that Muhammad was playing the role of God in fabricating things. If a God is really so desperate for gaining devotees by such sadistic ploys, then certainly He lacks the dignity. Such an ungodly God does not exist.

Liars get caught very often because they get entangled in their own lies. Muhammad's dishonesty in describing paradise is easy to catch because he often contradicted himself. He had included wine in the paradise-package, but how could he include it in the list when Allah had declared intoxicants as sinful? When others noticed this contradiction, Muhammad came out with a new design that the wine in the promised paradise is not intoxicating and therefore not sinful. But what the liar did not understand was that wine by nature contains alcohol which is intoxicating. Muhammad got tangled up in his webs of deception and eventually the truth came out. Allah condemned those who *"listened to music,"*, yet *"the angels sing."* How can we trust a God whose reward in paradise – drinking, listening music and fornication – is what He forbids on earth? Why would we trust a man who must lie – or be lied for – to validate his calling?

Allah is too comical. If anyone can remember Allah's ninety-nine names he will be allowed to enter paradise (Bukhari: 3.50.894). Paradise is not very high. A ladder would have been sufficient to reach there. Jihad is not necessary to enter paradise. All they have to do is to gather some wood and find a carpenter to build a ladder. Allah says in the Qur'an,

> *Or have they a ladder, by which they can (climb up to heaven and) listen (to its secrets)?* (Q: 52.38)

This is the height of Allah's stupidity or Muhammad's sick imagination or conscious fabrication – whatever we may call it. Right from the birth of Islam, there has been a clear and undeniable pattern of conscious manipulation, deception, and delusion; there is no end to it. Muhammad was willing to say and do anything in the name of God so long as it advanced his personal agenda, i.e., the sick and selfish ambition of a malignant Narcissist. It is such a conspiracy where even God is victimized. Allah was his "instrument" to fulfill his self-serving narcissistic desires. Muhammad knew that the advance of political Islam was possible only under the guise of a religious conviction, and its success depends upon this simple concept – "Serve me now, bring booty and women for me and if necessary die for my cause (Allah's cause) without expecting anything in return in this worldly life, and I assure you that Allah will reward you later – much later after your death". Bukhari recorded,

Narrated by 'Urwa Al-Bariqi; the Prophet said, "Good will remain (as a permanent quality) in the foreheads of horses (for Jihad) till the Day of Resurrection, for they bring about either a reward (in the Hereafter) or booty (in this world)'. (Bukhari: 4.52.104).

It is such a win-win situation. If they survive the battles, they secure booty and women; and if they fall, they are sure to enter paradise.

Having painted the lustiest picture of paradise, the liar proceeded to describe the sketch of hell. The malignant Narcissist is in an evil ploy again to fulfill his selfish needs. Allah created Islamic hell or *Jahannum* for serving two purposes – it is a torture chamber for all the infidels, and the idea of hell will terrorize people into accepting Islam. Muhammad was very specific in the Qur'an – who are the people destined to hell and the cause why they should go to hell.

But those who disbelieve and belie Our verses shall be the companions of the Fire, and there they shall live for ever. (Q: 2.39)

As for those who disbelieve and belie Our verses, they shall become the companions of Hell. (Q: 5.10).

Do you not see how those who dispute the revelation of God turn away from the right path? Those who have denied the Book and the message We sent through Our apostles shall realize the truth hereafter: when, with chains and shackles round their necks, they shall be dragged through scalding water and then burnt in the fire of Hell. (Q: 40.69-72).

In the hell; nonbelievers will burn forever in hellfire because they are vilest of creatures (Q: 98.5-8), a woeful punishment (Q: 33.8), garments of fire, scalding water will be poured upon their heads, melting skins and which is in their bellies, tortured with hooked iron rods, when they try to escape, they will be dragged, and will be told, "*Taste the torment of the Conflagration*" (Q: 22.19-22), when they cry out for help they shall be showered with water as hot as molten brass, which will scald their faces, evil shall be their drink, dismal their resting place (Q: 18.29), punishment will never be lightened, and they shall be speechless with despair (Q: 43.74-75), seized by their forelocks and their feet (Q: 55.41), chains, fetters and a blazing (fire) (Q: 76.4; 73.12), choking food and a painful punishment (Q: 73.13), roast the unbeliever in hell (Q: 69.31), neither shade nor shelter from the flames (Q: 77.31), you and your idols shall be the fuel of hell (Q: 21.98), and, food is Zakkum tree and foul pus (Q: 44.43; 69.36).

The hell is not for punishing the Muslim wrong-doers. They will go directly to paradise. Muhammad's recommendation is final and Allah cannot deny. Hence, all Muslim terrorists, murderers, rapists, cheats, thugs will go to paradise because they follow Islam. All they have to do is to recite the Kalima (incantation) – there is no God but Allah and Muhammad is His Prophet – and they will get free gate-pass to enter paradise. The "people of the book", idolaters and atheists are destined to hell for eternal suffering no matter how pious and God-fearing they may have been. Their good thoughts, good actions or piety are of no value. Bukhari recorded,

> *Narrated by Abu Huraira; Allah's Apostle said, 'All my followers will enter Paradise except those who refuse." They said, "O Allah's Apostle! Who will refuse?" He said, **'Whoever obeys me will enter Paradise, and whoever disobeys me is the one who refuses (to enter it)'***. (Bukhari: 9.92.384)

The above Hadith raises some disturbing questions. Why blind obedience to Muhammad is required to enter paradise? Why his recommendation is final and Allah cannot deny it? The answer is simple; Muhammad was playing the role of God. Zayn & Dibble (2007, p. 143) concludes, *"The Narcissist is a role-player. Because of the disorder he plays the main part in his created universe. This is a God-like role. The Creator of the Universe is said to have created the world and brought it into existence. The Narcissist feels he is 'omnipotent' and 'omniscient' and very unique and special. He believes his word to be 'the Gospel'. In his own mind he describes his false self as real, because he says it is."*

For Muhammad, everything was real inside his created universe and anything outside this universe was false. Since Muhammad was the creator of his own universe, naturally he was the God. Therefore, Muhammad was holding the key of paradise because all those misconceptions of paradise and hell belonged to his created universe, in other words, his sick imaginations. For Muhammad, his words were as true as Gospel; he had the final authority. Allah had hardly any importance. Now we know the reality of paradise and hell and which universe do they belong.

Next question; why Muhammad will not allow anyone to enter paradise who does not obey him blindly? As Zayn & Dibble continues, *"He even 'creates' people in his 'false' image to live in his world. His creations are supposed to live by his rules ... follow his 'commandments'... and if they refuse they are 'cast out' to live in a place that does not include the Narcissist, which in the Narcissist's psyche, would surely be Hell."* Muslims are the "created" people of Muhammad; they have no individual characters. Muhammad created them in his false image to live in his distorted world. They are like the pawns on a giant chessboard who live by the rules of Muhammad and follow his commandments. Hence, only Muslims will enter paradise; and for the same reason, the nonbelievers will go to hell.

What a sick and disgusting imagination, distortion of reality and narcissistic manipulation! Muhammad thought that people of other religions will convert to Islam out of sheer terror of hell. However, many rational thinking people around him did not believe him realizing that he was delusional. Qur'an says,

> *The hypocrites and those in whose hearts there is a disease said: 'Allah and His Messenger promised nothing but delusion'.* (Q: 33.12).

Muhammad had used the device of contradistinction to sharpen the appeal of his message for arousing human instincts of pain and pleasure to secure submission of ordinary man. Islam offers nothing to men but delusion and uses fear to suppress and stupefy the common Muslim masses. It worked wonder for Muhammad by enriching and empowering him during his lifetime. Today it works wonder for the Imams, Mullahs and tyrants alike. Islam was created for one malignant Narcissist's quest for narcissistic supply sources. It is utter foolishness to search for spirituality in Islam. In his childhood Muhammad was powerless, poor, and unloved. Therefore, his Islam was focused on power, money, and sex. His paradise reflected his wild fantasies, and his hell was a manifestation of the revenge he craved – a payment for the torment he had endured as a child. It is really sad that today more than a billion people still act like "laboratory guinea pigs" allowing a malignant Narcissist to experiment on them.

3.6.5.5: The Critics of Muhammad

Muhammad was constantly on the lookout for slights; he was hyper-vigilant. He perceived every disagreement as criticism and every critical remark as complete and humiliating rejection and a direct challenge to his mission. Gradually, his mind turned into a chaotic battlefield of paranoia. His thinking was dogmatic, rigid, and doctrinaire. He did not tolerate free thought or free speech. He demanded (and often got) complete trust and frequently dismissed his fellow Muslims from all decision-making. He was so afraid of being exposed that he ordered his followers to assassinate anyone who criticized him.

When a Narcissist feels that he is degraded by another person, typically in the form of criticism, he suffers from narcissistic injury which ultimately results in narcissistic rage. If his inflated but unstable false self is combined with his hypersensitivity to interpersonal feedback, the result may often be a tendency to hostile, aggressive, and even violent responding (Hook, 2007, p. 29). Insecure men are enraged by criticism; they will stop at nothing to silence anyone who irritates them. Often the Narcissist attempts to astonish the surroundings with apparent brilliance, bombastic announcements and the unnecessary and wrong uses of professional language. But beneath all these showmanship; he is shallow and devoid of real knowledge (Vaknin, 1999, p. 110). He is always fearful of being discovered and deceitful. Like a trapped animal, the Narcissist is forever on the lookout – was this comment a deliberate attack meant to humiliate me?

He cannot accept criticism for two reasons. First; he is simply the greatest, equal to God – the perfect being. The more he convinces himself, the better he feels. Such a person is above any type of criticism. He never admits to ignorance in any field. A Narcissist medical doctor would rather let patients die than expose his ignorance. Secondly, the Narcissist is very scared that by criticism, his true self may be accidentally discovered causing immediate collapse of the false self. This scares him to death. In this respect he is like a child. Deep down, he can be compared with a muddy shallow pond but pretending to be a deep ocean. At any cost the fantasy needs to be upheld. He does not dare confront the truth and admit it even to himself.

When he cannot handle criticism by displaying narcissistic rage, he may slip into depression – either real or pretended. He pretends depression to manipulate those around him, but when he actually experiences depression, it is usually a sign of being out of control. He may go to bed for several days (Zayn & Dibble, 2007, p. 83). In extreme cases, he may also entertain suicidal thoughts. For the same reason, he cannot share a joke which is directed to him as he cannot admit his vulnerability (Masterson, 1990, p. 96). He is dead serious about himself (Vaknin, 1999, p. 191). He likes to talk only about himself. Sometimes he may pretend to be interested to others but it is only with a potential narcissistic supply source.

The first victim of Muhammad's narcissistic rage was Ashraf, a young talented poet and a chief of the Jews tribe Banu Nadir. In an illiterate society, poets were the journalists of their day; their words swayed public opinion. Soon after Muhammad banished the Qainuka, Ashraf became concerned about his own people's security and visited Mecca to seek protection. He was courageous, and composed poems by praising the Meccans for their bravery and honor. When Muhammad heard about this, he assigned the job of killing Ashraf to one of his henchmen.

Narrated Jabir bin `Abdullah: Prophet said, "Who is ready to kill Ka`b bin Al-Ashraf who has really hurt Allah and His Apostle?" Muhammad bin Maslama said, "O Allah's Apostle! Do you like me to kill him?" He replied in the affirmative. So, Maslama went to him (Ashraf) and said, "This person (the Prophet) has put us to task and asked us for charity." Ashraf replied, "By Allah, you will get tired of him." Muhammad said to him, "We have followed him, so we dislike leaving him till we see the end of his affair." Maslama went on talking to him in this way till he got the chance to kill him. (Bukhari: 4.52.270)

After killing Ashraf, Muhammad murdered his friend, Abu Rafi. This time he sent Abd Allah bin Atik, another of his henchman to kill Abu Rafi (Tabari: VII.99; Bukhari: 5.59.370). The reason for his being killed was that he used to take the side of Ashraf against Muhammad. Tabari wrote,

*I [the murderer of Abu Rafi] came to my companions and said, 'By Allah, I will not leave till I hear the wailing of their women.' So, I did not move till I heard them crying for the Jewish merchant. I said, 'Deliverance! **Allah has killed Abu Rafi.**'* (Tabari: VII.100)

The above quote needs particular attention. The murderer did not say that he had killed Abu Rafi, instead he said "*Allah has killed Abu Rafi*". Each time Muslims kill someone they absolve themselves of the crime and blame their "God". While calling Allah an assassin seems odd, but Muslim mindset is different. For them calling their God a murderer is not a blasphemy.

When Muhammad gained power in Medina a man and his wife were murdered because they had written insulting poetries against him (Frieling, 1978, p. 33). On another occasion, Abu Azza, another of his critics was beheaded. Abu Azza used to write poetry urging the desert tribes not to join Muhammad's gang (Walker, 2002, p. 318). Next Muhammad permitted murdering Sallam Huqayq, another man of Khaybar (Tabari: VII.101; Ishaq: 482). Muhammad had now become a psychopath serial killer. Criticizing him became a deadly game and one after another of his critics started falling in pools of their own blood. There were no words more pleasing to a Muslim than "a critic of Muhammad is dead". They believed they were doing Allah a service by eliminating Muhammad's critics.

Muhammad's another victim was Abu Afak, a 120 year old poet from Medina. Afak lamented that people had surrendered their intelligence to Muhammad and became hostile to one another. Hearing this; Salim Ibn Umayr, a henchman of Muhammad, killed the old man when he was sleeping in an open place in a hot night (Sina, 2008, p. 42). When Asma bint Marwan, a Jewish mother of five small children, heard about the murder of Abu Afak, she composed a poetry cursing the men of Medina for allowing Muhammad to assassinate a venerable old man. Muhammad got her assassinated too. Ibn Ishaq wrote,

> '*You obey a stranger who encourages you to murder for booty. You are greedy men. Is there no honor among you?*' *Upon hearing this Muhammad said, 'Will no one rid me of this woman?' Umayr decided to execute the Prophet's wishes. That very night he crept into her home while she lay sleeping surrounded by her young children. There was one at her breast. Umayr removed the suckling baby and then plunged his sword into the poet. The next morning in the mosque, Muhammad, who was aware of the assassination, said, 'You have helped Allah and His Apostle.' Umayr said, 'She had five sons; should I feel guilty?' 'No,' the Prophet answered. 'Killing her was as meaningless as two goats butting heads.*' (Ishaq: 676)

Soon after receiving praise from Muhammad for the assassination of Asma, the killer went to her children, bragged about committing the murder, and taunted those little kids and the clan of the victim.

Muhammad was a man of extremes. He had created such an atmosphere of terror that nobody could disagree with him. Once, a blind Muslim murdered his slave woman by pressing a dagger in her belly. In the morning, Muhammad called the man to explain why he committed such a murder. The blind man stood up while trembling and said that the woman used to abuse and ridicule Muhammad and hence she was killed. Hearing this, Muhammad said, "*Oh be witness, no retaliation is payable for her blood.*" (Sunnan Abu Dawud: 38.4348). The message that Muhammad wanted to send was clear – "If anyone insults me, he should be put to death and the killer would not be charged".

This is a defense mechanism of the Narcissists. By showing that the man was not guilty of murder, Muhammad minimized the impact of the disagreement or criticism on himself. In psychopathology, this defense mechanism is known as "cognitive dissonance". This is a process of self-justification. Humans are sensitive to inconsistencies between actions and beliefs. When a person recognizes this inconsistency, it causes dissonance, which motivates an individual to resolve the dissonance. The easiest way to resolve dissonance between actions and beliefs is to change the belief by a simple "adjustment of thought". This is what Muhammad had achieved with this subtle manipulation. Through his words, Muhammad implanted a new way of "thinking" in the minds of his followers.

All those critics recognized Muhammad as a fake; they had every right to oppose him to save their clans from harming themselves. Muhammad's Qur'an recitals were conflicting; the stories could not be kept straight and new verses often abrogated old verses. They understood that internal contradiction was the surest sign that something was wrong. But neither Muhammad nor his Allah was able to refute his critics' claims in an intelligent manner. So the only option left to Muhammad was to kill them. Zayn & Dibble (2007, p. 102) wrote, "*The Narcissist realizes he is making bad choices, yet continues to make them anyway. And along the way many valuable, unknowing victims are cruelly wounded*". When Muslims cannot defend Islam logically, they insult, threaten and even kill the critics.

Deep down, Muhammad knew that those critics were right, but he was utterly helpless. By giving in to his cravings and cruelly using others, he demonstrated a defect (one of the many defects) in his personality. Muhammad knew that Qur'an could not stand mockery and criticism simply because it was false; probably he saw glimpses of his true self when those critics attacked him with their disapproval. He slipped into depression and on behalf of him Allah revealed the following verse,

> *When you hear His verses being disbelieved or mocked, do not sit with them until they engage in other talk, or else you will surely be like them. Allah will surely gather the hypocrites and unbelievers altogether in Hell.* (Q: 4.140).

When Muhammad was depressed, Allah was depressed; when Muhammad was helpless, Allah was equally helpless; when Muhammad was confused, Allah was likewise confused; when Muhammad changed his plan, Allah endorsed it; when Muhammad was furious, Allah sanctioned killing – what more evidence is required to show that Muhammad was only an invisible participant in the game of Qur'anic deception like the prompter in a stage play who takes a backseat behind the scene leaving the center stage for actors?

Why Allah forbade Muslims to ask questions? It was because there is no well-argued explanation for Islam. Islam is a layer upon layer deception; it relies upon ignorance and thrives in it. The deeper one digs, the more obvious the deception becomes. This is precisely why Muhammad protected his doctrine by killing those who criticized him, his book and his religion; he was scared to see the truth. A Narcissist is ever possessed with the inner sensation that he is really a petty crook who is vulnerable of being exposed and condemned by society (Vaknin, 1999, p. 110). In this situation, assassination is the easiest way out. It provides a quick way to end disputes, silence troublesome rivals, and above all, it instills fear into the hearts of those who are still alive. This is the most favored method for silencing the critics for all the notorious mass-murderers in the history – Stalin, Hitler, Saddam Hussein, Idi Amin, etc. The beloved Prophet of the Muslims was not an exception.

3.6.5.6: Narcissist Muhammad and his Collection of Women

Sex is a very important factor in the Narcissist's life, but it should be emotionless. When he cannot obtain adoration, admiration, approval, applause or any other kind of attention by other means (i.e., intellectually); he indulges in sex indiscriminately with multiple partners and becomes a lecherous man. He will consider his sex partners as objects not of desire but of narcissistic supply. Through this, the Narcissist derives his badly needed narcissistic fix. His inflated sense of entitlement may make him think that women owe him sexual favors (Hook, 2007, p. 32). Often he prefers complicated situations, like, sex with celebrities, adolescents, married women, etc (Vaknin, 1999, pp. 88, 89). The aim is; the more difficult the target, the more rewarding the narcissistic outcome. Otherwise the sexual philosophy of a Narcissist is same as an animal.

Muhammad was guilty of every sex crime known to the society – rape, incest, polygamy, adultery, fornication, sexism, pedophilia, abetting prostitution and sex-slavery. Qur'an (4.3) limits Muslims to four wives, but Allah revealed verses (Q: 33.49-50) telling Muhammad that he was exempt and could have any number of women he pleases, as wives, concubines or sex-slaves so that there might be no difficulty for him. During the lifetime of Khadija, Muhammad did not dare to bring another woman in the house. As a young man, he did not face any difficulty to sleep with an older woman, but all his difficulties appeared only during the last ten years of his life when he was old and suffering from all types of ailments. He took a total twenty-one wives, two concubines and many slave girls in his lifetime. No, doubt, Muhammad was a womanizer. Tabari wrote,

*They said (to a woman), 'What a bad thing you have done! You are a self-respecting girl, but **the Prophet is a womanizer.**'* (Tabari: IX.139)

It does not represent Muhammad a very loving and romantic person. On the contrary, it proves Muhammad's vulgarity, ugliness and instability of mind. This shows how he treated the institution of marriage. Even after having so many sexual outlets, Muhammad was a pedophile. When he was above fifty, he married a six years old child. He also stole his son's wife. After forcing young girls to watch his men execute their fathers and husbands, Muhammad and his followers raped them. Worst of all, he rewarded his mercenaries by dividing captured young girls among his followers. It is little wonder his Qur'anic paradise was so perverted.

Narcissists often prefer pedophilia (Vaknin, 1999, p. 264) for many reasons. First, it is easier to have emotionless sex with children. If the Narcissist is attached emotionally with a woman, then there is likelihood that his partner may discover his true self. But if a child is taken as a sexual partner, he is safe. Secondly, sex with a minor gives freedom of action with impunity. It enhances his magical sense of omnipotence and immunity; it thrills him. He can also defy the authority of the state and the edicts of his culture and society. The third and the most important advantage (from the Narcissist's point of view) is that, he can demand and obtain complete obedience by psychologically molding the child the way he likes. Sub-teen children are, as a Narcissist defines, "inferior". They are physically weaker, dependent on others for the fulfilment of many of their needs, cognitively and emotionally immature, and easily manipulated. Their fund of knowledge is limited and their skills restricted. Moreover, they are defenseless. The Narcissist can punish the child the way he wants to enforce discipline, and feels entitled to adulation and special treatment from his child-mate. This gives the Narcissist a feeling of superiority and control over the target (Zayn & Dibble, 2007, p. 8). His narcissistic stock goes up easily without much effort at the cost of the innocence of the child.

Pedophilia and child molestation had always been considered a psychiatric disorder agreed to by most clinicians (Marvasti, 2004, p. 6). The justice system sees pedophiliac behavior as a sex crime. The aims and acts of a sadist pedophile and a Narcissist pedophile are different. The sadist does it (always forcefully) to inflict damage on the child's body and mind. But for the Narcissist, forceful or deceitful pedophilia is, in essence, auto-erotic. He uses the child's body for auto-erotic sexual mono-game – sexual excitement by manual stimulation of his own genitals (Vaknin, 2006, p. 144). For a malignant Narcissist, this is a type of self-love. Unlike sadists, the Narcissist is not enticed by the children themselves but by their budding and immature sexuality or simply by their innocence.

At the age of fifty-one, Muhammad suddenly received a revelation from Allah that the six years old Aisha would be his wife. He knew that pedophilia was wrong and he was aware of society's view of his action as vile, corrupt, forbidden, evil, and immoral, but it was not a problem because he had Allah's recommendation for this. To please Muhammad with pedophilic sex, Allah did not hesitate to take the role of a marriage broker.

Aisha reported Allah's Messenger having said: I saw you in a dream for three nights when an angel brought you to me in a silk cloth and he said: Here is your wife, and when I removed (the cloth) from your face, lo, it was yourself, so I said: If this is from Allah, let Him carry it out. (Muslim: 31.5977)

Narrated 'Aisha: Allah's Apostle said (to me), "You have been shown to me twice in (my) dreams. A man was carrying you in a silken cloth and said to me, 'This is your wife.' I uncovered it; and behold, it was you. I said to myself, 'If this dream is from Allah, He will cause it to come true'. (Bukhari: 7.62.15)

However, Abu Bakr, the best friend and confident of Muhammad, had to agree to an immediate marriage. Much is written in Islamic sources about Abu Bakr, but we know very little about his relationship with his daughter. Law can forbid a father from killing his young daughter but this does not mean fathers truly loved and protected their daughters. Abu Bakr agreed to give his daughter in marriage, and the union was consummated when Aisha was nine. Sexual acts with a nine-year-old gave Muhammad freedom of action with impunity. It also enhanced the pedophile's magical sense of all-powerfulness and immunity. For Muhammad, Aisha was just a "sex-toy" for auto-erotic sexual mono-games.

Muhammad put his cheek and chest in between the naked thighs of a menstruating Aisha ... (Sunnan Abu Dawud: 1.270)

Narrated 'Aisha: The Prophet and I used to take a bath from a single pot... During the menses, he used to order me to put on an Izar (dress worn below the waist) and used to fondle me. While in Itikaf, he used to bring his head near me and I would wash it while I used to be in my periods. (Bukhari: 1.6.298)

Sucking the tongue, testing the saliva and drinking the leftover of Aisha, who was of his granddaughter's age, were favorite sexual activities of Muhammad. His sexual urges were abnormal.

Muhammad used to kiss and suck Aisha's tongue while they were fasting. (Sunnan Abu Dawud: 13.2380).

Aisha said: 'During menstruation, I used to bite off meat from bone, the Prophet would take the bone from me and place his mouth at the same spot to eat of it where I had been biting: when I drank water, he would take the vessel from me and place his lips at the same spot where I had put mine'. (Sunnan Ibn Majah: Vol. 2).

After the sexual mono-game Muhammad used to spoil his own garment and his child sexual partner took the job of cleaning it. How disgusting!

Al-Aawad and Hammam reported A'isha as saying: I used to scrape off the (drop of) semen from the garment of the Messenger of Allah. (Muslim: 2.567)

Incase I (Aisha) found that (semen) on the garment of the Messenger of Allah dried up, I scraped it off with my nails. (Muslim: 2.572)

Narrated Sulaiman bin Yasar: I asked `Aisha about the clothes soiled with semen. She replied, 'I used to wash it off the clothes of Allah's Apostle and he would go for the prayer while water spots were still visible'. (Bukhari: 1.4.231)

Narrated `Aisha: 'I used to wash the semen off the clothes of the Prophet and even then I used to notice one or more spots on them'. (Bukhari: 1.4.233).

To impose discipline on Aisha, Muhammad had raised his violent hand on her (Muslim: 4.2127). However, Muhammad's pedophilic lust was not satisfied with Aisha. Once he was attracted to a baby and wanted to marry her later. This is the height of ugliness of this hardcore pedophile.

The Apostle saw Ummu' when she was a baby crawling before his feet and said, 'If she grows up, I will marry her.' But he died before he was able to do so. (Ishaq: 311).

Muhammad was very ugly while dealing with children. Ash Shifa, (Tr. Aisha Abdurrahman Bewley, 2004, p. 184, cited Kasem, 2007) recorded that Muhammad had a disgusting habit of spitting in the mouths of suckling children. No doubt, he was at top of his ugliness with this type of acts. How a sane person can ever think of forcing the babies to drink his spittle? It is simply disgusting! Probably Muhammad used to get abnormal sexual pleasure by spitting in the mouth of the babies.

A Narcissist has no regards for women except fulfilling his own purpose. Since he cannot love himself (his true self), he is not capable of loving others. He may act lovingly, even pretends to be madly in love with a woman, but actually he displays love to achieve goals. It may be money, power, political strength, or a narcissistic supply (Masterson, 1990, p. 97). Once substitutes are available, the former ones are abandoned without a thought (Vaknin, 1999, p. 51). He does not feel guilty for it. Sometimes, the Narcissist disconnects himself from the lives of his partners in order to teach them a lesson (Zayn & Dibble, 2007, p. 88). Qur'an says,

It may happen that his Lord, if he divorce you, will give him in your stead wives better than you, submissive (to Allah), believing, pious, penitent, devout, inclined to fasting, widows and maids. (Q: 66.5)

The definition of love according to a Narcissist is totally different from that of a normal healthy person. Masterson (1990, pp. 109, 110) wrote, "*Love is the capacity to acknowledge the other's real self in a warm, affectionate way, with no strings attached ... true love is a union of two people each for the 'good of the other' where the other's best interest become at least equals to one's own... But the Narcissist defines love as the ability of someone else to admire and adore him, and to provide perfect mirroring."* In most cases, he prefers to be feared or admired, rather than loved. As Vaknin (1999, p. 358) wrote, *"When the Narcissist says 'I love you' he really means, 'I depend on you for the stabilization of my narcissistic supply and for the accumulation of the supply for the road ahead'."*

Narcissists always want something from others. They are not capable of giving anything to anyone, no matter how small, without asking something in exchange. When a Narcissist asks a person how you are doing, in his mind he actually does not intend to know about the well-being of the other person. Rather he is taking the "emotional temperature" of the person to see if he is reacting, because he is looking for that reaction. Even if the person is finally giving him a piece of his mind, the Narcissist is not listening; the statement simply goes in one ear and comes out from the other. Nothing makes a difference; the listening part is an illusion.

Muhammad did not know how to form a stable marital relationship. He simply could not postpone satisfaction. A Narcissist is the creature of "here and now" as he judges himself to be all deserving. He is immature in every walk of marriage and sex (Vaknin, 1999, pp. 139, 272-3). I can make a comparison – a person who has been in a wheelchair since childhood cannot have any idea of what it feels like to walk, run, jump, do gymnastics, ride a bike, etc. Similarly, the person with NPD is in an emotional cripple. His experience of life bears no resemblance to the ordinary person's. As Vaknin (1999, pp. 357, 195) wrote, *"The Narcissist never invests in anything, and never perseveres – so he never gets emotionally attached to anything ... if he does not get attached, he cannot get hurt"*.

For Muhammad, sex was an expression of power, both emotional and physical. Conquest of the body of a defenseless woman was a status symbol for him; this was the proof of his virility. This type of cruel activities allows a Narcissist to engage in vicarious narcissistic behaviors, to express his narcissism through the "conquered" women, transforming them into instruments at the service of his narcissism, into his extensions. For Muhammad, Rayhana and Safiyyah were two instant narcissistic solutions. He had no shortage of women; he could easily spare those two women who were in extreme grief, but he did not. He used sexual attack to "conquer" and "secure" new sources of narcissistic supply. The Narcissist likes to believe that he is the maker of the decision of which type of relationship he should establish and with whom. For Muhammad, Rayhana and Safiyyah must value his companionship sufficiently to sacrifice any independent expression of their own personalities. As Masterson (1990, p. 124) wrote, *"The exhibitionist [a person who shows expression of power] Narcissist would see the woman's sexual response as part of his entitlements and would say openly that he expects her to devote herself to his needs. He would manipulate her in such a way that she would have to accept his entitlement"*. This is heroism for a Narcissist and because of this attitude he often finds depictions of rape on video as enjoyable and sexually arousing (Hook, 2007, p. 33). A woman has no mind, only the "meat" of her body is "Halal" for Muhammad to enjoy. The "halal meat" of a woman's body has no individuality, no identity of its own – it is a toy for enjoyment.

Narrated Jabir bin 'Abdullah: When I got married, Allah's Apostle said to me, "What type of lady have you married?" I replied, "I have married a matron." He said, "Why, don't you have a liking for the virgins and for fondling them?"

Jabir also said: Allah's Apostle said, 'Why did not you marry a young girl so that you might play with her and she with you?' (Bukhari: 7.62.17)

When I returned to Medina, the Prophet met me in the market and said, 'Give me the woman.' I said, 'Holy Prophet of Allah, I like her, and I have not uncovered her garment.' Muhammad said nothing to me until the next day. He again met me in the market and said, 'Salamah, give me the woman.' I said, 'Prophet, I have not uncovered her garment but she is yours.' (Tabari: VIII.97)

The lascivious Prophet had a secret desire for his daughter-in-law, Zaynab bint Jahsh. It was not socially accepted for an Arab to marry his daughter-in law. But a Narcissist is not bind by any rule. It is the Narcissist who determines which laws to obey and which to break. He expects the society, his partners, his colleagues, his spouse, his children, his parents, his students, his teacher – in short; practically everyone in this world to abide by his rulebook. Muhammad broke all the social taboos by expressing his desire for the petite and elegantly attractive Zaynab. He retained the power to decide which contracts were to be scrupulously observed and which offhandedly ignored. By family obligation, Muhammad was supposed to be as her father. To fulfill his sexual desire for Zaynab, the Narcissist was in action again. What commences as an elaborate daydream ends up in a Narcissist's mind as a plausible scenario. The con artist silenced his critics with a simple solution – he claimed that Allah had instructed him to marry Zaynab, and that Allah himself would solemnize the marriage of Muhammad with his daughter-in-law. To fulfill Muhammad's desire Allah revealed the following verse.

... and when Zayd had accomplished what he would of her (divorce), We gave her to you (Muhammad) in marriage, so that there is no fault in believers concerning (marriage to) the former spouse of their foster children if they divorced them. The decree of Allah must be done. (Q: 33.37).

By marrying Zaynab, Muhammad proved that the society must attend to his needs whereas he was under no obligation to listen to or understand anyone. He did not feel shame at all because he had bypassed it. Whenever Muhammad took undue sexual advantages, he directed the shame to Allah as if whatever he did, he was actually following Allah's instruction. So it was never "my fault". The verses where Allah granted Muhammad special sexual privileges served only one purpose – it transformed "Muhammad's fault" to "Allah's fault". Hotchkiss (2003, p. 6) wrote, *"The shame is directed outward, away from the self. It can never be 'My Fault'".* In the following verse Allah takes away Muhammad's shame.

No fault shall be attached to the Prophet for doing what Allah has obligated for him. Such was the Way of Allah with those who passed away before the decree of Allah is a decree determined." (Q: 33.38)

Male Narcissists hate women virulently, passionately and uncompromisingly. His hate is original, inherent, and irrational. Though most of them learn how to disguise, even repress these untoward feelings, their strong hatred does swing out of control and erupt from time to time. Muhammad was a misogynist (strong hatred for women). In his farewell sermon he equated women to cattle. Tabari recorded,

> *Treat women well for they are like domestic animals and they possess nothing themselves. Allah has made the enjoyment of their bodies lawful in his Qur'an.* (Tabari: IX.113)

Since women are domestic animals, logically, the old stock can be replaced by new one, as Tabari and Ibn Ishaq recorded,

> *Ali [Muhammad's adopted son, son-in-law, and future Caliph] said, 'Prophet, women are plentiful. You can get a replacement, easily changing one for another'.* (Tabari: VIII.62; Ishaq: 496)

Elsewhere (Dagher, 1995, pp. 18-9), Muhammad is reported to have said, "*The woman has two things to cover her: the grave and the marriage*". When he was asked which one was better, the reply was, "*The grave*". Lastly, a quote from Imam Ghazali's work shows how much hatred Muhammad had for women.

> *The Prophet said: if husband would be covered with pus from head to toe, and wife would lick it, even then wife's gratitude to husband wouldn't be fulfilled.* (Imam Ghazali, from Ihya Ulum Al-Din, volume - 2)

There is a reason why Muhammad equated women with domestic animals. The ideal life partner of a male Narcissist is someone who is willing to become an extension of his fragile ego, to serve as an object of admiration, contempt, or often enough both, as if he had put a sign over the door ought to read "Abandon Self All Ye Who Enter Here" (Hotchkiss, 2003, p. 121). It means the life partner must obliterate her autonomy in the service of her husband's narcissism with doggy obedience. In sum; the husband cannot regard the separate existence of his wife as she does for her own. Such a woman is no way better than a domestic animal. Lastly, a quote from Russell (2009, p. 76) which is self-explanatory,

> *Those who have never known the deep intimacy and the intense companionship of happy mutual love have missed the best thing that life has to give; unconsciously, if not consciously, they feel this and the resulting disappointment inclines them towards envy, oppression and cruelty.*

3.6.6: Why Muhammad was Sinless?

Muhammad could not fathom the reciprocity in human relations, and as a result, slowly he became antisocial lacking in morale and in consequences. Muslims believe that Muhammad possessed special spiritual qualities, was *ma'soum* (or, *masom*, innocent) which means immaculate from sin (Nasr, 2007, p. 39). According to Qur'an, Allah forgave all past, present and future sins of His beloved Prophet. It means; whatever evils Muhammad wants to do, he can do without any remorse. He can loot, murder, plunder, rape – practically commit any crime known to the society with Allah's license. God himself is guarantor of his forgiveness. Qur'an says,

Lo! We have given thee (O Muhammad) a signal victory, That Allah may forgive thee of thy sin that which is past and that which is to come, and may perfect His favor unto thee, and may guide thee on a right path. (Q: 48.1, 2).

Narcissists are prone to magical thinking. In this respect they are like children. Muhammad never felt guilty for his cruel acts. He put Allah directly responsible for all his wrong doings and gave an impression to his followers that he was merely following Allah's instructions. A person who is carrying out God's order is not responsible for his actions, either directly or indirectly, and hence he is immaculate from sin. If Allah's decrees are delivered by Muhammad's tongue, then of course Muhammad is sinless.

Abu Musa reported the Apostle of Allah as saying: Make intercession to me, you will be rewarded, for Allah decrees what He wishes by the tongue of His Prophet. (Sunnan Abu Dawud: 3.5112).

Umar b Abu Salama said that Messenger of Allah, Allah pardoned thee all thy sins, the previous and the later ones. Upon this the Messenger of Allah said: By Allah, I am the most God conscious among you and I fear Him most among you. (Muslim: 6.2450).

The fact that nobody is perfect gives little comfort to the Narcissist. He thinks that he is an exception to this natural law. Thus, it is his challenge to find a way to stay pumped up inside in order to hold these harsh realities at bay (Hotchkiss, 2003, p. 7). He maintains his grandiosity and all-powerfulness through a connection to "someone", who can pump up to sustain the illusion of his chosen "specialness". For Muhammad, this "someone" was none other than the Allah, and the chosen "specialness" was, of course, "sinlessness".

A Narcissist does not feel that in any way he is related to his former "shelves". He blames the external world for his mishap. He is surprised by society's insistence that he should be punished for his deeds and be held responsible for them (Vaknin, 1999, pp. 49, 186). Even he may develop a feeling that he is being persecuted by powers greater than him. However, sometimes he realizes that people around him are sad and disappointed, and it has certainly something to do with his attitude towards them. But his grandiosity covers up his disagreeable state of things by convincing him – poor things, they can never fully understand him, they are so inferior, it is no wonder they are so depressed (Vaknin, 1999, p. 46). He cannot see through the defensive structures of his life, his thinking, his ways of perceiving reality. He senses, but cannot understand the hollow core at the center of his life. He had lived too long on deception and fantasy, and now he is the master deceiver (Masterson, 1990, p. 81). Allah wrote in the Qur'an,

And when We would destroy a township We send commandment to its folk who live at ease, and afterward they commit abomination therein, and so the Word (of doom) hath effect for it, and we annihilate it with complete annihilation. (Q: 17.16)

And We are not unjust to them, but they themselves were unjust. (Q: 43.76)

It was not We that wronged them: They wronged their own souls. (Q: 11.101)

This is how Muhammad immunes himself from sin. He is just carrying out Allah's instructions and the victims are suffering because of their own wrongdoings and Allah's curse. With Allah's authority, Muhammad can "*destroy a township*" and "*annihilate it with complete annihilation*" without taking a single grain of responsibility for it. So why should he feel guilty or accept the sin? For a person to be truly guilty, he needs to intend, to deliberate, to contemplate his choices and then to choose his acts. Muhammad had done none of these. A Narcissist, because he is deeply immersed in his delusion and grandeur, believes that his heinous acts have or will have a greater positive influence on humankind (Vaknin, 1999, p. 140). Let us analyze the most hateful verse of the Qur'an – "The Verse of the Sword".

When the sacred months are over, slay the idolaters wherever you find them. Take them and confine them, then lie in ambush everywhere for them. If they repent and establish the prayer and pay the obligatory charity, let them go their way. Allah is Forgiving and the Most Merciful. (Q: 9.5).

The above verse is one of the most frequently quoted Qur'anic verses. It is both offensive and defensive and meant for worldwide application. Muslim terrorists cite this verse to justify their violent jihad. However, this verse appears to be self-contradictory – Allah is instructing the Muslims to slay the nonbelievers, but at the same time Allah claims that he is "*forgiving and the most merciful*". But no; this verse is perfect if judged from a Narcissist's point of view. Muhammad knew that his instructions were immoral and would cause great pain to others, but his "magical thinking", i.e., his way of viewing the world convinced him that though his actions were against society and humanity, he could "get away" with this, because whatever he is doing today is for a long term benefit to the civilization. In the future, people will accept him as a true Prophet and his Allah as the most merciful and forgiving God. Therefore, this verse, though looks contradictory according to our moral standard and intellect, is meaningful if analyzed from Muhammad's point of view. Now we know what Muhammad's strength was. He was capable to "*destroy a township*" and "*annihilate it with complete annihilation*" without blinking an eye, and still could think himself sinless.

A Narcissist's magical thinking is so strange that if this "someone" cannot sustain his "chosen specialness", he may look for support from another object. But the very concept of his "chosen specialness" will never change. For Muhammad, Allah was merely an "instrument" whose only purpose was to certify Muhammad. If Allah had failed to pump up Muhammad's ego, Muhammad would have dumped Allah in a dustbin and picked up another God to uphold his prophetic position. This is narcissistic immunity. Muhammad had the immunity but God did not. Hence God changes, but Muhammad's "sinlessness" would not change at any cost. He would never take the responsibility of the harm inflicted on others by the results of his own decisions, opinions, beliefs, deeds and misdeeds, and, actions and inactions. He was above reproach and punishment.

In this situation Allah is helpless. In the hands of a malignant Narcissist, God is miserable. If Allah fails to prove Muhammad *ma'soum*, and does not take away Muhammad's moral responsibility to any of his misconduct; Allah's usefulness will cease immediately. Therefore, whenever Muhammad commits any crime, Allah is in a hurry to send a timely revelation to exempt him from taking any responsibility. This strange Allah-Muhammad relationship was noticed by Aisha, the child bride of Muhammad. She accused (Bukhari: 6.60.311; Muslim: 8.3453, 3454) Muhammad that whenever he desired something, magically a suitable verse was revealed. In other words, Muhammad commands Allah. Allah's survival solely depends on his approval. If Allah does not approve Muhammad by a suitable revelation, he will dismiss Allah immediately from His heavenly position and find another suitable God. Muhammad demanded "sinlessness" from Allah, and Allah granted it to protect Himself from the fury of His Narcissist messenger. Let us analyze some "witness" verses from the Qur'an.

We have sent thee (Muhammad) as a messenger unto mankind and Allah is sufficient as Witness. (Q: 4.79)

... and he (Muhammad) called Allah to witness as to that which is in his heart (Q: 2.204)

Enough is Allah for a witness between us and you: we certainly knew nothing of your worship of us. (Q: 10.29)

But Allah bears witness by what He has revealed to you that He has revealed it with His knowledge, and the angels bear witness (also); and Allah is sufficient as a witness. (Q: 4.166)

Allah (Himself) bears witness that there is no god but He ... (Q: 3.18)

Say (O Muhammad): What thing is of most weight in testimony? Say: Allah is Witness between me and you. And this Qur'an hath been inspired in me ... (Q: 6.19)

He (Muhammad) said: I call Allah to witness, (Q: 11.54)

The Unbelievers say: 'No messenger art thou." Say: "Enough for a witness between me and you is Allah, and such as have knowledge of the Book.' (Q: 13.43)

Say: Allah sufficeth for a witness between me and you. Lo! He is Knower, Seer of His slaves. (Q: 17.96)

Say: Allah is sufficient as a witness between me and you. (Q: 29.52)

... and enough is Allah for a Witness. (Q: 48.28)

In all the above verses, Allah was working hard to convince the nonbelievers that Muhammad was not a fake. Or, should we say that it was Muhammad, who was desperate to prove and uphold his prophetic status by citing Allah as a witness? Otherwise, there is absolutely no meaningful substance in the above quotes.

Malignant narcissism is such a deadly, evil and painful disease that it not only destroys the Narcissist, but infects and forever changes those people who are in touch with him by paralyzing their thinking capability. Muslims reason out this way – since Muhammad never felt guilty for his inhuman acts, therefore he was immaculate from sin. Since Muhammad was sinless, therefore all his cruel acts were godly. With this distortion of reality, Muslims came within the grip of Muhammad's narcissism and absorbed by his way of thinking. As a result, the sinless Muhammad himself became the object of worship to his followers along with Allah.

3.7: Malignant Narcissists, Muhammad and Vampires – A Comparison

Psychoanalysts often compare malignant Narcissists to vampires which makes much sense when breaking down the characteristics of the disorder. It also helps the students and novices to understand the destructive mindset of a malignant Narcissist in a better way. I have borrowed the analogy from the psychoanalysts and detailed it further by including Muhammad in the same comparison.

The fictional vampires are like ghost-like entities. They are cursed creatures and considered to be damned with their fate (Etheredge, 2005, p. iv). Malignant narcissism is a harmful, evil and torturous disease and the Narcissists are equally damned with their fate. Muhammad was a cursed human like the vampires. He was a slave of his superego as if he was possessed by an evil spirit. This master of darkness brought death and destruction wherever he went; it was his destiny. Muslims are also cursed for fully submitting to and trusting in Muhammad.

The vampire did not choose his fate willingly. Similarly, a malignant Narcissist is the product of faulty parenting who has not received enough love and attention. Because of this; the emerging 'self' was devastated, which forced him to split his normal healthy personality into a real and a false self. Chroniclers have recorded Muhammad's disrupted childhood which is also confirmed in the Qur'an.

The vampire uses people as tools and sources of supply to continue his existence. This is his constant, futile search for deliverance. A malignant Narcissist needs people to keep his false self upheld. Muhammad was helpless to his illness. Throughout he used others for his selfish needs. When the early Muslims fought, killed or got killed; it was Muhammad who benefited from their sacrifice.

Vampires are believed to be "soulless" with no conscience, a ruthless killer instinct, and a never-ending thirst for human blood (Zell-Ravenheart, 2004, p. 298). They are doomed to roam the earth and snatch souls from innocent victims. In real life we describe those who lack any kind of empathy, sympathy, mercy, and consideration for others as "soulless". Malignant Narcissists behave in the same way. Their victims often say, they feel as if their soul has been raped or even robbed by the Narcissist. Muhammad was deprived of all the human qualities and lacked sensitivity or the capacity for deep feeling. He was heartless and cruel like those soulless vampires. If the goal in life is the spiritual enlightenment to unite the conscious mind with the soul, then undoubtedly Muhammad was a great loser.

Vampires wait for suitable moments to attack a human to drink blood. It is difficult to recognize a vampire at first glance. They look just like and pass for any other normal human being from time to time. Others cannot really recognize them unless they reveal themselves to them (Bart, 2002, p. 217). Any reasonably clever Narcissist can act with saintly niceness for his own manipulative purposes. When Muhammad's divine mission was a complete failure at Mecca, luck favored him and he gained the trust of the inhabitants of Medina. Those foolish people failed to recognize Muhammad, gave him shelter, and allowed him to propagate his message at Medina. But, what Muhammad gave them in return?

A vampire cannot see his own image in the mirror because he is a spirit and not a physical being (Pucket *et. al*, 1981, p. 1123). Spirits do not cast a reflection. But when the spirit takes a physical form and sees his reflection, he becomes very pale with dark eyes and lips. Muhammad prohibited drawing his portrait because an image which may identify a certain period of his life is an "emotional handle", which always scared him.

Some stories about vampires detail vampirism as being a curse, acquired from ancient evils that must be passed on to innocent victims in more "satanic" methods. Narcissism breeds narcissism. The parents of the Narcissist are often Narcissists themselves, and they seem to transfer their narcissism to their children (Twenge & Campbell, 2010, p. 219). Allah was such an ungodly God that Muhammad needed the two satanic methods – use of sword and deception to sell this failed God.

According to the folklore, a human becomes vampire when a vampire bites him and drinks his blood. Even then the victim is not a true vampire until he makes his first kill of an innocent human and tastes his blood (Maberry, 2008, p. 229). Hence; a vampire can only be created by another vampire, and it happens when they come in close proximity. Muhammad had treated his followers as an extension of his own personality. It is through them Muhammad wanted to settle "open accounts" with the enemy world. Vaknin (1999, p. 11) wrote that people who are in daily contact with the Narcissists are "infected" and "changed forever". Narcissism is such a contagious disease that it spoils the lives of the victims even when their Narcissist leader is no more. Like the transformation into a vampire, slowly, the companions of Muhammad absorbed Muhammad's way of thinking and became as deadly as their leader just like the unfolding of a dark Shakespearean tragedy. They were programmed to materialize the unfulfilled narcissistic dreams and fantasies of their Narcissist leader. In doing so, they all became Narcissist themselves. This is how the terror survived Muhammad's death.

At the end; every vampire, every malignant Narcissist or every false Prophet is a loser. Destruction of the vampire comes when he is exposed to light. The false self of a Narcissist ceases to exist when his true self is brought to light. The myth of Muhammad's prophethood, his cult Islam, and his God Allah would be eradicated when his deception would be exposed. That day is not far away.

3.8: Correlating Muhammad's Neurotic Disorder and Narcissistic Urge

Faith is the basic element of a person's mental health. Theologically, faith is a gift of God, and it is entirely an individual choice to accept or reject it. But in the cold-eyed view of the trained psychiatrist, faith may also be a cover-up for deep inner anxiety and a strong narcissistic urge to power. This is the missing link between the neurotic disorder and the narcissistic delusion. Narcissism is all about achieving power at the cost of others, and if the Narcissist is also suffering from neurotic disorder, his hidden desires are often reflected in the symptoms of neurosis.

Freud, in his 1927 work *The future of an illusion*, regarded religion as "*the universal neurosis*". Initially his views were widely accepted by the researchers, but later on, they strongly opposed him. Not all religions are based on neurosis; there is a well-defined dividing line between healthy faith and neurotic faith. Neurotic faith is based on fear and hate, while brotherhood and peaceful co-existence are regularly stimulated by the healthy faiths.

Muhammad had a strong urge to establish himself a Prophet. As opportunity came, unconsciously, he exploited his neurosis to create a situation for others to believe in his genuineness. Before we proceed further, let us analyze how he used to receive the revelations from Allah.

Revelation came to the Apostle of Allah and he was covered with a cloth, and Ya'la said: Would that I see revelation coming to the Apostle of Allah. He (Omar) said: Would it please you to see the Apostle of Allah receiving the revelations? 'Omar lifted a corner of the cloth and I looked at him and he was emitting a sound of snorting. He (the narrator) said: I thought it was the sound of a camel. (Muslim: 7.2654).

Narrated Musa bin Abi Aisha; When Gabriel revealed the divine Inspiration in Allah's Apostle, he moved his tongue and lips, and that state used to be very hard for him, and that movement indicated that revelation was taking place. (Bukhari: 6.60.451)

In no way do I suggest that Muhammad was consciously staging a drama by artificially producing those acts, and they were merely a device by which he secured sanction for his revelations. He genuinely believed that he was receiving messages from God in that bodily condition or trance. It was his subconscious which played a trick on him and hence while distinguishing between the thoughts of his own mind and the revelations, Muhammad did "personally" enter (in his mind) into the latter and allowed them to give shape to his own developing prophetic consciousness, or more precisely his sick narcissistic ambitions. Allah's revelations found expression in Muhammad's consciousness rather than in his ears. Contrary to popular Muslim belief, the revelations were inspirational, something like "suggested" rather direct verbal revelation rote in the ears of Muhammad. Qur'an confirms it.

It is no less than inspiration sent down to him. (Q: 53.4)

Therefore Muhammad's own diseased mind shaped those revelations according to his subconscious wishes. Muhammad's own narcissistic thoughts came down as revelations, and his dramatic actions while receiving the revelations were "adjusted" accordingly to balance each other. Jung (1933, p. 44) commented, "*He [the patient] 'arranges' his symptoms and exploits [subconsciously] his neurosis to attain a fictitious importance.*" For example, when Muhammad fell in love with Zaynab and a verse (33:37) was revealed to him from the sky legitimizing his marriage with her, he knew what he had in mind. Therefore, when he had produced any psychological symptom at the time of putative revelation, he was inducing that state in himself by exploiting his neurosis unconsciously. The tenor of the passage would already have been fabricated in his mind.

This is the reason Islam is a neurotic and narcissistic faith. It is narcissistic, because the revelations were "censored" by the "suggestions" of a Narcissist, and obviously it is neurotic because it is based on fear and hate, as McCloud (2004, p. 37) observes, there is "*an irrational intensity of belief*" in the new doctrine. There are many symptoms, e.g., greater concern for form and theology than for ethical and moral principles, hatred of past beliefs and other's beliefs, intolerance of deviation, and the desire for martyrdom to prove devotion – all the symptoms of an unhealthy faith the whole world is witnessing in Islam for last fourteen centuries. It originated from Muhammad's neurosis and propelled by his abnormal narcissistic desires to achieve power at any cost. The followers of Muhammad, even since the birth of Islam, inherit his mental disorder simply by following his delusive faith.

3.9: The Intellectual Defeat of Muhammad

Muslims fraudulently claim that the Qur'anic Surahs stunned the early Arab intellectuals, but nothing could be further from the truth. Though the early Meccans were mostly illiterate and superstitious people ready to believe any sort of rubbish in the name of religion, there were many wise people amongst them who turned away from Muhammad knowing that he was deluded. We cannot blame them; they had seen many imposters like Muhammad. During those days, prophetic business was a thriving profitable industry in Arabia. Therefore, they ignored Muhammad as they ignored any other madman. The following verses confirm it.

The Hypocrites and those in whose hearts is a disease said: 'Allah and His Messenger promised us nothing but delusion; they have promised only to deceive us'. (Q: 33.11).

Then they had turned away from him and said: One taught by others, a madman! (Q: 44.14).

They take you not except for mockery. (Q: 21.36).
They said: 'Are we going to abandon our gods for the sake of a mad poet?' (Q: 37.36)

And when they see you, they treat you only as a mockery. (Q: 25.41).

But they were kind to Muhammad and left him alone in his fantasy world, and allowed him to believe in whatever fables he wanted. They were even ready to pay for medical advice to cure his mental disease. Utbah ibn Rabi'ah, a distinguished leader of Arabia, convinced the Quraysh at one of their community meetings to delegate him to approach Muhammad. So on behalf of the Quraysh, he came to Muhammad to assist him with different alternatives. Haykal (1976, chapter 5) recorded Utbah's words,

If you are unable to cure yourself of the visions that you have been seeing, we shall be happy to seek for you at our expense all the medical service possible until your health is perfectly restored.

As Muhammad's lies were exposed, Islam was destined to vanish in its infancy. To console Muhammad, Allah assured him by the following Qur'anic revelations,

By the Favor of Allah, you are neither a soothsayer, nor mad. (Q: 52.29).

Allah shall pay them back their mockery, and He leaves them alone in their inordinacy, blindly wandering on. (Q: 2.15)

In a state of anger Muhammad started calling the nonbeliever by different names. According to Qur'an, the nonbelievers are,

1. Harm-doers (Q: 2.59; 2.95; 2.145; 2.150; 2.165; 2.193; 2.229; 2.246; 2.254; 2.258; 2.270; 3.57; 3.86; 3.94; 3.128; 3.140; 3.151; 4.74; 5.29; 5.45; 5.107; 6.21; 6.45; 6.58; 6.135; 7.41; 7.47; 7.148; 8.54; 9.23; 11.31, etc)

2. Hypocrites (Q: 4.61; 8.49; 9.64; 9.73; 29.11; 33.1; 48.6; 57.13; 59.11; 63.1; 66.9, etc.)

3. Liars (Q: 6.28; 7.66; 9.77; 11.93; 39.3; 40.24, etc)

4. Evildoers (Q: 2.12; 2.26; 2.99; 3.63; 5.47; 5.108; 7.102; 9.24; 10.17; 11.18; 14.22; 17.47; 18.53; 19.86; 24.4; 29.4; 34.42; 37.22; 39.24, etc)

Indecent language is normally the jargon of low-bred, discourteous people who are lacking in civility and good manners. Is it conceivable that a God would use such vulgar language to address human beings? The answer is that such vulgar words and obscene language was the cultural heritage of illiterate Muhammad brought up in a desert. People who are evil attack others instead of facing their own failures. A curse uttered by a person who desires to harm another person, but finds him or herself physically powerless to do so, appeals to a supernatural power to inflict such harm.

The Arabs were certainly not harm-doers, hypocrites, evildoers or liars. Instead, those were the traits of Muhammad's own character. Let me analyze, what actually was going on in Muhammad's mind when he called the nonbelievers with such offensive terms. The mind of a Narcissist is limited to one line of thought as if he is playing according to a script where he is playing the lead role and he has total control over the play. Obviously, this "script" is written to conform his narcissistic ideas, but when others force him to see "glimpses of reality" by going against his script and pointing out his inconsistencies and faults, he is faced with a terrifying possibility of losing his "control" over the script (Zayn & Dibble, 2007, p. 142). At this time, he projects the negative qualities of his character onto others as a defense mechanism. For example; if someone were to call the Narcissist on some remarks he had made, but was now denying; the Narcissist, instead of admitting his mistake, might say – "You are a habitual liar! You have always been a liar! Nothing you ever say is true. You have spent your entire life lying and I can never believe a word that comes out of your mouth".

This sort of attack throws the victim off-track and causes him to become defensive in order to prove his honesty. Meanwhile the heat is off and the Narcissist is able to regain "control" (Zayn & Dibble, 2007, p. 93). Harm-doing, evil-doing, hypocrisy and lying were the negative qualities of Muhammad himself, and through the Qur'an, unknowingly, he had projected these qualities onto others; he simply exposed his true character. As Zayn & Dibble (2007, p. 93) wrote, "*When someone tries to convince the Narcissist of something that does not comply with the false self he has created, the Narcissist may project the real self onto that person. ... This type of projection is a common defense mechanism of the Narcissist*".

Now we know why the nonbelievers were called with such derogatory terms. All he wanted to do was to regain "control" of the situation. There are many verses in the Qur'an where Muhammad exposed various negative sides of his character without even realizing.

*And who is more unjust than **he who forges a lie** against Allah, or says: It has been revealed to me; while nothing has been revealed to him.* (Q: 6.93).

*Nay, the wrong-doers promise each other **nothing but delusions**.* (Q: 35.40)

*... but the unjust this day are in **manifest error**.* (Q: 19.38)

*And none but the **guilty led us astray**.* (Q: 26.99)

*Satan makes them promises, and creates in them false desires; but Satan's promises are nothing but **deception**.* (Q: 4.120)

*Then he caused them to fall by **deceit**.* (Q: 7.22)

*And lo! **In the love of wealth he is violent**.* (Q: 100.8)

Prophets are more evil doers than habitual liars and hypocrites, because the former commit crimes on the pretext of divine authority, but the latter only fabricate falsehoods of their own making. In sum, Muhammad had suffered a complete intellectual defeat and the most embarrassing social humiliation. He was mocked mercilessly by his people and faced extreme skepticism (Smith & Haddad, 2002, p. 147). Such critics were not merely the dead voices of the past. They were asking the same questions about his heavenly mission that we still ask in our time without getting any answers from the Muslim scholars. These questions are as old as Islam.

3.10: A Quest for the Impaired True Self of Muhammad

"Know thyself".

An ancient Greek aphorism

"I have often thought that the best way to define a man's character would be to seek out the particular mental or moral attitude in which, when it came upon him, he felt himself most deeply and intensely active and alive. At such moments, there is a voice inside which speaks and says, 'This is the real me!'"

William James in a letter to his wife, 1878

From his childhood, Muhammad was ill-fated and faced much psychological adversities. He lost his father before his birth and lost his mother's love and warmth during the time he needed these most. After his mother's death, he spent two years in the house of his grandfather, Abdul Mutalib, who also died shortly. It means whenever the child was emotionally attached to someone, he faced abandonment. It is a medically proven fact that adverse family and social situation often not only retard mental growth but the child may grow up with adjustment problems with others (Shepley, 2001, p. 3). This is called "attachment disorder". It arises from a failure to form normal attachments to primary care giving figures in early childhood, resulting in problematic social expectations and behaviors. According to the psychoanalysts (Flores, 2004, p. xii), the interpersonal breaches and traumas early in life are embedded (i.e. imprinted) in our brain and reflected in adult life in errant and compulsive behaviors.

During his early adult days Muhammad did not get a meaningful employment and remained unmarried till twenty-five which was quite a late marriageable age for the Arabs. Amongst them, the wealthy and the braves used to get better preferences in marriage. In this respect he was very unlucky. Neither had he money nor courage. Probably he was also physically weak. Arabs were good fighters and they really craved for the excitement of the battlefield, but Muhammad never fought a single battle personally. As Muir explains, "*Physical courage, indeed, and martial daring are virtues which did not distinguish the Prophet at any period of his career.*" (Sina, 2008, p. 33). In one of the battles, known as "Sacrilegious war", fought in Mecca, he assisted his clan by gathering up the arrows discharged by the enemy during the break in fighting and handing them to his uncles.

According to Bukhari (4.56.762; 8.73.140), Muhammad was "*shyer than a veiled virgin girl*". But once he became powerful at Medina, he was completely changed. As Twenge & Campbell (2010, p. 18) commented, "*A Narcissist has an overinflated view of his own abilities, similar to the kitten that sees himself as a lion on the popular poster.*" Now it would be disgusting if he behaves like a coward. He has gathered enough strength by becoming the leader of a band of criminals. The megalomaniac Prophet of Islam declared openly,

I will bring you slaughter. (Ishaq: 130; Tabari: VI.101)

Allah made me victorious with terror. (Bukhari: 1.7.331).

Deep inside in his heart, Muhammad still remained a coward in spite of having Allah on his side. Muhammad never put his life in danger in a battle. He often stood behind the fighting Muslims at a safe distance surrounded by bodyguards wearing two coats of chain-link armour, one on top of another and a helmet with a visor that covered his face. This double armouring would make him so heavy that his movements used to be very burdensome. He could not even stand in this condition without assistance from others, let alone walking. All he could do was to shout towards the front and encourage his men to show bravery and not to fear death.

During the battle of Uhud, Muhammad was beaten up by the brave Meccans and knocked down into a ditch. In a panic, he cried out loudly, "*Come to my help you Muslim there, come to me you Muslim there, I am the Messenger of Allah.*" (Ahmed, 2006, p. 173). He owed his life only to the devotion of his helpers, who shielded him with their bodies. Then Muhammad got up again all covered with mud and blood (Warraq, 2000, p. 141). Surely the battle of Uhud was the hardest day in Muhammad's life. Ahmed (2006, pp. 173-4) described,

> *Abd Allah Ibn Shihab was able to hit the Prophet on his forehead and caused a big cut on it. Ibn Qimah al-Harithi broke his nose and his shoulder. Then, he hit him with his weapon until two parts of it entered the blessed cheek of the Prophet. In all this, the Prophet was calling his friends to come for his help. Then, the Messenger of Allah fell in a ditch when Ibn Qimah made a second attack on him and strike his shoulder with full force. However, the two amours protected the Prophet from the strike but he continued to complain from the pain for a full month after Uhud.*

We often wonder where were Allah and the fighting angels on this fateful day. Why Allah did not send the angels to assist Muhammad and his gang when they needed the help most? However Muhammad's defeat immediately contradicts following two verses.

> *When thou didst say unto the believers: Is it not sufficient for you that your Lord should support you with three thousand angels sent down (to your help)?* (Q: 3.124).

> *When ye sought help of your Lord and He answered you (saying): I will help you with a thousand of the angels, rank on rank.* (Q: 8.9).

And this shameless spineless coward claimed to have a God on his side, and talked about bringing slaughter to the infidels. Allah and angels were Muhammad's delusions, and either conscious or subconscious fabrications of his diseased mind. When he said, "I will bring you slaughter", it was an act to hide the reality that he was a coward. He himself did not believe that Allah could save him. So he used to take extra precautions. Deep down, he knew that he was a fake. He knew that his prophetic claim was nothing but a concoction, a figment of his distorted thinking, that he could live only like a parasite in the guise of a Prophet. With falsehood, a number of people can be brainwashed, but in the harshness of battles, survival depends on courage, skill and physical strength. Sadly Muhammad lacked all these qualities and he was well aware of it.

Though the seed of narcissism was deep-rooted in Muhammad's mind much before he claimed the title of Prophet, no one saw his narcissistic outburst because he had no followers. He was a lone Narcissist. Most of the Narcissists are shy and humble when they have hardly any following. But the narcissistic monsters lurk inside them waiting for a suitable chance to come out. From the very childhood days Muhammad had a strong desire for recognition.

On the very same day, Muhammad started his mission; he lost several key capacities of his real self. When Muhammad got a strong foothold in Medina and started plundering the rich Meccan caravans, his real self was fully paralyzed by his false self. With this he lost his capacity to experience a wide range of feelings deeply with liveliness, joy, vigor, spontaneity and the excitement of creativity. From a helpless orphan to parasitic husband of a wealthy woman to a small-scale Prophet to a bandit king to the conqueror of Mecca to the *de facto* ruler of the whole Arabia to the founder of a world-threatening religion – Muhammad's journey along the path of his life is really amazing.

Muhammad was never a religious person. Islamic scriptures do not mention much about his religious views before his prophetic days. In Mecca; many Jews, Christians and, as some historians say, Hindus had settled and lived with harmony, but Muhammad had never showed any interest in the religious beliefs of other people. He did not even know that Jews and Christians have theological differences (Armstrong, 2006, p. 15). When he came to know, he was surprised. Let alone Jews and Christians, his knowledge about any religion of Arabia was very poor because of his illiteracy and lack of interest.

In fact, in the early Surahs, Allah's religious vocabulary was restricted to that which can be illustrated from the compositions of the pre-Islamic poets. But when Muhammad picked up bits and pieces about the religious doctrines of Jews and Christians, Allah's language in the Qur'an started changing accordingly. From the Qur'an itself we can see him gradually acquiring more and more information about other religions. In spite of this, when Muhammad established himself as a Prophet, Allah declared that Muhammad was a Prophet when the body and soul of Adam were still in the making. There is no limit of magical thinking; this charlatan was neither a mystic nor a messenger of any God but a Narcissist political leader who used God and his neurosis for his selfish needs.

Before his marriage to Khadija, Muhammad used to attend sheep with a miserly small payment. For the Arabs, this was an unmanly profession mostly reserved for girls. Muhammad took this unmanly job for two reasons – first, he was unsuitable for any better job. Secondly, it allowed him to avoid interaction with others with whom he (more correctly, his grandiose false self) was incapable of dealing as equal. Muhammad was a social misfit and his superiority complex was actually a mask of his inferiority complex. Haykal (1976, chapter 3) wrote,

Muhammad's occupation as herdsman during the years of his youth provided him with plenty of leisure to ponder and to contemplate. He took care of his family and neighbors' herds. Later, he used to recall these early days with joy.

Muhammad loved the job of a herdsman because he had adjustment problems. A study conducted by Lengua *et al*, (2000, pp. 232-4) with a sample of 231 children between the ages of nine and twelve provided data for the parental rejection and depressive symptoms. The study suggests that children who experience parental rejection and low levels of positive emotionality are more likely to exhibit higher levels of adjustment problems as they grow up. Muhammad had devalued himself (deflation of the false self) and became unduly sensitive. He was constantly envious of others and to witness the success and joy of others was too painful for him to see and too high a price to pay. So he had a favorite solution – social isolation. When things go wrong and we are hurt; the real self devises means to minimize and soothe painful feelings (Masterson, 1990, p. 42). It would never allow us to stumble in misery. Often one of the means is to interact with others or go to a therapist. But for a Narcissist, the situation is different.

Muhammad preferred to withdraw from the world and live in his dream-like sweet imaginary world. He used to retreat into his own thoughts. Even when he was a child, he avoided the company of other children. He hardly laughed because he thought it was silly. In his fantasy world, Muhammad was no longer the cast-off or unwanted child; rather loved, respected, praised and even feared. He was the one and the only one. He was so absorbed in his fantasy world that it became as real to him as the real world, only more pleasurable (Sina, 2008, p. 15). This is called "rescue fantasy". Neglected children often indulge in such fantasies. It is harmless, but it is a matter of grave concern when a grown up person cannot come out from these fantasies.

Masterson (1990, p. 83) wrote, "*Such rescue fantasies have great appeal to the young child who has not yet learned how to cope effectively with reality, and the same type of fantasies appeals to patients whose ability to deal with life as it is, is severely impaired by the false self*".

This attitude is common amongst those who have developed an utter negative attitude towards society. As Masterson (1990, p. 42) wrote, "*The real self does not block feelings or deaden the impact of emotions. It provides a sense of what is appropriate*". The Narcissist cannot be happy, because his feelings and expression of emotions are all distorted. He is chronically depressed and "anhedonic" (the inability to experience pleasure from activities formerly found enjoyable) (Vaknin, 1999, p. 193). Muhammad also suffered from anxiety disorder. Children with a diagnosable anxiety disorder reported lower levels of maternal acceptance than other children (Hazen, 2005, p. 8). Sina continued, "*He would often spend his time in pensive mood. He did not know how to be happy or have fun ... When reality became hard to bear and his loneliness overwhelmed him, he would escape into fantasy, where he could be anyone or anything he wanted to be.*"

The very thought of being inferior often drives a person to overcompensate, which results either in spectacular achievement or extreme "schizotypal behavior" (a need for social isolation, odd behavior and thinking, and often unconventional beliefs), or both. Haykal continued,

> [Muhammad used to] say proudly that 'God sent no Prophet who was not a herdsman . . . Moses was a herdsman; David was also a herdsman; I, too, was commissioned to prophethood while I grazed my family's cattle at Ajyad'.

This is an odd thinking. It is normal for a child but not for a person who is at his young adult days and matured enough to work as a herdsman. According to Vygotskii & Rieber (1998, p. 161), the lively fantasy of a child does not use the riches of his ideas. It has its roots in the great intensity and the easier excitability of his feelings. This way, a child's fantasy is significantly poorer than the adolescent's fantasy. These harmless fantasies are just commonsense thinking. But when the child's play ends in the fantasy of the adult, there is problem. When Muhammad still cherished such baseless, delusional and poor fantasies in his early adult days, certainly, he was not in touch with reality. As Jung (1933, p. 100) wrote, "*We are all thoroughly familiar with the sources of the problems which arise in the period of youth. For most people it is the demands of life which harshly put an end to the dream of childhood. If the individual is sufficiently well prepared, the transition to a professional career may take place smoothly. But if he clings to illusions that contradict reality, then problems will surely arise*".

When Muhammad secured a job to work for Khadija, a wealthy woman, the tough days of a herdsman were over. After some time, Khadija proposed him marriage. For Muhammad, the marriage with Khadija was a blessing because he found a financial security. This also allowed him to never work again. But still he was not happy because the childhood fantasies were haunting him. He left his wife at home to take care of several children and retreated to the caves around Mecca. This way he secluded himself from the world and wrapped himself in his own megalomaniac thoughts. His narcissistic fantasies also started developing and becoming rich and practical. As Vaknin (1999, pp. 74-5) described, *"The Narcissist feels miserably inferior and dependent. He rebels against this degrading state of things by partly escaping into a world of make-belief, daydreaming, pretensions and delusions of grandeur. The Narcissist knows little about himself, and finds what he knows to be abhorrent"*.

During later days when Muhammad established himself as a Prophet, his false self showed the same derogatory attitude toward others. Islam is a religion which was created from Muhammad's frustration and hate for the society. The foundation of hate was within Muhammad himself, which made his religion so hateful and destructive. However, this was the beginning of the outburst of his NPD. He was in distress because a "Narcissistic deficiency dysphoria" set in. In this situation, a Narcissist would behave very much as a drug addict would react to the absence of his particular drug. Vaknin (1999, pp. 85-6) wrote, *"The Narcissist will gradually turn more and more mechanical, detached and unreal. His thoughts will constantly wander or become obsessive and repetitive ... he will be far away, in a world of his Narcissistic fantasies where Narcissistic supply is aplenty. He will withdraw from this painful world which knows not how to appreciate his greatness, special skills and talents, potential, or achievements"*.

The real self allows us to be alone without feeling abandoned. It enables us to manage ourselves when there is no special person in our lives (Masterson, 1990, p. 46). Having a loving and caring wife and several children in the home, no way Muhammad could feel alone. Actually Muhammad's marriage with Khadija was only a financial security. There was absolutely no emotional attachment. During his frequent visits to the caves, a struggle was going on in his mind. His false self was continuously destroying whatever little humanity was still left in him. The monster which was lurking inside Muhammad was getting prepared to emerge with "clear authority" from Allah to take revenge by punishing the same cruel society which had neglected him.

At last, a timely hallucination caused by his neurosis, which Muhammad interpreted as a heavenly confrontation with the Gabriel, resulted in the final narcissistic explosion. Now he hates to look back to his true self. When the true self was in action, it had accepted and modulated various self-images, and resolved much apparent and temporary confusion. It also integrated various diverse aspects of his life and related them to each other to form a whole life and a whole self. But his true self failed to improve his status, by which he could command respect from others. Now it is time for the false self to transform the childhood fantasies into reality.

3.11: Conclusion

"What the world needs is not dogma, but an attitude of scientific inquiry combined with a belief that the torture of millions is not desirable, whether inflected by Stalin or by a Deity imagined in the likeness of believer".

Bertrand Russell (1996, p. 165)

Muhammad did not establish Islam to teach the pagans humanity. Spirituality is basically a non-existent subject in Islam. The only purpose of Islam was to enslave people. Qur'an was the work of this shrewd politician anxious to draw to himself by all possible means the greatest number of adherents. Muhammad's attitude was like a parliamentary candidate during his electoral campaign. He did not bother about the quality of his supporters, but the number, and to secure their votes he was ready to go any length. As situation demanded, he flattered his target group, promised paradise and threatened them of hellfire. The reason was obvious – he was striving to establish his doctrine not for sake of God, but for the sake of himself.

In religion, Prophet is a person who has been contacted by, or has encountered the supernatural or the divine, and serves as an intermediary with humanity by delivering this newfound knowledge from the supernatural entity to other humans. In Judaism, a Prophet is a person selected by a God who speaks as His formal representative, and the intention of the message is always to effect a social change to conform to God's desired standards. The charlatan Prophet of Islam adopted the same style of Judaism to shape his religion but in a twisted form. He had elevated himself instead of elevating the God. To achieve this he had discouraged free will (Allah's will is the only "freedom". Islam is based on predestination and fatalism), which is the origin of free thinking, enquiry and social progress, and set a great barrier for the unity of humankind. It imposed complete hegemony of fate on man. It is obvious that his prophethood has nothing to do with a God or a heavenly guidance, but it has everything to do with the manipulations of a malignant Narcissist.

Muhammad was an ambitious politician disguised as a spiritual leader. Though he started as a humble servant of Allah, his prestige and authority were truly unassailable when he got a strong foothold at Medina. This sudden change of his personality did not escape the notice of his contemporaries, *"That man aspires to dominate the Arabs"* said the Taiyite Chief Zarr Ibn Sadus. Abu Sufyan was to make the same observation, *"Prophetism is finished, the empire is beginning"* (Trifkovic, 2002, p. 45). They understood Muhammad's real intention of starting a new sect. They knew that Muhammad conceived his religion solely to satiate his lust for power, sex, and money; there was no way he could qualify as a true Prophet of God. Robert L. Snow (2003, p. 109) wrote,

Practically everyone has seen the cartoon with a character wearing the sandwich sign that proclaims, "The end is near". While this meant as a joke, throughout history, a large number of people have proclaimed with all seriousness that they have unique knowledge that the end of the world is coming. Through this proclamation, many Prophets of doom have attracted large group of followers who believe that these doom forecasters have some type of special insight, special vision or special relationship with God that gives them inside knowledge about the impending end of the world. Once this belief system is established, the doomsday forecasters then have tremendous control over the lives of the people who believe in them.

Muhammad did not perform any better. He demanded that he had unique knowledge about unseen and unknown, but it was not true. He spied everywhere in search of enemies, as Tabari recorded,

Muhammad sent out spies to obtain intelligence. But they came back with their joints dislocated. When he asked what had happened, they said, 'We saw white men on black horses. Before we could resist, we were struck as you see us now'. (Tabari: IX.6)

The Prophet asked, 'Who will go and spy on the enemy?' The Messenger stipulated that should he come back, Allah would cause him to enter Paradise. (Tabari: VIII.26).

The Messenger sent Amr to the Quraysh as a spy. (Tabari: VII.146).

Muhammad's spy brought him word that Ikrimah was coming out with five hundred men. (Tabari: VIII.71).

Abdallah married a woman but could not afford the nuptial gift. He came to the Prophet and asked for his assistance. He said, 'Go out and spy on the Jusham tribe.' (Tabari: VIII.149).

These were the sources of Muhammad's secret knowledge. After being tipped off by his spies, he used to say, "*Allah informed me...*", "*the Gabriel informed me.....*", "*Two angels of Allah informed me...*", "*a tree told me...*", "*I overheard dead bodies talking in the grave*", etc., and the deception went on. His habit of spying and eavesdropping was so nasty that many rumors spread about him. According to these rumors (cited Warraq, 2000, pp. 171-2), he not only saw behind his back but could see by day and by night, and he possessed a physical eye planted at the middle of his back or between his shoulders and his cloths did not prevent the light from passing through. Surprisingly, Muhammad never ran shortage of fools who wanted to be fooled by him, and his tribe of fools multiplied. Anyone who dared to question had been assassinated.

When Muhammad lost in the battle of minds, he won in the battle of swords and deception. Stout (2005, p. 182) observed, "*It would be difficult to refute the observation that people, who are completely unhampered by conscience, sometimes achieve power and wealth, at least for a while. Too many chapters in the human history book, from its first lines to its most contemporary entries, are organized around the stupendous success of military invaders, conquerors, robber barons, and empire builders.*"

Human cruelty increases when the malignant Narcissist gains an incredible, almost hypnotic control over a large number of people through brainwashing. Narcissism evolves through power. It manifests itself after the aggressive Narcissist finds a following and creates his mini cult. Wolman (1999, p. 136) wrote, "*History is full of chieftains, prophets, saviors, gurus, dictators, and other sociopathic megalomaniacs who managed to obtain support ... and incited people to violence*". Narcissists who are not successful in creating a cult live a reclusive life and their ambitions die with them.

The historical Muhammad is too privileged to be formally evaluated in the fashion a clinical psychologist would like. But given certain of his well-known and highly documented behaviors, it is certain that he would not be found to possess any intervening sense of obligation based on emotional attachment to others. As Stout (2005, pp. 93, 183) concludes,

> *Insidiously, when such a "savior" abducts the normal population to his purposes, he usually begins with an appeal to them as good people who would like to improve the condition of humanity, and then insists that they can achieve this by following his own aggressive plan.*

> *Brutal conquerors and empire builders are usually held in awe by their contemporaries, and during their life-times they are often seen as role models for the entire human race.*

Once Muhammad converted some foolish people to his cult who were ready to fight and die for him, there was nothing to look back. Wherever Muhammad and his hooligans went, death and destruction followed them. Islam had always relied on the sword. Muhammad's practice and constant encouragement of bloodshed are unique in the history of religions. Murder, pillage, rape seemed to have impressed the early Muslims with a profound belief in the value of bloodshed as opening the gates of paradise. "*Kill, kill the unbelievers wherever you find them*" is an injunction both unambiguous and powerful. Slowly Muhammad became a role model and his tribe prospered with hostility and bloodshed as Ayatollah Khomeini commented (cited Trifkovic, 2006, p. 25), "***Islam grew with blood***".

Chapter 4: Qur'an: The Thought-Journal of Muhammad

Muhammad claimed that Qur'an was his only miracle in spite of the fact that the Qur'an did not exist in its written form during his lifetime. For Muslims, the Qur'an is so sacred that no devout Muslim would touch it with his left hand. As Guillaume (1978, p. 74) wrote, *"[Qur'an is] the holy of holies. It must never rest beneath other books, but always on top of them. One must never drink or smoke when it is being read aloud. And it must be listened to in silence. It is a talisman against disease and disaster"*.

The claims are no doubt fascinating, but once we attempt to make an objective study of this book, we can find many "holes" in this supposed to be holy book.

4.1: The Authenticity of the Qur'an and the Authority and Responsibility of Allah

"While man must recognize his limitations, he must also become aware of the power in himself – the power to make use of his own reason and see the truth".

Eric Fromm (quote modified by the present Author)

Andrew Rippin, a leading expert on Qur'anic studies, lamented (1991, p. ix), *"I have often encountered individuals who come to the study of Islam with a background in the historical study of the Hebrew Bible or early Christianity, and who express surprise at the lack of critical thought that appears in introductory textbooks of Islam"*. Jeffery (1937, p. 1) wrote, *"Critical investigation of the text of the Qur'an is a study which is still in its infancy"*. Muslims will never allow a critical investigation of their book. In fact they cannot tolerate any criticism of Qur'an, no matter how small. As Mingana (cited Warraq, 1998, p. 80) concluded, *"The most important question in the study of the Qur'an is its unchallengeable authority"*. They begin with the Qur'an while pretending to conclude with it. Their logic is simple – Qur'an is from Allah because Muhammad said so, and Muhammad was the messenger of Allah because Qur'an says so. Both Allah and Muhammad demanded blind trust.

Put blind faith first, and then study the Qur'an ... (Sunaan Ibn Majah: 1.61)

Believe Muhammad blindly and he blesses you seven times ... (Tirmidhi: 1688, 1689)

A Muslim can live his whole life without considering an alternative view. But this is a circular reasoning, not a proof. What we need is; at least one concrete evidence, not logical fallacy.

The idea of revelation is the idea of something which is being shown – more strictly unveiled or unfolded. In Qur'anic revelations; Allah gave some instructions to the Muslims. He had also shown what He likes and what He expects from us. But unfortunately, Allah did not do that by showing us what it is like to be God. He only made Himself known through the chosen messenger Muhammad, even though the media Allah adopted was unusual one. But where is the "divine" verification for "divine" revelations? On this particular point the God of Islam failed miserably.

Why God wants us to accept a claim at random? Blind faith can be accepted up to certain extent but somewhere we should draw the line and must seek justification after that. It is for Allah to choose Muhammad as his last Prophet and there could be no question about it, only if we had sufficient evidence to believe in Muhammad's claim. Clifford (1897, p. 186) commented, *"[In religious belief] it is wrong always, everywhere, and for everyone to believe anything upon insufficient evidence"*. We know that Muhammad was insane; therefore, we need some external proof. Without evidence, neither Islam nor Muhammad has any stand.

In Allah's revelation, the mystery is more at the origin than at the substance of the communication, because these revelations are not revelations "of" Allah, but revelations "from" Allah. These revelations had revealed nothing about Allah. Only for this reason, the skeptics find Allah's revelations very difficult to accept, and these revelations drastically upset our logical way of thinking. We have to suppress our rational faculty to believe the genuineness of these revelations. As Lewis (1961, p. 228) argued, *"How do we know that the words which purport to tell us this are genuinely the words of God? What is the warrant for divine disclosure? What assurance do we have that it is God and not man who is speaking, or if it is in the first place the word of a man, what enables us to say that God speaks to us through him? How does a word become 'the word of God'?"*

Where is Allah's guarantee for His book, Qur'an? Can any divine disclosure be beyond any question and criticism as stated in the verses 5.101, 5.102? This would be like asking "Why should I believe the truth?" If something is true then we obviously believe it after confirming the facts by physical verifications or by reasons. There are likewise questions to ask about Qur'anic revelations. Why should I believe the Qur'anic revelations, unless I am sure that they are true? As Lewis (1961, p. 231) commented, *"There are two sides to revelation. It involves man as well as God and I do not see what a revelation could be like that does not involve the use of the faculties with which we are endowed as human beings."*

Lewis (1961, p. 265) wrote, *"It is in ethics that God comes nearest to us, and the link between ethics and religions is therefore very close. The voice of God is above all the voice of consciences. It is a Divine refinement of the working of conscience"*. There are several highly offensive verses in Qur'an, which promote hate, call for violence and murder, allow deception, curse the nonbelievers and prescribe severe punishment for them. These verses are highly unethical and if, *"it is in ethics that God comes nearest to us"*, is true; then Islam is not that right path which can lead a person to the real God. As Gandhi (1961, p. 10) wrote, *"One cannot reach truth by untruthfulness"*. Being guided by those absurd revelations, Muslims cannot reach the ultimate truth, i.e., the God.

Right reason is the rule of true faith, and we have no problem to believe in a religion so far as we see it agreeable to reason and no further. As Abelard (1836, p. 15) wrote, *"The first key to wisdom is assiduous and frequent questioning... for by doubting we come to inquiry, and by inquiry, we arrive at the truth... The faith should be founded in human reason and not in the contrary."*

"Revelation is not above reason", Caird (1956, p. 356) observed, *"Revelation, which is a necessary presupposition of religion, is often understood to fall outside science or philosophy."* Truth cannot be contrary to truth and reason, and since the study of philosophy does not merely to find out what others have thought, but what the truth of the matter is, truth cannot be contrary to philosophy also. Hence logically, there should be no disagreement between true revelation and philosophy. It is wrong to say that a proposition is false in philosophy and true in faith. Does the Qur'anic teaching conform to any other school of philosophical thought throughout the recorded history of humankind? Philosophy recognizes two ways in which humans may come to know whatever there is to be known – one way through experience (stressed by empiricism), and the other is through reasoning (Hick, 1993, p. 68). Aristotle, Socrates and Plato – the three great philosophers of the world did not claim to speak in the name of the revelation but with the authority of reason and their concern with man's happiness. Buddha was a great teacher. He did not speak in the name of a supernatural power but in the name of reason. He called upon every man to make use of his own reason to see the truth (Fromm, 1978, p. 38). These great teachers did not bring down any revelation, yet they had contributed much in the growth of the civilization. But Allah's guidance and instructions through the Qur'anic revelations had contributed nothing positive; human civilization would do much better if there were no Qur'an.

Some very early Muslim scholars openly acknowledged that the arrangements and the syntax of the Qur'an are not miraculous, and work of equal or greater value could be produced by other God-fearing people. Dasti concluded that Qur'an was not the word of God, since it contains many instances, which confuse the identities of two speakers – Allah and Muhammad. Dasti also noted more than one hundred Qur'anic aberrations from the normal rules (Warraq, 1995, p. 5). A belief must be shown to be sound in itself as well as in some consequences of holding it, as Sina (2008, p. iii) lamented, *"After reading the Qur'an, I was in shock. I was shocked to see the violence, hate, inaccuracies, scientific errors, mathematical mistakes, logical absurdities, grammatical solecisms and dubious ethical pronouncements in the book of God."*

Under the (mis)guidance of the Qur'anic revelations and sunna, Muslims live in a ghostly world of fearful piety, surrounded by devils, jinns crossing themselves a hundred times a day, imploring the intercession of Muhammad for afterlife, prostrating five compulsory prayers, awed by miracles performed by Muhammad, trembling over Allah's fury and selling everything to perform Hajj. A non-Arab Muslim family is a poor imitation of an Arab family within the principled confines of Islam.

Is there any scholar who can sincerely clarify the doubts raised on the Qur'anic revelations in this chapter? Let it be an open challenge to all of them. I am sure that the challenge would remain unanswered. If unanswered, then let this be an eye-opener to common Muslim folks. One point is very clear. Since, the authenticity of Qur'anic revelations is still remained unproven even after 1400 years of its reception; Qur'an has no authority to control Muslims' lives, not even for a single moment from cradle to grave and life thereafter, if any. An authority must produce its credentials and Qur'an has none. And, since there is no assurance regarding authenticity and authority of the Qur'an, it is safe to conclude that Allah has no responsibility for the welfare of the Muslims, or simply He does not exist.

4.2: Is the Qur'an Preserved?

Muslims believe that the original copy of the Qur'an (43.3 – "*the mother of the book*"; 55.77 – "*a concealed book*"; 85.22 – "*a well guarded tablet*") is kept in the heaven. To prove that Qur'an is superior to Bible, Muslims say that the Testaments are corrupted and changed. They say, for a holy scripture to be authoritative, it has to be preserved without any changes at all, and point to their Qur'an which claims to have been revealed word by word by Allah. Qur'an claims,

No change there can be in the words of God. (Q: 10.64)

There is none that can alter the words (and decrees) of God. (Q: 6.34).

But Qur'an itself confirms that God's word can be changed. This is called the "doctrine of abrogation" by which later revelations can cancel previous ones.

Revelations... We abrogate or cause to be forgotten. (Q: 2.106).

Not only two different Sunni and Shiaa Qur'ans; today we can present many other "authentic" Qur'anic manuscripts (dating from first century of Hijrah) which are different from existing standard forms. These Qur'ans were discovered in the Great Mosque of Sana'a (Yemen) which is one of the oldest mosques in Islamic history. The date of building goes back to sixth year of Hijrah. In 1972, during the restoration of this Great Mosque, laborers working in a crown space between the structure's inner and outer roofs stumbled across a amazing grave site containing an unappealing mountain of old parchment and paper documents, damaged books and individual pages of Arabic text, fused together by rain and dampness for over one thousand years.

By realizing the potential importance of the find, the President of *Yemeni Antiquities Authority* sought international assistance in examining and preserving the fragments because no scholar in his country was capable of working on this rich find. In 1979, he managed to interest a visiting German scholar who in turn persuaded the German government to organize and fund a restoration project. Soon after the project began, it became clear that the "paper grave" was a resting place for, among other things, tens of thousands of fragments from close to a thousand different codices of the Qur'an. Muslim authorities during early days cherished the belief that worn out and damaged copies of the Qur'an must be removed from circulation leaving only the unblemished editions. Also such a safe place was required to protect the books from looting or destruction if invaders come and hence the idea of a grave in the Great Mosque in Sana'a.

Restoration of the manuscripts was organized and supervised by Gerd R. Puin and H. C. Graf V. Bothmer. Carbon-14 tests date some of the parchments to 645-690. Calligraphic dating has pointed to 710-715. Some of the parchment pages seemed to date back to the seventh and eighth centuries (Islam's first two centuries), perhaps the oldest Qur'an in existence. Between 1983 and 1996, about fifteen to forty thousand pages were restored, specifically twelve thousand fragments on parchment and manuscripts dating back to the seventh and eighth centuries.

The rare style of fine and artistic handwriting fascinated both Puin and Bothmer, but more surprise was waiting for them. When these ancient Qur'ans were compared with the present standard one, both of them were shocked. The ancient texts were found to be devastatingly and disturbingly at odds with the existing form. There are unconventional verse ordering, small but significant textual variations, different orthography (spelling) and different artistic embellishment (decoration).

It scattered the orthodox Muslim belief that the Qur'an, as it has reached us today, is quite simply "*the perfect, timeless, and unchanging words of God*". It means; Qur'an has been distorted, perverted, revised, modified and corrected, and textual alterations had taken place over the years purely by human hands. The sacred aura surrounding this holy scripture of Islam, which remained intact for over fourteen centuries, is gone with this astonishing discovery and the core belief of billion plus Muslims that the Qur'an is the eternal, unaltered word of God is now clearly visible as a great hoax, a downright falsehood. Not only this, the Qur'anic claim that "*nobody can alter the words of God*" is also bogus. Muslims call the Qur'an "Mother of Books" and believe no other book or revelation can compare (Caner & Caner, 2002, p. 84). However, it is all gone now; the end result of whole Islamic struggle for fourteen centuries is a big zero.

As if that were not enough, many manuscripts showed the sign of palimpsests, i.e., versions very clearly written over even earlier washed off versions. The underwriting of palimpsest is, of course, often difficult to read visually but ultraviolet photography can highlight them. It suggests that the Sana'a manuscripts are not the only variants but even before that Qur'anic text had been modified and rewritten on the same paper. It means, Allah's claim (Q: 56.77-78; 85.21-22) that original text is preserved in heaven on golden tablets, which none can touch except angels, is also a fairy tale. Puin, after extensively studying these manuscripts, came to the conclusion that the text was actually an evolving text rather than simply the word of God as revealed in its entirety to Muhammad (Warraq, 2002, p. 109), "*So many Muslims have this belief that everything between the two covers of the Qur'an is just God's unaltered word. They like to quote the textual work that shows that the Bible has a history and did not fall straight out of the sky, but until now the Qur'an has been out of this discussion. The only way to break through this wall is to prove that the Qur'an has a history too. The Sana'a's fragments will help us to do this.*"

Puin even concluded (cited Taher, 2000), "*It is not one single work that has survived unchanged through the centuries. It may include stories that were written before the Prophet Muhammad began his ministry and which have subsequently been rewritten*". Elsewhere Puin (Lester, 1999) recalls, "*They [Yemeni authorities] wanted to keep this thing low profile, as we do too, although for different reasons. They don't want attention drawn to the fact that there are Germans and others working on the Qur'ans. They don't want it made public that there is work being done at all, since the Muslim position is that everything that needs to be said about the Qur'an's history was said a thousand years ago.*"

In fact, Puin and Bothmer knew for sometime during their study that Qur'an was an evolving text but they knew the possible implications of their findings and kept quiet. If Yemeni authorities come to know about this discovery, they may even refuse them further access. This is actually what Puin called "different reasons". So both sides kept quiet, and the research was carried on unabated. Puin's findings also confirm Wansbrough's theory on Qur'anic text. During the seventies, Wansbrough concluded that Qur'an evolved only gradually in the seventh and eighth centuries after a long period of oral transmissions and different sects used to argue furiously with each other on the genuineness of the revelations. The reason that no Islamic source material from the very beginning of Islam never survived is because it never existed. In fact Puin admitted that he was *"re-reading Wansbrough"* during the course of analyzing the Yemeni fragments (Warraq, 2002, p. 122).

Puin's other radical theory is that pre-Islamic sources have entered the Qur'an. He argues that two tribes it mentions, *As-Sahab-ar-Rass* (Companions of the Well) and the *As-Sahab-al-Aiqa* (Companions of the Thorny Bushes) were not part of the Arab tradition, and the people of Muhammad's time certainly did not know about them. He also disagrees that Qur'an was written in the purest Arabic. The very word "Qur'an" itself is of foreign origin. Contrary to popular Muslim belief, the meaning of Qur'an is not recitation. It is actually derived from an Aramaic word, "Qariyun", meaning a lectionary of scripture portions appointed to be read at divine service. Qur'an contains most of the Biblical stories in a shorter form, and is *"a summary of the Bible to be read in service"*.

Bothmer had painstakingly finished taking more than thirty-five thousand microfilm pictures by 1997 and brought the pictures back to Germany (Warraq, 2002, p. 109). It means; now Bothmer, Puin and other scholars will finally have a chance to scrutinize the texts and to publish their findings freely. Puin already wrote several short essays on their findings in various science magazines where he pointed out several aberrations between the ancient Qur'an and the present standard one. The extraordinary discovery of Puin had fascinated Rippin, as he concluded (cited Warraq, 2002, p. 110), *"The impact of the Yemeni manuscripts is still to be felt. Their variant readings and verse orders are all very significant. Everybody agrees on that. These manuscripts say that the early history of Qur'anic text is much more of an open question than many have suspected. The text was less stable and therefore had less authority than has always been claimed"*.

Warraq (1998, p. 14) has the same view as Rippin, *"Muslim scholars of the early years of Islam were far more flexible in their position, realizing that parts of the Qur'an were lost, perverted, and that there were many thousand variants which made it impossible to talk of 'the' Qur'an"*.

There is another proof that Qur'anic messages were distorted in the early days of Islam and nothing like "the" Qur'an does exist any more. Inscriptions of several Qur'anic verses are decorated on the Dome of Rock of Jerusalem which is most probably the first Islamic monument meant to be a major artistic achievement, built in 691 (Whelan, 1998, pp. 1-14). These inscriptions significantly differ from the present standard text. Coins from 685 have inscriptions that do not match today's verses (Warraq, 2000, p. 34).

Muslim criticism of Qur'an is very rare and almost nonexistent. Recently some websites critical to Islam are doing remarkable work on this. Otherwise whatever criticism is done on Qur'an are all by the Christian scholars. But Muslims should not take the Christian criticism as a mark of religious opposition. Christian scholars have done much more criticism of their own faith than Islam (Sproul & Saleeb, 2003, p. 17; Spencer, 2007, p. 1).

Once the findings of Sana'a are published, Islam will not be the same as it was for fourteen centuries. Muslims will cast doubt on Qur'anic sacredness and the very "romantic" concept of the Qur'an will gradually disappear, and a very interesting development can be observed. The first question which will appear in their mind is – which version is superior. But then, it is not possible to choose a Qur'an and discard the other copies by preference, because the Muslim belief also confirms that whoever denies a single verse of the Qur'an denies the entire revelation.

To protect the Qur'an from humiliation, Yemeni authorities had debarred Puin and Bothmer from further examination of the manuscripts. In fact, now they do not allow anyone to see those manuscripts except some very carefully selected non-Qur'anic parchments which are at display at the ground floor of Dar al-Makhtutat Library. But this is not going to help; the bird is already out of the cage and it is useless closing the door now. More than thirty-five thousand microfilms are out of Yemen before the authorities even came to know and already several duplicates are made. These microfilms, once published, will hammer the last nail in the coffin of Islam. Islam is in real danger now.

Ursula Dreibholz, a preservation expert who worked on the Sana'a project for eight years as the chief conservator, is much frustrated by seeing the lack of concern of Yemeni authorities to protect those manuscripts by using modern technology (1983, pp. 30-8). Neither the security devices are correct, nor is adequate attention being given to the manuscripts to avoid further deterioration (1996, pp. 131-45). In fact, Dreibholz (1999, pp. 21-5) said that it was her greatest concern to create a safe and reliable permanent storage system for the restored fragments. Also, there is poor storage, hardly any protection from insects and water. Most importantly, there is the lack of a fire prevention or detection system, keeping in mind the truly catastrophic fires that have destroyed important libraries and artworks around the world. The Yemeni authorities said neither they have money nor means to install efficient fire protection systems.

Obviously, by realizing the divine downfall within sight, many Muslims are disturbed and offended. The fundamentalists will not accept Puin's and Bothmer's work as having been done with academic objectivity, but see it as a deliberate attack on the integrity of the Qur'anic text (Taher, 2000). Naturally, those two German scholars will be at the forefront of their rage. Puin fears a violent backlash from orthodox Muslims because of his "blasphemous" theory, which he says, he cannot take lightly. By remembering the Salman Rushdie affair he wrote, "*My conclusions have sparked angry reactions from orthodox Muslims. They have said I'm not really the scholar to make any remarks on these manuscripts*". If Puin's views are taken up and trumpeted in the media, and if there are not many Muslims being rational about it, then all hell may break loose. There will be some hostile response and riots causing much death and destruction, may be another fatwa from Iranian Mullahs. But can they stop the truth from spreading?

4.3: The Trustworthiness of Allah and His Qur'an

The value and importance of truth is proclaimed in every religion. Bible does not condone or allow for deceit of any kind (Revelation: 22.15). Believers are commanded to keep their oaths even to their own detriment (Joshua: 9; Psalm: 15.4). Bible describes Jesus as Truth (John: 14.6) and instructs that the believers should be holy as God is Holy (Leviticus: 19.2; Peter: 1.16), you will know the truth, and the truth will set you free. (John: 8.32).

In Hinduism; the guiding principles of the Vedas are truthfulness and non violence. Traditionally Hinduism (more specifically Vedanta philosophy) considers itself to be *Sanatana Dharma* (eternal religion), and known to be Universalist and accepts all other religions to be true and valid. According to the authority of Bhagavad-Gita, the Absolute Truth is the objective of devotional sacrifice, which continues through many incarnations. As example; those who are devotees of other Gods and who worship them with faith actually worship only me (Lord Krishna) (Bhagavad-Gita: 9.23) and, I am the source of all spiritual and material worlds. Everything emanates from Me (Bhagavad-Gita: 10.8). In Sikhism, we find similar truth claims, as example; All Truth, all austere discipline, all goodness, all the great miraculous spiritual powers of the *Siddhas* (enlightened master or guru) without you, no one has attained such powers, Oh siblings of Destiny, follow the Guru's teachings and dwell in truth. Practice truth, and only truth, and merge in the true word of the *Shabad* (a sacred song) (Siri Guru Granth Sahib).

Muslim apologists repeatedly tell us that telling lies is an unpardonable sin in Islam. As Qur'an is a cheap copy of the Bible, it tries to condemn falsehood in few verses.

When you speak, be just, even if it affects your own kinsmen. Fulfill the covenant of Allah. (Q: 6.152).

Confound not truth with falsehood, nor knowingly conceal the truth. (Q: 2.42)

Now, based on the above verses, we should never expect Muhammad to tell lies, or to fervently incite other Muslims to gleefully resort to lies and deception, but no. The statement – lying is the greatest sin in Islam – itself is the greatest lie ever told. Both Muhammad and Allah were habitual liars. He even taught his followers how to lie and deceive because deception is an authorized Islamic strategy. In Islam lying is not only permitted, but actually fostered and sometimes even commanded. No doubt, lying is a core part of the religion of Islam. Though Muhammad did his best to pretend that he was chosen by the same God who gave missions to Moses and Jesus but with regard to lying and deceit, he stuck to his tribal culture. Allah claims at least thirty times in the Qur'an that he misleads people astray, and that He is the best deceiver (Wallahu khairul Makirin) (Q: 3.54; 4.88, 143; 6.39, 126; 7.178, 186; 8.30; 13.27, 31; 14.4; 16.93; 17.97; 30.29; 35.8; 36.8-10; 39.23; 40.33, 34, 74; 42.44, 46; 74.31). Even the first rightly guided Caliph Abu Bakr said (cited Khalid, 2005 p. 99), *"I swear to Allah that I do not feel safe from Allah's cunning even if one of my feet is already inside Paradise...."*.

God playing with men's souls is an embarrassing thing in a religion. How are Muslims to differentiate between Allah and Satan? How a "khairul Makirin" can be trusted? Satan does all he can to keep an unsaved person deceived and in darkness. For Muslims, Muhammad was the "perfect example" to be followed by all. This "perfect example" Muhammad believed that lying was acceptable and even taught his followers how to lie and how to expiate (make amends for) an oath. Bukhari recorded Muhammad's disgraceful words,

Narrated by Zahdam; Once we were in the house of Abu Musa ... by Allah, Allah willing, if ever I take an oath to do something, and later on I find that it is

more beneficial to do something different, I will do the thing which is better, and give expiation for my oath. (Bukhari: 4.53.361).

If we translate the above Hadith in common English, it means – "By the will of Allah, I am a liar; you should not trust me. You are forewarned". Now let us read the above Hadith in conjunction with following Hadith. These two quotes, if joined together, speak volumes.

Abu Musa reported the Apostle of Allah as saying: Make intercession to me, you will be rewarded, for Allah decrees what He wishes by the tongue of His Prophet" (Sunnan Abu Dawud: 3.5112).

Therefore, the conclusion is, Allah speaks through a liar's mouth. Nobody had seen or heard Allah, and Qur'an was revealed through a habitual liar. So where is the trustworthiness of Qur'an? The above two ahadith are enough to destroy the entire religious credential of Qur'an. How can a real God speak through an immoral and untrustworthy person? If Prophet is immoral, his God has to be immoral. Lying and deception had found a place in the Sharia law. It permits a Muslim to tell lies if and when necessary for the benefit of Islam. As Keller (1999, p. 745) commented, *"When it is possible to achieve such an aim (the victory of Islam) by lying but not by telling the truth, it is permissible to lie if attaining the goal is permissible."* Imam Jafar Sadiq (cited Richardson, 2006a, p. 170) said,

One, who exposes something from our religion, is like one who intentionally kills us.

You belong to a religion that whosoever conceals it, Allah will honor him and whosoever reveals it, Allah will disgrace and humiliate him.

This is called al-taqiyya (legal deception) in Islam which allows the Muslims to literally deny any aspect of their faith, and defined as, *"Taqiyya is merely uttering of the tongue, while the heart is comfortable with faith."* (Richardson, 2006a, p. 172). The ultimate purpose of taqiyya is to confuse and split the enemy so that they can be defeated easily. Deception for the cause of Islam was one of the main reasons Islam spread in Malaysia and Indonesia. Muhammad saw nothing wrong in practicing duplicity. According to Allah, treaties are not binding (Q: 47.35; 2.224, 225; 66.1, 2; 16.91, 94) and used to provide time to regroup and rearm. Muhammad's common practice was to say one thing and do exactly the opposite if something appealed to him otherwise. He sent men to kill people unaware in their homes and also gave them permission to tell lies in order to deceive the people being killed. No Muslim could ever believe that Muhammad would have ever denied that he was sent by Allah as a messenger. But Muhammad exactly did that.

When Allah's Apostle concluded a peace treaty with the people of Hudaibiya, Ali bin Abu Talib wrote the document and he mentioned in it, "Muhammad, Allah's Apostle." The pagans said, "Don't write: 'Muhammad, Allah's Apostle', for if you were an apostle we would not fight with you." Allah's Apostle asked Ali to rub it out, but Ali said, "I will not be the person to rub it out." Allah's

Apostle rubbed it out and made peace with them on the condition that the Prophet and his companions would enter Mecca and stay there for three days, and that they would enter with their weapons in cases. (Bukhari: 3.49.862).

An "immoral" god cannot be trusted. If a god needs to lie to propagate his faith there is a problem. The dishonest god of Islam is not worthy of a religion, devotion, sacrifice, or martyrdom. With such an ungodly god, the reliability of Qur'an is also gone. Islam is nothing more than a wicked plan of a malignant Narcissist for making profit. The deception is at the very core of Islam and Muhammad. I cannot find any difference between Muhammad and a con man on the street.

Muhammad was the most evil man who ever lived on the earth, and Islam is the most hateful and violent fraud ever perpetrated on humankind. Both Allah and Qur'an were created from the sick mind of a malignant Narcissist. Every established religion has produced some spiritual books which they claim to be holy. The trustworthiness of these books is often doubted by the rivalries. But Qur'an is a book which is proven to be the most untrustworthy and most hateful amongst all. The author of the Qur'an is a deceiving god and his spokesman is a confirmed liar by his own conviction. Though Qur'an claims to be a divine guidance, in reality it revealed the path to damnation.

I agree that to accuse someone of being a liar is quite an insult. But lying is practiced so much by common Muslims and the scholars alike that it became an integral part of their religion. So if I do not call them liars and put them on the same line with non-Muslims, it would be an insult to the rest of the humanity. Muhammad started it and it is continued throughout the history of Islam, and now the most respected scholars allow lying as a means to propagate Islam. According to Ibn Kathir's Tafsir - verse 3.28 (cited Richardson, 2006a, p. 173),

Abu Ad-Darda said, 'We smile in the face of some people although our hearts curse them'.

Sunnis often say that the doctrine of taqiyya is a Shiaa practice, but according to Ibn Kathir's Tafsir, taqiyya is indeed a doctrine for all Muslims and it is allowed until the Day of Resurrection. Taqiyya holds a central place in Islam. Since the god is not trustworthy, the holy book is not trustworthy and the Prophet was not trustworthy; how the followers can be trustworthy? A poisonous tree produces only poisonous fruits.

4.4: Who wrote the Qur'an?

The untrustworthy God of Islam made a big claim in the Qur'an,

Do they not consider the Qur'an (with care)? Had it been from other than Allah, they would surely have found therein much discrepancy. (Q: 4.82).

It means, Allah boasts that since this book is written by Him, there cannot be any error. This should hold true for all times, because God is supposed to be eternal. However, such is not the case. This book is full of contradictions. No one has to dig deep to find the truth. Even a quick reading of the Qur'an is sufficient to prove that it is a fraud. The opening Surah Fatihah of Qur'an is as below,

> *In the name of the Merciful and Compassionate God, Praise belongs to God, the Lord of the worlds, the merciful, the compassionate, the ruler of the day of the Day of Judgment! Thee we serve and Thee we ask for aid. Guide us in the right path, the path of those Thou art gracious to; not to those Thou art wroth with, nor of those who err.* (Q: 1.1-7).

The above words are addressed to Allah in the form of a prayer. But, is it Allah, who is praying to Himself? Or, is it Muhammad's words of prayer to God? Some Muslim compilers conveniently add the imperative "say" in the English translation of the Qur'an at the beginning of the Surah to remove the difficulty. This imperative form of the word "say" occurs at least 350 times in the Qur'an which is lacking in the original Arabic version. It is obvious that this word has, in fact, been inserted by later compilers to remove countless similarly embarrassing difficulties. So now we have direct evidence that the Qur'an starts out with the words of Muhammad.

But even after inserting the word "say" the difficulty is not removed. Qur'an, the perfect words of Allah, is supposed to be in existence even before the creation of humankind. This means, the above Surah has always existed as part of this eternal speech, and yet this is clearly a prayer that is being offered in worship to God. What sense does it make that God in eternity instructs people how to pray to him, when those people do not even exist? Who was offering this specific prayer before creation? Who are the objects of the plural pronouns that appear in the above Surah? It cannot be angels or jinns since they did not exist before creation, and it definitely was not humans. The only logical answer is that it is Allah who is praying here, that He is glorifying and praising Himself. Otherwise these are Muhammad's words put in the name of Allah.

There are many verses in the Qur'an where the speaker is clearly Muhammad.

> *I take refuge with the Lord of the Dawn.* (Q: 113.1)

If Allah is the only God, then who is the "Lord of the Dawn"? If this verse is true, then the "Lord of the Dawn" must be more powerful than Allah.

> *Indeed there have come to you clear proofs from your Lord; whoever will therefore see, it is for his own soul and whoever will be blind, it shall be against himself and I am not a keeper over you.* (Q: 6.104).

Who is the speaker of the line, "*I am not a keeper over you*"? Is it Allah or Muhammad? In fact Dawood in his translation adds a footnote that the "I" refers to Muhammad here. But what Muhammad's words are doing in the Qur'an?

> *For me, I have been commanded to serve the Lord of this city, Him Who has sanctified it and to whom (Belong) all things; and I am commanded to be of those who bow in Islam to Allah's Will.* (Q: 27.91).

Again, if the speaker is Allah, then who commanded him to serve the Lord of the city? Obviously the speaker is Muhammad, and here he is trying hard to justify killing of innocent Meccans who were not willing to follow his version of God.

So verily I call to witness the planets that recede... (Q: 81.15)

I swear by the afterglow of sunset, and by the night and all that it enshrouded, and by the moon when she is at the full. (Q: 84.16-18)

If the whole universe is created by Allah, why He needs to call to witness the planets and to swear in the name of the moon? Notwithstanding the fact that there is no sacred or supernatural being above Him, amazingly Allah swears oaths in the Qur'an, in seventy-four verses wholly and in seven verses partly (Sherif, 1995, pp. 30-1). It is only the liars who swear on all occasions, small or great, because their ordinary word is not believed. The true man's word, according to the proverb, is as good as his bond. Was it Muhammad's own words attributed to God? Muhammad was unable to disguise his pagan heritage. Pre-Islamic Arabs considered moon as holy deity.

Shall I seek other than Allah for judge, when He it is Who hath revealed unto you (this) Scripture, fully explained? Those unto whom We gave the Scripture (aforetime) know that it is revealed from thy Lord in truth. So be not thou (O Muhammad) of the waverers. (Q: 6.114)

Is Allah Himself asking a question to Himself, if He should seek a Judge? Does this verse make any sense if it is spoken by anyone else other than Allah?

Blessed is He in Whose hand is the Sovereignty, and, He is Able to do all things. (Q: 67.1)

How can Allah bless Himself?

Our Lord! Cause not our hearts to stray after Thou hast guided us, and bestow upon us mercy from Thy Presence. Lo! Thou, only Thou, art the Bestower. (Q: 3.8).

Our Lord! Lo! It is Thou Who gathered mankind together to a Day of which there is no doubt. Lo! Allah failed not to keep the tryst. (Q: 3.9).

In the above verses, Allah is addressing Himself "Our Lord". How can Allah use the pronoun "thou" to Himself? How can He grant mercy to Himself? It seems, every now and then Allah is forgetting that He Himself is Allah and Muhammad was forgetting that Qur'an is supposed to be Allah's words, not his.

Allah has said: Take not (for worship) two gods: for He is just One Allah: then fear Me (and Me alone). (Q: 16.51)

Who is the speaker of the words "*Allah has said*"? No way could Allah have expressed Himself in those words, and even if He did so, it proves that He was crazy. The later part of the sentence *"then fear Me"* indicates whom? It is definitely not Allah, because he already said before *"He is just One Allah"*. So this "Me" should be someone else and he is also the speaker of the verse.

A logical study of the Qur'an will show sufficient verses where the speaker was someone else other than Allah, or there were multiple authors of one single verse. As example, the following verse,

Nothing of our revelation (even a single verse) do we abrogate or cause be forgotten, but we bring (in place) one better or the like thereof. Knowest thou not that Allah is Able to do all things? (Q: 2.106)

If Allah is the only God, then "We" includes who else? Was it Muhammad? Does it mean Muhammad had the power of abrogating verses and bringing new verses? If it is true then in which respect Allah was greater than Muhammad? Same problem arises in the following verses,

And We have not taught him (Muhammad) poetry, nor is it meet for him. This is naught else than a Reminder and a Lecture making plain. (Q: 36.69).

Lo! We inspire thee as We inspired Noah and the prophets after him, as We inspired Abraham and Ishmael and Isaac and Jacob and the tribes, and Jesus and Job and Jonah and Aaron and Solomon, and as We imparted unto David the Psalms. (Q: 4.163)

The question is; who used to teach and inspire Muhammad besides Allah? Again, in the following verse; the use of the words like "He said", "your Lord says", "easy to me" in one sentence are not only confusing but also self-contradictory. The author of this verse is utterly confused.

He said: So shall it be, your Lord says: It is easy to Me, and indeed I created you before, when you were nothing. (Q: 19.9).

In the following verse, both Allah and Muhammad speak together.

Glorified be He Who carried His servant by night from the Inviolable Place of Worship to the Far distant place of worship the neighborhood whereof We have blessed, that We might show him of Our tokens! Lo! He, only He, is the Hearer, the Seer. (Q: 17.1)

A merciful, compassionate and all-wise God cannot praise Himself. The first sentence of the above verse is Muhammad's thanksgiving to God for His favor. In the second sentence Allah is speaking. The third sentence is clearly Muhammad's word.

The above verses lead to one conclusion – Muhammad was the actual author of this book. There is no way the Creator of the universe wrote a book devoid of context, without chronology or intelligent traditions. Muslims say that Muhammad was illiterate; therefore he could not be the author of Qur'an. In this case the next best logical conclusion is – he must have engaged several scribes to compose the verses conveying whatever he had in his own mind (the master plan of a malignant Narcissist). Muhammad had neither shortage of money nor all his gang members illiterate. Many of his advisors were literate. Then Qur'an was the handiwork of a few wicked people who were working for him. Finally, a timely ecstatic seizure, perspiration, foaming in the mouth, etc, or some kind of overacting used to give his fabrications divine approval. In fact Qur'an itself confirms the Meccan allegation against Muhammad that he forged the Qur'an with the help of other men. Their accusations were not without merit; Muhammad did have a lot of editorial help.

Those who disbelieve say: This is naught but a lie that he hath invented, and other folk have helped him with it, so that they have produced a slander and a lie. (Q: 25.4)

Let us analyze two more verses.

*So blessed be Allah, the **Best of creators!*** (Q: 23.14)

*Will ye cry unto Baal and forsake the **Best of creators**,* (Q: 37.125)

If Allah is the "best of creators", then there must be some other Gods besides Allah who are also "creators". Therefore, if Qur'an agrees that there are other Gods besides Allah, is Islam monotheism or polytheism? Hence "*There is no god but Allah*" is a false statement. It should be corrected as – "There are many Gods but Allah is the best". However the above two verses contradict the following verse.

Unto Allah belongs whatsoever is in the heavens and the earth. Lo! Allah, He is the Absolute, the Owner of Praise. (Q: 31.26)

If Allah has competitors and there exists other Gods who are also creators, then Allah cannot be the "*Absolute, the Owner of Praise*". According to me, this is the biggest blunder Muhammad made in his Qur'an.

Qur'an is not only a bundle of contradictions but also a volume of confusion. A true God is neither the author of confusion nor contradictions. These confusions and contradictions coupled with the historic blunders and errors may explain why Muslim scholars resist any serious analysis of the Qur'an.

Those who tell lies cannot get away so easily. Befooling others by telling lies in the name of God is a serious crime, and criminals always leave a clue behind. In all the above verses, the fake Prophet of Islam is caught red-handed. Allah was the rock God of Pagan Arabia. A rock cannot reveal anything to anyone; it is the superstition behind the rock that deceives the mind and the heart. Muhammad, the living God of the Muslims, revealed the Qur'an. And if we borrow words from J. von Hammer (cited Warraq, 1998, p. 97), "*We hold the Qur'an to be as truly Muhammad's word as the Muhammadans hold it to be the word of God*". As Cook and Crone (1977, p. 18) concluded, "*[The Qur'an] strikingly lacking in overall structure, frequently obscure and inconsequential in both language and content perfunctory in its liking of disparate materials and given to the repetition of whole passages in variant versions. On this basis, it can be argued that the book is the product of a belated and imperfect editing of materials from a plurality of traditions*".

In refuting the sacredness of Qur'an, Puin (cited Warraq, 2002, pp. 112, 121) commented,

My idea is that the Qur'an is a kind of cocktail of texts that were not all understood even at the time of Muhammad. Many of them may even be a hundred years older than Islam itself. The Qur'an claims for itself that it is 'mubeen', or clear. But [contrary to popular belief] if you look at it, you will notice that every fifth sentence or so simply does not make sense ... the fact is that a fifth of the Qur'anic text is just incomprehensible. If the Qur'an is not comprehensible, if it cannot even be understood in Arabic, then it's not translatable into any language. That is why Muslims are afraid. Since the Qur'an claims repeatedly to be clear but is not — there is an obvious and serious contradiction. Something else must be going on.

Allah loved Muhammad so much that Muhammad was allowed to change Allah's name in the Qur'an.

The Prophet said: Ubayy, I was asked to recite the Qur'an. I was asked: In one mode or two modes? The angel that accompanied me said: Say in two modes. I said: In two modes. I was again asked: In two modes or three? The angel that was in my company said: Say, in three modes. So I said: In three modes. The matter reached up to seven modes. He then said: each mode is sufficiently health-giving, whether you utter "all-hearing and all-knowing" or instead "all-powerful and all-wise". This is valid until you finish the verse indicating punishment on mercy and finish the verse indicating mercy on punishment. (Sunnan Abu Dawud: 1.1472)

Even Muslim scholars have accepted this; e.g., Professor Ahmad Hasan, the translator of Sunnan Abu Dawud, wrote, "*The Prophet was allowed to make minor changes in the name of Allah at the end of the verses. But ordinary persons cannot be allowed to do so*" (Hasan, 2001, p. 387, foot note 819). This way if Allah had allowed Muhammad to make minor changes in the Qur'an, how can we say that Qur'an is the pure words of God?

Critics often complain that Qur'an was written haphazardly. Sometimes Allah refers to Himself in third person singular (He), then shifts to first person plural (We) and sometimes to first person singular (I and Me). Why Allah used this unusual way of speech? If Qur'an is the words of Allah, then Allah cannot allude to himself in third person. If we read the Qur'an thoroughly, we will find this error in the entire Qur'an. Also, these shifting of pronouns are without any prior indication. According to a prominent Islamic scholar, Abdel Haleem (1992); the most common type of shifting is from third to first person (over one hundred and forty instances), then first to third person is the second largest (nearly one hundred instances), third to second person (nearly sixty instances) and second to third person (about thirty instances). For example, I have chosen some Qur'anic verses on intercessions. Unusual shifting of pronouns is highlighted.

Ask forgiveness for them (O Muhammad), [speaking in 1st person] or ask not forgiveness for them; though thou ask forgiveness for them seventy times Allah

will not forgive them [switching to 3rd person]. That is because they disbelieved in Allah and His messenger, and Allah guides not wrongdoing folk. (Q: 9.80)

So know (O Muhammad) that there is no Allah save Allah, and ask forgiveness for thy sin and for believing men and believing women [speaking in 1st person]. Allah knoweth [shifting to 3rd person] (both) your place of turmoil and your place of rest. (Q: 47.19)

And do not plead on behalf of those who act unfaithfully to their souls; [speaking in 1st person] surely Allah does not love [shifting to 3rd person] him who is treacherous, sinful. (Q: 4.107)

And never (O Muhammad) [1st person] pray for one of them who died, nor stand by his grave. Lo! They disbelieved in Allah and His messenger, [switching to 3rd person] and they died while they were evil-doers. (Q: 9.84)

And Noah called upon his Lord, [3rd person] and said: "O my Lord! surely my son is of my family! and Thy promise is true, and Thou art the justest of Judges!" He said: "O Noah! He is not of thy family: For his conduct is unrighteous. So ask not of Me that of which thou hast no knowledge! I give thee counsel, lest thou act like the ignorant!" [while talking to Abraham Allah uses the correct pronoun and when speaking to Muhammad Allah uses a wrong pronoun, suddenly speaking of himself in 3rd person] Noah said: "O my Lord! I do seek refuge with Thee, lest I ask Thee for that of which I have no knowledge. And unless thou forgive me and have Mercy on me, I should indeed be lost! (Q: 11.45-47)

Did Muhammad keep on forgetting that he should represent the Qur'an as word of Allah and hence Allah should not allude to Himself in third person? Many critics have noticed this inconsistency. Bell and Watt (1977, p. 66) wrote, "*The assumption that God is himself the speaker in every passage, however, leads to difficulties. Frequently God is referred to in the third person. It is no doubt allowable for a speaker to refer to himself in the third person occasionally, but the extent to which we find the Prophet apparently being addressed and told about God as a third person, is unusual*".

Muslim scholars have noticed this discrepancy too, but they have a readymade answer for this. They say that Qur'an is a masterpiece of Arabic literature. It is not just a bland piece prose in Arabic that was revealed to hand down some instructions to Muhammad. The unusual use of pronouns is actually a style of presentation. A reader who is not fully conversant with literary writings may consider this as an error of the author (in this case Allah). For this reason, the Qur'anic style of presentation should not be critically examined from the point of view of ordinary logic. In a brief, these apologists want to say that in Allah's language, wrong uses of pronouns add beauty to the language. But the fact is, switching from one pronoun to another without notice only creates confusion and it does not transform a prosaic writing into a masterpiece of literature. It only indicates that the author of the book was either an illiterate man or mentally unstable or both.

Now I should give a scientific explanation. Linguistic beauty is pure nonsense. At times of crisis, or danger, or depression, or when ample narcissistic supply is not available; a strange sensation sets in and pervades the psyche of the Narcissist, and he feels that he is watching himself from outside (Vaknin, 1999, p. 118). This is not an out-of-body experience. The Narcissist does not really "exit" his body nor does he believe that he is doing so, but he simply assumes. For a normal person, such assumption is absurd. In his delusion, involuntarily, the Narcissist takes the position of a spectator, a polite and silent observer, mildly interested of only one person – the Narcissist himself as if he is seeing himself in a movie (Zayn and Dibble, 2007, p. 105). On the screen, he observes events and people, his own experiences and loved ones of his own life. As a spectator, he finds some parts of this "movie" are exciting and some parts may be boring.

This detachment continues for as long as this crisis situation persists. During this time, the Narcissist cannot face who he is, or what he is doing, or what are the consequences of his deeds. Unfortunately, for a Narcissist, this is the case for most of the time, and he gets used to seeing himself in the role of the hero of a motion picture or of a novel. This strange pattern of behavior fits well with his grandiosity and fantasies. In sum; the Narcissist does not occupy his own soul, nor apparently does he inhabit his own body (Vaknin, 1999, p. 119). He is not fully there, entirely present.

In this situation, the Narcissist frequently talks about himself in third person singular. At times he calls his "other" narcissistic self in a different name (Vaknin, 1999, p. 118). Ultimately, this "motion picture solution" becomes the permanent one – an important feature of his own life. He will switch pronoun frequently and without prior notice. Often he will describe his life, its happenings, ups and downs, pain, excitement and disappointment in the most remote voice. So when Allah had sent down some "revelations" to Muhammad, it was, in fact, Muhammad received those instructions from himself while playing two different roles. He switched role frequently without any prior indication. This is the actual reason of using wrong pronouns in the Qur'an – the motion picture solution. As Muhammad changed role, naturally the pronouns were also changed. The very idea that shifting of pronouns makes the Qur'an a masterpiece of Arabic literature is utterly nonsensical. It makes much more sense to recognize this as being a very human error of the person who composed the Qur'an. If we apply the same reasoning to all parts of the Qur'an, there would not be much left as the word of Allah.

The problem is that the Narcissist practically "feels" this way. The presentation of "life as a movie", gaining control by "writing a scenario" or by "inventing a narrative" is a very common trait for a Narcissist. He really experiences his life as belonging to someone else and his body as just a dead weight or as an instrument in the service of some entity (Vaknin, 1999, p. 118). For Muhammad, it was Allah, his own mental figment. So when Muhammad claimed the title of Prophet of Allah, he really "felt" that way. If we say that Muhammad was sincere in his claim it was on which his sincerity based. Those Qur'anic revelations originated from his own sick mind. As Tisdall (cited Trifkovic, 2002, p. 75) concluded, "*The Qur'an is a faithful mirror of the life and character of its author. It breathes the air of the desert, it enables us to hear the battle-cries of the Prophet's followers as they rushed to the onset, it reveals the working of Muhammad's own mind, and shows the gradual declension of his character as he passed from the earnest and sincere though visionary enthusiast into the conscious imposter and open sensualist. All this is clear to every unprejudiced reader of the book*".

In this respect, every verse is meaningful if analyzed from a Narcissist's point of view. These revelations, put in the name of God, actually sanctioned Muhammad for his personal pursuit of sex, plunder and to fulfill his strong desire to achieve power even to solve his domestic problem. Now we know why Allah was always at readiness to entertain Muhammad.

Allah spies on Muhammad's wives and alert him on various domestic issues.

The Prophet confided a certain matter to one of his wives but thereafter she disclosed it, then Allah revealed what she had done to him. He made part of it known and another part not. And when he acquainted her with it, she said: 'Who has told you this'? He replied: 'I was told of it by the Knower, the Aware.' (Q: 66.3)

If both of you (wives) turn to Allah in repentance, even though your hearts inclined; but if you support one another against him, (know that) Allah is his Guardian, and Gabriel, and the righteous among the believers; and thereafter the angels are his reinforcers. (Q: 66.4).

We always wonder if God has nothing better job to do. A large portion of the Qur'an is preoccupied with the personal and political affairs of one man and his companions at one particular stage in the history. Most of these statements have no value to any other generation contrary to popular Muslim belief that Qur'an is eternal. Muhammad knew this fact very well. Therefore, he was never interested to compile the verses in a single book before his death.

Another important point needs to be noted. Muhammad said that he used to get revelations only when he slept with Aisha (Bukhari: 3.47.755). It is surprising; why not when he slept with other wives? Very few Islamic scholars will ever try to find out the answer. The fact is; except Aisha, all his wives were grown up and matured. They had seen the wickedness of life. It was not easy to convince these women about his divine communications with Allah via Gabriel. But Aisha was a kid. With all her childlike simplicity and innocence, it was easy for Muhammad to exploit her. She was completely dependent on Muhammad's maturity, and was ready to believe in whatever he told her about Allah, Gabriel, revelations, etc. Following Hadith will throw some more light on Muhammad's deception.

Narrated Abu Salama: 'Aisha said that the Prophet said to her "O 'Aisha' This is Gabriel and he sends his salutations to you." 'Aisha said, "Salutations to him, and Allah's Mercy and Blessings be on him," and addressing the Prophet she said, 'You see what I don't see'. (Bukhari: 4.54.440).

If Gabriel could come in front of Aisha to give Muhammad Allah's revelations, what made him shy to show his face to the child? Children are sinless; there was no reason why Gabriel could not show him to the child. But no; the Narcissist's manipulative capacity has its limits. Let alone Aisha; no one had ever seen Gabriel because all those divine confrontations were drama.

Bukhari recorded (6.61.512) that once a blind man corrected Allah's revelation.

Ibn Umm Maktum, a man from Mecca, requested Muhammad to correct a verse to exempt him to join in a jihad because of his blindness. When a jihadi verse was revealed, *"Not equal are those believers who sit (at home) and those who strive and fight in the Cause of Allah."* (Q: 4.95), Ibn Umm Maktum said, *"O Allah's Apostle! What is your order for me (as regards the above verse) as I am a blind man?"* Therefore Allah changed His mind and corrected His verse, *"Not equal are those believers who sit (at home) except those who are disabled (by injury or are blind or lame, etc.) and those who strive and fight in the cause of Allah."*

Thus, we can see how cleverly Muhammad had corrected, deleted, and modified the contents of a verse to suit his purpose. Qur'an itself confirms that there was a human hand which was involved in the construction of the Qur'an and his identification is also revealed.

*Rather, I swear by the returning orbiting, disappearing; by the night when it approaches and the morning when it extends, **it is indeed the word of an Honorable Messenger of power**, given a rank by the Owner of the Throne, obeyed, and honest.* (Q: 81.15-21)

Many Muslim scholars, unable to defend, concoct that the above verses refer to Gabriel, as the "Honorable Messenger" of Allah. Even then, those verses indicate that the Qur'an contains Gabriel's words and not completely Allah's words. However, the next two verses help us to recognize this Honorable Messenger. It was obviously not Gabriel.

And your companion is not gone mad. (Q: 81.22)

And of a truth he saw himself on the clear horizon. (Q: 81.23)

4.5: Internal Contradictions of the Qur'anic Verses: A Logical Explanation

The Qur'anic verses were revealed according to the caprices of Muhammad as if it was Muhammad who instructed God and Gabriel in what verses Allah must reveal to him. That is why many verses were revealed for worthless reasons while many other contradicted each other and laws of logic. When Muhammad was weak, Allah revealed the following verses,

And bear with patience what they utter, and part from them with a fair leave-taking. Leave Me to deal with the deniers ... (Q: 73.10, 11)

And do not dispute with the People of the Book (Nazarenes) except in the best manner, except for those among them who do wrong and say (to them): 'We believe in that which was sent down to us and that which was sent down to you. Our God and your God is One, and to Him we have surrendered. (Q: 29.46),

There is no compulsion in religion. (Q: 2.256)

But when he became strong enough to move from the stage of weakness to the stage of jihad, Allah revealed the following verses which were not so peaceful.

If anyone desires a religion other than Islam (submission to Allah), never will it be accepted of him; and in the Hereafter He will be in the ranks of those who have lost (All spiritual good). (Q: 3.85)

Fight those who do not believe in God and the last day... and fight People of the Book, who do not accept the religion of truth (Islam) until they pay tribute by hand, being inferior. (Q: 9.29).

Fight them, and Allah will punish them by your hands, cover them with shame, help you (to victory) over them, heal the breasts of Believers, (Q: 9.14)

Kill them wherever you find them, and drive them out from wherever they drove you out. (Q: 2.191)

Fighting is enjoined on you, and it is an object of dislike to you; and it may be that you dislike a thing while it is good for you, and it may be that you love a thing while it is evil for you, and Allah knows, while you do not know. (Q: 2.216)

Muslim scholars have noticed the contradictions too. According to them, it is impossible to understand some verses unless the reasons for the revelations were known, because many verses were revealed after certain incident or after a question was directed to Muhammad. But this cannot be true because Qur'an is supposed to be the eternal word of God.

Let us take a set of inconsistent verses – the verses concerning the consumption of alcohol are not in harmony. In the initial days of Islam, before Muhammad gained a following, he presented a moderate approach to intoxicants.

They ask thee concerning wine and gambling. Say: 'In them is great sin, and some profit for men; but the sin is greater than the profit'... Thus does Allah make clear to you the communications that you may ponder (Q: 2.219)

As his power grew, he presented a stronger position. It was not acceptable to Allah to have had any intoxicants close enough to prayers to fog the mind.

O you who believe! Do not go near prayer when you are intoxicated until you know (well) what you say ... (Q: 4.43)

When Muhammad's position was established and he had full control over his followers, Allah forbade the use of intoxicants entirely.

O ye who believe! Intoxicants and gambling, (dedication of) stones, and (divination by) arrows, are an abomination, of Satan's handiwork: eschew such (abomination), that ye may prosper. (Q: 5.90)

Satan's plan is (but) to excite enmity and hatred between you, with intoxicants and gambling, and hinder you from the remembrance of Allah, and from prayer: will ye not then abstain? (Q: 5.91)

Allah's final revelation calls the use of intoxicants "Satan's handiwork". But this put Allah in an awkward position because previously He had approved Satan's handiwork when He said that there was "*some profit for men*" in the use of intoxicants. One may wonder that if Allah is really omniscient and omnipotent and His word unchangeable, why did He not reveal the right verses to His Prophet from the beginning. However, this leads to some questions – Does God vacillate on sin? Would God approve of sin at one time and condemn it later? Does God sometimes loses his wisdom and makes mistakes?

Muslim scholars attempt to explain this contradiction by arguing a principle they call "progressive revelation". It means that a principle is first stated, later, it is elaborated upon, and finally, God's will concerning the matter is clearly stated. This process was deemed necessary because of the extremely corrupt nature of the society in which Muhammad lived. This interpretation technique provides a handy argument for explaining inconsistencies in the Qur'an. The claim is made that they are not really contradictions; they are steps in the progress of revelations.

The contradictions and the inconsistencies show that the Qur'an is incompatible in its assertions and teachings. An inconsistent or contradictory teaching cannot be from a real God. The idea that God would modify truth, which is what progressive revelation really claims, is absurd. Truth does not change.

But I want to give a scientific explanation. This is the typical thinking style of a Narcissist to keep his false self inflated at any cost – even let it be at the cost of the God. Allah revealed verses as situation demanded and as it suited Muhammad's self-serving needs. The Narcissist has a one track mind as if he is playing according to a written script. When difficulty arises he makes changes in the script and then starts all over again. Thus the script and dialogue change as situation changes. As Zayn & Dibble (2007, p. 89) wrote, "*When the things are not going the way the Narcissist intends, he simply rewrites the script. The Narcissist needs to maintain a sense of control in his relationships, so when the things are not going the way the Narcissist intends, a rewrite is necessary.*" When often appears to be mind games to us are merely new scripts for the Narcissist.

This was such a mind game of Muhammad. At any cost the Narcissist wants to ensure self-gratification. Sometimes there are sudden urgencies, sudden change of plan, some new selfish ideas need to be incorporated replacing the old ideas, etc. Muhammad achieved this by abrogating verses and/or revealing verses in perfect contradictory manner. At any cost the show must go on. As situation demanded, he just followed a new script leaving the old one invalid. If the new script demands violence, Allah's verses are violent and if the script is peaceful, the verses are also peaceful. Accordingly, the scene also changes – one moment it is peaceful and in the very next moment it might be violent. So when all the "old" and "new" scripts were compiled into one whole book, what we call Qur'an, the contradictions and irregularities were prominently visible.

Muhammad's followers often did not notice the contradictions because they were blinded in faith. This is the charisma of a Narcissist. But in many cases when the contradictions were prominently noticeable, they maintained silence due to fear – after all who has the courage to challenge Allah's authority. And when there were murmurs of disbelief, Muhammad simply abrogated the old verses with new one, or killed the critics. Surprisingly, these contradictions, inconsistencies and abrogation of verses never bothered Muhammad. Narcissists are goal-oriented and it really does not matter how he achieves his goal. Adding and removing from the script is a minor matter. Zayn & Dibble (2007, pp. 89, 92) described,

A Narcissist sees nothing unusual about it. After all he is in charge of his false self and the script that goes along with it. If he no longer wants to be related to someone a simple rewrite of the script is all that necessary. It is extremely simple.

Some Narcissists are so involved with their scripts and their false selves that they don't see beyond their self-created worlds. Therefore they really are oblivious to the feelings of others.

The Qur'an is, in principle, the source from which the Muslims have drawn their inspiration; but Muhammad had neither time, nor possibly even the intention of establishing an exact doctrine settled in all its details. In his anxiety to attract followers, he tried his best to please everybody. He was diplomatic rather than a legislator. According to circumstances, he expressed an opinion or a theory which he had no hesitation in repealing on the following day, if the interest of the moment demanded it.

4.6: Why Narcissist Muhammad needed the Qur'an?

Muhammad wrote the Qur'an to serve two specific purposes. First; Qur'an was like a status symbol of Islam – Muhammad's only proof of his prophetic claim. Secondly; through Qur'an Muhammad was capable of commanding Muslims in the name of God. He was more concerned for turning his people into a race of warriors. He bestowed on his people a character and determination that only a superb national reformer and a great patriot can do. The big lie of the Qur'an had skillfully and systematically paralyzed the rational faculty of those people who were forcibly converted to Islam. Thus a non-Arab Muslim's life is completely dominated by the spiritual hegemony of Arabia in the expense of his own national honor. Beyond this, this supposed to be holy book of Islam has no other purpose. This book is purely manmade and Muhammad was one of the authors. In acknowledging the claims of the Qur'an as the direct utterance of the divinity, the early manipulators had blocked all the criticism, which could otherwise have exposed it.

Now I will give a scientific explanation. A Narcissist always exaggerates his talents and achievements. He has a grandiose sense of self-importance and expects to be recognized as superior without commensurate achievements. He believes that he is unique and can only be understood by, or should associate with, other special or high-status people or institutions. But deep inside, he is hollow like a bubble – always fearful of being discovered as deceitful. To overcome his fear and to gain trust of the people, the Narcissists like to collect evidences of their dramatic talents, intellectual achievements, extraordinary performances, extreme sexual power or similar kind of things. As Vaknin (1999, p. 147) wrote, "*If he [the Narcissist] is an army man, he will show off his impressive collection of badges, his perfectly ironed uniform, the status symbols of his rank and if he is a clergyman, he will be overly devout and orthodox and place great emphasis on the proper conduct of rites, rituals and ceremonies"*.

In the case of Muhammad, he collected the Qur'anic verses as proof. Vaknin (1999, pp. 145-6) calls these objects as "Narcissistic Handles" which the Narcissist preserves almost compulsively. By interacting with these objects, the Narcissist recreates the narcissistic supply-rich situation. Vaknin (1999, p. 145) wrote, *"[the Narcissist wants to prove that] he is not hallucinating and that what he is telling others regarding himself, his grandiose fantasies, his achievements, brilliance, ideal love, fabulous wealth and regarding his past is true. Contrary to common sense, he is not out to prove anything to the outside world. It is he who is in doubt"*. Qur'an served this purpose for Muhammad. When the Narcissist cannot collect proof of his exaggerated talent, he writes autobiography. Adolf Hitler wrote his autobiography when he was still nobody, so did Stalin. For a Narcissist no subject is as important as his own self. Why would he waste his precious time and genius writing about insignificant things when he can write about such an august being as himself? At least Hitler and Stalin were educated, but Muhammad was illiterate.

Muslims have conditioned themselves to believe in this long existed deception of Muhammad. As a Narcissist, Muhammad projected his false self to his followers and constantly demanded "input" from the outside world. When his followers believed that the Qur'an was written by Allah; Muhammad was self-aware by watching their reactions, by listening to their words and by studying them. Without Qur'an the false self of Muhammad could not stand.

Qur'an was also a useful tool for him to use the fear factor for controlling obedience. There are 146 references to hell in the Qur'an. Out of this, only 6% of those in hell are there for moral failings – murder, theft, etc. The other 94% of the reasons for being in hell are for the intellectual sin of disagreeing with Muhammad – a political crime. Hence, Islamic hell is a political prison for those who speak against Islam (Glazov & Warner, 2007). Islam is actually a political movement in the camouflage of a religion – *"Fear Allah and obey me"* are pure political words. An integral part of Muhammad's prophethood was to build an Arab empire. In a political movement, there is no such thing as a universal statement of ethics. Muslims are to be treated one way and unbelievers another way. The goal is to dominate the entire world under Arab supremacy.

Muslim scholars often try to silence the critics by saying – "If Qur'an is a lie, how the lie survived for so many centuries?" Qur'an survived because Qur'an is not "A Small Lie", but "The Big Lie". The big lies are very powerful, and it always has a psychological effect on the listeners. It is a propaganda technique – the bigger the lie, the more believable it is. Adolf Hitler wrote (1925) in Mein Kampf, *"The broad mass of a Nation will more easily fall victim to a big lie than to a small one."*

Big lies are extraordinarily convincible because it offsets the scale of the listener's common sense, as Sina (2008, p. 179) explains; an ordinary person does not dare to tell a big lie thinking that it would not be believed and he would be ridiculed. Since there is no one who had never told a lie in his life, small lies are often detectable sooner or later. But the big lies are so strange that it often startle the listener. It offsets the scale of our common sense. When the lie is gigantic, the average person is left to wonder how anyone can have the courage, the impudence to say such a thing. Big lies always work wonder in politics. As George Orwell (cites Sina, 2008, p. 179) said, *"Political language ... is designed to make lies sound truthful and murder respectable and give an appearance of solidity to pure wind"*.

Islam is nothing but a pure Arab political movement. Whereas other belligerent nations require armed forces to subdue foreign countries, the Arabs need nothing of the sort. Qur'an does it all for them through an incredible process of brainwashing. It is a rare political skill. Hitler knew it, Stalin knew it – so was Muhammad.

4.7: Conclusion

"Where ignorance is bliss, 'tis [It is] folly to be wise".

Thomas Gray (cited Sagan, 1997, p. 12)

Qur'an is a highly confusing text. It contains commandments so contradictory that it would be difficult to extract any precise rules of conduct from it beyond the recognition of the unity of God and the mission of His messenger. Every single verse of the Qur'an directly or indirectly depicts the changing thought pattern of a severely confused author. Nothing is more foolish than dreaming of a paradise full of worldly pleasures as a reward for causing insult, injury and injustice to others. When the verses of the Qur'an are studied carefully with a critical mind, anyone who knows the different characteristics of narcissism will be able to, without any difficulty whatsoever, to detect that the author was a malignant Narcissist. Not only every verse; but every letter and every word of every verse is the product of Muhammad's own sick narcissistic imagination to achieve his own sick narcissistic ambition and to secure narcissistic supply sources. So, if Qur'an calls itself to be "mubeen", or clear, this is what it means; we have to study the book by the standard of a malignant Narcissist's sick judgment.

Also, Muslims' belief that Allah in heaven, before the advent of Muhammad, wrote the Qur'an on a stone tablet and its text is eternal and unchangeable, is also bogus. If not, the question remains, why then Uthman took the labor to standardize common text and destroyed all the "other" manuscripts? Moreover, we know that many people preferred to recite their own text over the Uthman's text and Uthman was compelled to use the threat of death to force the people to accept his revised text. In the early days, Qur'an was open for debate among different sects of Islam because they had witnessed that a large portion of the book was lost and corrupted. The authenticity of many verses had been called into question by the early Muslims themselves. Many Kharijites, who were followers of Ali, found the verses narrating the story of Joseph offensive, an erotic tale that cannot belong to Qur'an (Warraq, 1998, p. 17). We do not know when religious blindness crept in, but undoubtedly, those early Muslims after Muhammad were more liberal than the present generation we are seeing today. The Mu'tazilites (an Islamic sect, came into being in the second Islamic century) believed that the Qur'an was written by Muhammad himself and denied its revelation to the Prophet by God. They asserted that there is nothing miraculous in the Qur'an and that Arabians could have composed something not only equal, but superior to it, in eloquence, method, and purity of language. The Abbasid Caliph al-Ma'mun adopted the Mu'tazilites ideas about the Qur'an and ordered the chief officials in every province throughout the Islamic empire to publicly announce that the dogma in the Qur'an was created by Muhammad rather than Allah.

Muslims wrongly interpret the honesty Christians display about some variant readings of the Bible as weakness (Ali & Spencer, 2003, pp. 76-9). Christians, like Hindus, want to see their Holy book through scientific and historical point of view, as Rodinson (1980, p. viii) observed, *"[For Bible] the scientific attitude begins with the decision to accept something as fact only if the source has been proved reliable"*. When old manuscripts, or parchments of Christian faith, or ancient sacred manuscripts of Hinduism are discovered; Christian and Hindu scholars almost climb over each other's shoulder to gain an early access to them. Such findings cause great excitement to them. But sadly, no such excitement exists in Islam. Christians and Hindus are eager to see more and more light shed on the earliest manuscripts of their religions, while Muslims resist, often with strong determination. While both Hindu and Christian faiths are strongly backed up by archeological and historical evidence; so far neither any archeological exploration was allowed in Mecca and Medina, nor is there any prospect in the future (Peters, 1986, pp. 72-4). The contrast is really striking.

Since Muslims cannot argue their religion with reason (Islam cannot survive if argued with reason), they resort to pathological lying or narcissistic rage. We often hear two such arguments from them – the "language" argument and the "out of context" argument (Warraq, 2003, pp. 400-4).

When the Qur'anic contradictions, or absurdities, or the violent verses are pointed out, Muslims will ask aggressively, "Do you know Arabic?" Then they tell triumphantly, "You have to read it in original Arabic to understand it fully", or "These are not there in original Arabic Qur'an". With this the Western critics are generally taken aback. Now the question is how many Muslims have read the Qur'an in original Arabic? Since the majority of the Muslims are not Arabs, they have to rely on translations. Moreover the freethinkers and critics do not need to know Arabic; all they need is a critical sense, critical thought and skepticism. The language of Qur'an is a form of classical Arabic which is totally different from the spoken Arabic of today. So, even Arabs have to rely on translations to understand their holy text. Also, when the Muslims criticize Bible and other holy texts of Christianity; how many of them know a word of Hebrew, Aramaic or Greek? When they criticize the holy scriptures of Hinduism, how many of them know Sanskrit? Muslims do not understand that their flawed logic to defend Islam's foolishness goes against them. The Qur'an is indeed a confused text which confuses everyone – either he knows Arabic or not. Also, Muslims around the world preach Islam to make converts in languages other than Arabic. If Qur'an can only be understood in Arabic, why do they do this?

The second argument is, "You have quoted out of context". This "out of context" argument is an old, standby argument of crooked and lying politicians. Though Muslims try to silence the critics by this argument, actually they themselves quote the verses out of context to deceive the critics. This argument has two parts, Historical context and Textual context. Historical context is out of question because Qur'an is supposed to be the eternal words of Allah and its truth and validity must not be limited to a certain period of time. Also, as Spencer observed (2003, p. 127), reading the Qur'an is often like walking in on a conversation between two people with whom one is only slightly acquainted. Frequently they make reference to people and events without bothering to explain what is going on. In other words, the context is often not supplied. Therefore if the context is not given in the Qur'an, how a verse can be quoted out of context?

The remaining is the textual context. No doubt there are some peaceful verses in the Qur'an which were revealed in Mecca. Muslims want to prove that Islam is a peaceful religion by quoting these verses. But all the peaceful verses were abrogated by the violent verses of the ninth Surah because the ninth Surah was revealed later in Muhammad's career. In fact, most Muslim authorities agree that the ninth Surah was the very last section of the Qur'an revealed to him. Many Muslim theologians assert that the verse of sword (Q: 9.5) abrogates as many as 124 more peaceful and tolerant verses of the Qur'an (Spencer, 2007, p. 78; McAuliffe, 2006, p. 218). The ninth Surah is the only one of the Qur'an's 114 chapters that does not begin with "*Bismillah ar-Rahman ar-Rahim*" – "In the name of Allah, the compassionate, the merciful." It is because; Muhammad not only did not recite the Bismillah himself, but commanded that it not be recited at the beginning of this Surah. The *Tafsir al-Jalalayn* explains Muhammad's command by saying that the Bismillah is security, and ninth Sura was sent down when security was removed by the sword. Ali ibn Abi Talib agrees, saying that the Bismillah "*conveys security while this Sura was sent down with the sword. That is why it does not begin with security.*" (Oliver, 2006, p. 537; Spencer, 2009, p. 200). Ibn Kathir declares that the verse of sword (Q: 9.5) has "*abrogated every agreement of peace between the Prophet and any idolater, every treaty and every term ... no idolater had any more treaty or promise of safety ever since the Sura Bara'ah (the ninth Sura) was revealed*" (Spencer, 2003, p. 134). Ibn Juzayy, another commentator, agrees that the verse of the sword's purpose is (Spencer, 2005, p. 25), "*abrogating every peaceful treaty of the Qur'an*".

Therefore, the tolerant verses are practically meaningless. The problem began when Uthman collected the verses of the Qur'an and arranged them in a way that the abrogated verses were mixed up with the abrogating verses (Ahmed, 2006, p. 77). This arrangement led to the appearance of discrepancies and contradiction in the Uthmanic Qur'an, which is used until our present day. The second proof is that the Sharia law does not take into account the peaceful verses because these are abrogated. Like a Narcissist tries to fool the victims with his delusional thoughts, Muslims try to fool the non-Muslims with their twisted logic and pathological lying. They repeat the same lies again and again thinking that it will become true if often repeated. "Islam is a peaceful religion" is a lie which is as old as the birth of Islam. Why do not we find the Taliban terrorists singing the peaceful verses from the Qur'an while beheading the captives? In November 2002, Osama bin Laden quoted eight jihadi verses from the Qur'an in a "Letter to the American People" and in his 1996 declaration of jihad against the USA, he quoted sixteen jihadi verses (Spencer, 2003, p. 125). Long history of lying has caused the Muslims to believe their own lies; they are delusional like their Prophet.

When the Narcissist tells a lie, he is the first person to believe his own lie. Though it looks contradictory, Narcissists are self-delusional. Deep inside, they are capable of distinguishing between a truth and a lie. Muslims distort the meaning of the Qur'anic verses as per their needs and they are well aware of it. As example; though Allah allowed Muslims to marry maximum four wives, many Arab kings, noblemen and oil-rich Sheikhs have a large collection of wives. Akbar, the Mughal Emperor had more than 5000 women (Early, 1977, p. 642). Muhammad's grandson

Hasan had up to 300 wives. How they manage to have so many wives when only four are sanctioned to each of them? It is very simple, only a little manipulation is required. Allah said in the Qur'an (4.3) that Muslims are allowed to marry what seems good to them by two, three or four. This instruction was interpreted in different ways by different Qur'anic scholars – one scholar added two, three and four and got nine wives. Another got a total of eighteen wives by doubling two, three and four and added the results (Eraly, 1997, p. 666).

Secondly, reinterpretation of Qur'anic verses is officially allowed. Sheikh Youssef Alqardawi, the most famous Muslim scholar in the Arab world, appeared on Al Jazeera's weekly program "Sharia and Life", to discuss issues related to Islam and answer some of the questions put to him, through phone calls. On February 22 2009, he rejected the evolution theory, because the Qur'an says otherwise; but he reassured his audience that Muslims do not need to worry about the evolution theory as long as it remains a theory. Only if it becomes a recognized scientific fact, the Muslim scholars would reinterpret the relevant verses in the Qur'an to bring them in line with proven scientific facts (Salih, 2009). Muslims claim that Qur'an is divine, but shamelessly reinterpret the Qur'an by twisting the language and changing the meanings of the words or even introducing completely new meanings. Their logic is simple, "The Qur'an is correct even when it is wrong". Is not it ridiculous?

Throughout the recorded history of Islam; Qur'an, the most unholy religious book, had turned men into monsters – there have been millions of murderers, millions of rapists and millions of terrorists. They commit all sorts of crimes with a clear conscious and in the name of Allah. But while committing crimes in the name of God, they do not question the credibility of the revelations in this book. The God who created man would not deceive him or led him to hell as Allah does. Nor would He order men to terrorize, mutilate, rob, enslave, and slaughter the followers of other scriptures He claims He revealed, wiping them out to the last.

Chapter 5: The Allah Delusion

"Question with boldness even the existence of a God; because if there is one, he must more approve of the homage of reason than that of blindfolded fear".

Thomas Jefferson, 3rd U.S. President

"All religions, with their gods, their demi-gods, and their prophets, their messiahs and their saints, were created by the prejudiced fancy of men who had not attained the full development and full possession of their faculties".

Mikhail Bakunin (1814 - 1876)

All the existing religions acknowledge that God is the Creator of the universe. As Creator of the universe, God must be distinct from the world, and His existence cannot depend on any of His creation. Hence, he is absolutely different from anything else that exists that makes him totally unknowable. Although God Himself is unknowable, we can, to some degree, understand His relationship to the universe. In this manner, we speak of God through His "attributes of action". Though we cannot know what God is, we can learn much by realizing what He is not.

Muslims use the remotest language possible to explain Allah. They try to make Allah as awe-inspiring as possible in order to discourage people from conducting research on him. If a Muslim is asked to define Allah, he will just beat about the bush, ascribing attributes to Allah that neither belong to Him nor befit Him. But Allah is not really as mysterious as Muslims would like the world to believe. When the falsehood of Qur'an is exposed, the falsehood of Allah is also exposed. He has been at the Ka'ba stone all along before Muhammad commenced preaching his religion. Since God is eternal, there is no creator of God. However, since Allah is not a God but pretending to be God, he has a creator. In this chapter I want to find out who had created Allah and how he was created and why he was created.

5.1: Allah: The Ungodly God

"In what concerns Divine things, belief is not appropriate. Only certainty will do. Anything less than certainty is unworthy of God".

Simone Weil (1909 - 1943)

For past several thousand years, there had been two main religious groups predominant in much of the civilized world. One of them was sun worshippers and the other was moon worshippers. The main solar religions thriving today are Hinduism, Christianity and Buddhism (Buddhists follow largely lunar calendar but the main characteristic and many important doctrines and traditions are solar); whereas lunar religions are Islam and Judaism. Hitti (2002, p. 97) writes that the moon-worshiping is principally a pastoral society and the sun-worshiping is mainly an agricultural society.

Allah is at the centre of the Islamic faith. He has quite an interesting history. In ancient Arabia, much before Muhammad, the desert Bedouins used to worship a deity by the name Allah. Those half-starved anarchic tribes had a nomadic life as they were incapable of sustaining an agricultural society (Rodinson, 1980, p. 17). Daytime travel was nearly impossible due to the unbearable heat of the sun. Most journeys were undertaken at night, on moonlight and beneath a sky bedecked with glittering stars. Those indigent Bedouin Arabs were so intimately connected with the moon and its phases that their lives were literally governed by the moon. To them, the moon was their life-sustainer; an absolute holy entity to be worshipped and revered with utmost zeal.

After Muhammad forced Islam on these desert Arab indigents; these neo-Muslim Bedouins still continued with the practice of their age-old belief. Therefore, they associated Allah with the moon – *Allah Taalaa*, the supreme God. Islam is intimately connected with the moon. All its rituals are based on the sighting of the moon or on the moon calendar. Every religious act and ritual, jihad and Islamic bloodshed, attack on non-Muslims and every Islamic law is designed for only one purpose – to please Allah.

Allah revealed the Qur'an to Muhammad but did not reveal Himself in the Qur'an. This is especially puzzling because Allah wants us to know His will even more than we want to know it. He preferred to remain a mystery to the Muslims. In fact this mysterious, intangible nature of Allah is the essence of Islam. Through Qur'anic revelations, Allah notifies the humankind what He likes and expects from us, and what He forbids. But why He does not do that by showing us what it is like to be God? Allah wants absolute obedience and He does not like to be questioned, but in this case how do I know that Allah had really appointed Muhammad to act as a Prophet? In this regard Allah failed miserably. If there was a strictly direct disclosure of Allah, then we could have no further doubt about his existence. As Caird (1956, p. 60) concluded, "*A God who does not reveal Himself ceases to be God; and religious feelings, craving after a living relation to its object, refuses to be satisfied, with a mere initial and potential revelation of the mind and will of God - a God who speaks once for all, and then through the whole course of history ceases to reveal Himself.*"

For us, this is a crucial problem. If there were a direct disclosure of Allah, and we could see Allah strictly as He is, then there could be no doubt about him and his revelations would carry an absolute guarantee in itself and we knew it was Allah who spoke. If it is Allah's intention to confront us with his presence as personal will and purpose, why has this not been done in an unambiguous manner – by some overwhelming manifestation of divine power and glory? As Lewis (1961, p. 228) concluded, "*If God wants to communicate with us in terms of what we understand as finite beings, if He has to make Himself known within the human situation, how are men able to recognize the ways in which He does this, how does an occasion which is in substance a finite one carry with it some reference or overtone which is more than finite?*"

Why Allah did not disclose himself? Is he ashamed of his own creation? As Shaikh (1998a) wrote, "*The cause of God would have been served better if He were to show His face to mankind frequently for assuring them that He is there*". If a child refuses to open his clenched fist to show what he has in it, we may feel sure that it is something wrong – something he ought not to have. Is not the same logic applicable to Allah? Allah did not disclose himself because he lacks one element of perfection, namely "existence", and those Qur'anic revelations are actually a parody of Allah for his imperfection. In fact Allah did not disclose himself to Muhammad also. Qur'an confirms that even Muhammad did not have much knowledge of his Allah. No doubt, Allah was playing a sick game with Muhammad.

I had no knowledge of the Highest Chiefs when they disputed; It is revealed unto me only that I may be a plain warner. (Q: 38.69-70).

What a heavenly paradox – Muslims have to put their trust on Qur'an because their bread and butter in the afterlife will depend on Allah's heavenly pension, but in doing so, they are actually mocking Allah for his imperfection.

Goodness and love are treated as two attributes of God. If Allah is a perfectly loving God, Allah must wish to abolish all evil; and if Allah is all-powerful, Allah must be able to abolish all evil. But evil exists (and more amongst the Muslims); therefore Allah cannot be both omnipotent and perfect loving. So when a revelation describes Allah as all-powerful and merciful, the revelation must be false.

In several verses, Allah prescribes eternal torment of hell for the disbelievers which logically cannot be true. It is unjust for God to burn a disbeliever in hell forever. A disbeliever, being a finite being, can only commit a limited amount of sin in his entire life. Eternal torment of hell is an infinite punishment. It is unfair to punish for a finite amount of sin with infinite torment. Also, since such punishment would never end, what constructive purpose will it serve? Can this give any solution to the problem of evil? Why Allah is silent on this issue and did not send a suitable revelation to justify his divine decision? If eternal torment is Allah's will, then on what basis He is "most gracious, most merciful"?

If God really punishes or rewards a man at His judgment, it is more justified to say, "*Good conduct will be rewarded, and bad conduct punished, either here or in a life hereafter*" (Durant & Durant, 1961, p. 187). In fact, this is same as the "Law of Action and Reaction" (the doctrine of Karma) in Hinduism (Abhedananda, 2005, p. 79). But these moral values are in contradiction with the Qur'an. In countless number of verses Allah punishes a human only because he does not accept Islam. Why Allah needs to resort to sex, violence and torture to gain followers? Why our good conducts have no value? Radhakrishnan (1970, p. 19) wrote, "*We can believe only in a just God, who is impartial to the saint and the sinner even as the sun shines on those who shiver in cold or sweat in heat. God is not angered by neglect or placated by prayers. The wheels of His chariot turn unimpeded by pity or anger. God is not mocked.*"

Thomas (cited Durant, 1950, p. 969) agrees with Radhakrishnan, "*The highest knowledge we can have of God in this life is to know that He is above all that we can think concerning Him*". What we humans are doing always concern Allah. He is believed to watch us day and night like a hawk just waiting for us to disobey Him even once. He is jealous, revengeful, hateful and proud. If Allah is the only God, then he is jealous on whom? How can I call Allah a perfect God? Why is He so upset and suffering from inferiority complex?

When Muhammad started preaching his religion in Mecca, there were never-ending arguments going on between the Meccans and Muhammad over his lack of prophetic credentials. In this regard Allah seemed to be very puzzled in the Qur'an,

Is it that their mental faculties of understanding urge them to this, or are they an outrageous folk, transgressing beyond the bounds? (Q: 52.32)

The above verse demonstrates Qur'an's lack of divine inspiration. A God can never ask such a question if He is all-knowing. We wonder, whose inadequacies are reflected in the above verse, Muhammad or his Allah? The above verse also directly contradicts the following verses.

He (Allah) is the Wise, the Knower. (Q: 43.84)

He hath perfect knowledge. (Q: 2.29)

In fact, Allah itself is a very confusing God. During those days there was much idolatry in practice with hundreds of deities around. This made Muhammad utterly confused. Therefore he experimented with various brands of Allah, but the Meccans disappointed him and hence he changed his mind several times. Every time, as situation demanded, he made some necessary changes to his version of Allah. Finally he designed his own Allah to go well with his requirement and hence Allah has the likes and dislikes similar to Muhammad.

Such a God is an absolute fake. Allah is one of the most famous fictional superheroes of all time. Muhammad had developed a reverse (benign) form of paranoia which is very common to the Narcissists. A Narcissist feels constantly watched over by senior members of his group or frame of reference, the subject of permanent criticism, the center of attention. If a religious man, he calls it divine providence. For Muhammad it was Allah, the superego of his false self.

In the following few pages of this chapter, we will re-discover Allah, wrest him out from the hands of the Islamic clerics, pull him down from his divine position and put him under the limelight for everyone to see his true color. But before we attempt to recognize Allah as Muhammad's superego, we should try to understand the very concept of superego and its importance in the structural model of a human mind, how superego forms, and how much influence does superego can have on the day-to-day business of a normal person (normal in the sense, he is not suffering from NPD) and of a malignant Narcissist.

5.2: Theology versus Psychology and God versus Superego

"Psychology has questions that need to be answered. Theology has answers that need be questioned."

Unknown

"Man is a strange being; he cannot make a flea, and yet he will make gods by dozens."

Michel de Montaigne (1533 - 1592)

"Guilt: Punishing yourself before God doesn't."

Alan Cohen (1954 -)

The basic concept of superego makes common sense to us. Most of us, as adults, often hear of our own superego, while some of us hear it very often. It is the voice in our heads that commands us, "Do not harm others" or screams, "Thou shalt not kill". This internalized authoritative figure which has such a tremendous influence over us and direct us with such a strident voice, is called superego by the psychologists.

Ever since the beginning of human civilization, men have tried mightily to pin down "good" and "evil" and to find some ways to account for those who amongst us seems to be inhabited by the later. In the fourth century, a Chinese scholar Saint Jerome introduced the Greek word "synderesis" to describe the innate God-given ability to differentiate between good and evil (Stout, 2005, p. 27). It was the interpretation of Ezekiel's Biblical vision of four living creatures emerging from a cloud *"with brightness round about it and fire flashing forth continually"* (Barthelemy & Ryan, 1963, p. 112). Each creature had the body of a man but four different faces. The face in front was human, on the right a lion, on the left an ox and the face in back was of an eagle's. The human face represents the rational part of a man, the lion reflects the emotions, ox symbolized the appetites and the eagle's face represents our sinfulness when we are overcome by evil desires.

Augustine, Jerome's contemporary, agreed with Jerome and concluded, *"Men see the moral rules written in the light which is called truth from which all laws are copied"* (cited Bowie & Bowie, 2004, p. 146). However a noticeable problem still remained even after the above theological explanation. If the truth – the absolute knowledge of good and evil – is given by God to all human beings, why all human beings are not good? This question remained at the centre of the theological discussion for several centuries and gave birth to two more questions – Did God withhold the truth from a few of His servants? Why God had created the evil and had distributed it randomly among all the types and enterprises of humanity?

After much debate on the above issues for centuries, the theologians came to the conclusion that if only human reason were perfect, there would not be any bad behavior. Again after much discussion that centered around the relationship between human reason and divinely given moral knowledge, the theologians asked – is there a divine loophole wherein reason asks us to do something "bad" in order to bring something "good"; e.g., a "just war"? In sum; though the theological theories were developed in renowned theological schools throughout the centuries, the confusions were never totally dispelled. To many people it appeared that the God hypothesis was more of a muddle than a mystery.

In the beginning of twentieth century, the theories of a physician/scientist (also a hardcore atheist) on psychology were so revolutionary that they were to *"agitate the sleep of mankind"* (Strachey & Gay, 1961, p. ix). This brilliant researcher was none other than Sigmund Freud, and he argued that religion and science are mortal enemies. Freud dealt with the problem of religion and psychoanalysis in one of his most profound and brilliant books, *The future of an illusion*. His analysis attempted to show why people formulated the idea of a God. The internalized authoritative figure, as proposed by Freud, is not of a divine origin but all-too-human. He called this authoritative figure as "superego".

With this discovery of the superego, Freud effectively wrested "God" out of the hands of theologians and placed him in front of the psychologists for further study. The psychologists and the psychoanalysts are now slowly occupying the priest's domain and the symbol of psychology is overshadowing the symbols of religion. A violent opposition between them is unavoidable once the psychological jargons start contaminating the word of God.

5.3: The Importance of Superego in the Structural Model of a Human Mind

Freud saw the adult personality structured into three parts, the id (real self), the ego (false self) and the superego; all developing at different stages in our lives. All these components are functions of mind, not parts of the brain or in any way physical. They are separate aspects and elements of the single structure of the mind. For Freud, the "eternal struggle" among these forces that occurs at an unconscious level, constitutes the problematic of the human condition. In sum; throughout his analysis, Freud saw "man" as a closed system and this theory characterizes the mental apparatus as a "*dynamic union of opposites*" (Marcuse, 1972, p. 35). In previous chapters, I have already discussed in details the functions of true self and false self and how they interact with each other.

In the initial days when Freud put forward his theory on narcissism, he did not have much clear idea about the function of this third component, superego. In 1914, Freud published the paper *On narcissism: An introduction* where he suggested that the adults are often devoted to an ideal ego which sets up within himself. Freud then put forward the notion that there may be a "special psychical agency" whose task it is to watch the actual ego (the false self) and to measure its strength performance. He attributed a number of functions to this agency, including the normal conscience and certain paranoid delusions. In another 1917 paper *Mourning and Melancholia*, Freud insisted more definitely that this agency is independent and apart from the rest of the ego. In 1921, Freud published one more paper where this was made still more clear. In 1933, Freud concluded that the superego is "*the vehicle of the ego by which the ego measures itself*" (Riviere *et al*, 1960, p. xxxvii). Having securely established the concepts of the ego and the superego, Freud became preoccupied with the relationship of the ego to superego. When the new account of the analysis of the mind was established, it formed the subject of many more new writings which came in rapid succession.

The psychologists have different opinion on when the superego develops. Freud proposed, with much opposition from the existing researchers, that in the normal course of development, young children's minds accrue an internalized authoritative figure (Stout, 2005, p. 30). Eventually this internalized authoritative figure becomes a free standing force when the mind is still developing unilaterally judging and directing the person's behavior and thought. Ultimately it emerges as superego; it is the commanding inner voice that says "NO" even when no one is around.

Therefore, superego might be called the moral part of the mind. It provides guidelines for making judgments. The tension it creates is called by us the sense of guilt and it expresses itself as a need for punishment (Freud, 1989, p. 70). But if the person does something which is acceptable to the superego, he experiences pride and self-satisfaction. It means the person had taken the ideas of punishment, reward, right and wrong into himself. Superego helps the false self to control the urges of true self. It consists of two systems.

The conscience – Conscience is the ability or the faculty that distinguishes whether one's actions are right or wrong. It propels us outward in the direction of other people and punishes us through causing feelings of guilt. It also rewards us when we behave "appropriately" by making us feel proud. Conscience takes the people to streets to protest a war or makes a human right's worker to risk his life. When conscience is combined with surpassing moral courage, we see the great personalities like Mother Teresa, Mahatma Gandhi and Nelson Mandela. In various ways, genuine conscience changes the world.

The ego-ideal – In Freud's psychoanalytic theory of personality, the ego-ideal is the part of the superego that includes the rules and standards for good behavior. These behaviors include those that are approved of by parental and other authority figures. Obeying these rules leads to feelings of pride, value, and accomplishment. In sum; the ego-ideal is an imaginary picture of how we ought to be, and represents career aspirations, how to treat other people, and how to behave as a member of the society.

Stout (2005, p. 31) summed up Freudian theory of superego, "*The superego is not just a voice; it is an operator, a subtle and complex manipulator, a prover of points. It prosecutes, judges and carries out sentences, and it does all these quite outside of our conscious awareness. While the superego, in the best case [for a healthy person], it can help the individual to get along in the society, it can also become the most overbearing and perhaps the most destructive part of his personality*". Superego yammers at us inside our minds everyday of our lives. Some people's superegos are rather more insulting than others.

With the discovery of the superego and a clear understanding of how it influences us, Freud showed us that our usual respect for law and order is not simply imposed on us from the outside. We obey the rules, honor the virtues, help the poor, self-sacrifice cheerfully for the benefit of the others, primarily from an internal need to preserve and remain embraced by our families and the larger human society in which we live.

5.4: The Superego of a Malignant Narcissist

Now we will see how the superego functions in the sick mind of a Narcissist, more precisely, a malignant Narcissist. The malignant Narcissist lacks in a fully developed and healthy superego. It means; these two essential systems of superego, conscience and ego-ideal, do not work well because of their immaturity.

A person with an unhealthy conscience has no intervening sense of obligation to others because he does not feel any emotional attachment with anyone. He also does not know what are the rules and standards for good behavior because his ego-ideal is faulty. Such a person is not structured by regular moral standards because he does not have the ability to distinguish whether his actions are right or wrong. In sum; there is no inner moral judge to teach him moral values. Religious views of conscience usually see it as linked to a morality inherent in all humans, but for the malignant Narcissist, he can become an unattached, conscienceless manipulator, deceiver, and killer. He simply does not have the capacity of seeing himself from the point of view of another person.

Therefore the malignant Narcissist has a twisted superego that plays a very important part in his narcissistic tendency. Though superego claims its position on the basis of the principle of parental authority for the healthy people, it becomes the internal chaos monster of the narcissistic disorders; the patient suffers from various types of obsessions and compulsions. The superego of a Narcissist is very harsh, cruel, uncompromising and punishing and its command is very powerful. In fact, the Narcissist's sense of self-worth is totally at the mercy of his superego. It haunts him every moment of his life to such a degree that he is always at unrest. The concepts of the superego and narcissism are linked at the roots and that superego pathology should be seen as a determining factor in the formation of a narcissistic disorder. The false self of a Narcissist cannot stand without authorization. Here lies the very importance of superego. The term "superego" itself indicates that it dominates the ego (the super inflated ego i.e., the false self); the tension between the two agencies take the form of moral anxiety, mistrust and paranoia.

Superego is as false as the false self of a Narcissist. But while the false self is directed to the outside world, the superego is directed to the Narcissist himself. It punishes the Narcissist for the deeds and misdeeds of his false ego (Vaknin, 1999, p. 328). This punishment creates within the Narcissist a strong feeling of paranoia and injustice. Malignant Narcissists, because of their disorganized superegos and consequent lack of the capacity for self-exploration, are often erratic which leads to self-destructive behaviors and a loss of reality testing (Goldner-Vukov & Moore, 2010, pp. 396-06). He feels punished without any wrongdoing. Just like the false self is the inflation of the true self, the superego is the inflation of the false self. The superego of the malignant Narcissist is very primitive; it has a general propensity for cruelty. Often it is the self-destructive unconscious wish of the Narcissist.

The superego of the Narcissist often takes the authoritative position of God or some kind of superior power which has full authority and control on him. He, by mistake, takes it as a representation of a spiritual call toward enlightenment. When he is deluded, he experiences a higher spiritual state of mind.

The relationship between the false self and superego is very strange. A sadistic, idealized superego and a grandiose, manipulative false self interact with each other mechanically, like master and a slave; there is absolutely no emotional attachment. It is always a terror based abusive relation. The slave is terrorized by the master; he has no free choice. Malignant Narcissists often act like robots, and no robot is capable of introspection. With such an ideal, sadistic, rigid, primitive, and punishing superego, he eventually becomes a zombie lacking in morals and in conscience and becomes antisocial. The superego commands the Narcissist with criticisms, negative evaluations, and angry or disappointed voices. It berates him for failing to conform to his unattainable ideals, fantastic goals, and grandiose or impractical plans.

The behavior of the malignant Narcissist is a product of these manipulative dualistic forces. His false self serves as a barrier and as a shock absorber between the true self and the sadistic, punishing, immature superego (Vaknin, 1999, p. 156). He is trapped; he cannot escape these two determining forces which underlie his actions. Every moment of his life is strictly supervised by the exceptionally strict court of superego.

However, the superego does not terrorize the malignant Narcissist all the times. There are moments, when it can be rewarding also. Freud observed that there is also a pleasure that is derived from the interplay between the false self and the superego. Freud calls this "Narcissistic reward". Therefore, a rewarding superego is the other side of the superego coin. Most of the time when the Narcissist is overly punitive, he has very limited ability to be rewarding. Certainly part of helping a person deal with an overly punitive superego would be to help him balance it with a rewarding superego. The victory of the false self over the true self can only occur if, by way of compensation for this renunciation, a narcissistic reward is accorded by his cruel superego (Sheridan, 1999, p. 199).

Without a strong and dictatorial superego, the Narcissist cannot move forward. He is so helpless that he cannot detach himself from the tyranny of his superego. Deep inside of his mind, he knows that he is a fraud. He does not trust his ability to manage his own affairs and to set practical aims and realize them. This is why he needs the superego as a guardian and regulator of his own affairs, more specifically the affairs of his false self. It is such a self-contradicting mission.

When the Narcissist is fooled into thinking that the voice of this internalized "judge" is coming from God or some supernatural power, he becomes addicted to religion. His inner voice confirms him of his divine mission and he thinks about himself of "being chosen" or of "having a destiny" or "clear authority". He believes he has a "direct telephone line" to God. Sometimes this God "serves" him through divine intervention. This inner voice scares him, confuses him, misguides him and manipulates him to submission. Slowly the malignant Narcissist becomes paranoid and this false God which is produced by his sick mind starts running the show. As Freud (Riviere *et al*, 1960, p. 33) concluded, *"It [superego] contains the germ from which all religions have evolved"*.

As Britton (2003, p. 71) concluded, *"The language of theology is the natural, or supernatural, language of the superego, and I therefore make no apology for using it. We may have decided with Nietzsche [a 19th-century German philosopher and atheist] that God is dead, but certainly his internal representative – the superego – is not"*.

As Vaknin (1999, pp. 148, 166) described, *"A Narcissist often entertains the delusion that God (or an equivalent institutional authority) is an active participant in his life in which constant intervention by this God is a key feature. God is included in a larger picture, that of the Narcissist's destiny and mission ... the Narcissist firmly believes that he is unique and that he is thus endowed because he has a mission to fulfill a destiny, a meaning to attain"*.

According to Freud (1989, p. 72), a great change takes place in the mind when the authority is internalized through the establishment of a superego. This particular change makes the malignant Narcissist very destructive because the authoritative superego changes his perception of the situation radically. Owing to the omniscience of the superego, the difference between aggression intended and aggression carried out just loses its force. Freud concluded, *"The phenomena of conscience then reach a higher stage ... at this point, the fear of being found out comes to an end; the distinction, moreover, between doing something bad and wishing to do it disappears entirely, since nothing can be hidden from the superego, nor even thoughts"*.

On rare occasions, the punishing superego is so harsh that the false self cannot take it any more. Untamed, it may become the "ego-destructive superego" (Britton, 2003, p. 73). This is the time the false self and the tyrannical superego compete with each other to establish superiority on each other, and the Narcissist contradicts himself the most. He wishes to reverse the (real) situation and thinks this way – "If I were the father and you were the child, I should treat you badly". After much struggle, the false self can wrest the position of arbiter, just as a child can become an adult who takes over from the parent the function of self-assessment. Self-assessment and self-observation are ego functions, not superego functions (Britton, 2003, p. 72). On the one hand, the Narcissist accepts the authority of his superego by disregarding the fact that the superego is inhuman to him; on the other hand, he confronts this authoritative personality with clear proofs of its fallibility. With the above confrontation, any of the three things happens. Either the Narcissist becomes more desperate to secure more narcissistic supply sources, or suffer from lifelong depression even to the point of committing suicide, or serious doubts creep in which may free him at last, i.e., he recovers from his narcissism.

5.5: Allah: The Superego of a Malignant Narcissist

Now it is time to reveal the true identity of Allah. If this mysterious moon-god of Islam is put under the searchlight of psychological analysis, it is not difficult to understand that Allah was the superego of Muhammad. Qur'an confirms that Allah gave authority to Muhammad.

Do not rise up against Allah, I come to you with clear authority. (Q: 44.19).

Those who swear allegiance to you (Muhammad) indeed swear allegiance to Allah. (Q: 48.10).

According to Muslim belief, Muhammad was the final authority for Allah's revelation here on earth. In other words, his false self kept its narcissistic "balloon" inflated with the strong authority of his superego, Allah. Without a strong and dictatorial Allah, Muhammad could not move forward in his divine mission. But what are Allah's credentials? Such questions are forbidden in Allah's religion and may lead to a grave danger.

Narrated Abu Huraira: Allah's Apostle said, Satan comes to one of you and says, 'Who created so-and-so?' till he says, 'Who has created your Lord?' So, when he inspires such a question, one should seek refuge with Allah and give up such thoughts. (Bukhari: 4.54.496)

It is narrated on the authority of Abu Huraira that the Messenger of Allah said: Men will continue to question one another till this is propounded: Allah created all things but who created Allah? He who found himself confronted with such a situation should say: I affirm my faith in Allah. (Muslim: 1.242).

He (Allah) will say: 'Dispute not with each other in My Presence: I had already in advance sent you Warning'. (Q: 50.28).

He cannot be questioned for His acts, but they will be questioned (for theirs). (Q: 21.23)

By this way Allah debarred any possibility of criticism in Islam and the authority remained unchallenged. Allah wanted to be shrouded in a mystery because

Muhammad himself did not have a clear idea of his Allah. So Muhammad told Muslims to affirm their faith in Allah and to give up such thoughts.

The relationship between Allah and Muhammad was not friendly. Their liaison was not like father and son; it was purely that of a master and slave. Like a child who is under compulsion to obey his cruel parents, the false self is obliged to submit itself to the unconditional command of his superego. Allah, the superego of Muhammad, never gave him the intimate love that a father gives to his son. Muhammad had spent many years among Christians and Jews and adopted many of their customs and stories in Qur'an, but he never wanted to adopt the "father and son" theological concept of the Jews and Christians. He simply could not imagine that God could be loveable. Hence the God-Prophet relationship was one of a slave to his master, with obedience, rather than love, being the primary impulse.

Narrated 'Umar: I heard the Prophet saying, 'Do not exaggerate in praising me as the Christians praised the son of Mary, for I am only a Slave. So, call me the Slave of Allah and His Apostle'. (Bukhari: 4.55.654)

And when the slave of Allah stood up in prayer to Him (Allah)... (Q: 72.19)

A common Muslim name is Abdallah, which literally means "servant of Allah" or "slave of Allah". Allah makes it clear that humans are His slaves, and slaves have no freedom, except do what the master orders.

But in other religions, the view is different. In Hindu belief, the whole universe is one self same reality (teachings of Upanishad). There is no distinction or duality between God (*paramatma*) and the soul (*jivaatma*) except in our perception. God and the soul are one and the same. There is nothing like a soul separating itself from God and then entering the body as a separate entity. It means, every human being is a part of God. Therefore the core teaching of Hinduism (The Vedanta Philosophy) (Beckerlegge, 1998, p. 297) is: "Do not injure another. Love everyone as your own self because the whole universe is one. In injuring another, I am injuring myself; in loving another, I love myself". In Talmudic Judaism; God is the creator, law-giver, and protector. Hence He is called "Father". In Christianity, God is called "Father" not only for the same reasons, but because of the mystery of the father-son relationship revealed by Jesus Christ. This is the revelation of a sense in which fatherhood is inherent to God's nature – an eternal relationship.

But Muhammad's Islam does not match to any of these great theological concepts. He interacted with Allah mechanically. There was absolutely no sense of divine union. Muslims often claim that the Christians and Muslims pray to the same God, but this is a deceitful attempt to misguide and gain converts from Christianity. While Christianity is based on love, brotherhood and forgiveness; Islam is based on hatred, lust and revenge.

Allah is very cruel. Neither He trusts others nor is He trustworthy at all. The Qur'an describes Allah as the best deceiver and a liar who is not above using the same evil and wicked schemes of His opponents. Qur'an calls Allah "al-Makr" (the word for deception/deceiver/schemer is Makr); in fact, Allah is the best Makr in the world. Muhammad thought that he was under constant watch of Allah.

Indeed, your Lord is ever watchful. (Q: 89.14).

Who sees you when you stand up. And your turning over and over among those who prostrate themselves before Allah (in worship). (Q: 26.218-9).

Allah is so cruel that He likes to see people afraid of him. Muhammad equated love with fear.

Whosoever fears the Merciful in the Unseen, and comes with a contrite heart. (Q: 50.33).

Anas b. Malik is reported to have said that Allah's Messenger recited this verse: 'He is the fount of fear. He is the fount of Mercy (Q: 74:56)'. Then he said, "Allah, the Mighty and Glorious, has said, "I deserve that I am feared and no other god is appointed with Me. So he who fears that no other god is appointed with Me, then I am competent to forgive him. (Sunaan ibn Majah: 5.4299)

Narrated Abu Musa: The sun eclipsed and the Prophet got up, being afraid that it might be the Hour (i.e. Day of Judgment). He went to the Mosque and offered the prayer with the longest Qiyam, bowing and prostration that I had ever seen him doing. Then he said, 'These signs which Allah sends do not occur because of the life or death of somebody, but Allah makes His worshipers afraid by them. So when you see anything thereof, proceed to remember Allah, invoke Him and ask for His forgiveness'. (Bukhari: 2.18.167)

Allah demands unquestionable obedience, fear, and affection from His slaves. If the slaves fail to please Allah with those emotional needs, Allah is furious and acts like a child. He gets mad and fires His outburst in an uncontrollable manner, and then proceeds to destroy His slaves who made Him angry.

My (Allah) Anger should fall upon you, and upon whosoever My Anger falls has assuredly fallen. (Q: 20.81)

Allah warns you to be cautious of Him, the arrival is to Allah. (Q: 3.28).

Superego is often relentless and cruel on his insistence on perfection (Engler, 2009, p. 48). But this ideal perfection may be quite far from reality or possibility. Allah wants to be perfect. He cannot coexist with other Gods of other religions because in that case He is not the supreme power. Hence, Allah repeatedly said (Q: 3.19, 3.85, 6.153, 12.40) that no other religion except Islam is acceptable to Him. Allah is the most uncompromising God in the history of religions.

Superego's power to enforce rules comes from its ability to create anxiety in the false self of the Narcissist. The false self observes itself in a realistic light and the superego in a moral light (Britton, 2003, p. 72). Often the rules, demands and wishes of the superego are very unrealistic. Allah made Muhammad's life miserable. If Muhammad cannot perform well in propagating Allah's religion, Allah threatens him to send a beast as the final messenger of humankind. This continuous degradation of his false self by his superego made Muhammad a violent person. He was at unrest.

And when the Word falls on them, We will bring out from the earth a beast that shall speak to them: 'Indeed the people were not certain of Our verses'. (Q: 27.82)

In the above verse Muhammad was receiving extreme humiliation from his superego; otherwise, this verse is meaningless. How a beast can perform better than a man in preaching a religion? Which beast can speak Arabic? What kind of beast will replace Muhammad? Muhammad also claimed to be the last Prophet of God (Q: 33.40). Therefore if verse 33.40 is right then the verse 27.82 must be wrong. Another Hadith further proves that Muhammad was under tremendous pressure from his cruel superego which was the main reason of his aggressiveness.

Narrated Aisha: Allah's Apostle never took revenge (over anybody) for his own sake but (he did) only when Allah's Legal Bindings were outraged in which case he would take revenge for Allah's sake. (Bukhari: 4.56.760).

The expression "*Allah's Legal Bindings*" needs particular attention. Allah, the internalized "judge" of Muhammad haunted him in every moment of his prophetic career. Given the tumultuous history of his prophetic career, with its raids, wars, and assassinations it is undeniable that terror was Muhammad's legacy. Allah was too rigid and did not care for justice or decency. In fact Allah rewarded him well.

Allah's Apostle said, 'I have been made victorious with terror. The treasures of the world were brought to me and put in my hand.' (Bukhari: 4.52.220)

(Muhammad said) 'Rejoice, Allah has promised us victory after tribulation. This increased the Muslims faith and submission'. When cities were conquered Muslims used to say, 'Conquer for yourselves whatever seems good to you because all treasures were given to Muhammad'. (Tabari: VIII.12)

And much booty that they will capture. Allah is ever Mighty, Wise. Allah promised you much booty that ye will capture, and hath given you this in advance, and hath withheld men's hands from you, that it may be a token for the believers, and that He may guide you on a right path. (Q: 48.19, 20).

If we make a close observation of the doctrine of jihad, we will find that it is a gross insult to the very concept of God because this violent doctrine depicts Him as a bloodthirsty dictator, who allows murder, rape, death and destruction of the infidels on a permanent basis only because of their "crime" of not believing in Him. Such a God cannot be the real creator of the universe. Now we know it was Muhammad's rigid and punishing superego which had commanded him in such an uncompromising voice and Muhammad mistook it as a divine decree. If Allah hates the non-Muslims, then based on what logic He created them? Why Allah had not created all humans as Muslims to remove the need for such atrocities that His followers are required to commit as jihad? If Allah has to depend on the Muslims to do His bidding, then He cannot be Almighty. As Shaikh (1999, p. 162) wrote, "*Just ponder over the vastness of this universe, which exceeds trillions of stars and planets bound by the authority of an unbending and natural law. If God is the controller of such an immense and wonderful world, He cannot be so mean, miserable and miscreant to terrorize mankind into submission."*

It is difficult to imagine that the God of humankind acts like a terrorist. God has to be merciful, loving and liberal. We, human beings, need God's mercy and understanding owing to our inborn weaknesses. Allah is merciful only in theory. He even expects a share of booty from Muhammad.

And know that whatever ye take as spoils of war, lo! A fifth thereof is for Allah, and for the messenger. (Q: 8.41)

Allah divided the booty stolen from the first caravan after he made spoils permissible. He gave four-fifths to those He had allowed to take it and one-fifth to His Apostle. (Ishaq: 288)

According to Freud (1979, p. 297), what the false self regards as danger and respond to with an anxiety-signal is that the superego may be angry with him or it will punish him or cease to love him. The biggest fear of the false self is that his superego may die (i.e., stop interacting). This is what the Narcissist is even scared to think. His false self is on absolute dependence on the superego, more specifically, on the authorization of the superego. The Narcissist is merely acting as a robot. If the superego dies, the false self will immediately collapse.

Now, let us understand Muhammad with the above Freudian analysis. If Allah cannot survive as a God, in other words, if no one worships Allah, Islam will collapse. If Islam collapses, then what would be the value of Muhammad? Who would accept Muhammad as a Prophet? A Prophet has no stand without a God. On the day of battle of Badr (March 13, 624), Muhammad cast a glance at the mighty infidel army. The vastly numerical superiority of the enemy terrified him. He then prayed to Allah to grant him victory.

It has been narrated on the authority of 'Umar b. al-Khattab: When it was the day on which the Battle of Badr was fought, the Messenger of Allah cast a glance at the infidels, and they were one thousand while his own Companions were three hundred and nineteen. The Holy Prophet turned (his face) towards the Qibla. Then he stretched his hands and began his supplication to his Lord: 'O Allah, accomplish for me what Thou hast promised to me. O Allah, bring about what Thou hast promised to me. O Allah, if this small band of Muslims is destroyed. Thou will not be worshipped on this earth'. (Muslim: 19.4360).

Narrated Ibn 'Abbas: The Prophet, while in a tent (the battle of Badr) said, 'O Allah! I ask you the fulfillment of Your Covenant and Promise. O Allah! If You wish (to destroy the believers) You will never be worshipped after today'. Abu Bakr caught him by the hand and said, 'This is sufficient, O Allah's Apostle! You have asked Allah pressingly'. (Bukhari: 4.52.164)

Though it appears strange that a man is telling his God what would happen if He does not listen to him, it is not odd at all. Muhammad's concern was not for Allah but for his own selfish interests. In the above quotes, a Narcissist was expressing his fear that his superego might sink into oblivion if the battle was lost.

If the superego fails to exist, who would give authority to the false self, and how the false self would survive? Let us analyze another two ahadith.

Narrated 'Abdullah: The Prophet said, "... And there is none who likes to be praised more than Allah does. (Bukhari: 9.93.500)

Abu Huraira reported that Allah's Messenger said, 'If anyone did not supplicate to Allah, Hallowed be He, Be becomes angry with him.' (Sunaan Ibn Majah: V.3827)

All these phrases e.g., "praise to Allah" and "supplicate to Allah" were not for God but for Muhammad himself. His survival depended on Allah's survival. Allah was a paper tiger, no better than a scarecrow – impotent and powerless. The more Allah is praised and supplicated, the stronger He becomes. The simple formula – the stronger the God is, the stronger the Prophet is.

The punishing superego sometimes crosses the limit in its cruelty so much that the false self cannot tolerate it anymore. As Britton (2003, p. 73) commented, the superego is *"an internal object hostile to the ego – an enemy within – not simply a tyrant"*. Allah often became so ruthless and uncompromising with Muhammad that at different points in his carrier he abandoned the unity of God (i.e., the Narcissist disobeyed the command of his superego) and his claim to the title of the Prophet (Warraq, 2000, p. 340). Undoubtedly, this is an unacceptable image of Muhammad. Viewed from psychology, it was the withdrawal symptom of the Narcissist. On one hand, Muhammad had to accept the authority of Allah by disregarding the fact that Allah was cruel and ungodly; on the other hand, he confronted his cruel superego, by defying the sovereignty of Allah. As Freud (Riviere *et al*, 1960, p. 61) explained, *"The ego [false self] gives itself up because it feels itself hated and persecuted by the superego, instead of loved. To the ego, therefore, living means same thing as being loved – being loved by the superego. When the ego finds itself in an excessive real danger which it believes itself unable to overcome by its own strength, it is bound to draw the same conclusion. It sees itself deserted by all protecting forces and lets itself die"*.

Though Muhammad's prophetic life was full of contradictions, undoubtedly, this was the time when he contradicted himself the most. Muhammad was on the path of recovery through self-realization and was very close to free himself from the tyranny of his superego which he mistook a God. But no, he could not. If he could, then certainly Islam would have died shortly after this, but he dived deep into his sick narcissistic world in persuasion of further narcissistic supply sources and Islam survived.

5.6: Conclusion

"Do not pray in my school and I won't think in your Mosque."

Unknown

"There can be but little liberty on earth while men worship a tyrant in heaven."

Robert Green Ingersoll (1833 - 1899)

Superego is the unconscious wish of a malignant Narcissist, which is projected back at him. Allah was "everything" what Muhammad wanted to be. Since they were parts of the same sick mind, they were often identical. They thought alike and their preferences were also similar. They also commanded together. The pivot of Islamic faith is the political genius Muhammad, not Allah.

If ye obey him, ye will go aright. But the messenger hath no other charge than to convey (the message) plainly. (Q: 24.54)

If ye do love Allah, Follow me (Muhammad): Allah will love you and forgive you your sins: For Allah is Oft-Forgiving, Most Merciful. (Q: 3.31)

Allah's Apostle said, 'Whoever obeys me, obeys Allah, and whoever disobeys me, disobeys Allah, and whoever obeys the ruler I appoint, obeys me, and whoever disobeys him, disobeys me.' (Bukhari: 9.89.251)

Allah expresses all his wishes through Muhammad. While the Narcissist Muhammad projected his false self to the outside world, his superego Allah directed itself to him (i.e., his false self). Since Muhammad could not prove his prophethood, his Allah also could not prove that He was the real God. Muslims can attribute anything to Allah, but Allah was a dummy, a clever myth. Neither a dummy has the power to throw anyone in hell nor can it reward anyone with paradise. Longing for praise and greatness is human weakness and it does not fit to a true God.

When Muhammad felt a sexual desire for Aisha, a child of only six years old, or to Zaynab, his daughter-in-law; his God sanctioned it. Why Allah did not scold him for his abnormal desires? Why Allah made special laws of sexual enjoyments for him to the total exclusion of other Muslims? It is this exclusivity that cancels out Muhammad's claim that he was the behavioral model for his followers. Though Muhammad did not follow Qur'anic instructions and on occasions placed himself in a position higher than Allah, he is still an *"excellent example"* (Q: 33.21) and *"great morality"* (Q: 68.4). This is confusing, but a quote (Riviere *et al*, 1960, p. 48) from Freud scatters all doubts, *"The superego owes its special position in the ego, or in relation to the ego, to a factor which must be considered from two sides."* Now let us read the above quote again from an Islamic perception. Allah granted divine dispensation for Muhammad because, *"The Allah (superego) owes its special position in the Prophet Muhammad (ego, false self), or in relation to the Prophet Muhammad, to Islam (a factor) which must be considered from two sides"*.

The strange relationship between false self and superego does not remain same throughout the life of a Narcissist. As the false self matures with continuous input of narcissistic supplies, his perception of his superego also changes considerably. This is one main reason; Allah was such a confusing God. The morality of the Qur'an, its anachronism, and its many unethical commandments make an unprejudiced reader doubt that Qur'an was Muhammad's own composition. If the Surahs are arranged chronologically (in order of their composition) and compared with the events in Muhammad's life, we see that there is much truth in the statement that the passages were – not, as Muslims say, revealed, but – composed from time to time, as occasion required, to sanction each new departure made by Muhammad.

If we look at the ninety-nine names of Allah, we will find many abusive names;

e.g., *Al-Mutakabbir* (The Proud One), *Al-Jabbar* (The Dictator), *Al-Qahhar* (The Subduer), *Al-Khafid* (The Abaser), *Al-Mudhell* (The Humiliator), *Al-Mumit* (The Death Giver), *Al-Muntaqim* (The Avenger), *Ad-Darr* (the Creator of the Harmful), *khairul Makirin* (The Best Deceiver) and *Al-Warith* (The Inheritor). These are not divine qualities. This can be explained by Freudian analysis. The implication in Freud's thinking is that the superego is a more primitive mental structure than the false self. The superego of a malignant Narcissist takes the same place equal to that of a small child's view of parental authority. If the parents are tyrannical, these are the same terms the small child attributes to his parents, while having the harshness and arbitrariness that a small child would have as a judge. Also, though a Narcissist's sense of self-worth is totally at the mercy of the superego, he can make a judgment on his own conscience even though still subjected to the reproaches of the superego (Britton, 2003, pp. 72-3). This explains why in spite of being such a cruel mass-murderer, some of the Qur'anic verses have moral standards. Muhammad was perfectly capable of differentiating between good and bad, but he was not capable to control his behavior.

One does not need a scholastic review of Allah to disprove Him. Qur'an exposes Allah quite nicely – a real God cannot sponsor rape, incest, thievery, kidnapping for ransom, the slave trade, mass murder, and worst of all, world conquest by way of sword and deception. Also, God does not need to plagiarize. He would know history and science and thus would not have made such a fool of Himself. There was nothing genuine in Muhammad's claims. This malignant Narcissist led nearly all of his own people astray and the evil progressed through generations. Human can follow in the footprints of a human, but cannot measure up to the conduct of someone who occasionally gives the impression of a man but often claims the privileges of a God. In this case both the claimant and the God are frauds.

Chapter 6: Islam: The Purpose-built Religion of a Malignant Narcissist

"The more I study religions the more I am convinced that man never worshipped anything but himself."

Sir Richard Francis Burton (1821 - 1890)

"Religion cannot be overriding morality. Man, for instance, cannot be untruthful, cruel or incontinent and claim to have God on his side".

M. K Gandhi (cited Rao, 1990, p. 54)

Religion not only teaches morals and guidelines to follow through life, but also teaches hope. Through religion people feel more comfortable with the fact that one day everyone will die because they believe they are going to a better place. People fear the unknown because it is just that, unknown. No one knows what to expect; it could be good or bad. All the world religions thrive in this uncertainty.

6.1: The Purpose of Creation of Islam

"Islam was not a torch, as has been claimed, but an extinguisher. Conceived in a barbarous brain for the use of a barbarous people, it was – and it remains – incapable of adapting itself to civilization. Wherever it has dominated, it has broken the impulse towards progress and checked the evolution of society".

Andre Servier (French Writer)

The entire purpose of this divine planning, what we call Islam, was to install Muhammad as the holiest of holies. His entire leadership under the authority of Allah was a sick game played ultimately for the sake of himself. For the Narcissists, what matters is power. It is their ultimate goal to achieve supremacy. More power means more victims for narcissistic needs, because the more power they have, the more freely they can diminish others to keep themselves inflated (Hotchkiss, 2003, p. 14). Sometimes, the Narcissist looks for the weak points of his potential victims, and then project himself (his delusions) in such a clever manner that his grandiosity may seem to offer something that is missing from their lives. Sometimes his hunger of admiration makes him want to please the targets which the unsuspected victim may feel like real love. Therefore; narcissism and religion go well together (Vaknin, 1999, p. 147). He wants to feel unique and a "purpose-built" religion permits him to feel unique.

Religious supremacy and pretended divine authority allows the Narcissist to exercise his control over his followers openly and unabated. He can taunt and torment his followers, bully and punish them, berate them, abuse them spiritually, or even sexually. He can also extort money by some pretence. With religious authority, he can easily obtain obedient and unquestioning slaves upon whom he can exercise his capricious and wicked mastery. He can transform even the most harmless and pure religious sentiments into cultish rituals and a virulent hierarchy. In sum, his followers become his prey. He preys on the gullibility of the innocents and his own followers, at last, become his hostages. Following table demonstrates how religion is viewed by a normal healthy person and by a malignant Narcissist.

	Normal healthy people	The malignant Narcissists
1	Religion encourages people to live by a set of rules; both spiritual and moral.	Religion encourages a Narcissist to develop his own set of rules and get divine sanction for these. He believes he has a "direct connection" to God. Morality and spirituality are not important issues.
2	Religion brings people together as a community of believers. It discourages selfishness and encourages mutual cooperation. With more religious devotion, people are more loyal to their group and the members of that group.	Religion brings the Narcissist closer to his community of believers, but the group must magnify the Narcissist, echo and amplify his life, his views, his knowledge, and his personal history. This intertwining and enmeshing of individual is what makes the Narcissist most comfortable. He considers himself above the group.
3	Religion instills a belief in "something" greater than ourselves – and not just "something", but a being to which we are held to account.	Religion instills a belief in a Narcissist that he is this "something". In playing God, he is convinced that he is merely being himself. Even he has no hesitation to put people's lives or properties at risk.
4	People search for truth in religion.	Narcissists search for more narcissistic supply sources. They are interested in a tailor-made religion.

Islam was such a purpose-built religion of Muhammad. He was a cold-blooded imposter; he knew what he was supposed to do to secure his needs. The best way of enslaving people was to create a religion. By this way, Muhammad was safe and unquestioned. It was his strong dominance urge that forced him to rise above Allah. Hence Islam was Allah's religion by name only; actually it was the religion of Muhammad. Vaknin (cited Sina, 2008, p. 66) observed, "*Narcissists use anything they can lay their hands on in the pursuit of Narcissistic supply. If God, creed, church, faith, and institutionalized religion can provide them with Narcissistic supply, they will become devout. They will abandon religion if it cannot."* Muhammad was at the center in his clever plan of self-elevation. The Islamic theory of guidance simply means following Muhammad blindly; any question or hesitation is tantamount to blasphemy which leads to hell.

Muhammad achieved this self-elevation by watching his steps carefully. First he introduced himself as a humble spokesman of Allah, claimed that he had the authority, preached the oneness of Allah and advocated the destruction of all the idols of Ka'ba so that they should not rival Allah. When his followers accepted his advocacy, the supremacy and oneness of Allah were firmly established. Now He took the second step very judiciously. He put himself in a rank higher than Allah by becoming an object of *"praise of Allah and His angels"* (Q: 33.56). How nicely he used Allah's authority to devalue Allah – the same God who had authorized him. If Allah and His angels shower praises on Muhammad, obviously, all the believers are bound to follow this pattern of human worshipping otherwise they are disobeying Allah's instruction. After some hesitation, when the Muslims agreed to Muhammad-worshipping, Muhammad took the ultimate bold step. He forced his Allah to accept the same Muhammad-worshipping along with the common Muslims. Now, Allah salutes Muhammad and confirms His humiliating status by a revelation.

> *... and **when they (nonbelievers) come to thee, they salute thee, not as Allah salutes thee, (but in crooked ways)** . .. Enough for them is Hell: In it will they burn, and evil is that destination!* (Q: 58.8)

How many Muslims have ever noticed this dirty trick of Muhammad? In the history of Gods no God is as miserable as Allah. What other proof is required to show that Muhammad was actually an imposter, and the religion he preached was a fake? Narcissists do not promote themselves directly because by this way they would be exposed shortly (Sina, 2008, p. 69). Hence, Muhammad first found a suitable God, elevated that God over other Gods and then elevated himself over the same God at His cost. Vaknin (1999, p. 147) commented, *"[The Narcissist believes that] God 'serves' him in certain junctions and conjunctures of his life, through divine intervention. He believes that his life is such momentous importance, that it is micro-managed by God"*.

A popular Persian saying goes like this, *"**BaKhuda Diwana Bashad Ba Muhammad Hoshiyar**"* (Faith & McCallum, 2005, p. 132), which means; "Take liberties with Allah, but be careful with Muhammad". It proves my point. Allah is just a decorative convenience. Praising Muhammad is an integral part of the daily prayers of the Muslims – *"La ilaha illa Allah wa-Muhammad rasul Allah"*. This is called *Shahada* (Muslim declaration of faith). It means; "There is no god but Allah and Muhammad is the messenger of God". A Muslim utters those words several times a day. The *Shahada* is also recited in the muzzein's call to prayer, included in the *Salat* (daily ritual prayer) and incorporated in Sufi meditative prayer. It is also recited in the moments before death. Muhammad associated himself with Allah in such a way that practically they became inseparable. By recitation of this confession of faith, the early Muslims were fulfilling the narcissistic needs of Muhammad as they are still doing it today. Muslims are actually the "slaves of Muhammad".

The Narcissist wants to leave a legacy (Sina, 2008, p. 66). He fears death because he realizes that he would not have same type of control in the afterlife (Zayn & Dibble, 2007, p. 92). On his deathbed, Muhammad instructed his followers to continue their jihad against the infidels. Non-stop jihad is the fruit of Islam which is the means to raise Muhammad above the mark of divinity. Muhammad wanted to be eternal like God. For achieving this he left behind him a devoted, dedicated and determined band of followers. Therefore, when a Muslim sacrifices his life in jihadi terrorism thinking that he is doing a service for Islam and Allah, actually he is carrying the personal flag of Muhammad. In this sense Islam is idolatry.

Many of the early Meccans and contemporaries of Muhammad recognized him as an imposter. There was large scale apostasy amongst those early Muslims.

Those who believe, then reject faith, then believe (again) and (again) reject faith, and go on increasing in unbelief, Allah will not forgive them nor guide them nor guide them on the way. (Q: 4.137)

I heard the Apostle say, 'I have never invited anyone to accept Islam who has not shown signs of reluctance, suspicion and hesitation.' (Ishaq: 116).

Immediately after Muhammad's death Islam fell apart in Arabia and most of the tribes returned to their original faith. Ninety percent of all Arabs refused to pay zakat, and thus turned renegades (Shaikh, 1995, p. 48). Muslim historians state that most Arabs considered Islam synonymous with plundering and loot. After the death of Muhammad, Arabs thought that with Muhammad out of the picture, there would be no more lucrative raids or wars to line their pockets and satisfy their lust. Hence, many of the tribes repudiated Islam and became renegades. Some of them said, if Muhammad had really been God's messenger then he would not have died. Others mentioned that his religion would only last during his lifetime (Warraq, 2000, p. 145). In sum; those apostates completely discarded Muhammad and looked at Islam with much suspicion. The leaders of the opposition to Islam posed as Prophets and political leaders, hoping to emulate Muhammad. The opposition movements that arose took one of two forms. One group challenged both the political control of Medina and the religious claims of Islam by proposing rival ideologies. The second type of rebellion was more political in character. It was a tax rebellion against the Islamic state. Let alone the rebels; even the Muslims had hardly shown any respect to Islam.

Narrated Hamza bin `Abdullah: My father said."During the lifetime of Allah's Apostle, the dogs used to urinate, and pass through the mosques, nevertheless they never used to sprinkle water on it (urine of the dog)". (Bukhari: 1.4.174)

Islam started with a purely political motive. It was a political struggle with many competitors to achieve power. Many other Prophets were at rat race with Muhammad. Most of the murders organized by Muhammad in the name of Allah were political murders and his political agenda was advanced by securing and dividing plunder. As Sina (2008, p. 169) wrote, *"Islam was not created to teach humans spirituality, nor make them enlightened. The spiritual message in Islam is secondary or virtually nonexistent. Piety in Islam means emulating Muhammad, a man who was far from pious. Rituals like prayers and fasting are mere window dressing to lure unbelievers inside, to give Islam the appearance of sacredness and spirituality. False Prophets can deceive only in sheep clothing".*

Many religious aspects of Islam were later additions. After Muhammad died, the Caliphs realized that the cult of Muhammad was an excellent tool that could be used to raise a strong and spiritually dedicated army, to gain power and to become rich. In haste, they compiled the Qur'an to keep Islam steady going. Ahmed (2006, p. 100) gave one example of the wars of apostasy (Muslim historians denote this as Hurb al-Riddah) that Caliph Abu Bakr waged against some Arab tribes; "*Abu Bakr's wars were political wars and had nothing to do with religion. He waged his wars against those who refused to accept his claim to lead the Muslim community. In order to justify his wars, Abu Bakr clothed them with divinity. He fabricated hadith to justify the killing of the Muslim Arabs and attributed the hadith to the Prophet*". Early history of Islam was full of forgeries, because Muslim historians often suppressed the facts.

Sina (2008, p. 67) commented, "*It is a mistake to think of Islam as a religion. The religious/spiritual aspect of Islam was created later by Muslim philosophers and mystics who gave esoteric interpretations to Muhammad's asinine words. His followers molded the religion according to their penchant, and with the passage of time, those interpretations inherited the seal of antiquity and thus credibility*".

Sina's assertion is true. The early Muslims were hardly religious in the strict sense of the term. Islam has hardly anything new which were not there during pre-Islamic days. It is pagan beliefs plus the prophethood of Muhammad. Muhammad was not an original thinker; his intention was to borrow from other religious scriptures everything that seemed capable of strengthening his doctrine and attracting followers. Whatever good exists in Islam was all shamelessly plagiarized from Judaism and Christianity. This "ignorance" and "spiritual bankruptcy" of Islamic doctrine and pre-Islamic rituals continued well in the first Islamic century. Indeed Islam could not be properly said to have existed in the sense of a fixed dogma until later (Warraq, 2003, p. 42). The "indoctrination" of Islam continued taking shape when Islam had to confront Christianity, a much more advanced rival religion. Many of the early Muslims were pure hypocrites. Qur'an says,

Of the people there are some who say: "We believe in Allah and the Last Day;" but they do not (really) believe. (Q: 2.8)

They had no respect for Muhammad. When the booty captured at Hunayn was divided among the Muslims, some of the followers of Muhammad were not happy. They became violent with Muhammad.

Narrated Jubair bin Mut`im: That while Allah's Apostle was on his way back from Hunayn, the Bedouins started begging for things so aggressively that they forced him to go under a Samura tree where his outer garment was snatched away. On that, Allah's Apostle stood up [in his undergarments] and said, 'Return my clothes. If I had as many camels as these trees, I would have distributed them amongst you; and you will not find me a miser, liar or coward.' (Bukhari: 4.53.376)

[The rebels in demanded] 'Muhammad, divide the spoil and booty of camels and cattle among us'. They [the rebels] forced the Prophet up against a tree, and his robe was torn from him. Muhammad cried, 'Give me back my robe. If

there had been more sheep I would have given you some. You have not found me to be niggardly, cowardly or false. (Tabari: IX.31; Ishaq: 594)

This is what happens if the bandit leader cannot pay his accomplices.

Narrated by Anas bin Malik; Muhammad prayed, O Allah! I seek refuge with you from distress and sorrow, from helplessness and laziness, from miserliness and cowardice, from being heavily in debt and from being overcome by men. (Bukhari: 4.52.143).

This was how Muhammad saw himself, and in fact, it was what he had become in the hands of his greedy followers. This lazy and blood-sucking Prophet of Islam never earned a meal by any honest means. He had no idea how hard-earned money looks like. All his money and property were looted from others. He did not know how to value capital or labor. Therefore, no matter how much he robbed, he always felt that it was less for him. He was scared of running heavily in debt.

Even Muhammad's close associate Hamza did not show him respect. Once Hamza was drinking in this house with others, and a girl singer was singing. At one moment the girl said in her song, *"Hamza, get up for slaughtering the fat she-camels."* (Muslim: 23.4879). Hearing this, Hamza rushed to his sword and cut off the Ali's camels' humps and cut their flanks open and took out portions from their livers. Seeing this Ali started weeping and complained to Muhammad and then,

Narrated 'Ali: The Prophet started blaming Hamza. Hamza was drunk and his eyes were red. He looked at the Prophet then raised his eyes to look at his knees and raised his eyes more to look at his face and then said, "You are not but my father's slaves." When the Prophet understood that Hamza was drunk, he retreated, and walking backwards went out. (Bukhari: 5.59.340)

This is the height of insult Muhammad had to take from others. He was not a very respectable figure in the eyes of many of his followers. They were hardcore bandits and rapists and they had joined Muhammad only for opportunities. They had seen Muhammad closely and they knew that Muhammad was delusional and his claims were untruthful. However, the fact cannot be denied that some of his followers truly believed in his claims and his descriptions of heaven and hell. Sina (2008, p. 67) commented, *"If we think of religion as a philosophy of life to educate, to bring forth human potential, to elevate the soul, to stimulate spirituality, to unite hearts and to enlighten mankind, then Islam surely fails that litmus test completely. Therefore, by this measure, Islam should not and cannot be regarded as a religion".*

6.2: Islam: The Cult of a Malignant Narcissist

"Without deceit and sword, Islam would have been stillborn."

Craig Winn

"No matter how you look at Islam it turns out to be a foolish religion."

Ali Sina (Ghamidi *et. al*, 2007, p. 211)

The term "cult" was originally used to denote a group which follows strange or sinister ritual practices. The cult leader uses some form of coercive persuasion or mind control to recruit and maintain members by suppressing their ability to reason, to think critically, and to make choices in their own best interest. Mind control is a pure psychological manipulation. Slowly, the followers turn into totally dependent on the group and the leader. They are even ready to abandon their friends, families, and the community to show their devotion to their leader. Cults are at high risk of becoming abusive to the members – physical, financial and psychological.

Many cults are peaceful and harmless, but there are some deadly or destructive cults where the cultist twists some harmless beliefs into dangerous activities that present a serious threat, both to their members and the common people. There are many recorded incidents where these cults have physically injured or killed other individuals deliberately, or have a high probability of causing harm to others.

All these cult leaders are Narcissists in one form or another. First they tell a lie, and then they sincerely believe their own lie. By seeing their sincerity, people around them think that they have some type of special insight, or relationship with God that gives them inside knowledge (Snow, 2003, p. 109). This way, when this belief system is established, these false Prophets can have tremendous control over the lives of the people who believed in them. As Vaknin (cited Sina, 2008, p. 63) explains, *"The Narcissist is the guru at the centre of a cult. Like other gurus, he demands complete obedience from his flock: his spouse, his offspring, other family members, friends, and colleagues. He feels entitled to adulation and special treatment by his followers. He punishes the wayward and the straying lambs. He enforces discipline, adherence to his teachings, and common goals. The less accomplished he is in reality – the more stringent his mastery and the more pervasive the brainwashing."*

Can we find some similarities? Muhammad never thought of the spiritual upbringing of his followers. He tried to subvert the human will with total and complete obedience to him, the proxy God of Islam. Muhammad needed admirers. He drew an imaginary circle around himself where he was the center. The purpose of other people was to serve him.

Narrated by Anas; The Prophet said: None of you will have faith till he loves me more than his father, his children and all mankind. (Bukhari: 1.2.14)

Vaknin continues, *"He alone determines the rights and obligations of his disciples and alters them at will ... The Narcissist is a micro-manager. He exerts control over the minutest details and behaviors. He punishes severely and abuses withholders of information and those who fail to conform to his wishes and goals... Within his cult, he expects awe, admiration, adulation, and constant attention commensurate with his outlandish stories and assertions. He reinterprets reality to fit his fantasies"*.

For Muslims everything is "*Insha'Allah*" spoken through Muhammad's tongue. In theory, Allah and Muhammad together command the Muslims, but in practice, Muhammad alone determines the rights and obligations of his followers. As Vaknin wrote, *"The Narcissist does not respect the boundaries and privacy of his reluctant adherents. He ignores their wishes and treats them as objects or instruments of gratification. He seeks to control both situations and people compulsively... His thinking is dogmatic, rigid, and doctrinaire*" (cited Sina, 2008, p. 63). Muhammad's jihad was directed to these "reluctant adherents". In Islam, all non-Muslims, due to their non-believing status, are reluctant adherents. Muhammad had a strong urge to control both the people and circumstances.

Financial fraud is involved in almost all the destructive cults. The cult leader attempts to obtain all the worldly possessions of their members. These "cults of greed" promise the target groups that if they join them and follow their special program for success, they will be very rich. Often they will hold up their leader as example and explain that if the member does what the leader says then he would be successful too. As example; the *Chonjonhoe* cult lured its members by promising material and spiritual rewards and deceived them some thirty-four million US$, which the leaders spent for living in luxury. Muhammad was greedy. His only source of income was looting of caravans, ransom and slave-trade. He encouraged his followers to spend money in the cause of Allah. In Islam, Allah borrows money from Muslims to wage jihad against the non-Muslims. More precisely, Allah uses Muslims' money (hard cash) to buy war implements to fight the non-Muslims.

Ye will not attain unto piety until ye spend of that which ye love. And whatsoever ye spend, Allah is Aware thereof. (Q: 3.92).

Who is it that will lend unto Allah a goodly loan, so that He may give it increase manifold? Allah straiteneth and enlargeth. Unto Him ye will return. (Q: 2.245).

The likeness of those who spend their wealth in Allah's way is as the likeness of a grain which groweth seven ears, in every ear a hundred grains. Allah giveth increase manifold to whom He will. (Q: 2.261).

All that you spend in the Way of Allah shall be repaid to you. You shall not be wronged. (Q: 8.60).

If ye loan to Allah, a beautiful loan, He will double it to your (credit), and He will grant you Forgiveness: for Allah is most ready to appreciate (service), Most Forbearing. (Q: 64.17).

And whatsoever ye spend (for good) He replaceth it. And He is the Best of Providers. (Q: 34.39)

Those who lend a good loan to Allah, shall be repaid in multiples. They shall receive a generous wage. (Q: 57.18).

In the above verses who is asking money from the Muslims? God does not need money but the god-man does. All the beggars teach that others should give. It was Muhammad who needed money for his military expeditions to expand his empire, not Allah. But Muhammad was reluctant to spend from his own pocket. There is not a single verse where Allah tells Muhammad to spend from his own share. Is not this a financial fraud?

Narrated Abu Huraira: The Prophet said, "Every day two angels come down from Heaven and one of them says, 'O Allah! Compensate every person who spends in Your Cause,' and the other (angel) says, 'O Allah! Destroy every miser.' (Bukhari: 2.24.522)

Many cult leaders also require to the members to sever all outside relationships with their families and friends (Snow, 2003, p. 28). They believe that the families are part of enemy system because they harm one's total dedication to the cause. Muhammad destroyed happy family ties. Qur'an says,

We have enjoined on man kindness to parents; but if they strive to make thee join with Me that of which thou hast no knowledge, then obey them not. Unto Me is your return and I shall tell you what ye used to do. (Q: 29.8).

O ye who believe! Lo! Among your wives and your children there are enemies for you, therefore beware of them. And if ye efface and overlook and forgive, then lo! Allah is Forgiving, Merciful. (Q: 64.14)

Your ties of kindred and your children will avail you naught upon the Day of Resurrection. He will part you. Allah is Seer of what ye do. (Q: 60.3)

Allah's instruction was very clear. He wanted the Muslims to disobey their parents and abandon them, if they stand on their way to accept Islam. Centuries later, another tyrant used the same technique. The Hitler Youth Program taught young Germans to inform on their parents if they dissented from the Nazi party line. Allah's verdict about the separation of relatives and children on the Judgment Day has the same implication. We cannot separate Islam from other deadly cults which had caused much harm not only to the cult members but others also. Few notorious cults and cult leaders are Jim Jones, David Koresh, Order of the solar temple, Heaven's gate and Charles Manson.

When Jim Jones started preaching in 1965, he had a handful of followers. He stressed the need for racial equality and integration, and helped the poor. When the followers started multiplying, he gradually assumed the role of Messiah and named his cult "Peoples Temple" and shifted to Jonestown. With time he demanded more obedience and loyalty which his followers were more than eager to comply. He convinced them that the world would be destroyed in a nuclear holocaust and if they followed him, only they would emerge as survivors. This picture reflects Islam in similarity. In the beginning, Muhammad was a peaceful preacher; he called people to believe in God and fear the Day of Judgment. Accordingly the early verses were peaceful. But when his influence grew and number of followers increased, he showed his real face. He became a bandit and threatened his followers with Allah's punishment if they did not obey him. When Muhammad wanted his followers to migrate to Medina, he had exactly the same plan in his mind as Jim Jones. Many were reluctant, so Muhammad turned his more loyal followers against those who did not want to leave. Allah revealed the following verse,

Surely those who believed and fled (their homes) and struggled hard in Allah's way (to establish Islam) with their property and their souls, and those who gave

shelter and helped-- these are guardians of each other; and (as for) those who believed and did not fly, not yours is their guardianship until they fly; and if they seek aid from you in the matter of religion, aid is incumbent on you except against a people between whom and you there is a treaty, and Allah sees what you do. (Q: 8.72)

Everything was going well within Peoples Temple, however during 1978, his group members killed five people including one politician who came to Jonestown for a fact-finding mission. Following this incident, Jim gathered his followers and told them to drink cyanide-laced beverage along with sedatives. Jim was reported to have said, *"We must die with some dignity. Do not be afraid to die"*. For those who were afraid to die, Jim advised (cited Pafumi, 2010, p. 91), *"Death is just stepping over into another plane. We did not commit suicide; we committed an act of revolutionary suicide protesting the conditions of an inhuman world"*.

Muhammad advised Muslims to die in the cause of Allah. For Jim it was *"an act of revolutionary suicide protesting the conditions of an inhuman world"*, and for Muhammad, *"Allah has purchased from the believers their selves and possessions, and for them is Paradise. They fight in the Way of Allah, slay, and are slain."* (Q: 9.111). But for both of them suffering for the faith constitute a powerful testimonial.

According to Jim, death is friendly; it is just entering into a new dimension. He convinced his people that by killing themselves they were not committing suicide. Muhammad convinced his followers that dying for Allah was martyrdom. Allah confirmed that the Muslims who are killed in his cause would enter paradise.

You must not think that those who were killed in the way of Allah are dead. But rather, they are alive with their Lord and have been provided for rejoicing in the Bounty that Allah has given to them and having glad tidings in those who remain behind and have not joined them, for no fear shall be on them neither shall they sorrow. (Q: 3.169, 170).

For those who fought and were killed in My Cause, I shall blot out their sins and admit them indeed to Paradise. (Q: 3.195)

Holy jihad is a religious duty of every Muslim. The exact phrase is *"al-jihad fi sabil Allah"* – striving in the cause of Allah (Arimbi, 2006, p. 88; Willis, 1967, p. 396). Jim led 909 of his followers (includes 276 children) in a mass suicide, which was for him *"death as the final proof of faith"*. Muhammad asked his followers for an ultimate test of devotion to the cause of Allah by glorifying martyrdom. When Muhammad was told that the only chance of martyrdom was dying in the battle, he is reported to have replied, *"Then the number of martyrs in my community would be small"* (Cook, 2007, p. 35). In fact, Muhammad glorified the status of a martyr to such an extent that many Muslims sought to attain it without the inconvenience of actually going out to fight.

Neither Jim nor Muhammad ever valued the preservation of human lives. Both of them put themselves in the place of God. As Vaknin (1999, p. 148) commented, *"In playing God, the Narcissist is completely convinced that he is playing himself. He will not hesitate to put people's lives and fortunes at stake"*. Muhammad was indistinguishable from Allah.

Those who deny Allah and His messengers, and (those who) wish to separate Allah from His messengers, saying: "We believe in some but reject others": And (those who) wish to take a course midway. They are in truth (equally) unbelievers; and we have prepared for unbelievers a humiliating punishment. (Q: 4.150-1)

Vaknin continued, "*He feels part of a grand design, a world plan and the frame of affiliation, the group, of which he is a member, must be commensurately grand. Its proportions and properties must resonate with his. Its characteristics must justify his and its ideology must conform to his pre-conceived opinions and prejudices. In short, the group must magnify the Narcissist, echo and amplify his life, his views, his knowledge, his history*".

Similar to Jim Jones, another deadly cult was Heaven's gate where thirty-nine members committed suicide. Yet another cult led by Charles Manson ordered his followers to enter the houses of rich people randomly, kill them, and make it look as if it has been done by the blacks. Charles had a cause which was preservation of air, trees, water, animals (ATWA). He made his cause look so important that it justified murder. All these cult leaders had something in common. They were capable of subverting individual's sense of control over their own thinking, behavior, emotions, or decision-making by using various psychological tactics.

The cult leaders use a belief system as their base. It can be any standard religion or they may have invented their own belief system. In the beginning, this belief system often appears innocent. When Charles talked about preservation of ATWA, or when Jim stressed the need for racial equality and integration and his group helped the poor, or when Muhammad started preaching peacefully in Mecca, no one could see anything wrong in it. What makes a cult leader dangerous is that they make the people zombies by controlling their minds, not what they believe. If the Muslims want to believe in oneness of Allah and Muhammad's prophethood, it is fine; the world has no inconvenience. The problem starts when the poisonous teachings of Muhammad infect their minds, and the brainwashed Muslims turn their religion into a killing machine. That is why the notion of mind control is so central in the cult issue.

The cult leaders desperately trick the unsuspecting people into joining and coerce them into staying. They are after the obedience, time and money of the potential victims. They have to use deception because if people knew their motives beforehand, then they would not join. Hence the leader needs to hide the truth from the potential victim until he is sure that the person is completely under his grip. For example, if Jim Jones was open and honest about the group and had said to new recruits – "Join us, give me all your money and then drink poison and die happily", he would not have any takers. If the leader of the Heavens Gate cult had told their new entries that the name of his cult was a misnomer and the more appropriate name should be "Gateway to Hell", were there any possibility for the leader to establish his cult? If Muhammad had shown his "feet of clay" at Mecca, would Islam have survived?

Cult leaders control a person by controlling his behavior. When a new person first goes to a cult, the cult members will practice "love bombing", where they arrange instant friends for him. It seems wonderful; how could such a loving group be wrong! But the new member soon learns that if he ever disagrees with them then he will lose all the supports. This unspoken threat influences the member's actions in the cult. This is "control of behavior" (Hassan, 1990, p. 60). Things, that usually would have made him complain, will pass by silently because he does not want to be ostracized.

Cults also try to cut the member off from his friends and family because they hate others being able to influence him. The members are forced to accept; "All that is good is embodied in the leader and the group. All that is bad is on the outside". This is "control of thought" (Hassan, 1990, p. 60). Also, members are taught never to feel for themselves or their own needs but always to think of the group and never to complain. They are never to criticize the leader but criticize themselves instead (Hassan, 1990, p. 64). This is "control of emotions".

Then there is "control of information". Free thought is not allowed. The leader convinces his victims that any information from outside the cult is evil, especially if it is opposing the cult. They are told not to read it or believe it, and these should be discarded as "spiritual pornography", or "apostate literature". The victims are told that such critical information should be destroyed immediately and the members should not even entertain the thought that the information could be true (Hassan, 1990, p. 65). Only information supplied by the cult is true. This is what Muhammad had instructed in his Qur'an.

> *When you hear His verses being disbelieved or mocked, do not sit with them until they engage in other talk, or else you will surely be like them. Allah will surely gather the hypocrites and unbelievers altogether in Hell.* (Q: 4.140)

All these evidences make Islam a cult in the guise of a religion. It is not only the biggest and most successful cult but also the most dangerous.

6.3: Islam and Apostasy

In a pure religious organization, the members would not have any trouble with the people in authority to move to another religion or to a different sect within the same religion because it is the belief system that matters, not membership in an organization. As example; when a Christian wants to change his faith, he can do it without much resistance from the members of his former faith. Similarly, when he moves from one church to another, he can still be a Christian. But in the cults the leaders tell that the members can only be "saved" (or can only be successful) in their organization alone and nowhere else. No other organization has the truth; all others miss the mark. Narcissists strongly disapprove of others' personal autonomy and independence. So it is not the belief system that decides the member's future, but the belief system together with his membership with that particular group. This is a major difference between a cult and a religion.

The Islamic leadership is feared like a cult leadership is feared. To disagree with the leadership is same as disagreeing with God. The cult leaders claim to have direct authority from God to control almost all aspects of the followers' lives. Even questioning the leaders or the agenda is still seen as a sign of rebellion and stupidity. Under Islamic law an apostate must be put to death. There is no dispute on this among classical and modern Muslim scholars. But there is a controversy as to whether Qur'an prescribes any punishment for apostasy in this world or the apostates are threatened with punishment in the afterworld (Warraq, 2003, p. 17). In some verses (3.85, 2.217, 16.106) apostasy is not acceptable to Allah. However, in the following verses Allah commands Muslims to kill the apostates.

*Therefore, do not take a guide from them until they emigrate in the way of Allah. Then, **if they turn back take them and kill them wherever you find them.** Do not take them for guides or helpers.* (Q: 4.89).

*Say; flight will not avail you, **if you flee from death or slaughter, you would enjoy (this world) only for a little (time).*** (Q: 33.15, 16)

Some ahadith describes how apostates were tortured and killed by Muhammad and his companions.

*Narrated Ikrima: Ali burnt some people and this news reached Ibn 'Abbas, who said, "Had I been in his place I would not have burnt them ... I would have killed them, for the Prophet said, **'If somebody (a Muslim) discards his religion, kill him.'*** (Bukhari: 4.52. 260)

*Narrated Abdullah: Allah's Messenger said, The blood of a Muslim who confesses that none has the right to be worshipped but Allah and that I am His Messenger, cannot be shed except in three cases: ... and **the one who reverts from Islam (Apostate) and leaves the Muslims.*** (Bukhari: 9.83.17)

*Narrated Abu Bruda; Abu Musa said, **He was a Jew and became a Muslim and then reverted back to Judaism.** Then Abu Musa requested Muadh to sit down but Muadh said, "I will not sit down **till he has been killed. This is the judgment of Allah and His Messenger,"** and repeated it thrice. **Then Abu Musa ordered that the man be killed, and he was killed.*** (Bukhari: 9.83.58)

Some of the apostates, during Muhammad and the early Caliphs, were poor people. They were of no threat to the Muslims. Despite this, they were brutally murdered. Sometimes the apostates fought the rule of Islam; in other cases they simply rejected Islam by realizing the evil in Islam. However always leaving Islam was the fundamental reason to kill them because the apostates hurt Muhammad's narcissistic feelings. A Narcissist feels devalued once his victims desert him. As Vaknin (1999, p. 199, 273) wrote, *"The Narcissist never really separates from his sources of Narcissistic supply until and unless they cease to be ones. They never say real good bye ... He would do everything to lead to the fulfillment of his greatest horror: being deserted"*.

However, Allah's hatred towards the apostates is the direct violation of the Article 18 of the Universal Declaration of Human Rights, which states;

Everyone has the right to freedom of thought, conscience and religion; this right includes freedom to change his religion or belief, and freedom, either alone or in community with others and in public or private, to manifest his religion or belief in teaching, practice, worship and observance.

Muslims living in Islamic countries have no problem with the rule of putting apostates to death but those living in the West are embarrassed because the Western nations value the freedom of thought and speech which Islam does not. These virtues have never blossomed under Islamic rule.

Muhammad valued only those people who were his narcissistic supply sources. The value judgment was not for the sake of the followers but what they provided him. If that production comes to a standstill and the person ever comes to discover the true nature of the Narcissist hidden underneath all his colorful layers, he is quickly and thoroughly devalued and demonized. Thus, the Narcissist becomes panicky and sometimes violently reacts to the "drop-outs" from his cult. There are many things the Narcissist wants to keep under wraps. Abandonment threatens his precariously balanced personality. Hence apostasy is a serious offence in Islam. It is recorded in Muslim hadith (9.29) that during Muhammad's lifetime, and the lifetimes of the next four Caliphs, hundreds of thousands of Muslims left Islam.

On a large scale, the Caliphs made war on groups that chose to leave Islam and massacres of apostates occurred. On a smaller scale, individual apostates were executed. Many of those apostates became violent and attacked Medina and other centers of Islam. They were led by many false Prophets amongst their individual groups. This group included the rebellion of the Bani Asad in the Najd led by Talha Ibn Khalid, who claimed to be a new Prophet; the opposition of the Bani Hanifa in Yamama, led by Maslama Ibn Habib, who also considered himself a Prophet; the uprising of clans of the Bani Tamin and the Bani Taghlib in northeastern Arabia, led by a woman, called Sajah, who claimed to be a Prophetess and ultimately joined forces with Maslama and the Bani Hanifa; and the insurrection of the Bani Ans in Yemen, led by Aswad al-Ansi, another self-proclaimed Prophet. In the wars these apostates waged against Muslims, fifty or sixty thousand people were killed, and the number of casualties is unprecedented in Arab history (Warraq, 2003, p. 32). Dealing with the apostates in an inhuman way is an aspect of Islam that portrays one of its most ugly faces. This religion is a ridiculous unspiritual belief system; it functions as a religious mafia, forbids men to think and choose for themselves.

6.4: The Force of Narcissism

The malignant Narcissist seeks to dominate every space in which it participates, both on individual and group levels. This strong urge of domination is the origin of narcissistic force. Hotchkiss (2003, p. 9) commented, "*Narcissists exude a powerful force field that is difficult to stay clear of and nearly impossible to control once you [the victim] have been drawn in*". Vaknin (1999, p. 34) compares the force of narcissism with the psychological element of drug addition. It is only interested in, committed to, and obsessed with power and control by any means, and it will sacrifice people and resources indiscriminately to achieve domination.

When the narcissistic defense mechanism is operating in an interpersonal or group setting, the Narcissist does not show the grandiose part of his character in public. He presents a front of patience, friendliness, and confident rationality. However, beneath the surface it is supremely smug and superior. It is "confident" that it can deceive the "fools".

The Narcissists resist the audience in a methodical and calculated manner. The commonly employed methods are misinformation and blocking access to funding and other resources, and if necessary, they even indulge in character assassination. The target person is often unaware of his narcissism; hence he will often be unable to recognize the presence of a narcissistic force which is trying to enslave him, or already have enslaved him. Narcissistic forces are also critical; they can be harsh in their judgments of anything short of perfection, can be bullying and abusive in their verbal criticism, daring others to challenge their destructive communication tactics. Recognizing the presence of narcissistic forces is the only way for a potential victim to save himself. Otherwise, sooner or later everyone around him becomes his victim. Vaknin (1999, p. 114) commented, *"People are sucked – either voluntarily or involuntarily"*.

Narcissists are everyday people like we meet in a general crowd. Often these people are very appealing. They are very cold and calculated type and rarely act out of passion. Some of them are masters of the art of flattery. In real world, the bad people do not look the way they are supposed to. They do not resemble werewolves or a psychopath staring at a corpse on a rocking chair. Famous crime psychologist Rajat Mitra (2007, p. 36) commented, *"[These people] can be very charming and caring if they want to be. In fact they may appear normal to people around them. They have this remarkable ability of hiding other darker self from the world."*

They do not want the targets to know that they have set a trap for them. Unless one has the experience of dealing with narcissism, it is difficult to appreciate how strong a force drives the grandiosity of the narcissism. Only a very small fraction of the psychopaths and malignant Narcissists land in the asylum. A great majority of them are undetected and considered to be "harmless" and "normal".

6.4.1: The Force of Narcissism of Muhammad and the Early Muslims

"A belief in a supernatural source of evil is not necessary; men alone are quite capable of every wickedness".

Joseph Conrad (1857 - 1924)

The strong force of narcissism of Muhammad makes Islam a die-hard religion and Muslims are the first victims. Islam, the legacy of Muhammad, is a powerful force field which is very difficult to stay clear of. Qur'an says,

This day have those who disbelieve despaired of your religion, so fear them not, and fear Me. This day have I perfected for you your religion and completed My favor on you and chosen for you Islam as a religion. (Q: 5.3)

The above verse cannot be from a God. If Islam is a favor bestowed upon the Muslims, then why Allah said, *"Do not fear them, but fear me"*? Actually it was not a warning from the God but from a Narcissist to his victims. In plain English he intended to say; "After my death do not lose your fear in me and be faithful to me and me only". This is a fear based control mechanism designed by the Narcissists to keep their victims in their control. When a malignant Narcissist instills fear in his victims' minds, he has tremendous power over them. The very strength of Islam is this "fear factor". Muhammad had achieved what he desired through his Qur'an.

Anyone who, with a basic knowledge on narcissism, makes an objective study of the Qur'an will find an unmistakable signature of a malignant Narcissist on every page of this supposed to be holy book. Qur'an contains only deception, lies and meaningless blabbering of a mentally sick person. By putting their trust on Qur'an, the Muslims not only become a narcissistic supply source to Muhammad but also inherit his mental illness. This way, the ghost of Muhammad is still haunting the Muslims. Muslims fail to recognize Muhammad as a hardcore criminal and ruthless tyrant. For them, Muhammad was a holy Prophet and Islam made bad men good. Here lies Muhammad's success. Born Muslims are indoctrinated by their parents, relatives, or at Madrassah that start at childhood. The irony is that the programming is done by those people who themselves are the victims of Muhammad's narcissism. Converted Muslims are often misguided people. When a sane person converts to Islam, he automatically becomes a mental slave of Muhammad.

Muslims are unaware of their victimization. Once a person comes within the grip of Islam, it is difficult for him to detach himself from this evil force. The closer one gets to Islam, the more one surrenders to its calling. The more one emulates its Prophet and follows the Qur'an, the more perverted one becomes. While offering five obligatory prayers, Muslims think that they are praying to God, but actually their prayers go to Muhammad. Muhammad is the real God of Islam, not Allah. Earth has several time zones, which differ from one another gradually. It means; every moment there is some Muslim, who is praying to Muhammad, securing his narcissistic supply needs!

Today a billion plus people affirm their Muslim faith. This is the sweet dream of a malignant Narcissist. Muhammad put himself in an extremely enviable position to all Narcissists. A Narcissist never assumes responsibility of the welfare of his victims. Muhammad's followers died happily in battles for him, but it never turned him. Narcissists are emotionally invalid (Vaknin, 1999, p. 28). Even today, when a Muslim picks the burden of Islamic jihad he fails to see the truth. This is the height of Muhammad's brainwashing capability on the Muslims. As Mirza Malkam Khan had a slogan of unraveled cynicism (cited Sina, 2008, p. 66), *"Tell the Muslims something is in the Qur'an, and they will die for you."*

6.5: Inverted Narcissism

Inverted Narcissism (also called covert Narcissism, co-dependency, Narcissist's magnets, self-effacing) is a Dependent Personality Disorder. An inverted Narcissist is a co-dependent who relies exclusively on and actively seeks relationships with the Narcissist (Zayn & Dibble, 2007, p. 108). They prefer to live with the Narcissists, to cater to their needs and to succumb to their whims regardless of any abuse inflicted on them by the Narcissist. This is the way they have been conditioned. They feel alive, stimulated and excited only with Narcissists. The world glows in multicolor in the presence of a Narcissist and decays to sepia colors in his absence. The Narcissist is the only meaningful, crucially significant figure in the inverted Narcissist's life.

Inverted narcissism can be compared with "Stockholm syndrome". This term is used to describe a paradoxical psychological phenomenon wherein hostages express empathy and have positive feelings towards their captors. This occurs when the hostages tend to identify emotionally with the captors rather than with the police. In this sense, the captor becomes the person in control of the captive's basic needs for survival and the victim's life itself. Similarly, the inverted Narcissists tend to remain in those situations because that is what they "know". They feel empty and unhappy in relationships with any other kind of person. This is the Narcissist's leverage over the inverted Narcissist.

The inverted Narcissists are typically insecure because they have not been valued for themselves, and have been valued by the Narcissist only to the extent that they meet their Narcissist's needs. They develop their self-concepts based on their Narcissist's treatment of them and therefore often have highly inaccurate ideas about who they are.

6.6: Pre-Islamic Arabia and the Dawn of Islam

Narcissism affects society and culture in profound ways (Vankin, 1999, p. 11). The Narcissists always try to modify the environment to make it conductive to his narcissistic needs. Muhammad did the same. Not only he had enslaved people but also changed the Arab society and the culture. His influence was utterly negative; he destroyed the "humanness" of the Arabs and brought jungle rule in a rather peaceful society through Islam.

Islam is condemned by history. Hence Muslims often rewrite it and try to give a rosy picture. Scholars write hundreds of books every year exaggerating the "chaos and confusion" that prevailed in pre-Islamic Arabia. One such book, published in India, claims that pre-Islamic Arabs used to drink the blood of their enemies in the battlefield, sisters and mothers were often raped by brothers and sons, and when Islam came, it civilized the Arabs. Another author (Kotb, 2004, p. 193) wrote that the pagan Arabs used to bury their female children alive, make women dance naked in the vicinity of Ka'ba during their annual fairs, and treat women as mere chattels and objects of sexual pleasure possessing no rights or position whatsoever, and when Qur'an was revealed Arabs became civilized.

But the history says something else. The revisionist image of pre-Islamic Arabs as skilled fighters is widely accepted by the historians. But its derogatory overtones are preached because they are essential to show Islam as a divine religion which makes bad people good. Muslim scholars try hard to paint the pre-Islamic period, called *Jahiliyyah* or "Period of Ignorance" in the worst possible light. They demonize Arabs to make the resulting Islamic society, arguably the most ignorant and brutal in history, look good by comparison. But whatever little evidence we have of these people, their lives, and their customs, indicates that they did not act foolishly. Unlike their descendants in the twenty-first century; seventh century Arabs were a free, brave and peace-loving people who cherished family values and honored tribal commitments.

There is no historical evidence of Arabs conquering their neighbors before Islam. They were illiterate, isolated, and perhaps even ignorant about the outside world. But there is no evidence at all that they were bloodthirsty criminals who terrorized and looted in violent raids. However, that all changed with the advent of Muhammad. After Islam, religious intolerance crept in, and Muslims conquered much of the world. When Muhammad could not establish his religion peacefully, he became a criminal. When Muhammad took control as a leader, the Muslims put

Arabia in turmoil, spilling blood for plunder. They became a gang who terrorized and raided settlements and caravans alike. They knew terror, rape, murder, thievery and slave trade were wrong, yet they did these things in the name of God. Their consciences were simply paralyzed by a malignant Narcissist's powerful force. They became inverted Narcissists of Muhammad. Muhammad and his Allah said that booty was good, that raping the infidel women pleases God, and that killing the enemies was the surest way to reach the paradise, and people believed him. The Narcissist leader gave a sacred aura to crime and terrorism.

Islam turns good men bad, destroys civilization and replaces it with barbarism; it brings sickness to a rather healthy society. For this reason, today's Muslims find it essential to revise their past and invert truth. Deep inside, they are afraid, the truth might come out. This is why Muslims strongly resist Qur'anic criticism, does not allow any archeological exploration in Mecca and Medina, and stopped all further research on Sana'a manuscripts. But it is their true past, their actual history, their pre-Islamic superior culture which accuses them and haunts them. Simply stated – Islam perverts men and erodes culture.

Muhammad's narcissistic force had a very bad influence on Arab society and culture. During Muhammad and his successors, prostitution diminished for a time (Durant, 1950, p. 220). It was not because Muhammad had a high regard for women and he worked for the welfare of the fallen women. But it was because Muhammad lowered the status of married women to the lowest level of sex-slavery and prostitution. He allowed sexual appetite so many outlets within the Islamic law that the prostitutes became jobless. Muhammad viewed women as domestic animals. There is enough evidence that prior to Islam's aggression, women were much more respected and used to enjoy more rights than at any time since.

Before advent of Islam, many Arab families had a matriarchal (mother is the ruler of the family) system. There were many dominant queens during the pre-Islamic era; e.g., Zabibi, Shamsiyah, Zenobia, and above all, the queen of Sheba (her original name was Bilqis), whose beauty had bewitched Solomon (Shaikh, 1999, p. 16). Muhammad's first wife, Khadija was a powerful merchant-woman. It is surprising that Allah neither commanded Muslim women to veil nor allowed Muhammad to practice polygamy despite the fact that Khadija was fifteen years older than him and had been married twice before. Only after Khadija's death all these unfair Qur'anic verses started coming down. It is also a misconception that in pre-Islamic Arabia female infants were murdered and Islam abolished that practice. If that were true, how did Arab men marry multiple times? Muhammad allowed his followers to marry four women and he himself had more than a dozen. How could it be possible, if there were female infanticide in practice?

Pre-Islamic Arabs were mainly polytheists. Every tribe had their own idols in Ka'ba. Christians, Jews, Zoroastrians, Sabeans (an extinct monotheistic faith) and also some Hindus used to live in peace and harmony with one another. There were many self-proclaimed Prophets. The followers of different faiths had equal freedom and dignity. But Muhammad was a breath away from destroying all of that. He would transform his world into a killing machine poised to plunder Arabia and then the world. Today Saudi Arabia is the most extremist of the Muslim states.

For the centuries before Islam, tribal alliances had formed the foundation of peace in the Arab world. There were no policemen or courts, as none were needed. Caravans traveled safely and people lived in harmony because they had established a means to work together and to work things out. They were fond of poetry. Poets were the journalists during those days. Apart from the Jews, most Arabians were illiterate, so poetry became the most effective means of disseminating a message. Walker (2002, p. 79) wrote, "*The court poets were preoccupied with form and style, the melody of words, the rhythms of balanced phrases, the music and harmony that emerged from the interplay of vowels and consonants, and the beauty of expression. They discovered new metres and new rhythms, developed to the full opportunities their language offered for poetic eloquence, and set standards for excellence that later poets were long to emulate*".

Later on, poetry composed by Hanifs became the initial ingredient in Islam. But once Muhammad became a ruler, he cursed the poets. In pre-Islamic days, the poets used to meet during Ramadan in a great seven day national gathering with their compositions at Okaz. But once Muhammad attained power, he put an end to the contests (Walker, 2002, p. 80). He had developed a strong detest for the poets.

Those who go astray follow the poets. (Q: 26.224)

Narrated Ibn `Umar: The Prophet said, 'It is better for a man to fill the inside of his body with pus than to fill it with poetry'. (Bukhari: 8.73.175)

Narrated Abu Huraira; Allah's Apostle; said, It is better for anyone of you that the inside of his body be filled with pus which may consume his body, than it be filled with poetry. (Bukhari: 8.73.176)

Original works of pre-Islamic poets did not survive much after advent of Islam. Within hundred years of Muhammad's taking over of Mecca, the Arab genius of poetry was completely erased (Warraq, 2000, p. 151). As Taha Husayn, an Egyptian scholar, writing in 1925, lamented that little of any genuine pre-Islamic literature had survived (Krizeck, 1964, p. 60). Most of those poets were Christian Arabs. But Muhammad and his followers had wiped out almost everything through deliberate neglect. Wherever Muhammad went; bloodshed, death and destruction followed him. He destroyed everything good whatever he found close by. Muslims followed his instruction and carried out his order blindly.

Ethics and religion are not only interdependent but have great influence on each other. A religion without ethical values cannot be called a religion. As Lewis (1961, p. 257) wrote, "*If religion is true, we should expect religion and ethics to have much importance for one another... Religion is itself nothing but ethics – or ethics with relatively incidental accompaniment*". The moral teachings of the Hindu, Christian, Buddhist, and Jain religions have enormous positive influence on the progress of the modern civilization. But the poisonous teachings of Qur'an gave us nothing except violence, misery, poverty, cruelty, death and destruction. Can any good thing ever come out from Muhammad's teaching? Was Pope Benedict XVI, far away from truth when he quoted, "*Show me just what Mohammed brought that was new, and there you will find only evil and inhuman, such as his command to spread by the sword the faith he preached*"?

Every culture changes itself slowly, but it can also change in a dramatic way. Full-scale cultural transformation usually happens only under the threat of force (Twenge & Campbell, 2010, p. 307). The best example is Iran, where a group of

Mullahs imposed strict Islamic practice on a largely unhappy population. Germany was one of the richest and most peaceful nations in Europe, yet under the Nazis the urge to ride roughshod over weaker nations and impose an iron fist across Europe proved irresistible (Morse, 2010, p. 2). However, when a cultural change takes place under pressure, the core cultural ideas co-opt themselves to fit a new vision. As example, Hitler turned German culture something very ugly and twisted, but he did it using core ideas from the existing culture. He rose to power by wielding Teutonic myths, stories of Aryan history and the ancient symbols like swastika. Muhammad imposed religious fanaticism on a rather peaceful pre-Islamic culture by including most of the pagan practices in his religion. Hitler and Muhammad were cut from the same cloth – fully committed, ruthless and totally dedicated fanatics. Hitler was stopped, Mein Kampf was exposed, and Nazism was eradicated, as they could not coexist with a civilized world. Once the grip of Islam loosens, the culture of Arabia might revert back to its pre-Islamic form.

6.7: How Muhammad Enslaved the Early Muslims?

People cannot survive in a social isolation. Everyone wants to be a productive member of the community to feel proud and to give support to others. This built-in instinctive need is very strong. Logic is not as strong as our need to be accepted in a community. Since this is a strong need, some immoral people can exploit it in a cult for money and power. People join cult thinking that it is a healthy group; they want to be ethical and responsible for one another. By trusting the leader they allow themselves to be reprogrammed by the leader. Slowly the leader convinces them that they are required to accept a lot of new information on faith, and once they accept that, they start seeing reality relative to that new information they are working with. Ultimately the leader's teachings become absolute truth. Muhammad, as the founder of Islam, performed no different. His early followers were mostly slaves and stray people who had no stand or no hope in the society. Though he started his mission as a humble spokesman of God, gradually he became the single powerful leader of his cult. He focused full attention on himself and became more of a source for "truth" than God.

The early Muslims who fought, killed or got killed for Allah were ordinary individuals who had once led peaceful lives. But something made them vulnerable and needy. Searching for something to fill the holes in their lives, they had the misfortune of meeting a charismatic malignant Narcissist and falling under his spell. Gradually, more and more isolated, they were indoctrinated into the mind set of Islam, and ultimately Muhammad's word and teachings became absolute truth. They became inverted Narcissists.

Voltaire (1694 - 1778), a French enlightenment writer and philosopher famous for his advocacy of civil liberties, including freedom of religion, had immense hate for Muhammad. He wrote a Muslim blasphemous play *Mahomet,* performed in 1742 and dedicated to Pope Benedict XIV, where Muhammad was presented as an imposter who enslaved men's souls (Spencer, 2005, p. 20). This play was a study of religious fanaticism and self-serving manipulation based on an episode in the traditional biography of Muhammad in which he orders the murder of his critics. Voltaire (1745) described the play as, "… *written in opposition to the founder of a false and barbarous sect to whom could I with more propriety inscribe a satire on the cruelty and errors of a false Prophet"*. Today, with the development of psychology and personality disorder studies, thanks to Freud, Jung, Kernberg, Kohut, Vaknin, Masterson, Hotchkiss and many others, we know how true Voltaire was. Muslim's perpetual mental slavery is repugnant and awful, and because of this perpetual mental slavery, Muslims cannot write an honest biography of their Prophet that does not hide the truth. They have to defend Islam's foolishness, more precisely; the inverted Narcissists have to protect the Narcissist.

Muhammad had used various methods to manipulate people in his cult.

6.7.1: The Fatal Attraction of Muhammad's Fantasy World

The fantasy world of a Narcissist has a seductive allure which promises the potential victim in its specialness. Except few people; like, Abu Bakr, Uthman, Ali and Omar; most of Muhammad's early followers were a bunch of slaves and socially outcast people belonging to the dignitaries of the Quraysh. Due to their poverty, these slaves were vulnerable and deprived of many things in their lives. Muhammad gave them hope – "Accept Allah as God and me as messenger of God. Obey my command and paradise is assured for you".

Allah's erotic paradise is the sweetest bait that was ever dangled before the Muslims to motivate them to fight. In the God-Prophet relationship, Muhammad was the dominating force, and the message was clear – "Fight the infidels. If you win you will get sex and booty and if you die Allah will reward you". It was such a win-win situation. Muhammad's paradise was glittered with the fulfillment of all kinds of worldly desires and sense enjoyment. It was a sinister ploy to recruit those who had no hope or expectation of ever getting those things in their present lives.

Distortion of reality is a common practice of the Narcissists; it works wonder. The lure of paradise, booty and women were simply irresistible to those early Muslims. If we say, "A belief system is a lens through which we can see God", then Muhammad had distorted this lens and it resulted in distorting their picture of God. The minds of the Muslims were "kidnapped" by Muhammad.

6.7.2: The Superficial Charm of Muhammad

The superficial charm of a Narcissist is enchanting. They often appear simple, saint-like, colorful and exciting as they draw the innocent targets into its web. Often they pretend to be wonderful and entertaining. Sometimes there is extreme and unrealistic flattery. But, under this cover-up, they always look for the narcissistic vulnerabilities of the targets. Muhammad had a pleasant personality. He used to greet people (obviously whom he liked) with a sweet smile. He hardly laughed, and if he did, he covered his mouth. He loved perfume (Muslim: 7.2700). It is a fact that we, consciously or unconsciously, judge a person's character by his appearance. Osama bin Laden was very soft-spoken and had a saintly face, Saddam Hussein had an uncle-like friendly ear-to-ear smile, and Hitler had a comical face with a funny moustache. Yet all of them have committed crimes that are beyond imagination. There is no "face of evil".

Moreover, many of the Narcissists are fully aware of the power of oratory. A great speech requires eloquence, a moment of consequence and ideas of importance. Both bin Laden and Hitler had the gift of the gab. They could mesmerize people with their talk. Laden was a truly gifted orator, and his amazing oratory skill had inspired hundreds of youth to lay down their lives as suicide bomber. Muhammad had the ability to talk readily, fluently, and convincingly. He believed that "*in eloquence there is magic*" (Sunnan Abu Dawud: 4.4994) and used to say, "*Some eloquent speech has the influence of magic*" (Bukhari: 7.62.76). Elsewhere he boasted, "*I have been given the keys of eloquent speech and given victory with terror*" (Bukhari: 9.87.127).

The superficial charm and high charisma of Muhammad was a tactics used to get his way. By acting nicely on the surface, he concealed his true personality. His charm was entirely insincere. He used his "skills" to gain the trust of unsuspecting people and then lured them into his narcissistic trap.

6.7.3: Muhammad's Mental Instability

The mental instability of their Prophet often confused the early Muslims. There was a vast difference between what he had preached and what he had followed. He presented himself as an honorable messenger of God, but lived the life of a criminal. This "Jekyll and Hyde" unpredictability and the swift changes of mood and priorities of a Narcissist often deny the people around him their autonomy, their unperturbed development and self-fulfillment and their path to self-reorganization. It compels the people to live in a constant fear and anxiety – what next?, where next?, who next?, when next? This fear of uncertainty, anxiety and unpredictability make them an instrument to the Narcissist. The victim no longer knows what is true and right, and what is wrong and forbidden. These are recreated for them by the Narcissist. This cripples his judgment and makes him feel like a child constantly insecure and frightened. In the uncertainty and frightening atmosphere, the victim has only one sure thing to cling to, i.e., the Narcissist himself. Once they start compromising, there is no end of it.

Muhammad sometimes overvalued his potential victims and then completely devalued them. Once he declared that he was the foretold Prophet of the Jews, but afterwards he devalued them completely and condemned them. Same was true for the Christians also. This contradictory behavior of valuation and devaluation of the same people often makes other people nervous. People are worried – is it my turn after them? They suffer from emotional insecurity, an eroded sense of self-worth, fear, stress, and anxiety. They unconsciously try very hard not to upset their leader. In psychology this is called "walking on eggshells" (it means; to watch what you say or do around a certain person because anything might set him off). Gradually, emotional paralysis ensued and the Muslims came to occupy the same emotional wasteland inhabited by their Narcissist Prophet.

This influence remains stable, even when the Narcissist leader is long out of the lives of the followers. Even today, after fourteen centuries of their leader's death, Muslims cannot see that their beloved Prophet was actually some kind of mafia lord, because they still want to remain in the good-book of Muhammad. They are compromising ever since the birth of Islam.

6.7.4: Muhammad's Misleading Signals

A Narcissist's deceitful emotional messages often mislead people around him because he can mimic real emotions artfully. Most people are misled into believing that he is more human than common. As Vaknin (1999, p. 358) wrote, "*Narcissists deceive their environment in more than one way. Even when they express emotions it is because they have discovered the efficiency of this instrument in obtaining Narcissistic supply*". When the Narcissists display outburst of emotions they are actually putting on a calculated response to obtain a certain result. They do not value warm or caring relationships and are unmoved by things that would upset the normal person, while outraged by insignificant matters. They are bystanders to the emotional life of others, perhaps envious and scornful of feelings they cannot have or understand. At the end, the Narcissists are cold, with shallow emotions, living in a dark world of their own.

Muhammad's emotional messages were fraudulent and purposeful. He was capable of witnessing or order acts of utter brutality without experiencing a shred of emotion. While visiting the tomb of his mother, Muhammad cried for his long dead mother but Allah did not allow him to pray for her. This was a fake emotion. In reality, Muhammad had an overly complicated relationship with her. He simply could not forgive her. By mimicking real emotions artfully, by shedding few drops of crocodile tears, Muhammad made other people to believe that he was more human than others.

One of the strongest of human emotions is fear – healthy or unhealthy. Fear is good as long as it takes up a protective role, helping a person to rightly recognize and respond cautiously to impending dangers and possible threats. As example, a fear that makes a passerby to wait patiently before crossing a busy road for safety reasons is certainly a healthy fear. The fear of death, which functions to make us alert in dangerous situations, is a very healthy emotion because it helps a person to reason more clearly. But often fear turns unhealthy; it overpowers an individual's power of reasoning and other positive attributes that make him see things in clearer light. Muhammad based his religion on this unhealthy human weakness – the fear for unknown and unseen.

Muhammad and Allah continually repeated the words, "*fear me, fear me, obey me, obey me*" in Qur'an. When Muhammad successfully instilled the unhealthy fear in the minds of the Muslims, he snatched their freedom. Allah's wrath, doomsday, hellfire – all these clever emotional tricks drove them to seek refuge with him. A healthy fear is a healthy life force, but the kind of fear that we see in Islam tramples self-confidence. It is simply not the fear but "addiction to fear".

Another strong emotion is love. Narcissists know this human weakness very well. When a new member goes to a Narcissist, he experiences a sudden "overflow" of love, as if suddenly he has become the most lovable person in the world. If he is not aware that the Narcissist had set a trap for him, he will be in danger. Gradually he will be locked in the Narcissist's web and the exit gate will be closed. Initially Muhammad had set such a "love-trap" for the Jews and Christians. With a typical "love bombing", i.e., his deliberate show of affection or friendship, he tried to elate the Jews and Christians, praised them, their scriptures and their Gods and Prophets. These fake misleading emotions of love were specially forged for the Jews and Christians. Accordingly, Allah became too active and started sending down many verses praising the Jews. But Muhammad's all attempts to gain the Jews as convert to Islam failed though he was partially successful with the Christians.

All these manipulative faked emotions confuse many people around the Narcissist (Vaknin, 1999, p. 358). For him this is a game and he can spend his entire life getting better at the game. The victims often feel that something is wrong but due to utter confusion cannot tell what went wrong. They even do not understand that in their perplexed condition, they are slowly coming within the narcissistic grip of the manipulative leader.

6.7.5: Pathological Lying

Pathological lying (also called *Pseudologia fantastica, mythomania*), is one of several terms applied by psychiatrists to the behavior of habitual or compulsive lying. For a Narcissist, telling the lie makes the game more interesting. But while playing this game of deception, others are left in a state of confusion. Since they do this all the time and seldom tell the truth, that makes them pathological liars. With many years of practice, they become very convincing liars. They lie coolly and easily, even when it is obvious they are being untruthful. It is almost impossible for them to be consistently truthful about either a major or minor issue. They lie for no apparent reason, even when it would be easier and safer to tell the truth. It actually makes him feel great when the game becomes more and more cruel. He feels like he is one damn special, distinguished, famous and unforgettable person. He is just an image, not a real person. Muhammad's claims were very strange. He declared, "*The very first thing Allah Almighty ever created was my soul, first of all things, the Lord created my mind, I am from Allah and believers are from me. Just as Allah created me noble, he also gave me noble character.*" (Sina, 2008, p. 62). Allah declared very generously that He had created the universe for Muhammad (Tabaqat, Vol.1), and gave him an "*exalted standard of character*" (Q: 68.4).

All these claims were fabricated in Muhammad's lie factory. Certainly he did not have a noble character; rather all evidences confirm exactly the opposite. This type of lies of a Narcissist is also called "crazy lying". Confronting their lies may provoke an unpredictably intense rage or simply a Buddha-like ear-to-ear smile. These plagiarists and thieves are rarely original thinkers and they seldom credit the true originators of ideas. For them, objective truth does not exist. The only "truth" is whatever will best achieve the outcome that meets their needs. When a Narcissist tells a lie, he repeats it often and sticks to it. This is the art of lying; all expert liars and politicians know it.

When Muhammad recounted his tale of ascending to the seventh heaven, many Muslims lost their faith on Muhammad and left him. His closest friend, Abu Bakr, was at first taken aback. He was puzzled; he had two choices either to abandon Muhammad by accepting that he was a fraud, or remain with him by believing his absurd tales. Ibn Ishaq wrote,

Many Muslims gave up their faith. Some went to Abu Bakr and said, 'What do you think of your friend now? He alleges that he went to Jerusalem last night and prayed there and came back to Mecca.' Bakr said that they were lying about the Apostle. But they told him that he was in the mosque at this very moment telling the Quraysh about it. Bakr said, 'If he says so then it must be true. I believe him. And that is more extraordinary than his story at which you boggle'. (Ishaq: 183)

The particular words of Abu Bakr need to be read between the lines. "*If he says so then it must be true. I believe him*" – it means, Abu Bakr saw some credibility in Muhammad's absurd story and believed him. This is the power of big lie; there is always certain force of credibility. Muhammad knew it, so was Hitler.

6.7.6: The Method of Projection

To change the victims, the Narcissists often use the method of projection. To understand it better, let us take the example (Hotchkiss, 2003, p. 10) of a Narcissist mother who is conflicted about her own sexual desires. To hide her own inferiority and to inflate her false self, she will call her innocent teenage daughter a sexual pervert when actually the daughter did not even have any experience in sex. The mother repeats her tough words so strongly and so often that a time comes, the young woman is subconsciously forced to accept that label and starts behaving promiscuously. It is as if the daughter is a blank screen on which the mother has projected her unacceptable lust and impressed upon the daughter the immoral character of the mother.

Muhammad had used the same method of projection on his followers to secure their confidence. He was illiterate. To hide his own inferiority and to inflate his false self, Muhammad declared himself the guardian of illiterates sent by Allah (Bukhari: 3.34.335). According to him, Allah loves illiterate people and hates educated people and Allah had promised the first entry to paradise to the illiterate Muslims and the last entry to the educated Muslims (Sunaan Ibn Majah: 5.4290). By this way Muhammad not only glorified his shortcoming but projected it towards his followers. Qur'an says,

Those who follow the Apostle, the unlettered Prophet, whom they find mentioned in their own (Scriptures), in the Law and the Gospel ... so believe in God and his Apostle, the unlettered Prophet. (Q: 7.157, 158).

The message of holy illiteracy served three purposes for Muhammad. First; since Muhammad was a fraud and he could prosper only through deception, he had encouraged Muslims to hate and have contempt for knowledge, which in turn secured the survival of Islam. Illiterate people can be fooled more easily. Second; when Muhammad declared himself a guardian of the illiterates, his followers felt a better emotional bond with him. Muhammad became the "dearest" of his followers as if all Muslims were his own people and Muhammad was one of them. Allah has sent an illiterate man to guide the illiterates. It boosted up the confidence of the slaves and stray youth who were his early followers. Third; since Allah likes illiteracy, therefore illiteracy must be godly. In simple words, Muhammad used his shortcoming as an advantage. This is a manipulation through projection.

Muhammad's declaration of holy illiteracy as Allah's preference had a terrible influence on the Muslims. As example; Akbar, the Mughal emperor of India was an illiterate, and surprisingly, it was not a shame for him but a pride. This stupid Muslim emperor, in his own eyes, had one qualification to be a Prophet. "*The Prophets were all illiterates*", he used to point out frequently and sincerely believed that, in order to honor their Prophet, it is the essential duty for every faithful Muslim to keep one of their sons illiterate (Eraly, 1997, p. 909). This shows how much Muhammad's method of projection had worked on the Muslims.

Muhammad used method of projection to impose Arab supremacy on the non-Arab Muslims. It should be rightly termed as racism. Few quotes from Islamic sources (cited Shaikh, 1995, pp. 29, 30, 32) are as below,

1. He, who aggresses against Arabia, shall not win Muhammad's love, nor will he intercede for him.
2. Muhammad told Suleiman Farsi, a freed Persian slave who fought for Islam, "*If you bear a grudge against Arabia, you bear grudge against me*".
3. The Quraysh are the rulers of men in vice and virtue until the Day of Judgment.
4. The right to rule (Caliphate) shall belong to Quraysh, even if two men existed.

Muhammad even wanted his followers to look culturally different from the nonbelievers.

1. When the Prophet saw Abdullah bin Amr as wearing clothes dyed in saffron (during that time, a significant number of Hindus settled in Mecca), he forbade them to wear that on the ground that such cloths were worn by the nonbelievers.
2. The Prophet said, "*The Jews and the Christians do not dye (grey) their hair, so you should do the opposite what they do.*"
3. Arabic is the most sacred language for a Muslim, more than his own mother-tongue.

Muhammad projected Mecca, his home place.

O Mecca, by Allah, you are better than any part of the earth and dearer to me than the rest of the world. The Mecca is the best place and dearer than any other place. Had my Nation not driven me out, I would not have lived in another place.

And, ultimately Muhammad declared,

No person attains faith till I am dear to him than the persons of his household, his wealth and the whole of his mankind. (Muslim: 1.70)

Now let us see what the outcome of these deceitful manipulative games is. Since none can enter paradise without Muhammad's intercession, the believers find it absolutely necessary to follow the Prophet in every detail with utmost sincerity. As Shaikh (1995, pp. 43-4) wrote, "*The faith has come to mean, not only to pray, fast and perform Hajj, the way the Prophet used to do, but also look like him, that is cut hair like him, wear cloths like him, walk like him, talk like him, sleep like him, eat like him, adopt his manners and above all, love and hate what he loved and hated"*. Imitation is the worst kind of flattery.

Muhammad's method of projection works so much on the Muslims that they willingly and submissively self-denigrate to become a partner in his narcissistic game. It has a devastating effect on the national character of the non-Arab Muslims. When a non-Arab person accepts Islam, he is forced to love Arabia and its traditions at the expense of the culture, honor and pride of his own motherland. Mecca is now more favorite than his birthplace and Arabic more than his mother-tongue. Since Muhammad hated the infidels, a non-Arab Muslim must hate his own people of his own nation who are following the faith of their ancestors. In fact, the non-Arab Muslims have to hate their own forefathers to love and glorify the Arab heroes. The Pakistani, Afghan, Bangladeshi and Indian Muslims have immense hate for their Hindu counterpart. Can they deny the fact that their forefathers were forced to accept Islam under sword and through deception? Every Asian Muslim is a blood relative in the direct line of descent of Hindu parents. But they have to "sincerely" hate the Hindus to remain in the good-book of Muhammad. In Egypt, the glorious land of ancient Pharaohs, no one call themselves Egyptians any more. All of them had become Arabs. Muhammad's deceptive game of projection worked on them and changed their worldview. Naipaul (1998, pp. 1, 72) wrote,

Islam is not simply a matter of conscience or private belief. It makes imperial demands. A convert's worldview alters. His holy places are in Arab lands; his sacred language is Arabic. His idea of history alters. He rejects his own: he becomes, whether he likes it or not, a part of the Arab story. The convert has to turn away from everything that is his. The disturbance for societies is immense, and even after a thousand years can remain unresolved; the turning away has to be done again and again. People develop fantasies about who and what they are.

The sacred Arab places have to be the sacred places of all the converted peoples. They have to strip themselves of their past; of converted peoples nothing is required but the purest faith (if such a thing can be arrived at), Islam, submission. It is the most uncompromising type of imperialism.

Slowly, a non-Arab Muslim becomes a cultural refugee in his own country because he does not have any real love, respect or loyalty for his own motherland and ancestors as we notice in almost all the Indian Muslims. After being completely devoid of National honor, slowly these rootless Muslims develop a strong slave mentality for the Arabs, because whatever they think or do must conform to the patterns of thinking and doing set by the Arabian soil and culture. This type of self-contradiction is not there in any other religion.

6.7.7: Alienation from an Individual's Own Powers

Islam is an authoritative religion. In this religion, man is controlled by a higher power. Allah is entitled to obedience, reverence and worship. But the reason for worship, reverence and obedience lies not in the moral qualities of the deity, not in love or justice, but in the fact that the deity has control, i.e., has power over man. Allah, the higher power, has the right to force man to worship Him and that lack of reverence and obedience constitutes sin. Therefore Allah is the sole possessor of what was originally man's. The more perfect Allah becomes, the more imperfect becomes the man. A Muslim projects the best he has unto Allah and thus impoverishes himself. Now, Allah has all love, all wisdom and all justice. Man is deprived of these qualities; he is now empty, poor, completely powerless and weak and pathetic. Ultimately the man is alienated from himself. His only access to himself is through Allah. Having lost his own he is completely at Allah's mercy. This mechanism is the very same which can be observed in interpersonal relationships of a masochistic, submissive character where one person is awed by another and attributes his own powers and aspirations to the other person. The alienation from his own powers makes the Muslim slavishly dependent on Allah. Slowly he becomes a man without self-confidence. That is why everything is *Insha'Allah* (if Allah wills it – fatalism)for a Muslim. His religious experience is always authoritarian, never blissful.

Deprived of everything, such a person's only hope is Muhammad. Only through Muhammad, a Muslim can beg Allah to return some of his humanity and for this the Muslim is ready to reserve his full life for Islam. He always feels himself to be a sinner (living without humanity is sinful). The more he praises Allah, the emptier he becomes. The emptier he becomes, the more sinful he feels. The more sinful he feels, the more he praises Allah – and less he is able to regain himself. The less he is able to regain himself, the more he comes within the evil grip of Muhammad. This is the same mechanism that makes people endow the leaders of even the most inhuman systems with qualities of super wisdom and kindness. Whether the people worship a punishing, awesome God or a similarly conceived leader makes little difference.

6.7.8: Introducing Errors in the Thought Process

Probably the most important cause humans differ from animals is that the humans are able to use information to reason and solve problems even when the information is partial or unavailable, as Descartes said, *"Cogito ergo sum"* – I think therefore I am (Evans, 1984, p. 18). Reasoning is the process by which we use the knowledge we have to draw conclusions or infer something we know about the domain of interest.

Reason and freedom are interdependent. If everything is *Insha'Allah* or God willing, then why we need to use our thinking capability? If there is no drive for progress in a human, mind stagnates. Once the mind rebels at stagnation, the man loses the capacity to make sense of things, to establish and verify facts and to change or justify practices, institutions and beliefs. This is the time various thinking errors creep in the mind and ultimately the mind becomes dysfunctional.

Muhammad infused this *Insha'Allah* very skillfully in the thought process of his followers to make it dysfunctional. He taught his followers that they should shun everything that is opposed to Islam. Islam is the only belief system where the followers do not aspire for freedom because the clerics tell their victims that it is the will of Allah. This is why there will never be true democracy in the Muslim world.

Muslims' mental slavery to their Narcissist Prophet starts from this dysfunctional thinking process. Few examples of dysfunctional thinking are as below,

1. Polarized or all-or-nothing thinking (seeing things in black-and-white categories) – dar-ul-Islam and dar-ul-harb, believers and nonbelievers, Muslims and non-Muslims, paradise and hell.
2. Catastrophic thinking (delusional anxieties by thinking about irrational worst-case outcomes) – Jews and Christians are secretly conspiring to destroy Islam, Jews are controlling the world economy.
3. Discounting the positive, accentuate the negative – all the non-Muslims are enemies of Muslims, no infidel can be trusted as a friend.
4. Overgeneralization (making sweeping negative conclusions) – vilest creatures in Allah's sight are Jews and Christians.
5. Labeling (An extreme form of over generalization) – Jews are pigs, Christians are rats, put a global label on nonbelievers as Kafirs.
6. Mind reading – Muslims know that the non-Muslims are always opposing Islam and behaving negatively because of Islam, Allah is the best plotter.
7. The Fortune Teller Error (you anticipate something will happen and are convinced your prediction is already sealed) – Allah will destroy all the infidels, paradise for Muslims and hellfire for nonbelievers.
8. Mental filter and Tunnel vision (only see things in the Islamic way) – Qur'an is the only truth, Islam is the only perfect religion and all other religions and competing philosophies are false, Islam has perfect answers for science, politics, government, economics, psychosocial problems and human life.
9. Personalization (see oneself as the cause of some negative event when in reality he had little connection with it) – Israel exists on one tiny piece of land surrounded by much larger Arab nations such as Jordan, Syria, Saudi Arabia, Iraq, and Egypt. In spite of this, the Arabs were repeatedly defeated by the Israeli Jews. Because of this many non-Arab countries have made Jew-bashing as the cornerstone of their foreign policy with a view to winning the Arab sympathy.

When the thought process is dysfunctional, the followers are ready to believe anything what their leader would say. Without realizing, the victims just give up their own rights and allow themselves to be directed by the Narcissist leader.

6.8: Who Benefited from Islam?

Muslim scholars and sympathizers often portray Muhammad as a poor man who led a very simplistic life and dedicated his life for the service of God and society. But this is an absolute falsehood; during his prophetic career, Muhammad gathered a vast wealth for himself and at the time of his death he was one richest man in Arabia. He was not shy to admit that he loved money,

Narrated by Abu Huraira; Allah's Apostle said; I have been made victorious with terror (cast in the hearts of the enemy). The treasures of the world were

brought to me and put in my hand. (Bukhari: 4.52.220)

Terror was Muhammad's legacy and one of his strongest motivations was money. Another motivation was sex with captured women.

Narrated by 'Adi bin Hatim; .... the Prophet further said, 'If you live long enough the treasures of Khosrau will be opened and taken as spoils. You will carry out handfuls of gold and silver'. (Bukhari: 4.56.793)

Narrated by 'Uqba bin 'Amr; the Prophet said, 'I have been given the keys of the treasures of the world by Allah'. (Bukhari: 4.56.795)

Ali [Muhammad's adopted son, son-in-law, and future Caliph] said, 'Prophet, women are plentiful. You can get a replacement, easily changing one for another.' (Tabari: VIII.62; Ishaq: 496).

The simple reason Muhammad could not be poor is that he maintained a large family. We cannot say exactly, how many times he married, but it is generally agreed that at one stage he had at least nine wives. Marriages were costly social activities during those days as it is today. When Muhammad married his daughter-in-law, Zaynab, it is recorded that he celebrated for a week; hundreds of goats were slaughtered to provide lavish meals for the residents of Medina (Bukhari: 6.60.314-7; 7.62.84, 92, 95, 97, 99, 100). Throwing such a lavish party for a week for the entire population of Medina can hardly be called a simplistic life style. Today only millionaires can provide such party.

Secondly, marrying multiple wives was a sign of wealth in Saudi Arabia and still so in these days. As example, king 'Abd al-'Aziz of Arabia had 300 wives. (Pipes, 1983, p. 180). Each of Muhammad's wives had her own house independent of another, maids and slaves to look after them. This is one example of his "simplistic" life style. Also, he had a good number of slaves, servants, slave girls, personal assistants, and bodyguards. Then there were many mules, horses, donkeys, goats and camels stolen and looted from others. Such a man could be anything but a poor or simple man.

Muhammad used to take one-fifth share of the booty in Allah's name which obviously became his wealth at the end. The amount of wealth he gathered from his raids was not small. After the battle of Hunayn (February 1, 630), Muslims captured 24,000 camels, 40,000 sheep and goats, 4,000 ounces of silver and 6,000 prisoners. They were removed to the neighboring valley of Al-jirana and sheltered there (Shaikh, 1999, p. 20). Ishaq recorded,

The Apostle held a large number of captives. There were 6,000 women and children prisoners. He had captured so many sheep and camels they could not be counted. (Ishaq: 592)

In another expedition, Muhammad suddenly attacked Banu Mustaliq without warning while they were heedless and their cattle were being watered at nearby places. Their fighting men were killed and their women and children were taken as captives (Bukhari: 3.46.717). In this war (cited Sina, 2008, p. 34), "*600 were taken prisoners by the Muslims. Among the booty there were 2,000 camels and 5,000 goats"*. Now, one-fifth of this amount Muhammad earned from this battle alone. Considering the number of battles he fought in his lifetime and countless number of women and children he captured as slaves; no doubt he died as one of the richest man of Arabia.

After the Khaybar massacre, Muhammad subdued the Jews of Fadak and took half of their land. This half land of the entire city was his personal property. But the sad part is that, even after earning so much by plundering, Muhammad was not satisfied. His greed increased with his age. When he became *de facto* ruler of Arabia, many Muslim noblemen used to visit him for advice. Muhammad found a good opportunity to make a profit. Allah, through a timely revelation, prescribed certain amount of money to be paid to the Prophet by anyone who wanted to meet and talk to him and the payment should be made before the consultation.

O you who believe! When you consult the Messenger, then offer something in charity before your consultation; that is better for you and purer; but if you do not find, then surely Allah is Forgiving, Merciful. (Q: 58.12)

By seeing the greed of Muhammad, the visitors preferred to stay away from him. This frustrated Muhammad and the next verse was revealed.

Is it that ye are afraid of spending sums in charity before your private consultation (with him)? If, then, ye do not so, and Allah forgives you, then (at least) establish regular prayer; practice regular charity; and obey Allah and His Messenger. And Allah is well-acquainted with all that ye do. (Q: 58.13)

In another verse Allah addresses His messenger directly and orders him to take alms from the wealthy Muslims, in order to purify and pardon them.

Take alms out of their property, you would cleanse them and purify them thereby, and pray for them; surely your prayer is a relief to them; and Allah is Hearing, Knowing. (Q: 9.103)

Narcissists are "interpersonally exploitative", i.e., they use others to achieve their own ends. Muhammad never put his life in danger by fighting a battle. But when it was time for collecting booty or women, he was well ahead of others. His followers died happily for his cause. They thought they were fighting for Allah's cause, but actually they laid down their lives to fulfill the narcissistic desires of Muhammad. They buried their intelligence in Muhammad's cult and allowed the bloodthirsty Muhammad to have the last laugh.

The companions of Muhammad were equally greedy. The character which Ibn Ishaq gave to the companions in *Sirat Rasul Allah* was rarely pleasing. All of them gathered large wealth and lived a luxurious life. As example, Muhammad's cousin Zubair was found to be having estates of total value of fifty million and two hundred thousand dirham. Fabulous figures are quoted for other companions also. A son of the Caliph Omar had one thousand slaves at the time of his death. Within short decades after Muhammad's death, Mecca and Medina were transformed from obscure settlements to the religious and political capitals of a mighty empire. A

Meccan house which had been purchased in pagan days for a skin of wine was afterwards sold for 60,000 dirham – and this was far below its value (Margoliouth, 1914, pp. 136-7). Huge fortunes were built up out of the plunder which reached Mecca and Medina in camel loads from Persia, Syria and Egypt. Some more examples (Ahmed, 2006, pp. 55-6) would show how much those companions robbed from the countries they invaded.

1. When the third Caliph Uthman was murdered, he had thousand of thousand and five hundred thousand of dirham and one hundred thousand dinar. This is equal in our today counting several million of dollars.
2. Al-Zibair Ibn al-Awam had fifty-one thousand of thousand dirham and two hundred thousand dinar. Besides that he had houses and estates in Basra, Alexandria and Kufa. When he died, he left behind him a large garden if it had been sold it would have brought thousand of thousand and six hundred thousand dinar.
3. When Abd el-Rahman Ibn Awof died, he left gold that others used axes to cut.
4. Sa'ad Ibn Abi Waqas left behind him two hundred and fifty thousand of dirham.
5. Ibn Masood left ninety thousand dirham.
6. Talha bin Abid Allah had in his hand a ring of gold which had diamond in it. His daily income from his land in Iraq was one thousand dirham, or four hundred thousand or five hundred thousand dirham annually. When he died he left two thousand and two hundred thousand of dirham and two hundred thousand of dinar. Moreover he left hundred jars full of gold.
7. Umar bin al-A'as left behind him seventy jars of pure gold. While he was dying he offered his gold to his sons but they refused to accept it because they believed it had been taken unjustly.
8. When Zayd bin Harith died he left behind him gold that had been cut by axes.

Muhammad enjoyed everything whatever he needed in his life, and his companions followed his footstep after his death. Margoliouth (1914, p. 137) wrote, "*No empire can be anything other than worldly, the pious Caliphs were as anxious about the revenue as were the impious.*" The first Umayyad Caliph was reported to have said that he had enjoyed all that it was possible to enjoy in a lifetime.

From a destitute orphan to a shepherd, to a parasitic husband of a wealthy woman, to a humble messenger of God, to a desert bandit to one of the richest men of Arabia – Muhammad slowly transformed himself as opportunities came to him. No doubt he was a man of caliber.

6.9: Who are the Pathetic Losers?

Though Muhammad and his companions gathered a vast wealth and lived a lavish life and the economy of Mecca and Medina prospered, the conditions of the common Muslims deteriorated with time. There were large scale deaths in warfare leaving women and children of the dead Muslims helpless which neither bothered

Muhammad nor those Caliphs. Common Muslims were convinced that Allah loves poverty and illiteracy and hates wealth, prosperity, education and the rich people. According to Ghazali (al-Ghazali, 1993, pp. 2.28, 3.181, 3.201); prayer, a big family and poverty will ensure paradise. To promote further admiration of poverty among the Muslims, Ghazali wrote that Allah and His Prophet praised one who remains satisfied with poverty. He even exhorted Muslims to condemn wealth and to praise poverty; poverty is better than wealth. But he never explained – if Allah really loves poverty, why Muhammad and the early companions gathered so much wealth? For common Muslims, Muhammad said,

Narrated Abu Huraira: I heard Allah's Apostle saying, "The example of a Mujahid in Allah's Cause-- and Allah knows better who really strives in His Cause --- is like a person who fasts and prays continuously. Allah guarantees that He will admit the Mujahid in His Cause into Paradise if he is killed, otherwise He will return him to his home safely with rewards and war booty. (Bukhari: 4.52.46).

If you are loyal to this undertaking it will profit you in this world and the next.' They said, 'We will accept you as a Prophet under these conditions, but we want to know specifically what we will get in return for our loyalty.' Muhammad said, 'I promise you Paradise.' (Ishaq: 205)

The Believers fight in Allah's cause, they slay and are slain, kill and are killed. (Q: 9.112).

And what though ye be slain in Allah's way or die therein? Surely pardon from Allah and mercy is better than all that they amass. (Q: 3.157)

What is the difference between "Allah's cause" and "Muhammad's cause"? If the Muslim fighter dies, Muhammad and his companions lose nothing but if he returns with booty and women, Muhammad takes one-fifth share of the booty and the woman of his choice, and the companions' wealth also grows. Poverty was glorified in Islam for their self-serving purposes. If Muslims remain poor, then Muhammad and his companions could gather more wealth. Muhammad's thinking was simple – "Fight the infidels, gather booty and capture women for me. Allah will give you much more after your death. If you obey me you will enter Allah's paradise and if you don't obey you will go to hell". For Muhammad, the Muslims were mere instruments. Allah revealed two verses to console the Muslims,

Whoso is removed from the Fire and is made to enter paradise, he indeed is triumphant. **The life of this world is but comfort of delusion.** (Q: 3.185)

… and in the Hereafter there is grievous punishment, and (also) forgiveness from Allah and His good pleasure, **whereas the life of the world is but matter of delusion.** (Q: 57.20)

If life is a comfort of delusion, why Muhammad and his early companions gathered so much wealth? As Vaknin (1999, p. 115) commented, "*A Narcissist sees no reason in dedicating thought to their needs, wishes, wants, desires and fears. He derails their life with easy and benevolent ignorance".*

Muhammad did not recognize the individuality or rights of the poor Muslims; he only recognized himself as human. He never hesitated to tell lie or deceive his devoted followers. Muhammad's needs were greater than his followers and he denied equal justice and equal opportunity to all. A Narcissist does not realize or accept that the world contains other human beings. He also does not know how to feel sorry for what he does. He does not like to put himself in the shoes of his victims. If we make a careful study of the Qur'an and ahadith we will find there are umpteen number of cases where Muhammad had benefited at the cost of the lives of his followers. There were many instances where common Muslims had laid down their lives in the name of Allah just for a small benefit of Muhammad. Today if a billion plus Muslims adore Muhammad as their Prophet it was possible because of those early brainwashed followers who sacrificed their lives happily to make Muhammad what he is today. Without them, what was Muhammad's contribution to the success of Islam?

Muhammad saw those around him as objects, targets, or opportunities or anything but human being. Most probably, he had no true friendship with anybody in his band. He had only partners in crime and victims. As it is going to be shown shortly; his accomplices frequently ended up as victims. For Muhammad the ends always justified the means. There was no place for feelings of remorse, shame, or guilt. Muhammad felt justified in all his actions because he considered himself the ultimate moral judge. Nothing gets in the way of a malignant Narcissist. Life was a superficial game for Muhammad and his followers were pawns on his board.

6.9.1: The Demoralizing Influence of Muhammad's Teaching on the Arabs

Narcissism is such a vile disease that causes others to suffer. It is a mental epidemic and a curse to humankind. Anyone who comes in contact with a Narcissist is bound to be a loser. As Vaknin (1999, p. 11) wrote, "*It is a destructive, evil and torturous disease, which affects not only the Narcissist, but it also infects and forever changes people who are in daily contact with the Narcissist*". One of the very strange things to deal with after being the victim of a Narcissist is that most people will not want to believe what happened to the victim, even if they saw it with their own eyes! This is the height of the manipulative capability of a Narcissist. Narcissists often reverse the role with the victims. The victim is represented as mentally disordered and the Narcissist – the suffering soul.

The Narcissist is forever the same; it is the victim who changes. Victims are unable to separate themselves from the Narcissist. For the Narcissist there is no place for feelings of remorse, shame, or guilt. He scapegoats the followers and blames the victims, and the victims allow themselves to carry the guilt and responsibility on their own shoulders (Zayn & Dibble, 2007, p. 105). Blame is a powerful reinforcer of passivity and obedience, producing guilt, shame, terror, and conformity in the followers.

Even after all the miseries caused to the victims, still there is something more terrible. Narcissism is a contagious disease; it spoils the lives of the victims even when their Narcissist leader is no more. The influence is really that much. Slowly, the victims absorb the Narcissist's way of destructive thinking. It means, though the Narcissist leader is dead or has abandoned his victim, the force of narcissism will still haunt the followers. The Narcissist is still alive deep inside the traumatic memories waiting for an opportunity to act out. The victims are modified and they are not even aware of it as we read in the science fictions of alien snatching the human bodies. As a summary, any sane person who has put a single grain of trust on his Narcissist leader is destined to suffer.

Almost everyone who came in direct contact with Muhammad had suffered miserably. The early Arabs, though illiterate, hotheaded and superstitious, were generally innocent. They had high sense of self-respect for which they were ready to die. But when they came within the narcissistic grip of Muhammad, they became murderous and greedy. Now they are ready to die for Allah's cause instead of dying for the preservation of self-respect. Now they are the mental slaves of their leader – fanatics of no honor, no self-respect.

With the deterioration of their character, the early Arabs not only lost their property and self-respect but also the lives of their children, relatives even their own. At the end of the day those disappointed and disillusioned pathetic losers returned with empty hands. Almost all of them died a dog's death. Muhammad had invaded their mind and changed their attitude completely, and modified them by his powerful force of narcissism, so much so that now they are nothing but a shadow of their former selves. Now they have contacted the disease of narcissism. They have been infected and poisoned; they have been branded.

I cannot say for sure when demoralizing influence of Muhammad's teaching began to be felt, but in all probability, it started when Muhammad became the head of a criminal gang. From this time Muhammad began introducing errors in the thought process of the Muslims through his poisonous teaching which slowly made it dysfunctional. It was then those Muslims who had never broken an oath were convinced that they might evade their obligations, and to those Muslims, to whom the blood of their clan had been as their own, began to shed it with impunity in the "cause of Allah". Also, lying and treachery in the cause of Islam received Allah's approval. Muslims learned that raiding and murdering innocents, enslaving their children and raping their wives were godly acts which please God. Muslims also learned from their Prophet that by committing all these brutal acts they would enter paradise. No doubt, initially many of his followers became suspicious about the true divine origin of the revelations but slowly they absorbed Muhammad's way of destructive thinking. The mindset of the Muslims changed as they lost their self-worth and honor.

Booty is always easy money. When the Muslims were addicted to this source of easy money, they lost their productivity, ethics and the sense of moral obligation to the society. They were so much changed that even after Muhammad's death, the force of his narcissistic maneuverability was still conning them. The malignant Narcissist was still alive deep inside the memories of the companions waiting for an opportunity to act out. In sum, the early victims of Muhammad were modified even without being aware that they were victimized by their master.

Here I wish to discuss about some prominent companions of Muhammad, e.g., Abu Bakr, Omar, Uthman, Ali and Fatima to show how the force of Muhammad's narcissism ruined them all. Abu Bakr, the closest male friend of Muhammad, was the first of the so-called four "rightly guided" Caliphs. He ruled for two years and then died. Other three Caliphs; Uthman, Omar and Ali were murdered. Fatima, the daughter of Muhammad, died some six months after Muhammad. Because of their closeness to Muhammad they were more open to Muhammad's narcissistic grips. No doubt they were the most devoted Muslims and put their complete trust on Muhammad but Allah gave them nothing in return. Qur'an says,

He is the one who has strengthened you and the believers with His help through putting affection in their hearts. If you had spent all that is in the earth, you could not have so united their hearts; but Allah has united them. He is Mighty, Wise. O Prophet! Allah is all-sufficient for you and for the believers who follow you. (Q: 8.61- 64)

However, instead of uniting those people, God cursed them by bringing them divisions and hatred. When Muhammad died, he had left a huge wealth which he had earned by all sorts of criminal activities. Before death, Muhammad proclaimed that he would not be leaving inheritance to his family members (Muslim: 19.4355). But the very next day of Muhammad's death, greed overcame all the people, and nasty and hateful events began to transpire. Fatima, along with Ali and Al-Abbas, demanded her share in the inheritance, but Abu Bakr refused (Muslim: 19.4349). She left angrily and did not talk to him till her death (Tabari: IX.196, 197). After Abu Bakr's death, Omar became Caliph, but Ali and Abbas had never allowed the dispute to die out – they still wanted the money. Greed for Muhammad's wealth was equally displayed by his wives also (Muslim: 19.4351).

Muhammad's dead body was barely cold and here they were demanding their share of inheritance. There was no real period of mourning, no spiritual reflection or drawing close together of Muhammad's near and dear ones. Instead, people were moving on the money right away as if they were waiting for Muhammad to die. Their minds were completely filled up by greed and hatred and they started calling one another a *"sinful, treacherous, dishonest, liar!"* (Muslim: 19.4349). No doubt, a number of dark and powerful negative sentiments were at work there. The hatred continued for a long time and ultimately it resulted in bloodshed.

There was another dispute. At the time of his death, Muhammad did not declare a successor. There was strong disagreement about who should be the next ruler. On Muhammad's death, his most intimate friends, Abu Bakr and Omar abandoned the corpse and left it without a burial place in a hurry to ensure his political succession (Warraq, 2000, p. 182). This resulted in strong arrogance and rebellion. Ali wanted to be the Caliph but Abu Bakr became a Caliph because Omar supported him. Seeing this, Al-Zubayr drew his sword, saying, *"I will not put it back until the oath of allegiance is rendered to Ali."* (Tabari: IX.188, 189). However Abu Bakr became Caliph without bloodshed. Ali was compelled to give a token pledge of allegiance to Abu Bakr though in his heart he rejected him.

When Abu Bakr became Caliph, Abu Sufyan was very unhappy. He hated Abu Bakr, because Abu Bakr was coming from a lowly clan of Mecca. Sufyan hated to take orders from this lowly nobody, and even agreed to a future bloodshed if it would be required to rid this perceived wrong (Tabari: IX.199). He was a shrewd politician and had his eye on power. At the time of Muhammad's death, the Muslim community was not at all unified; rather, they were nearly at each other's throats.

After deep hatred and greed; next came, ambivalence, moral corruption and murder. When Abu Bakr died, Omar became the Caliph but he was murdered by one of his slaves who claimed to have been cheated by him. Uthman was the next Caliph. Under his leadership, life became more difficult for Muslims. There were charges of clan partiality, financial mismanagement, corruption and elitism against Uthman (Tabari: XV.143, 162, 167). Soon a large Muslim army rose up in arms against him and three large bodies of men, from Egypt, Kufa, and Basra, moved against him and marched on Medina (Tabari: XV.186, 187). Even his own adopted son rose against him. The dark attitudes that were implanted in the Muslim's hearts and minds by Muhammad's force of narcissism found an opportunity to grow, spread roots, and now more blooms of Islam's real fruit started blossoming.

Uthman called for help from his various governors, but nobody came. The tribesmen of Uthman did little or nothing to defend their Caliph. They knew that if he fell, they could perhaps be the next Caliph (Tabari: XV.185). Ultimately Uthman was murdered and one of his murderers was Muhammad b. Abi Bakr (Abu Bakr's son). Tabari recorded how cruelly Uthman was killed,

> *He [the murderer] came over to him with a broad iron headed arrow and stabbed him in the head with it.... They gathered round him and killed him.* (Tabari: XV.190, 191).

Uthman was stabbed nine times, throttled and one of his hands was severed. After killing him, one of the murderers rejoiced at his death,

> *By Allah, I have never seen anything softer than his throat. By God, I throttled him until I saw his soul shaking in his body like the soul of a jinn.* (Tabari: XV.205).

So at each progressive step in the history of Islam, the picture becomes darker and darker. In less than fifteen years, the Islamic community began to become corrupt. Within a generation of Muhammad's death, the true fruit of Islam ripens. Now the most precious Islamic blood is being spilt, and that at the hands of the best Muslims. Muhammad's companions were now murdering one another. The Islamic community's heart had become so full of sin that their emotions were now giving way to brutal actions. Men that stood with Muhammad through thick and thin, lived through poverty with him and fought side-by-side in the most difficult days of Islam are now clashing violently against each other. The Islamic empire is now beset with moral, political, and financial corruption from Medina to its outskirts. Muhammad's best friend's son has just butchered the supreme ruler of the Islamic empire in his own home and the Islamic community was nowhere to be found. They turned a blind eye, or turned their backs on their ruler, indulgent as he was. They desired power, wealth, and vainglory, and for this they betrayed and murdered one another. In less than one generation the Islamic community had become a pack of dogs set on devouring one another. Spiritual corruption had established itself from the Caliphate on down and now this spiritual death bore its fruits in the physical realm.

Up to this point we have seen the evil seeds of greed, hatred, envy, and discord grow from deep within the hearts of many prominent Muslims. Following Uthman's murder, confusion began to spread in the Islamic community, and the search was on for a new leader. Eventually, in Medina, Ali was recognized as the Caliph. But

Aisha, Muhammad's most beloved wife, moved against Ali. She gave a passionate speech in Mecca, heating the desert blood within the Muslims' hearts. She cried for justice and vengeance (Tabari: XVI.41, 43, 51, 53). Implicitly, she implicated Ali in Uthman's murder, and the people knew that fighting for justice would be fighting Ali. Finally, Ali marched towards Basra and Aisha and her followers gathered their full strength to meet him. Soon a violent battle started and neither side yielded much ground. Men from both sides were fierce, brave warriors. They did not fear death that day and fought like lions. In Islamic history this battle is known as "Battle of Camel". The various accounts of the casualty count were very high.

Those killed at the Battle of the Camel numbered 10,000, half from Ali's followers, and half from Aisha's. It was said that in the first battle 5000 Basrans were killed and a further 5000 in the second battle [there was a pause in the battle], totaling 10,000 Basran fatalities and 5,000 Kufans. (Tabari: XVI.164).

In the battle of camel, two prominent Muslims Talha and Zubayr died, both of them were most beloved of Muhammad's companions. However, more bloodshed lay in store for Ali. The long underlying conflict between Muhammad and Abu Sufyan re-appeared and the bitterness revived. Ali and Mu'awiyah (Abu Sufyan's son) played the opposing roles. Mu'awiyah, the governor of Syria, was a kinsman of Uthman, the murdered Caliph. He wanted the murderers brought to justice. Seeing that war was inevitable, Ali gathered his forces and Mu'awiyah raised the entire country of Syria against Ali and gave order "*In that case, Oh Abu Abdallah, prepare the men!*" (Tabari: XVII.2). In the history of Islam, this battle is known as "Battle of Siffin", which continued for a long time. It was actually a series of day by day battles. Ali tried to negotiate with Mu'awiyah to end the battle but he received much humiliation. In this battle, one notable person Ubaydallah, the son of Caliph Omar was murdered (Tabari: XVII.63). After Ali's humiliation, Mu'awiyah turned to Egypt where Muhammad b. Abi Bakr (Uthman's murderer, Abu Bakr's son) was appointed as governor. Soon he was captured and murdered.

Slowly Mu'awiyah gained in power. By seeing Ali in a miserable condition, his hand-picked governors, his own relatives and friends rebelled against him (Tabari: XVII.210, 211). Eventually Ali was murdered. By hearing the news about Ali's death, Aisha rejoiced.

And she threw down her staff and settled upon her place of abode, like the traveler happy to return home. (Tabari: XVII.224).

After Mu'awiyah died, his son Yazid claimed the Caliphate. But Ali's son and Muhammad's grandson Husayn opposed Yazid and likewise claimed the Caliphate. This again led to war. At this point Yazid was very powerful. Husayn encountered Yazid's force near Karbala with about forty-five horsemen and less than one hundred foot soldiers. In the battle, Husayn was captured and beheaded, and his severed head was sent to Yazid (Tabari: XIX.167, 176).

I cannot see any type of brotherhood amongst the leading Muslims; instead I can see war, hatred, envy, lies, deceit, bitterness and massive bloodshed in the lust for power. Also, there were wholesale slaughtering, cruel brutalities and bitter oppression and absolutely no spiritual fruit worth mentioning. Allah could have prevented this long, painful conflict just by giving Muhammad a revelation about the succession. Why did not He? He issued revelations on far less important matters. And what should we say about the Qur'anic verse 8.63 now? – "*And united their hearts; had you spent all that is in the earth, you could not have united their hearts, but Allah united them; surely He is Mighty, Wise*".

Instead of spiritually building them up, Muhammad's narcissistic force had poisoned them, ruined them and completely destroyed them. Little by little, Muhammad's narcissistic poison worked in the spiritual bloodstream of those Muslims which dishonored and demonized them. They would have been better if they did not have sold their soul to their Narcissist Prophet.

It was just a dark Shakespearean tragedy unfolded in front of us. Hatred, envy, and bitterness, were rooted in the hearts of the leaders of the Islamic community. Some foresaw civil war down the road even before the death of Muhammad. The seeds of narcissistic wickedness ran deep within the hearts and minds of those, the best Muslims, from the beginning. All the seven deadly sins (shamelessness, magical thinking, arrogance, envy, entitlement, exploitation and bad boundaries) of a Narcissist were prominently present in them because they came in direct contact with Muhammad more often than others. Muhammad's narcissism infected them and changed them completely. Even the sons of the Caliphs were striving to kill one another. The greed and lust for power was so strong that even Muhammad's wives could not come out from this.

Where is the root of all these negative qualities that poisoned them? If we make a careful study of Muhammad's biography, we will not fail to see that all these evils originated from Muhammad. The greed, last for power, hatred, envy, lies, deceit, bitterness, shamelessness, exploitation, bloodshed – practically all the evil actions were the trademarks of Muhammad. He left a legacy that manufactured many clones of Muhammad, e.g., Bakr, Ali, Omar, Uthman, Osama bin Laden, Saddam Hussein, Mullah Omar, Ahmadinejad, Khomeini, etc. A poisonous tree produces poisonous fruits. A mass-murderer cannot preach Gandhian nonviolence.

In every community, there are good and bad people. The tragedy is, Islam's poison strengthens the wicked side of a good man and subdues his moral faculty. Each of the prominent players of early stage of Islam shed the blood of tens of thousands of Muslims only to secure what they thought they were entitled for. But at the end they got nothing and most of them died miserably like stray dogs on the streets.

Chapter 7: Psychology of Islamic Terrorism

7.1: Introduction

"Satan, laughing, spreads his wings."

Black Sabbath War Pigs Song

Terrorism has surely existed since before the dawn of recorded history. Human nature has not changed. People become terrorists in different ways, in different roles, and for different reasons. Perceived injustice, need for identity, need for belonging, religious indoctrination and mental illness are common vulnerabilities among potential terrorists. Though there is no particular "terrorist personality" or any accurate psychological profile of the terrorist, research shows that childhood abuse and trauma, and themes of perceived injustice and humiliation often are prominent in terrorist biographies. However this theory does not really help to explain the root causes of Islamic terrorism.

There is one common point amongst all the terrorist groups. They provide a set of beliefs that justify and mandate their destructive actions. No one wants to kill innocent people or destroy property for nothing. They believe in their cause which they regard as absolute, and they behave in such a way that are serving a meaningful cause, either by promoting the cause or by destroying those who oppose it (the question of point of view – one man's terrorist is another man's freedom fighter – public glorification of terrorism under the mask of selflessness). Though terrorism is among the gravest of threats the world is facing today, little research and analysis has been conducted on terrorist psychology. Many important factors (e.g., analyses of incident-related behaviors) are neglected. Apart from a drive for truth, political psychological theory advises that the better a target group understands the roots of the terrorist mind-set, the better that group may develop policies to effectively manage the risk (Clayton *et. al*, 1998, pp. 277-311). Despite the compelling need for such an understanding, many theoretical and practical impediments have delayed, and perhaps even derailed, the objective scientific psychological study of terrorism (Reich, 1998, pp. 261-79). Concerned governments spend in billions to protect their citizens but their efforts often lack a theoretical – let alone observation, experiment or experience based foundation for understanding terrorists and their violent acts.

First of all, the case studies and "inside information" of a terrorist group are not always readily available. These are very difficult to obtain even for intelligence bureau without having a spy or paid police informer within a terrorist group. Thus, the analysis of the groups and their leaders often remain incomplete. Secondly, researchers have little, if any, direct access to terrorists, even imprisoned ones. Occasionally, if a researcher has gained special access to a terrorist group for interviews and discussions, etc, usually he has to do it at the cost of compromising the credibility of his research. Even if he obtains permission to interview a captured terrorist, such an interview would be of limited value. Most terrorists would be reluctant to reveal their group's operational secrets to their interrogators, let alone to journalists or academic researchers, whom they are likely to view as representatives of the "system" or perhaps even as intelligence agents in disguise. Even if terrorists agree to be interviewed in such circumstances, they will not be honest in answering questions. Terrorism research may involve expensive and inconvenient travel to politically unstable regions, is potentially dangerous, and raises ethical issues that may challenge institutional review boards. Lastly; it is a matter of safety for the researcher himself, because he could face retaliation. These issues may explain why journalists, rather than academics, have published a substantial proportion of the available literature reporting behavioral observations of terrorists.

All these drawbacks are serious challenges to terrorism research. It also affects every level of the government, which starts from policy level decisions (how a state should respond to terrorism) to individual-level decisions. Although all types of terrorism are equally condemnable, in this chapter our basic aim is rather modest. We do not anticipate identifying or discovering or analyzing the explanation for all terrorism. Rather we will focus only on the analysis of Islamic terrorism.

7.2: Frequently Asked Question: Does Islamic Ideology Promote Terrorism?

One of the greatest concerns of all civilized cultures is the alarming incidence of Islamic terrorism in today's world. Wherever terrorist and subversive activities take place, one is sure to find the presence of Muslims. Since the tragic events of September 11, 2001, attention has shifted to the psychology of Islamic terrorism. There is a dearth of published literature describing psychological studies of Muslim extremists. A stereotyped question is always asked – what exactly is it that makes Muslims so viciously engaged in violent crimes against the rest of humanity? Why are all terrorist activities that target innocent non-Muslims always abetted by Muslim terrorists? This stereotyped question becomes more pressing everyday and it is often responded by a readymade answer that the fault lies with only a handful of misguided Muslims who are not adhering to Islamic principles and hence indulge in terrorism. Some critics, who are knowledgeable about the Islamic ideology, tell us that Islam by its very nature and through its essential principles openly supports, encourages and propagates terrorism of the worst kind. Therefore the Islamic terrorist is in fact the most devout Muslim because he is following exactly what Islam teaches through the Qur'an.

I do not deny that Islamic ideology plays a crucial role in a Muslim terrorist's target selection, and the Qur'an functions as the central terrorist manual that urges them to slaughter, rape, torture, pillage, mutilate and molest all the non-Muslims. No doubt, Qur'an supplies them with an initial motive for action and provides a prism through which they view events and the actions of the non-Muslims; but are the Qur'an and other Islamic scriptures alone responsible for growing Islamic terrorism incidents?

I seriously doubt.

In this world there is no shortage of destruction-oriented ideologies. All the religious doctrines have some violent preaching in them. But, all of us, except Muslims, have learned to separate those from our day-to-day thinking, and because of this, all the religions coexist peacefully other than only Islam. Therefore it is not the destructive ideology alone which is responsible for promoting terrorism. Israeli psychology professor Ariel Merari is one of the few people to have collected systematic, empirical data on a significant sample of Muslim suicide bombers. He examined the backgrounds of every modern era (since 1983) suicide bomber in the Middle East, and concluded (cited Schmid, 2011, p. 136),

"In itself, the ideology is not enough to convince a person to engage in terrorism".

Islamic ideology may help inform an understanding of terrorist behavior of the Muslims, but unfortunately, it does not explain everything. The non-Muslim nations need to know the answer so that a public policy can be planned accordingly.

7.2.1: Better Answers through Better Questions

All the destruction-oriented ideologies generally are based on a set of shared beliefs that explain and justify a set of agreed upon behavioral rules. For Muslim terrorists, the confirmed beliefs of Islam provides them the moral and political vision that inspires their violence, shapes the way in which they see the world, and defines how they judge the actions of people and the society.

If we just say that the ideology controls actions (which may apparently be true), we are oversimplifying the problem. What we fail to understand is – **why or how this control occurs**. There is something which helps to regulate and determine a Muslim terrorist's behavior. We want to know what the strength of this behavioral control is. It is not just the appeal of the rhetoric that determines whether violent mandates will be followed but definitely something else – a mysterious dark force which makes a sane person insane. This dark force destroys all the human qualities and fills up the mind with unjustified hate for the non-Muslims. For a better understanding, we need to take a suitable approach to Islamic terrorism analysis.

There are various approaches to terrorism analysis, as example, the multicausal approach, the environmental approach, the organizational approach, the role of media approach and the psychological approach (Hudson, 1999, p. 15). Out of all these, our only concern is the psychological approach. A detailed examination of other approaches is outside the scope of this book.

7.3: The Psychological approach: An analysis of sociologically-based Explanations of Islamic Terrorism

"While nothing is easier than to denounce the evildoer, nothing is more difficult than to understand him".

Fyodor Mikhailovich Dostoevsky (1821 - 1881)

[Note: "Sociologically-based explanations" is the more appropriate term of the phrase "root causes"]

The Muslim terrorist mindset can best be understood through psychological approach. But it would be helpful first to examine whether and how psychology and other behavioral sciences have sought to explain violent behavior more generally.

The first generation of psychological research on terrorism commenced from late-1960s to the mid-1980s. The term "research" is used loosely because virtually none of the professional literature was based on any practical studies. Rather, the writings that were produced during those days were based largely on assumptions, theoretical formulations and Freud's psychoanalytic theory. Freud (Strachey & Gay, 1961, p. 8) assumed, *"One has, I think, to reckon with the fact that there are present in all men destructive, and therefore anti-social and anti-cultural trends, and that in a great number of people, these are strong enough to determine their behavior in human society"*.

During 1969, Feuer put forward his famous "conflict of generations" theory, which was largely based on Freudian interpretation of terrorism as a psychological reaction of sons against fathers (Crenshaw, 1986, pp. 390-1). The idea that terrorism is rooted in childhood abuse (often unconscious squeal) is a relatively common theme, and is still held by some contemporary analysts. However, many early psychologists also attempted to understand and explain terrorism from a different angle. Within a psychodynamic framework, they focused on the trait of narcissism as a defining and driving factor of terrorism. In the next few pages of this chapter, we will try to understand Islamic terrorism through narcissism.

7.3.1: Narcissism as the Driving Force of Terrorism

The possible linkage between narcissism and terrorism was first advanced by Gustave Morf (1970) in his ground-breaking work, *Terror in Quebec - case studies of the FLQ*. Morf conducted clinical examinations with prisoners held as members of the Front for the Liberation of Quebec (FLQ) and reported that these individuals exhibited narcissistic traits, wishing to put themselves at the center of the universe, but did not fulfill the criteria for a full-blown narcissistic personality disorder. He further concluded that a "permissive society" was responsible for their narcissism. Morf's hypothesis was immensely popular and soon many researchers took deep interest in his work; e.g., Lasch (1979), Crayton (1983), a combined work by Haynal, Molnar and Puymege (1983), Post (1984, 1986, 1990), and Pearlstein (1991) (cited McCormick, 2003, pp. 473-507). Their collective valuable works helped us to develop our understanding on the co-relation between narcissism and terrorist behavior. The common basic argument is that terrorist behavior is rooted in a personality defect that produced a damaged sense of self. According to Risto Fried (1982), the target or victim is treated as a "discardable object," which psychoanalyst and famous political scientist Richard Pearlstein cited as evidence that terrorism is a *"spectacularly vivid example of narcissistic object manipulation."* The essence of pathological narcissism is an overvaluing of self and a devaluing of others. It is not difficult to see how one might observe these traits among terrorists.

Crayton (1983, pp. 33-41), by using Kohut's concepts to guide his argument, suggested the psychology of narcissism as a framework for understanding terrorist behavior. According to Crayton, the two key narcissistic dynamics are a grandiose sense of self and "idealized parental imago" (The thinking goes like this – "If I cannot be perfect, at least I am in a relationship with something perfect"). Young adolescents are plastic in their political orientation and open to indoctrination. With regard to the effect of groups, he argues that the narcissistically vulnerable persons are drawn to charismatic leaders and that some groups are held together by a shared grandiose sense of self. As others have posited, he suggested that narcissistic rage is what prompts an aggressive response to perceived injustice. Crayton's views are supported by Pearlstein. By using a Freudian analysis of the self and the narcissistic personality, Pearlstein eruditely applied the psychological concept of narcissism to terrorists and concluded (cited Burum, 2004, p. 19) that narcissism is the "*most complete and thus most intellectually satisfying theory*" for explaining terrorism.

Some researchers suggested "narcissistic rage" as the primary drive for terrorist aggression. As children, the nascent terrorists are deeply traumatized; they have suffered chronic physical abuse and emotional humiliation. This creates a profound sense of fear and personal vulnerability that becomes central to their self-concept. To eliminate this fear and to create a more tolerable self-image, such individuals feel the need to "kill off" their view of themselves as victims. They buttress their own self-esteem by devaluing others. The result of this devaluation of others muffles their internal voice of reason and morality. Furthermore, whatever sense of "esteem" has developed in that process is extraordinarily fragile, which makes the individual particularly vulnerable to any slights, insults or ideas that threaten to smash the pretense of self-worth (Akhtar, 1999, pp. 350-5). This is narcissistic injury. Crayton (1983, pp. 37-8) wrote, "*As a specific manifestation of narcissistic rage, terrorism occurs in the context of narcissistic injury,*" For Crayton, terrorism is an attempt to acquire or maintain power or control by threats. Those individuals with a damaged self-concept have failed to integrate the good and bad parts of the self, which are instead split into the "me" and the "not me." They need an outside enemy to blame for their own inadequacies and weaknesses.

7.3.2: Muhammad's Narcissism as the Driving Force of Islamic Terrorism – Strong Evidences

There is no shortage of evidence that narcissism is the primary driving force of Islamic terrorism. Muslims' thought process exactly reflects the distorted thought process of their Narcissist Prophet as if their Prophet is talking through them. Deep down, there is unhealthy envy and paranoia which force them to decompensate and act out in a violent manner. Muslim terrorists are in a constant state of deficient narcissistic supply. They want to bring "down to their level" (by destroying it) the object of their pathological envy, the cause of their seething frustration, and the symbol of their dull achievements; it is always incommensurate with their inflated self-image. They seek omnipotence through murder, control through violence, prestige, fame and celebrity by defying figures of authorities, challenging them, and humbling them. They attribute evil and corruption to their enemies and foes.

When members of al-Qaeda, Islamic jihad, al-Aqsa Martyrs' Brigade, and Hamas were asked why they were killing the non-Muslims, they said, "***Islam. We are following Muhammad's orders***" (Winn, 2004, letter to the reader). Habis al Saoub quoted in his Arabic document, entitled *A Martyr's will* (Spencer, 2003, p. 23), "*The Prophet Muhammad's seventh-century assertion that abandoning the cause of jihad is a disgraceful act tantamount to leaving the Islamic religion*". Mahmood Ghazi, Pakistan's Minister for Religious Affairs, openly supported Kashmir jihad stating that it was "*in accordance with the teachings of Prophet Muhammad*" (Spencer, 2003, p. 45). This is how Muhammad is directly responsible for today's Islamic terrorist attacks.

When Muhammad killed his opponents he justified it by Allah's name, "*Allah made me victorious with terror*". After 9/11 attack, Laden claimed that the terrorist attack was in defense of own people and was the will of Allah (Lachkar, 2008, p. 30). He called the Muslims, "*to comply with God's order to kill the Americans and plunder their money, whenever and wherever they find them*" (Bjorgo, 2005, p. 59). It was as if Laden was the new messenger of Allah, only relaying the commands of Allah which were justified with verses from the Qur'an. Both Muhammad's and Laden's distorted thinking pattern is mirrored in this quote from Brigadier S.K. Malik's (Pakistani Army) controversial book, *The Qur'anic Concept of War* (2008, p. 57), "*We see that, on all the occasions when God wishes to impose His will upon His enemies, He chooses to do so by casting terror into their hearts*".

During 1995, The Armed Islamic Group of Algeria (GIA) commented in a press release, "*Everyone should know that the killing, massacring, slaughtering, expulsion, burning, taking of captives that we do, these are sacrifices for the sake of Allah*" (Cook, 2005, p. 171). Where from these destructive thoughts are coming? This is what Muhammad had convinced the Muslims in the Qur'an.

Say: Truly, my prayer and my service of sacrifice, my life and my death, are (all) for Allah, the Cherisher of the Worlds. (Q: 6.162)

GIA collapsed in 1998 and the dissidents formed a new terrorist group – Jama'a al-Salaffiya. Its first communiqué tells the tale, "*[Those who] grasp the tails of cattle, are satisfied with farming, and [if you] have left Jihad, then God will cause humiliation to overtake you that will not leave you until you return to your religion*" (Cook, 2005, p. 120). Who is uttering these words? It is not the terrorists, but the ghost of Muhammad is talking through them. Muhammad had no experience with agricultural production. His livelihood was totally dependent upon raids and plunder. According to Bukhari (3.39.514), Allah had a great disdain for agriculture and agricultural implements.

A pan-Arab daily newspaper published an article on February 23, 1998, where some advice was given to all Muslims and a Qur'anic verse was cited. The advice was, "*The ruling of killing Americans and their allies whether civilian or military is incumbent upon every Muslim who is able and in whichever country is easiest for him*" (Cook, 2005, p. 175), and the relevant verse was, "*And fight them until persecution is no more, and religion is for Allah...* " (Q: 2.193)

The words "Allah wishes" and "sacrifices for the sake of Allah" need particular attention. No God had revealed the Qur'anic verses; it was the narcissistic wishes of Muhammad in the form of divine revelation. Muhammad had never sacrificed any worldly pleasure for the sake of Allah, his followers did it for him during his lifetime and present day Muslims are still doing it. Malik (2008, pp. 59, 60) wrote, "*Terror struck in the hearts of the enemies is not only a means, it is the end in itself ...* **Terror is not a means of imposing decision upon the enemy; it is the decision we wish to impose upon him.**".

Where did Malik get such destructive ideas? He was simply repeating Muhammad's words. Did not Muhammad say in his Qur'an (8.12), "*I will instill terror into the hearts of disbelievers*"? Malik continued, "***It [terror] can be instilled only if the opponent's faith is destroyed. Psychological dislocation is temporary, spiritual dislocation is permanent ... to instill terror into the hearts of the enemy, it is essential, in the ultimate analysis, to dislocate his faith***".

Did Muhammad not use the sword to convert pagans into his faith? Malik's advice of *"dislocating the spiritual faith of the enemy"* originates from Muhammad. Did Christ ever say; "Know that paradise is under the sword"? Did Confucius ever say; "I will instill terror into the hearts of the unbelievers"? Did Buddha ever tell his followers to behead the non-Buddhists in war and slice off their fingertips? Did Adi Shankara kill people and steal their wives? Did Mahavira Jain promote killing in the name of God? Had anyone of them ever asked the followers to collect booty and share it with him and God? Muhammad made all those statements and more. In fact, no founder of a major world religion has ever resembled Muhammad. No other Prophet grew rich stealing the property of innocents. No one else kept a harem, or assassinated poets, or was a child molester or mass-murderer, or had promoted slavery. Hate is the basic tenet of Islam and violence is the conclusion.

The terrorist leaders or the planners of a suicide attack never offer their own children as martyr. When a suggestion was made to one such planner; the planner, Sheikh Yassin replied smartly, *"We do not choose the martyrs to die. Allah chooses them."* (Richardson, 2006, p. 158). Yassin was echoing Muhammad's words,

Allah has purchased from the believers their selves and possessions, and for them is Paradise. They fight in the Way of Allah, slay, and are slain. (Q: 9.111)

The simple fact is that an advocate of suicide bombing will never put his neck where his mouth is. Why he does not do the suicide mission by himself and take the first opportunity to enter paradise? No one has ever seen an Islamic cleric or one of his relatives strapping on a bomb and detonating it to receive the divine reward of a trip to paradise, yet they enjoin others to do so. Muhammad encouraged martyrdom but never fought a battle where his life would be in danger.

Muhammad was megalomaniac. The Muslim terrorist leaders are equally megalomaniac. As a fine example, I quote a passage from Abdullah Ocalan (the founder and leader of Kurdistan Workers' Party, also known as the People's Liberation Army of Kurdistan). He said in a press conference with the Turkish Daily Newspaper in December 1998 (Hunsicker, 2006, p. 41), *"Everyone should take note of the way I live, what I do and what I don't do. The way I eat, the way I think, my orders and even my inactivity should be carefully studied. There will be lessons to be learned from several generations because Apo [Ocalan - "Apo" means uncle] is a great teacher"*.

Turkish journalists who had interviewed Ocalan came back with the impression of a "megalomaniac" and "sick" man who has no respect for or understanding of the "superior values of European civilization". Ocalan underlined his personal hunger for absolute power at the helm of the organization in a 1991 party publication (Hunsicker, 2006, p. 41), *"I establish a thousand relationships every day and destroy a thousand political, organizational, emotional and ideological relationships. No one is indispensable for me. Especially if there is anyone who eyes the chairmanship of the PKK, I will not hesitate to eradicate them. I will not hesitate in doing away with people"*.

Barkey & Fuller (1998, p. 40) describe him as, *"[He is] secretive, withdrawn, suspicious, and lacking in self-confidence. He does not like group discussion; his close associates reportedly seem uncomfortable around him. He does not treat others as equals and he often demeans his subordinates in front of others, demands self-confessions from his lieutenants, and keeps his distance from nearly everyone*"

Ocalan is mentally sick like Muhammad because he had inherited the mental disorder of Muhammad. He is a Narcissist himself. To the Narcissist, there are only friends or foes – either for or against their vision. There is no middle ground.

Muhammad's Qur'an is full of statements about how evil the Jews are and how the Muslims must fight the Jews until they are subjugated, which I have already discussed in details in previous chapters. Could grievances of the Palestinians such as "the Evil Jews violently and unjustly took away our land" originate from such apparently unrelated statements in the Qur'an? According to Palestinians; the Jews are something like bloodthirsty sadistic monsters. This creation of paranoia that has its roots in the paranoia created toward Jews in the Qur'an going back to Muhammad himself. This is called "evil gene delusion". This is the delusion that if a group of people did something wrong a thousand years ago, that means their modern day descendents are evil as well. The Nazis assumed that all non-Aryans were inferior and evil due to their genes. Muhammad's paranoia as reflected in the Qur'an is transferred through generations of the believing Muslims. They hate the Jews mainly because they believe that Jewish tribes betrayed Muhammad and that therefore the Jewish descendents of those tribes and all other Jews are treacherous as well. Today, the twenty-first century nuclear Prophet of Islam, the Hitler of Middle East, suffers from the same delusion. Mahmoud Ahmadinejad, the clown President of Iran took the Jews hating one step further. He is desperate to obtain a nuclear weapon. If he gets, he will use it against Israel within no time. This is his goal and he made it very clear. He said it literally that he wants to destroy Israel – "*wiped off the face of the map*" (Cohen, 2007, p. 9). Lastly, a quote from Sina,

> *Muslims, as a whole, by virtue of taking on the life of Muhammad, leave behind their own, forsaking their humanity and to a large degree, their individuality. As they come to inhabit the narcissistic bubble universe of their prophet, and to the extent that they follow his examples, they become extensions of him. Muslims are twigs from the tree of Islam and the root of that tree is Muhammad. They share his character, his attitude and his mindset. You could say each Muslim is a mini Muhammad of a sort.* (Sina, 2008, p. 4).

7.3.3: Inter-sect Terrorism: "Narcissism of minor differences"

Inter-sect violence between major sects of Islam i.e., Shiaa, Sunni, Ahmadiyya, Kurd, Ismaili, etc, occurs in countries like Pakistan, Bangladesh, Afghanistan, Iraq, Sudan, Nigeria, Somalia, Lebanon, Algeria and elsewhere. Often sectarian conflict leads to a violent civil war. This can be explained by Freud's theory "Narcissism of minor differences". Freud undertook a clinical study of group aggression, and concluded, "*It is precisely the minor difference in people who are otherwise alike that form the basis of feelings of strangeness and hostility between them*" (Ignatieff, 1998, p. 48). Narcissism of minor difference is not an individual behavior; rather it is implicated as a group behavior.

This term "Narcissism of minor differences" describes the manner in which negative feelings of a group are sometimes directed at people who resemble them, while the group takes pride from the "small differences" that distinguish the group from the other (Lyon, 2006, p. 11). This dynamic is the critical factor underpinning the Muslims' sudden outbreak of inter-sect violence that we often see in various Muslim countries. The religious rituals of every sect have minor differences from other sects, and each sect believes that they are practicing the real Islam. As a result, these "minor differences" between sects are transformed to major conflict amongst them. It is narcissistic because narcissism implies a focus on the self and a disregard or "devaluation" for the circumstance, interests and rights of others. Moreover, narcissism also asserts that outsiders have no understanding or place within the boundaries of one's own group.

Inter-sect narcissistic hate is too much in Islam. The violent Shiaa-Sunni conflict in Pakistan and Iraq shows that there are virtually no sanctuaries left – neither home, nor mosque or the hospital or even the graveyard; and being innocent is not the issue. Just "being" is enough – being Shiaa or Sunni. Lashkar-e-Jhangvi, an outlawed Sunni group has been responsible for murders of untold Shiaas (Pearl, 2003, p. 74). Let alone Shiaa and Sunni sectarian violence; now two different schools of thought of Sunni sect, Barelvi or Deobandi clash violently against each other. Not surprising, most of the civil wars are raged amongst Muslims and a majority of the world's refugees spill out from the Islamic countries. From 1975 to 1990, the Lebanese civil war cost at least 150,000 lives. Most of them belonging to Palestinians which is more than ten times as many deaths as Israel has inflicted in fifty years of combat (Manji, 2004, p. 140). The eight year long Iran-Iraq war caused death of likely more than one million people and property loss of US$ 1.19 trillion. In the genocide of Bangladeshis during '71 war, three million people were slaughtered, a quarter million women were raped and many babies were burned alive (Bhattacharyya, 1987, pp. 119, 186). More than ten million refugees had to flee to the safety of neighboring India to escape the brutality of the marauding soldiers from Pakistan. In Darfur alone, violent deaths are close to one million. The common Muslim thinking (Ignatieff, 1998, p. 59) is like this – "It is not the desire to be the master in your own house, but the conviction that only people like yourself deserve to be in the house".

7.3.3.1: The Root Cause of Inter-sect "Narcissism of Minor Differences"

Inter-sect narcissistic violence in Islam started during Muhammad's lifetime. The Narcissism of minor differences what we are seeing today amongst the Muslims is the direct consequences of Muhammad's narcissism, or more precisely Muhammad's narcissistic paranoid delusion and lust for power.

Paranoia is an unhealthy thought process which is heavily influenced by anxiety or fear, often to the point of irrationality and delusion. Muhammad had a pervasive distrust and suspiciousness of others such that their motives were interpreted as malevolent and hence he called for the destruction of rival mosques. He suspected, without sufficient basis, that others were trying to exploit, harm, or deceive him.

Muhammad ordered the destruction of an opposition mosque at Dhu Awan during April 631 after accusing its builders of being unjust. He sent a band of Muslims to destroy the freshly constructed mosque by burning it down (Tabari: IX.61). Muhammad concocted the story that he suspected that the builders of the "Mosque of Dissent" were planning to assassinate him. This was paranoid delusion of Muhammad. Allah promptly sent down verses justifying the destruction.

And as for those who chose a place of worship out of opposition and disbelief, and in order to cause dissent among the believers… (Q: 9.107).

Never stand (to pray) there… (Q: 9.108).

Is he who founded his building upon duty to Allah and His good pleasure better; or he who founded his building on the brink of a crumbling, overhanging precipice so that it toppled with him into the fire of hell? Allah guideth not wrongdoing folk. (Q: 9.109).

The building which they built will never cease to be a misgiving in their hearts unless their hearts be torn to pieces. (Q: 9.110).

These verses (9.107-10), when taken in true Islamic spirit, call for the destruction of rival mosques. The question is – which mosques are genuinely Islamic and which mosques are not. The irony is that there is no central authority in Islam to decide on this, so naturally it leads to confusion. Thus Sunni kills Shiaa, Shiaa kills Sunni and both these groups kill Ahmedi or Kurdish Muslims and so on.

On top of this religious chaos, a Hadith (Sunnan Abu Dawud: 3.40.4744) just added fuel to the fire. It instructed Muslims to kill anyone whoever is suspected to create disunity in Islam. This is similar to handing over a fatwa to virtually every sect of Islam. Naturally every sect of Islam is at loggerheads with each other and eliminating each other as per their belief(s) in a perfect Islamic way.

Secondly, when a Narcissist is in the position of authority, sometimes he even justifies butchering of his own people by claiming that they intended to assassinate him, devastate the economy, harm the nation or the country, etc (Vaknin, 2004). We have seen this tendency in notorious Narcissist leaders like, Saddam Hussein, Stalin and Hitler. On several occasions, Muhammad's cruelty turned to his own people.

The Prophet said, 'burn all those who had not left their houses for the prayer, burning them alive inside their homes.' (Bukhari: 1.11.626)

Therefore, the concept of "Universal brotherhood" in Islam is for name only. Muslims will never stop loving each other to death with joy in their hearts. From the very beginning of Islam, Muslims were never a unified community. They are only united in their hatred for the non-Muslims.

7.4: The Thin Boundary Line between a Terrorist Muslim and a Peaceful Muslim

"*Islam, just like the Roman God Janus, has two faces*".

Abul Kasem

"*The militant Muslim is the person cutting the head of the infidel while the moderate Muslim holds the victims feet*".

Dr. M. Sabieski

In a country when Muslims are a minority they demand more and more privileges and rights for minorities from the host country. When their number grows by birth or immigration, they want to impose the Sharia rule. When they become majority, they start bringing death and destruction to the host nation and start ethnic cleansing. This is the worst type of disloyalty and hypocrisy.

Is not this the same what Muhammad did to the early Meccans? When he was weak, he brought down verses which were peaceful. He even uttered some verses which praised the pagan gods (the satanic verses) to make the Meccans happy. But when he became powerful his darker side began to emerge and the Qur'anic verses started losing their beauty. Once he conquered Mecca, he showed his true color to everyone – either convert or die by the sword.

The policy-makers often fail to see this point. They are making the same mistake what the early Meccans did. They realize the impact of radical Islam but fail to pay attention to moderate Islam. Little do they understand that the moderate Islam is much more dangerous than the radical Islam because it grows and silently kills the host. Islamic jihad has many faces. Jihad is not just slaughtering people for Islam; it is also a systematic suppression of truth and propagation of lies. If not, how can the moderate Muslims boldly assert (despite hard evidence to the contrary) that Islam is a peaceful religion?

The slogan "Islam is a peaceful religion" is about 1400 years out of date. The seed of terrorism is germinating inside every Muslim. Anyone who has put a single grain of trust on Muhammad and his Qur'an fills up his mind with unjustified hate and paranoia, and he is bound to have similar destructive ideas like his Prophet. The dark force of Muhammad's narcissism immediately starts working in him. Several years into the war on Islamic terror, but still often we hear Islam is a religion of peace. While those so-called peaceful Muslims use this term for obvious reasons, those who know Islam use this term sarcastically. Terrorism is there in every cell of Islam. Islam cannot survive without terrorism because terrorism is the life-giving force of Islam. Those who are against terrorism have no place in Islam; they are infidels. The Muslim terrorists are not "hijacking" Islam; they are, at least in their own view, restoring it. Without terrorism Islam will suffocate and collapse. The peaceful face of Islam is the political Islam and it is the mask of violent Islam. As the Turkish Prime Minister commented, *"These descriptions are very ugly. It is offensive and an insult to our religion. There is no moderate or immoderate Islam. Islam is Islam and that's it"* (McCarthy, 2010, p. 39).

The only difference between a peaceful Muslim and a terrorist Muslim is that the terrorists are openly in action and they are not at all shy to make their agenda known to the non-Muslims, whereas the peaceful Muslims are silently in action and hypocrite. In the wake of two London bombing, one of the most radical Islamic groups in Britain, al-Ghurabaa stated (Dawkins, 2006, p. 307), *"Any Muslim that denies that terror is a part of Islam is kafir (nonbeliever)"*. And a similar statement from Zakir Naik (Al-Kindy, 2005, p. 86; Downing, 2009, p. 354) is, *"Every Muslim should be a terrorist"*. Islam and terrorism are blood brothers.

The so-called peaceful Muslims are very calculative, and proceed sophistically. They give long speeches on human rights and democratic values and sing the peaceful verses of Qur'an but once Islam becomes powerful they will start singing another tune. The fundamental concepts of human rights, developed in the West with the help of John Locke and other enlightenment thinkers, have not had any impact on Islam even to this day. Hard-line Muslims have openly admitted this fact. In January 1985, Saeed Raja'i-Khorasani, the permanent delegate to the United Nations from the Islamic Republic of Iran, declared, "*The very concept of human rights is 'a Judeo-Christian invention' and inadmissible in Islam.*" (Spencer, 2002, p. 104). The so-called peaceful Muslims would not hesitate to implement Jyzia tax on Christians and Jews, and slit the throats of Hindus, Buddhists, Sikhs, ex-Muslims, atheists and agnostics according to the Sharia law. Deep down, every "believer" is potentially the judge and executioner of every "nonbeliever". After all, both the terrorists and the peaceful Muslims are working for the same cause – to dominate the world in the name of Islam.

Since the noblest goal of a Muslim is to assist Islam rule the world, these moderate Muslims shamelessly lie about Islam to deceive the infidels. As Imam Ghazali says (cited Shienbaum & Hasan, 2006, p. 63), "*Speaking is a means to achieve objectives. If a praiseworthy aim is attainable through both telling the truth and lying, it is unlawful to accomplish through lying because there is no need for it. When it is possible to achieve such an aim by lying but not by telling the truth, it is permissible to lie if attaining the goal is permissible.*" The peaceful Muslims and the terrorist Muslims are two sides of the same coin.

For a peaceful Muslim, it is very easy to become a terrorist. Hate for the non-Muslims is the basic tenet of Islam and violence is the conclusion. As Ayatollah Sadegh Khalkhali, a hard-line Islamic Iranian Judge (Peterson, 2002, p. 201) openly declared, "*Those who are against killing have no place in Islam. Our Prophet killed with his own blessed hands. Our Imam Ali killed more than seven hundred on a single day. If the survival of the faith requires the shedding of blood, we are there to perform our duty*". So when a so-called peaceful Muslim emerges as a terrorist, it does not involve a discrete choice to change status. A terrorist is lurking inside every Muslim waiting for a chance to come out. One such example (Martin, 2010, p. 195); Qur'an says, "*When the sacred months have passed, slay the idolaters wherever ye find them...*" (Q: 9.5). A son of Pakistani businessman was inspired by this verse and took an oath, "*I state in the presence of God that I will slaughter the infidels my entire life. May God give me strength in fulfilling this oath*".

Islamic terrorism is a complex phenomenon; hence, the personalities of the terrorists change from person to person. It would be useless to attribute a simple and global characteristic to all of them. In Islam, terrorists can assume many different roles – only a few will actually fire the weapon or detonate the bomb or become a human bomber. The "personality" of a Muslim politician, or a Mullah, or a financier of Islamic terrorism, or an illiterate Muslim woman who gives birth to a dozen kids because a large family pleases Allah, or the simple pious bearded Muslim who pays regular *Zakat* to the mosque, is different from that of an administrator, or strategist, or an assassin, or a suicide bomber. This is the essence of jihad that had been widely discussed in Islamic books on religious laws. Though some systematic differences might be discerned between those who engage in terrorism and those who do not; deep down, they have identical psychological set up. As Taylor and Quayle, the two well known researchers of the present age religious terrorism, commented (1994, p. 197), "*The active terrorist is not discernibly different in psychological terms from the non-terrorist; in psychological terms, there are no special qualities that characterize the terrorist*". Who can deny that the clerics and the militant community leaders are elected by these moderate Muslims?

In reality, peaceful Islam does not exist. *"Al Islam huwa al hall"* (Islam is the solution) is not a slogan raised by Muslim terrorists only but by all the Muslims (Phares, 2005, p. 251). The nouns "terrorist" or "terrorists" do not necessarily refer to everyone within a terrorist organization. In an army not everyone carries a gun. There are many non-fighting members, e.g., accountants, cooks, fund-raisers, logistics specialists, medical doctors, nurses or recruiters – who may play only a passive support role. But all of them have the same ultimate goal, i.e., to defeat the enemy. Similarly, there are many ways to support jihad, besides personal violence. The peaceful Muslim we know is commanded to give money to Islamic charities and the charities give the money to the actual fighters. They are playing this passive support role and the ultimate goal is to conquer the world for Islam.

7.5: Conclusion

"Minarets are our bayonets
Domes are our helmets
Mosques are our barracks
Believers are our soldiers".

A Ziya Gokalp poem (Coughlin, 2006, p. 195)

"Educating the children to Jihad and to hatred of the Jews, the Christians, and the infidels is what is needed now".
Sermon of Sheikh Muhammad Saleh al-Munajjid in Al-Daman, Saudi Arabia

"The history of Islam, for instance, tells us that Islam needs blood to thrive. Human blood is the life-line of Islam, violence its hallmark, and hate its foundation ... As a car needs gasoline to run, so does Islam need human blood just to run its own course, set by Muhammad, its Prophet".

Abul Kasem

"Whenever one looks along the perimeter of Islam, Muslims have problem living peacefully with their neighbors. Islam's borders are bloody, and so are its innards."
Samuel Huntington (1996, pp. 256, 258)

Islamic terrorists have a very self-contradictory outlook. They ridicule Western culture as false, meaningless, dangerous, corrupt common values, and rotten social values; but at the same time they devote their entire life to the elimination and pulverization of this "insignificant" entity. To justify this self-contradiction, the Islamic terrorists cast themselves as an altruistic savior of the Muslim Ummah "endangered" by the enemies. Sometimes they are driven by messianic delusions. They are always self-appointed and self-proclaimed, rarely elected. However, this is another self-contradiction. They accuse the western nations of being a failed civilization interfering ignorantly and sacrilegiously in the affairs of Islam and exporting this contagious failure to Islamic societies by "infecting" them with the virus of its own terminal decline. Paradoxically, the same Muslim fanatics who believe that the West is dying also decry its overwhelming military, technological, and financial superiority.

Militant Islam is not a cancerous mutation of the "true" and "peaceful" Islam. It is the purest expression of its nature as an imperialistic religion which demands unmitigated obedience from its followers and regards all non-Muslims as both inferior and avowed enemies. In Islamic faith there is nothing to pervert. It is simply "bloodshed in the name of God". This murderous cult lacks objective justification and does not have any demonstrable standard to pervert.

Practically every "lunacy", every hypocrisy, and every terrorist act of Muslims can be explained from the point of view of Muhammad's narcissism. The sadistic cruel nature of Prophet Muhammad is reflected in the behavior of the Islamic terrorists. Muhammad's entire prophetic life was based on victimizing innocents. He was a criminal of worst type humanity had ever seen. Today's Muslim terrorists are not doing anything new what their Prophet had not done fourteen centuries ago. Every Muslim is carrying the personal flag of Muhammad. It is like the invasion of the body snatchers as we see in horror movies and Muslims are not even aware of it. Muhammad affected his victims by infiltrating their psyches and by penetrating their defenses. Like a fatal virus, the evil curse of Muhammad established a new genetic strain within the Muslims which generates obedience and reverence and awakens a profound feeling of awe that manifests itself both as fear and as being strongly attracted towards Muhammad's cult. Now the evil spirit of Muhammad echoes through them, talks through them, walks through them, hates through them as if Muslims do not have a mind of their own to think rationally, sanely or sensibly. This is the origin of the mysterious dark force as if Muhammad took rebirth in every Muslim to finish his unfinished job – to conquer the world – the ultimate dream of a seventh century malignant Narcissist.

Chapter 8: The Legacy of Muhammad

"Have we not seen that millions of people, misguided by their irrational passions, can believe in ideas which are not less delusional and irrational than the products of a single individual?"

Erich Fromm (1900 - 1980)

Muslims adore Muhammad like a slave adores his Master for the fear of punishment. One poet (cited Noor Allah Marqadah, 2010) was not shy about it.

Muhammad Ki Ghulami Hay Sanad Azaad Honay Ki.
Khuda Kay Daman-e-Tauheed Mein Abaad Honay Ki.
Muhammad Ki Muhabbat Deen-e-Haq Ki Shart-e-Awwal Hay.
Agar Is Mein Ho Khami Tow Sab Kuch Na Mukammal Hay.

(Slavery of Muhammad is the guarantee of forgiveness of Allah. It is the only way to get to the divine light. True love with Muhammad is the first condition of true Islam. If there is any doubt in it, nothing is complete or acceptable to Allah.)

Muhammad resides deep inside of the heart of every Muslim. No wonder, praising him is an integral part of their daily prayers. By judging him a mercy and by praising him in the daily prayers, every Muslim automatically becomes a victim of his narcissistic force. This is the legacy of Muhammad. The ghost of Muhammad haunts the Muslims every moment. Like aliens snatch the bodies of the victims; Muhammad had invaded and modified the minds of Muslims and brought them to his bubble universe to serve him. This way, when the Muslims adopt Muhammad's way of thinking, all the seven deadly sins of a Narcissist start blooming in them. As Sina (2008, pp. 59, 60) commented, *"The personality disorder of one man has been bequeathed like an inheritance upon his followers, where one man's psychosis, spectacular in its depth of self-absorption, has been spreading to millions of his followers, rendering them, in the same way, self-absorbed, irrational, and dangerous"*. By this logic, Islam is the mental illness of the Muslims.

8.1: No Other Religion except Islam Promotes Narcissism

All the world religions, except Islam, traditionally put a brake on narcissistic behaviors. Some of them directly reduce narcissism or related concepts; like, pride, hostility and selfishness, and teach us that the society is something which is larger than the self. The core message is that each of us should live according to certain rules that apply to everyone, and the value of a community of fellow believers. The individualistic (also narcissistic) motto "Do what is right for you" does not fit very well with the same-for-everyone rules and beliefs of most religions. But in Islam, the God is full of pride, the Prophet was perverted, the book is full of hate; hence the religion is bound to promote narcissism.

In Christianity; the Gospels are full of verses that praise the humble and meek, and chastise the proud. A verse on Proverbs (15.26) says, *"The Lord will destroy the house of the proud.*" A sermon on the mount advises that "*Blessed [are] the meek: for they shall inherit the earth*" (Matthew: 5.6). Christianity also emphasizes on forgiveness (especially for one's enemies) and humility which is just opposite of narcissism. "*Turning the other cheek*" is definitely not a narcissistic act. Christianity also teaches that you should treat others as you would like to be treated is another dictum counter to narcissistic ethos.

Eastern religions, as example, Hinduism, focus directly on egoism as a source of suffering. In Hindu theology, the saint is considered one who has completely annihilated his ego. Hindu seers had encouraged humankind to shun egoism and to focus on the development of a virtuous and good mind called *Sumati.* There are many Vedic prayers that invoke the noble and upright mind (Badlani, 2008, p. 85). In Hindu Katha Upanishad there is a story, according to which the knowledge about the secrets of immortal soul is more valuable than the material goods and social status. Buddhism, which was a mutation of Hinduism, takes the Hindu wisdom a step further. Zen (a school of Mahayana Buddhism) has several stories describing the negative consequences of narcissism. As example (Twenge & Campbell, 2010, p. 246); the Prime Minister of Tang Dynasty once asked a Zen master, "*What is egoism according to Buddhism?*" The master shot back in a harsh tone, "*What kind of stupid question is that!?*" Insulted, the Prime Minister became angry. The master then smiled and said, "*THIS, your Excellency, is egoism.*"

Islam is all about this egoism the Zen master and the Hindu seers had warned us again and again. This is coupled with many destructive thoughts, like; revenge, hate, envy and self-glorification. Every religion has some inherent truth and beauty which Islam lacks completely. No religion other than Islam competes for adherents. Other religions give people what they need spiritually, but Islam demands. Therefore Islam cannot enforce narcissism reducing practices.

8.2: Islam: The Narcissism Epidemic of the Muslims

On September 30, 2005, twelve editorial cartoons, most of which depicted Muhammad, were published in the Danish newspaper *Jyllands-Posten.* They were neither works of art by any account nor very amusing. Only one cartoon showed Muhammad's turban shaped like a bomb. A group of Danish Imams protested, but the Danish Prime Minister took the view that what a newspaper had done was not his business because the freedom of the speech in Denmark meant that newspapers were beyond the control of the government.

Some Imams then took their campaign to condemn the Danish government to Saudi Arabia and Egypt. But they took as their evidence not only those twelve cartoons but three more, including one with Muhammad as a demonic pedophile and one with a pig snout. This was reported in a Danish tabloid *Extra Bladet* and not denied (Desai, 2007, p. 8). The third fake cartoon was a praying Muslim being raped by a dog. The three extra cartoons were more offensive and more insulting to both Muhammad and Islam than the original twelve cartoons. Clearly, the Imams added them to fuel outrage by giving the Arabs an idea, how hateful the atmosphere in Denmark is towards Muslims. However, this controversy led to protests across the Muslim world, some of which escalated into violence (resulting in more than 100 deaths), including setting fire to the Danish embassies in Syria, Lebanon and

Iran, storming European buildings, and desecrating the Danish, Norwegian, Dutch, French and German flags in Gaza city.

This is an abnormal behavior. Muslims rioted in far away places such as Nigeria and Turkey, killed innocents and destroyed property, yet they call their religion a peaceful religion. In Islamic countries many Christian churches and Hindu temples are regularly destroyed, Jews are routinely labeled "apes and pigs" in the state-controlled media, and in Saudi Arabia carrying a Bible is forbidden, but still Muslims quote some peaceful verses from the Qur'an to show that there is no compulsion in religion. Why this hypocrisy? If some innocent cartoons wounded the delicate sensibilities of the Muslims, then, in the same way, labeling Jews with offensive terms equally wound the sensibilities of the Jewish community.

The cartoon incident highlights the fact that Muslims cannot be good citizens of any country where another religion and culture is dominant. It means; Muslims cannot be a loyal minority, and as their numbers and strength build up they will demand to impose their Muslim laws and systems on their hosts. In fact the Qur'an instructs them not to live as minorities, but try to take over. Their allegiance is always to the wider world of Islam over any national boundaries.

The cartoon rage was a repetition of the fury unleashed by Salman Rushdie's 1988 novel *The Satanic Verses*, and of Pope's criticism of Muhammad on September 12, 2006. The dying Ayatollah Khomeini of Iran declared in a fatwa that Rushdie and those associated with the publication and distribution of the book should be killed. Following Khomeini's dictum, a mob attacked the USIS office in Islamabad, the capital of Pakistan, and huge public demonstrations with ritualistic burning of Rushdie's novel were arranged from the streets of Dhaka, Bangladesh, to the streets of Bradford, England. As a protest of Pope's criticism, many churches were burnt down, several Islamic terrorist organizations gave a joint threat to Vatican, and an Italian nun of sixty-five years was killed.

How should we explain such mad furor over cartoons, or works of fiction, or a comment from Pope that so readily seize Muslim sensitivities, and then spill over into the streets with appalling consequences? What is to be made of the cartoon controversy, the Rushdie's novel and Pope's comment? And what is the implication, if any, of such conduct on the part of Muslims for the West?

Muslim rage over the minor issues can be explained by Kohut's psychoanalytic theories on narcissism first published in 1972. According to Kohut; the frustration and suppression of the grandiose self is displayed by means of narcissistic rage which is a result of the shame and fear at being faced with failure. When a Narcissist's grandiose sense of self-worth is under attack, typically in the form of criticism, he suffers from narcissistic injury. The natural reaction is to rage and pull down the self-worth of others to feel superior to them. By showing rage, he wants to pacify his internal pain and hostility and rebuild his self-worth.

Muslims cannot tolerate even a small criticism of their Prophet. The depiction of Muhammad with a bomb in the turban indicates that Islamic terrorism is closely related to Muhammad (surely it is!). Since Muhammad is the Prophet of all the Muslims, it indirectly points negatively to the Muslims and their religion. It caused narcissistic injury, and hence they raged. By killing more than one hundred innocent people and destroying property in riots everywhere in the world, the Muslims felt superior to others, i.e., non-Muslims.

Narcissistic rage comes in many forms, but all pertain to the same important thing, revenge. When angry Muslims rioted, attacked churches, or issued fatwa on Rushdie's head, the only thing that was in their mind was revenge. Narcissistic rage is the outcome of shame and fear. The shame is that they follow a Prophet who is more of a criminal and less a Prophet, that all other religions are more spiritual and progressive and logical than their own. The fear is that, their Prophet would be exposed by criticism, that the spiritual bankruptcy of their religion would be discovered. For the very same reason free thought and freedom of expression is not allowed in Islam.

There are many evidences that Muslims are suffering from mass narcissism. By taking the example of Saddam Hussein, Twenge & Campbell commented (2010, p. 266) that much of the Muslim world has already been infected by narcissism. This way, every Muslim is a "mini" Muhammad. The beast of Muhammad is very much alive in the hearts of the Muslims. Whenever it gets a chance, it makes its presence known to the world ferociously, sometimes without any logical provocation.

Paranoia is a common trait of narcissism. It is actually pervasive among normal people and among groups of people. Groups can also be considered to suffer from mental illness. Amongst Muslims there is massive creation of paranoia toward the infidels which originated from Muhammad's paranoia. Muhammad used to see conspiracies everywhere. Throughout his career, Muhammad addressed the infidels with offensive terms and talked about how they were plotting against him, opposing his religion and persecuting him and his followers. Muslims also see conspiracies everywhere. They "know" that the filthy infidels are always plotting against them, opposing their religion and persecuting them. Any healthy criticism is taken as personal slight. Gradually, their minds turn into a chaotic battlefield of paranoid fear. When Muslim terrorists destroyed twin towers, some Muslims believed that it was the work of Mossad or the CIA. In India, Muslims refuse to allow their children to take polio vaccination because the Hindus have polluted the vaccines. Jews have invented the cartoon show Tom & Jerry because Allah equates them to rats and they want to prove that rats are cute. USA agreed to give militarily support to Israel, because Monica Lewinsky was an agent of Mossad (Razzaque, 2008, p. 45). USA attacked Afghanistan and Iraq to loot their resources. Afghan children are told in Madrassah that Afghanistan is a poor country because of the disproportionate wealth of the Americans. Some of these conspiracy theories are so ridiculous that Muslims often make themselves a laughing stock. But they believe all these nonsense because illogical fear and distrust in instilled in their minds.

Muslims cannot accept any criticism of their faith. Questioning of their beliefs, no matter how trivial, is met with evasiveness, defensiveness, irritability and hostility. This is called persecution complex. Narcissists develop a feeling that they are persecuted by higher powers. Muhammad never had shortage of critics. They described him as motivated by a combination of political ambition and sensual lust. Muhammad never engaged in any meaningful debate with them, rather he silenced them by killing them. Exactly same type of persecution complex is observed in Muslims. They are hyper-vigilant and constantly on the lookout for slights. They take every realistic criticism as personal insult. Neither they can question their own faith nor will they allow anyone to do so. Muslims are always eager to prove that Islam is a nonviolent religion, but once the violent verses are shown to them they become furious. Persecution complex can strike anyone, regardless of belief, creed or religion. Once the Muslims start believing that the whole world is against them, they begin to justify any actions by the presumed hostility of the world.

Next topic of discussion is delusional disorder. The patient who is suffering from delusional disorder holds one or more strange fixed beliefs implanted deep inside in his mind. Often vivid hallucinations related to the content of the delusion may be present. He may successfully function in daily life and may not exhibit odd or bizarre behavior aside from these delusions. Common Muslims suffer from delusional disorder like Muhammad. They believe that they will enter paradise only because they are Muslims and all the nonbelievers are destined to hell. How do I know that it really happens, had anyone ever come back from his grave and told us that he had seen Muslims and non-Muslims in their afterlife? How do I know that Muhammad did not lie to propagate his mission? These questions will never arise in Muslim mind. After all, Muhammad was a mentally deranged criminal. How much could he be trusted? When a Muslim transforms himself from a human being to a human bomb, all these questions do not occur in his mind. A Muslim's delusional disorder has an undue influence on his life. He is oversensitive in his belief, because he has no logical explanation. But he cannot come out of his delusion.

From the very deep bottom of his heart, every Muslim knows that his religion is a violent religion, that Muhammad was an aggressive man, that the real God cannot be unethical, that Islam is a mental prison; but he cannot express himself. So he lies to himself. He knows that something is seriously wrong with his religion, but he is confused. He understands that people around him are not happy with him, but he is helpless. In his mind, he agrees to every accusation of the critics of Islam, but he cannot stop putting his trust in Muhammad. He had succumbed to his mental illness which he had inherited from his Prophet. This is the gift of Muhammad to Muslims.

8.3: The Demonic Recipe of Narcissist Muhammad

Islam is the legacy of a malignant Narcissist. By following Islam, Muslims inherit all the seven deadly sins – shamelessness, magical thinking, arrogance, envy, entitlement, exploitation and bad boundaries – all included in the demonic recipe of Narcissist Muhammad. These sins are deadly because they invade and annihilate the integrity of everyone they touch, and sinful because they destroy the sinner as well. These seven deadly sins not only harm others, but also prevent the Narcissist from developing a real self.

8.3.1: Shamelessness (Bypassed shame)

Shame is a healthy emotion, but people who bypass shame become obsessive which results in low self-esteem and leads to anger and lowliness. Bypassed shame can set up explosive chain reaction, like, acute panic (a shame-fear alternation), resentment (shame-anger alternation, with anger directed out), and guilt (shame-anger sequences, with the anger directed in) (Scheff, 1999, pp. 88, 93). Muslims appear to be "thick-skinned", but actually they are extremely shame-sensitive. Today being Muslim itself is a shameful act. Deep inside, a Muslim feels pathetic and foolish deserving of mockery and humiliation. Allah repeatedly cursed the infidels, but the infidel world is progressing well; it is the Muslims who are at the lowest people in a society. Two-thirds of world's poorest people live in Muslim countries. With all their oil-wealth, there is no Muslim nation among the top thirty of the world's richest nations. Democracy and rule of law is practically non-existent (Trifkovic, 2002, p. 3). Most of the Muslim nations are like living hell which is one of the reasons Muslims immigrate to more civilized Western nations. Some Muslim nations are so poor that their people will simply die from starvation if USA stops financial aid to them. Though Muslims show cool indifference to all criticisms, all of a sudden they surprise us by reacting – acute panic, resentment or guilt.

We often hear from the Muslim clerics that Islam is in danger. When some progressive Muslims talk about female education, equal rights, drawbacks of Madrassah education, etc, the clerics are in panic. One reason is that they fear to lose their control. They are scared of free thoughts, because if freedom of thought and speech is encouraged, Islam will be exposed. But the second reason is that the bypassed shame changes into panic (a shame-fear alternation). When we talk about reformation of Christianity and Hinduism – another two world religions; Christians and Hindus are very open to logical and constructive criticism. But for Muslims, the bypassed shame vents out as panic.

Violent rage (shame-anger alternation, with anger directed out) is the second explosive chain reaction. The three best examples of this are; as stated before, Danish cartoon, Rushdie's novel, and Pope's criticism. All these are shame-based rage. When Muslims feel humiliated, embarrassed, or ridiculed and their already low self-esteem takes a further drop; they rage to cut off these bad feelings.

The third point is guilt, i.e., the shame-anger sequences, with the anger directed to himself, his religion and his Prophet. In this process, the Muslim doubts his Islamic faith but he may not leave Islam immediately. He dives deep into Islamic studies, goes to mosque more frequently, attain more religious seminars and apparently become more devoted to his religion. But all these actions are superficial as if he is trying to trick himself. This is not permanent; sooner or later he stops fooling himself and guilt overcomes him. Ultimately he leaves Islam.

8.3.2: Magical thinking

Magical thinking is one of the hallmarks not only of malignant narcissism, but of many other mental disorders. There is no cognitive logic in magical thinking; the Narcissist just knows it. The same way Muhammad knew that killing, raping, looting and torturing the infidels are all divine acts which satisfied Allah. One part of the Muslim mind is always engaged in magical thinking. As Hotchkiss (2003, p. 10) wrote, "*Magical thinking, exploitive idealization, and the devaluation of others via shame-dumping and belittling are all attempts on the part of the Narcissist to avoid feeling defective and insignificant*". Magical thinking is one of the most dangerous mind-altering substances.

It explains why the Muslims made it a practice of Jews-bashing. The prosperity of the Jews gives them heartburn. So they inflate their narcissistic balloon by ridiculing the Jews, by labeling them "apes and pigs" or decedents of "monkeys and pigs". But, what they hardly understand is that in both theory and practice, magic does not conform to reality. Universe is not ruled by wishful thinking, but by immutable laws. Today these "monkeys and pigs" are the most educated and most advanced people on the earth (followed by Christians and Hindus). And where do the Muslims stand? They are at the bottommost level and live a pitiful life both in the Islamic world as well as Western world. But in spite of knowing all these facts Muslims cannot come out of their magical thinking. This is abnormal.

Ever since the birth of Islam, this religion had not changed. In spite of that there are many Muslims who believe that Islam can be reformed like Christianity and Judaism. In fact the Shiaas of Iran even have a "Hidden Imam" who will come back any day now and set things right.

Muslims often take childlike pleasure glorifying the golden age of Islam, which is actually a myth. Muslim Ummah was equally backward during those days as it is today. Spencer (2005, p. 91) reported that there is no historical proof to support the idea that Islam inspired a culture which outstripped others. Tisdall wrote (2005, p. 91), "*No great civilization, no scientist of note, no renowned school of philosophy, has ever arisen on purely Mohammedan ground*". He believed that even several Muslim scholars had accepted this fact. Islam had never encouraged scientific knowledge. The only knowledge it accepts is Qur'anic knowledge. Diderot (Gunny, 1996, p. 168) stated that during Caliph al-Mamun, people were heard shouting for his death because he had fostered science at the expense of the "holy ignorance" of the faithful believers.

With so much glorification of illiteracy and dislike for science, there is little doubt that Islam's golden age was a clever myth. It is infidel's education, science, technology and endurance, based on which the human civilization had spread everywhere including Islamic world itself on which the Muslim community has no contribution. The sheikhs of Islam could not do anything better than stand silently as spectators to infidel's prosperity. Trifkovic (2002, p. 196) concluded, "*Whatever flourished, it was not by reason of Islam, it was in spite of Islam.*" The glorious past of Ummah is a wishful thinking of the Muslims. When they look at the infidel prosperity, it is their challenge to find a way to stay pumped up inside in order to hold these harsh realities at bay.

Magical thinking is very common amongst children. There is no harm in it for them because they are in a growing stage. They create imaginary worlds while playing and start knowing the differences between fantasy and reality by the age three or four, though they usually still believe (with adult encouragement) in Santa Claus, the Tooth Fairy or similar many. But when the adults cannot emerge from this stage, we know something is wrong with them. Mental dysfunction of Muslims should not be taken lightly because they not only could harm themselves and their society but to those around them. Can we ignore the magical thinking of the suicide bomber and his concrete belief in Allah's reward? Reality is the most potent check on runaway magical thoughts and if we want to stop Islamic terrorism we have no other way but to fight Muslim's magical thinking with reality.

Muslims' appetite for such irrational beliefs is rooted in Muhammad. The sense of having special powers often put people in threatening situations, as we have seen not only in Muhammad, but other monstrous leaders, like, Hitler, Alexander and Genghis Khan as well. Muhammad's illusion of divine power is the basic cause of Muslim's magical thinking throughout the course of Islam. Magical thinking is more or less common with every religion but for the Muslims it knows no bound; an orthodox Muslim can spend his whole life in it, e.g., the Urdu poet, Mir Taqi Mir (cited Geisler & Saleeb, 1993, p. 88) wrote, "*Why do you worry, O Mir, thinking of your black book? The person of the seal of the Prophets is a guarantee for your salvation*". For Muslims magical thinking goes beyond "belief without evidence" to the point of "belief in the face of overwhelming evidence to the contrary".

Neither Muhammad was a Prophet, nor was Qur'an from God. This book is full of contradictory ramblings of a sincere but delusional man. Giving one's life for such a religion, far from being evidence of its truthfulness, was nothing less than insanity. Most of the Qur'anic sciences are proven to be wrong by modern science. There is no Prophet and no God who can stop the progress of science. Magic does not matter, only facts matter. In the end it is the facts and the reality they represent, that determine our opportunities and limitations.

8.3.3: Arrogance

Almost everything of the Western civilization offends the sensibility of the Muslims. The list is a long one; ranging from religious liberty, sexual equality, and the right of gay people, to music, alcohol, dogs, and pork. Everyday new items are added to this list. Muslims demand and expect their host country to satisfy all their claims. Western nations have given every right to the Muslims. Muslims have freedom of religion. They have the right to speak against their host country, no one will kill them. In fact they can burn American flag on any street in the USA. But they are reluctant to give same type of freedom to the minorities in Muslim majority nations. In Saudi Arabia, the practice of any religion openly besides Islam is strictly prohibited now, just as it was during the time of Muhammad (Hagee, 2007, p. 29). The minorities are not allowed to build churches or openly read Bible in Saudi Arabia. It is a punishable act. Saudi Arabia is building mosques in America with riches from America's gas tanks, but if anyone goes to Saudi Arabia and try to worship any other God than Allah, he can be killed.

This is narcissistic tendency. A Narcissist expects and needs admiration and seeks out situations in which that requirement can be met. Even after this, he expects to be treated with respect, deference, and admiration. When such admiration is not forthcoming, the Narcissist may respond with surprise, hurt, or even rage. Hotchkiss (2003, p. 14) wrote, "*They can be quite sensitive to other's opinions and often have unrealistic expectations of unconditional approval and admiration*".

Is this the superiority complex of the Muslims? No, it is just the opposite. The arrogance comes from their inferiority complex. Narcissists are often double-faced. The face which they present often comes across to others as a "superior being" but, "*behind the mask of arrogance is a fragile internal balloon of self-esteem that is never satisfied with being good or even very good – if they are not better than, then they are worthless. Value is always relative, never absolute. From their point of view, if someone else's stock goes up, theirs automatically goes down... For them, there is nothing acceptable about being ordinary or average – if they cannot be superior, they are nothing.*" (Hotchkiss, 2003, pp. 11, 13). Arrogance is a defense mechanism against shame as well. It attempts to fill their inner emptiness with an ego rather than allowing that emptiness to blossom into humility. Hotchkiss continued, "*At the root of the harm inflicted to others is the need to get rid of the exaggerated shame of real or imagined inferiority*".

Arrogance is some kind of "unwarranted pride". The arrogant assumes his views and opinions as "the truth". A Narcissist is often arrogant because he sees first himself. Rather than offering respect to all, he demands respect from all. When Muslims show their tremendous hate and arrogance for Western civilization, they are actually showing the empty edifice of their ego. Muslim's this type of unhealthy narcissistic arrogance is deep-rooted in Muhammad.

All forms of religious arrogance lie well beyond the path of true spirituality. Neither Muhammad nor the Muslims understood this simple fact. They see their path as the one true way and attempt to convert others, even over protests of disinterest. For Muslims this is their religious duty but for a psychologist, this is the perfect example of narcissistic arrogance.

8.3.4: Envy

Envy occurs when a person lacks another's superior quality, achievement, or possession, and either desires it or wishes that the other lacked it. There is hardly anyone in this world who had never been envious to others in some time of their lives. Envy can be both constructive and destructive. Aristotle's emphasis (Salovey, 1991, p. 9) was that some forms of envy motivate people to improve themselves whereas other types motivate people to take good things away from others. The first type of envy is non-malicious envy. Some psychologists do not consider non-malicious envy to be envy at all. Muslim's envy is narcissistic pathological envy. In pathological envy, the envious person is not only unhappy by his envy but also wishes to inflict misfortune on others. This is when it becomes dangerous.

When there is a social comparison between Muslims and non-Muslims, the "self-image" of the Muslims is threatened. For them, to witness the success and joy of the non-Muslims is too painful and too high a price to pay. So they devalue the source of their frustration and envy. Envious thoughts are daily struggle for most of the Muslims and it is well portrayed in Iqbal's poetry. Muhammad Allama Iqbal was a great poet of Pakistan. His poetry inspired many Indian Muslims to fight the war against their Hindu countrymen and divide the Nation in two, Pakistan and India; which they called "independence". The prosperity and power of the infidels caused Iqbal to complain to Allah, which in Urdu called *Shikwa* (expressing dissatisfaction). This is a long poetic work.

In the beginning, Iqbal reminds Allah that Muslims are totally devoted to His cause. They wandered in the deserts, mountains and oceans with Allah's message and died happily for the grandeur of Allah's name. They honored Ka'ba and put the Qur'an to their hearts. Still Allah is not happy with them. Iqbal wrote,

Phir Bhi hamsey ye gila hai ke wafadar naheen
Ham wafadar naheen too bhi to dildar naheen.
Rahmaten hain teri aghyar ke kashanon par
Barq girti hai to becharey musalmanon par.

(Still you complain that we are lacking fealty. If we are lacking fealty you also are not generous. Thy graces descend on the other people's abodes. Lightning strikes only the poor Muslims' abodes.)

In the next stanza, Iqbal laments that the idols in temples say "The Muslims are gone", the hudi singers are also gone. In frustration Iqbal wrote,

Khanda zan kufr hai ehsaas tujhe hai ke naheen
ApniTauhid ka kuch paas tujhe hai ke naheen?

(Infidelity is mocking the Muslims. Do you have some feeling or not? Do not you have any regard for your own Tawhid or not? The concept of monotheism in Islam is Tawhid – Author)

Aaj kiyun seene hmare sharar aabaad naheen?
Ham wohee sokhta saamaan hain tujhey yaad naheen?

(Why are not our breasts filled with love's sparks now? We are the same lovers, do you not remember now?)

In the next stanza, Iqbal is burning in envy by seeing that Allah gave all the blessings to the infidels; the Muslims got misery, poverty, infirmity and ugliness.

Ye shikayat naheen hain unke khazane maamoor
Naheen mahfil men jinhen baat bhi karne ka shaoor
Qahr to ye hai ke kafir ko milen hoor-o qasoor
Aur becharey musalman ko faqat waida-i hoor
Ab wo altaaf naheen ham pe inaayaat naheen
Baat ye kiya hai ke pheli si madaraat naheen.

(We do not complain that their treasures are full. Who are not in possession of even basic social graces? Outrageous that infidel are rewarded with Houries and palaces. And the poor Muslims are placated with only promise of Houries. We have been deprived of the former graces and favors. What is the matter; we are deprived of the former honors.)

Ultimately, in deep frustration, Iqbal calls Allah unfaithful.

Kabhi hamse kabhi ghairon se shanasai hai
Baat kahney ki naheen too bhi to harjai hai.

(You are changing friendship between us and others. It is difficult to say but you are also unfaithful.)

Iqbal's *Shikwa* is the voice of every Muslim either they express their feelings publicly or not. Anywhere in the world, Muslims are in a pitiable condition. They are at the bottom-most level in any society. Many of the destructive acts of Muslims are motivated by their envy, just in the same way Muhammad was envious of the Jews which caused the destruction of many of them. But Muhammad did not show his envy publicly. Narcissists act as if they want people to envy them, but in reality they envy others which make them crazy, and they "act out". Muhammad gave an impression that the Jews were envious of him. Ishaq wrote,

Jewish rabbis showed hostility to the Apostle in envy, hatred, and malice, because Allah had chosen His Apostle from the Arabs. The Jews considered the Prophet a liar and strove against Islam. (Ishaq: 239).

What treasure Muhammad had for which Jewish Rabbis should show hostility to him with envy, hatred, and malice? Ali, the son-in-law of Muhammad, used to carry water for brick making by the Jews. He received a date for each bucketful of water and he shared his tiny meals with Muhammad, who had nothing (Margoliouth, 2010, p. 235). According to Bukhari (4.53.357), people used to give (as alms) some of their date palms to Muhammad till he conquered Banu Quraiza and Banu Nadir. The Jews were much wealthier and cultured than the Arabs. Muhammad wanted to show that the Jews were envious to him, but in reality, it was Muhammad who was envious to them. To see the prosperity of the rich Jews was too painful for him. So he devalued the source of his frustration by attacking and massacring them. This is narcissistic pathological envy. The Narcissists are constantly envious of other people; they envy their successes, their property, their character, their education, their children, their ideas, the fact that they can feel, the religion they follow, their good mood, their past, their present, their spouses – practically everything.

Today Muslims are doing the same thing. They have strong grievance against Western civilized world. Their complaint is about the democratic process and all the freedom the infidels cherish and their education, prosperity and happiness. Muslims are envious because of the way the infidels love and pursue life, the way the infidels peruse wealth, the way the infidels relate to each other with respect, the way the infidels look at each other as equally under the law and in the eyes of God. Muslims are also envious because of the way we, the infidels respect our wives taking sincere care for all her needs, the way we give love to our children and educate them and teach them moral values.

Muslims are confused when they look at the Christians. The religion of the Christians teaches them to love others, to practice brotherhood and to show absolute forgiveness to the enemies. Muslims are also confused when they look at the religious teachings of the Hindus, Buddhists, and Jains. The main guiding principle of Hinduism is *Sarva Dharma Sambhava* (equal respect for all religions; Bhagavad-Gita: 7.21), and Buddhism and Jainism talk about virtues and strict nonviolence. All these moral values simply puzzle them.

After seeing all these when they look at Islam, they find that it is completely a different teaching. When they compare Muhammad with Jesus Christ or Buddha, they silently lower their face in shame. They understand that all other religions are spiritually superior to Islam and Islam is at the lowest position in the pantheon of all religions. It frustrates them and the narcissistic frustration transforms into envy and rage. Somehow they have to secure a sense of superiority in the face of infidel's ability by using contempt to minimize them. This is the source from where all the destructive thoughts of Muslims generate. As Hotchkiss (2003, p. 17) wrote, "*Envy knows intuitively that the best defense is a good offence, so he [the Narcissist] begins to look down at his colleague*".

Muslims' narcissistic envy, fueled by the desperate need to be superior, is something far darker. Both together make them more dangerous. When the twin towers of World Trade Center came down, Muslims cheered everywhere. The entire Muslim world does not have the technology to build a mighty structure like the twin towers but they can obviously bring them down within hours. Muhammad's hate for the infidels larks deep inside the heart of every Muslim. This dark force within Muslims cheers when the grand and glorious are toppled from their pedestals. They love to see the flaws and misfortune of the infidels because it means that they are not so much distant from the Muslims. Since the Muslims cannot pull themselves up to the level of the infidels, it is the infidels who should bring their standard down.

8.3.5: Entitlement

Narcissists hold unreasonable expectations of particularly favorable treatment and automatic compliance because they consider themselves uniquely special. Any failure to comply will be considered an attack on their superiority and the perpetrator is considered to be an "awkward" or "difficult" person. Defiance of their will is a narcissistic injury that can trigger narcissistic rage. They have a strong feeling that they have a right to be entertained. Vaknin (1999, p. 48) wrote, "*Most of them are insistent. They demand treatment on a preferential and privileged basis*". Hotchkiss (2003, p. 20) wrote, "*In social situations, you will talk about them of what they are interested in because they are more important, more knowledgeable, or more captivating than anyone else... In personal relationships, their sense of entitlement means that you must attend to their needs but they are under no obligation to listen to or understand you*".

Throughout his prophetic career, Muhammad ordered killing thousands of innocent people, raped women mercilessly, destroyed their houses, stole their property, sold women and children in the slave market and claimed one-fifth share of the booty in Allah's name because he felt a strong sense of entitlement of having special privileges. He followed no code of ethics because he was specially entitled to defy Allah's rules. His behavior even stunned his followers. He justified all his actions by bringing Allah's revelations whenever he liked. Those who doubted him were punished by death. When he took Safiyyah to bed for sex on the very same night he had killed her husband and many male relatives after attacking Khaybar, and when he took Rayhana to bed on the same night he had killed her male relatives of Quraiza tribe; he justified his action because he felt entitled for it. Narcissistic entitlement can be appropriately presented by two simple words, "**I deserve**".

Muslims come to Western countries for better living standard. But once they overcome their initial hardship, they become rude and demanding. There is something in Islam that makes it impossible for Muslims to fit into Western, liberal societies. They demand to be treated the way they would be in Muslim majority countries but then get offended when they are not. They do not value Western culture. While Jews, Hindus, Christians, Buddhists and followers of other religions have no problem to be loyal citizens of other countries at the same time peacefully maintaining their own religious beliefs, culture and identity; Muslim arrogance demands that once they have their heavy footprints in any place, and their demographics grow to a substantial level, the land automatically becomes theirs for all time. They aim to set up "special Muslim rights" contrary to the laws of their host country where they have immigrated almost like "refugees". They want tolerance from the Christians in Western nations but they are utterly intolerant of Christianity in almost all Muslim countries.

Why this double standard? There are two reasons. First, there is a natural conflict between being a devout Muslim and living in a civilized society. Secondly, Muslim's narcissistic sense of entitlement, i.e., the "I deserve" mentality. As example, let us discuss the "burqa" controversy.

The full-faced veil (the niqab, burqa or chador) of the Muslim women causes such deep reactions in the West not so much because of its political or religious symbolism but because it is extremely impolite. Just as it is considered rude to enter a Hindu or Buddhist temple wearing shorts or shoes, so, too, it is considered rude, in a Western country, to hide one's face in common places and work stations. To a Western child, or even an adult, a human clad from head to toe in black looks like a scary ghost. Muslims protect veiling their women saying that religious freedom is a right every one should enjoy. Indirectly, Muslims want to say that their right to practice their religion is more important than anyone else's right. In this case, why they do not allow carrying Bibles by Christians in Saudi Arabia? Christians also have their religious rights.

Western societies are multicultural. The culture of the host society necessarily needs to be respected by the guests. Those who feel it necessary to practice their religion to such an extent, have no absolute right whatsoever to make the rest of the world adapt to their practices. They are free to stay home and wear whatever they choose but they are not free to demand the "right" to jobs that put their religion at odds with the job requirements. In Britain, France and most of Europe; this type of demands of Muslims has gone way beyond "rude" or "impolite".

This attitude is in narcissistic psychopathology of the Muslims. Patients with this type of attitude always want more; they are never happy. Whatever good is done to the Muslims is never good enough for them. Muslims also generally show no gratitude or express any thanks even when someone goes out of his way for them. Like the most spoiled of royalty, they merely expect that they should be the center of all the attraction at all times. They demand "respect" for their religion, even as their religion dismisses and denigrates others. They immigrate to countries that are polite enough to let them in and allow them to practice their religion in peace, but they threaten violence unless those countries are willing to alter their own traditions and subvert their own values in adopting the Islamic perspective. These attitudes of Islamic narcissistic entitlement are all around us these days.

These Islamic Narcissists not only want to be tolerated by the society they live in and freedom to practice their religion even in the most multicultural sensitive nations but also they want the society or nation they live in to completely submit to their values and religious practices and to acknowledge their obvious superiority – or else. Giving into their sense of entitlement only leads to more and more demands for attention and acknowledgement of their narcissistic superiority. Muslims will never express gratitude or thanks, and always view others as mere extensions of their own damaged self. The only way to deal with such narcissistic behavior is to set clear limits and expectations, and then stick to them. Tolerating the unceasingly intolerable behavior and demands that modern Islam exhibits will only reinforce the underlying psychopathology and accentuate the bottomless narcissistic entitlement.

8.3.6: Exploitation

"After coming into contact with a religious man I always feel that I must wash my hands".

Nietzsche (1844 - 1900)

In Islam, exploitation is subtle and dangerous because it operates under the guise of religiosity. There are thousand and one ways people had been and are being exploited today in the name of Allah. The present day Muslim clerics employ Islam to promote sex-slavery, fear, insecurity and alienation. As example; Islam promotes pedophilia. Muhammad practiced pedophilia, hence, in many Muslim countries this heinous social practice is protected by law. In fact there is no minimum legal age for marriage for either men or women under Islamic law. As Ayatollah Khomeini said, "*A man can have sexual pleasure from a child as young as a baby. However, he should not penetrate, sodomising the child is OK*" (Payeur, 2006, p. 83). According to Saudi Arabia's most senior cleric, the grand mufti Sheikh Abdul-Aziz al Sheikh, "*Ten-year-old girls are ready for marriage, and those people who think that ten or twelve-year-old girls are too young to marry, are 'unfair' to them.*" (Mantos, 2009, p. 132). In early 2002, the researchers in refugee camps in Afghanistan and Pakistan found half the girls were married by the age thirteen. In an Afghan refugee camp more than two out of three second grade girls were either married or engaged and practically all the girls beyond second grade were already married. One ten year old girl was engaged to a man of sixty. Khomeini married a ten-year-old when he was twenty-eight (Spencer, 2006, pp. 171-2). We have no statistics, how many children had been sexually exploited "legally" following these decrees of Khomeini and Sheikh Abdul-Aziz.

In the eight year long Iran-Iraq war (1980-88), the Islamic clerics of Iran would tie China-made plastic keys to the neck of children ten years of age or younger and send them over Iraqi minefields. They would tell them that those were the keys to paradise and then, after martyrdom, they could open the door of paradise with the keys and step inside for eternal fun. There were about one million casualties in that war, but not a single cleric or member of their families was lost. It is amazing that no suicide bomber has ever asked a bloodthirsty cleric who enjoins others to blow themselves up along with innocent bystanders, "If it is such a great divine act rewarded by immediate admission to paradise, why are you not doing it yourself?"

For the clerics Islam is an excellent tool for domination. For them, Islam is not a religion but a means of livelihood. In the Islamic justice system, the functions of the jury, defense lawyer, prosecutor, and judge are all relegated into the hands of a mullah, called Qazi (the Islamic judge), whose verdict is authoritative. These Qazis have chosen a parasitic position; they target the lower class illiterate Muslims. They exaggerate the spiritual power of the Prophet and the wrath of Allah; this is their brainwashing tactics. It is a tragedy but the worst part of the tragedy is that most of these clerics are hypocrites and do not even believe in Muhammad or his teachings – some of them are plain atheists. They sell Islam in the market of religion; it is the best commodity to barter for anything they desire (Shaikh, 1995, p. 91). If Islam were to suddenly disappear more than a million of these Islamic parasites would instantly be out of work.

Islam as an "agenda" sells well in politics. Before election in Bangladesh, a powerful Mullah issued a fatwa that whoever votes for the Muslim politicians would go to heaven and whoever votes for the Hindu politicians will go to hell. *Islamic Oikyo Jote* (a hardcore Islamic fundamentalist political party of Bangladesh) declared that voting for them is equivalent to the Hajj pilgrimage (Roy, 2007, pp. 358-9). The deceptions and exploitations in the name of Allah have no end. The average Muslim does not know what is written in the Islamic scriptures. He simply assumes that since Muhammad was the "Holy Prophet", his teachings must be holy which as a Muslim he should value. The Muslim politicians and theologians exploit his ignorance and mobilize him for street riots by ascribing to enemies of Islam what is in fact contained in their own scriptures. As Voltaire (cited Dawkins, 2006, p. 306) wrote, "*Those who can make you believe absurdities can make you commit atrocities*". Those Muslims, who know the facts, turn a blind eye to this deception and misguidance of the common Muslims. This is religio-political exploitation. When religion is mixed with politics, it has tremendous brainwashing capacity. Muhammad knew it, so does the Islamic clerics and politicians.

8.3.7: Bad Boundaries

Muhammad never valued the privacy or individuality of anyone. He spied everywhere who posed as his detractors. He even encouraged his believers to spy on each other (Sina, 2008, p. 102), and claimed (Bukhari: 1.11.686-7; Muslim: 4.872) that he could see behind his back. But why he needed to see behind his back? The reason is simple. He wanted to keep a vigil eye on his followers.

Muhammad did not trust his wives. He was sexually weak. Apart from sucking Aisha's tongue and fondling other wives, he could not perform any better. Having a large collection of wives with low sexual capacity is dangerous. So he had to keep an eye on his wives' activities. Allah did the spying job for him.

When the Prophet confided a fact unto one of his wives and when she afterward divulged it and Allah apprised him thereof, he made known (to her) part thereof and passed over part. And when he told it her she said: Who hath told thee? He said: The Knower, the Aware hath told me. (Q: 66.3)

The act of secretly listening to the private conversation of others without their consent is invasion of privacy. It is not only unethical but also the biggest insult to God saying that He invades other's privacy. A real God definitely has something better to do than eavesdropping married women. Since Allah and Muhammad thinks alike, Allah's sense of bad boundary reflects Muhammad's own bad sense. But, Muhammad was too sensitized and erected rigid boundaries to protect him and demonstrated paranoid rigidity and vigilance.

O ye wives of the Prophet! Whosoever of you committed manifest lewdness, the punishment for her will be doubled, and that is easy for Allah. (Q: 33.30).

O Ye who believe! Enter not the dwellings of the Prophet for a meal without waiting for the proper time, unless permission be granted you. But if ye are invited, enter, and, when your meal is ended, then disperse. Linger not for conversation. Lo! that would cause annoyance to the Prophet, and he would be shy of (asking) you (to go); but Allah is not shy of the truth. And when ye ask of them (Muhammad's wives) anything, ask it of them from behind a curtain. That is purer for your hearts and for their hearts. And it is not for you to cause annoyance to the messenger of Allah, nor that ye should ever marry his wives after him. Lo! that in Allah's sight would be an enormity. (Q: 33.53)

Narrated Sahl bin Sa'd As-Sa'idi: A man peeped through a hole in the door of Allah's Apostle's house, and at that time, Allah's Apostle had a Midri (an iron comb) with which he was rubbing his head. So when Allah's Apostle saw him, he said (to him), "If I had been sure that you were looking at me (through the door), I would have poked your eye with this (iron bar). (Bukhari: 9.38.2)

Muhammad was unaware that other people might have similar types of well-defined boundaries which were as valuable as his own and needed to be respected. He had adulterous desires for a married woman, Zaynab, the wife of his adopted son Zayd. When Zayd divorced her, Muhammad married his son's divorcee. This shameful intrusion of a married woman's privacy, who was also happened to be his daughter-in-law, is a clear proof that Muhammad did not learn to recognize that other people had boundaries which were not to be invaded.

While criticizing and ridiculing the pagan Meccans for the polytheistic belief system, Muhammad never thought that his faith could similarly be criticized and ridiculed. He wanted respect from others but was not ready to give respect to them in return. Allah forbad all criticism of Islam by Qur'anic verses 5.101-2, but never prevented the Prophet from criticizing other faiths. It was because Muhammad was unsure of similar type of religious right of other people. The lack of experience with healthy boundaries made him confused and unsure when an "invasion of privacy" was occurring. In Muhammad's fantasy world there are separate rooms, but there is no door; then how can he knock the door before entering? We can see a child-like tendency in Muhammad's attitude. Like a two-year-old child, he threw temper tantrums believing that he was at liberty to get his own way. He believed that having power gave him the right to treat others the way he liked. In his behavior, where were those personal boundaries, the guidelines, rules and limits?

When a Narcissist is resisted by others, he develops an anxious, apprehensive attitude towards them and violates their rights in some way. In fact, sometimes he is so confused that he is unsure if truly an invasion is taking place. He reads others personal diaries, mails and personal journals; ignore closed bathroom and bedroom doors; purses and wallets are rifled through; expensive and private possessions are "borrowed" without asking; conversations are eavesdropped; extremely personal questions are asked and unsolicited opinions are offered (Hotchkiss, 2003, p. 30). But once he is confronted with these violations, he is annoyed and mystified and the common reply is; "You are misunderstanding me" or, "That's not how you feel", or even, "This is who you are".

Muslims suffer from an unhealthy and confused sense of personal boundary. In Islam, your privacy is my business. Sina (2008, p. 102) wrote, *"Muslims are vigilant toward each other's words and actions; each Muslim spies on others to see whether the laws of Islam are properly observed. An ambience of terror is created in all Islamic countries, where hardly anyone dares raise the slightest question of the tenets of Islam. Your own father, son or brother could report your infidelity, which, of course, would mean certain death to you"*. A tree is known by its fruit. The mistrusts and suspicions which separate father from daughter, brother from sister and mother from her son originates from the following Qur'anic verse.

O you who believe! Take not for protectors your fathers and your brothers if they love infidelity above Faith: if any of you do so, they do wrong. (Q. 9:23)

Muslims are over-absorbed into the web of religious society and maintain Islam by a process called, "collective surveillance". Here the social life is completely focused on the ethics of religious group, the individual ego is overwhelmed by the religious ego, and own individual expression is not permitted. There is no personal boundary and the individual ego does not develop in a healthy way. Hence the individual has very little independence from group life. This social claim upon their allegiance is maintained through collective supervision and strict surveillance that extend throughout this society, leading to similarity in beliefs and social observance. This is why all the Muslims have similar mindset. The indoctrination of a Muslim mind starts from childhood.

Though Muslims have developed a rigid boundary for themselves, they are puzzled when they violate the personal boundaries of others (non-Muslims). When few cartoons of Muhammad are published, or, Rushdie writes a book, or Pope criticizes Muhammad; Muslims are offended and fatwas are issued. But when the Taliban destroyed the Bamiyan Buddha statues in Afghanistan, or churches are regularly burnt down and Christians are raped / killed in Indonesia and Pakistan, or thousands of Hindu temples are destroyed in Bangladesh, or Jews are regularly named as "descendents of monkeys and pigs" in government controlled media of Saudi Arabia or other Islam nations; we cannot see any fatwa against them. What kind of twisted, distorted "morality" is this?

Muslims do not understand that the non-Muslims are also unique individuals who have private thoughts, personal feelings and a body that belongs only to them. They demand that the rest of the world treats their violent, bloodthirsty Prophet, with "respect". Do they show their respect to Christ, Adi Shankara, Buddha, Guru Nanak or Mahavira Jain? Muhammad is the Prophet of all Muslims worldwide, and Muslims may respect him, but we the infidels do not revere him as a Prophet, rather we identify him as a criminal of worst kind. Today, Muhammad is the most hated historical personality. If Muslims want to revere this man, they are free to do so, but their arrogant assertion that the whole world must hold him in high esteem is absolutely ridiculous. This is obviously a mental flaw. Muslim's one track thinking goes this way – "How the non-Muslims are treating me"; but it never occurs in their mind – "How I am treating the non-Muslims". They manage to blame everyone else for their problems. Unless the Muslims come out from their distorted logic, they can never have a healthy relationship with the non-Muslims.

8.4: The Collective Mental Sickness of Muslim "Ummah"

"Truth is a fact and not a judgment."

Carl Jung

According to Hotchkiss (2003, p. 30), when most of the seven deadly sins are present in an individual, that person is diagnosed with a NPD. In Muslim mindset, all the seven deadly sins are prominently present. It means the whole Muslim Ummah is suffering from mass narcissism – a collective mental sickness. This is the reason for the madness of the Muslims everywhere.

Muslims live in a truly dysfunctional and sick society composed of people with sick beliefs. They sincerely believe that only Islam is the true religion and rest all religions are false, and those with no religion whatsoever or atheists are even worse. But the fact says almost all the terrorists come from this supposed to be true religion. All the major conflicts in the world are between Muslims and rest of the infidels. In addition, there is inter-sect violence also. If we take a statistical average, Muslims, as a group, are thirty-six times more likely to resort to violence for conflict resolution than the rest of humanity (Sina, 2008, p. 5). Muslim character is same everywhere; in Iraq, Sudan, Somalia, Afghanistan, Kashmir, Algeria, Iran, Bangladesh, Pakistan, Indonesia, Nigeria, Palestine, Morocco, Egypt, Saudi Arabia, – practically every corner of the world where Muslims have a majority. As Sina (2008, p. 3) raised his doubt, "*Why? What makes sane people commit such evil? Why are Muslims, as a lot, so angry with others, so at war with the world that they are often quick to resort to violence? Millions of Muslims riot, protest, and kill completely innocent people anytime, anywhere, when someone says something about Muhammad. This kind of behavior is not rational. Yet the perpetrators are completely sane people. How can we explain this paradox?*"

The answer is that Muslims are cursed people – Muhammad's narcissism works on them like an evil curse. The Islamization of the Muslim mind starts from the birth and continues throughout his/her life. It is the most extensive brainwashing process a human can ever be subjected to. After birth, an adult holds the newborn and recites the azan (the call for prayers) directly into ears of the baby. This way, the child hears the blessed names of Allah and Muhammad before he hears anything else. As the child grows up, he reads and hears more about Qur'an. He sees people performing prayers and walls are decorated with posters of Arabic calligraphy of some Qur'anic verses. He also hears the azan repeated five times a day in every mosque in the area, and it becomes the most frequently heard sound by him. In the process of growing, his ears soon gets used to hearing the endless recitations of the Qur'an that go on almost continuously.

If the kid goes to Madrassah, further indoctrination continues. Various thinking errors, e.g., Allah's wrath, Allah's hate, Muslims are best of people (Q: 3.110) and unbelievers are vilest of created beings (Q: 98.6), paradise and hellfire, etc, are systematically programmed in him. This is coupled with illogical thoughts and twisted logic to make the child to believe that Muhammad is the best man Allah ever created, or will ever create to the end of time, and Allah (like the Big Brother) is watching every Muslim and he should behave strictly according to Allah's will.

The fear factor starts working and soon the innocent mind of the child gets the message that there is something very special about the Qur'an, which he is destined to read hundreds of times without ever understanding it, and except Muhammad, no one should be taken as guidance. For this, if necessary, the Madrassah teacher even punishes him both mentally and physically. Muhammad recommended (Sunnan Abu Dawud: 2.495) thrashing the child for not performing prayer.

Soon the child gives up and forcefully convinces himself and becomes deluded. His mind and senses are crippled and Muhammad's mental illness is implanted in his mind. When the child grows up and becomes an adult, he continues the same brainwashing process to his children and grandchildren. When this cycle continues for few generations, the whole society becomes mentally sick.

When the child inherits Muhammad's narcissism, he fails in his "reality test" – the ability to distinguish the actual from the imagined. Neither he can confront the truth nor can he admit it even to himself. His sick mind fervently believes in

Muhammad's infallibility, brilliance, heroism, and perfection. Slowly, Muhammad becomes his drug, his addiction. Without Muhammad, it is a world of black and white. With Muhammad it is a colorful show complete with drama, thrills, fun and full of excitement. Now he is fully within the grip of Islam. He is in a mental prison. He simply cannot dare to cross the narrow limits specified by Qur'an and ahadith. Now he can see things only through the eyes of Muhammad. This will continue for throughout his life. Once belief systems are rigidly instilled – they are virtually impossible to modify belatedly. Let us read four self-explanatory quotes,

However pure Gandhi's character may be, he must appear to me from the point of view of religion inferior to any Musalman, even though he is without character. Yes according to my religion and creed, I hold an adulterous and a fallen Musalman to be better than Mr. Gandhi. (Muhammad Ali, the Khilafat leader and a close associate of Mahatma Gandhi; cited Ralhan, 1998, p. 221).

Our Prophet gave to humanity a Charter of Human Rights fourteen centuries ago. (Muhammad Anwar in World Muslim Conference, 2004).

One of the most noticeable things about the Prophet Muhammad as described by the Koran is that he spoke of mercy for humankind. (Mohammad Ahmadullah Siddiqi, the founder of "Students Islamic Movement of India" after 2006 Mumbai bombing; cited Spencer, 2006, p. 183)

Don't forget that killing [unbelievers] is also a form of mercy. (Khomeini; cited Bjorgo, 2005, p. 58)

All the above four speakers are looking at the outside world through the eyes of Muhammad. They simply do not realize how illogical their remarks are because they have lost their capacity to distinguish between reality and delusion. Like drug-addiction, they are addicted to Muhammad; they are co-dependent on Muhammad. While talking about the codependent-Narcissist relationship, Vaknin (cited Sina, 2008, p. 76) wrote, *"The inverted Narcissist can only truly FEEL anything when he is in relationship with another Narcissist. The inverted Narcissist is conditioned and programmed from the very beginning to be the perfect companion to the Narcissist – to feed their Ego, to be purely their extension, to seek only praise and adulation if it brings greater praise and adulation to the Narcissist."*

The inverted Narcissist makes excuses for his dependency on the Narcissist and fills in for him as necessary. Rappoport (2009) wrote, *"The Narcissist is on stage, performing, and needing attention, appreciation, support, praise, reassurance, and encouragement, and the co-Narcissist's [inverted Narcissist] role is to provide these things ... the co-Narcissist serves as the audience".*

It explains perfectly why Muslims are addicted to Muhammad. They are all inverted Narcissists; they are so much dependent on Muhammad that they are ready to give any excuse to remain with him. Muslims feel insecure because they have not been valued for themselves, and have been valued by a malignant Narcissist only to the extent that they meet their Prophet's needs. They develop their self concepts based on their Prophet's treatment of them and therefore often have highly inaccurate ideas about who they are. Vaknin (2003) wrote,

To "qualify" as an inverted Narcissist, you must CRAVE to be in a relationship with a Narcissist, regardless of any abuse inflicted on you by him/her. You must ACTIVELY seek relationships with Narcissists and ONLY with Narcissists, no matter what your (bitter and traumatic) past experience has been. You must feel EMPTY and UNHAPPY in relationships with ANY OTHER kind of person. Only then, and if you satisfy the other diagnostic criteria of a Dependent Personality Disorder, can you be safely labeled an "inverted Narcissist"... This is a Narcissist who, in many respects, is the mirror image of the "classical" Narcissist."

This is why a Muslim can neither confront the truth about Muhammad nor admit it to even himself. He needs Muhammad for his emotional gratification and the performance of his own false self or his daily function. Muslims are not only needy and submissive, but fear abandonment, cling and display immature behaviors in their effort to maintain the "relationship" with their Prophet. Islam had made the Muslims' lives miserable, but no matter what abuse is inflicted upon them, they prefer to remain in the good-book of Muhammad. Without Muhammad they feel empty and unhappy. This is Stockholm syndrome – the hostages express empathy and have positive feelings towards the captors. It is really that painful to practice Islam. Vaknin continued,

These Narcissists [inverted Narcissists] are self-effacing, sensitive, emotionally fragile, sometimes socially phobic. They derive all their self-esteem and sense of self-worth from the outside, are pathologically envious (a transformation of aggression), are likely to intermittently engage in aggressive/violent behaviors.

The Inverted Narcissist is liable to react with rage whenever threatened, or when envious of other people's achievements, their ability to feel wholeness, happiness, rewards and successes, when his sense of self-worthlessness is diminished by a behavior, a comment, an event, when his lack of self-worth and voided self-esteem is threatened. Thus, this type of Narcissist might surprisingly react violently or wrathfully to good things.

Can we agree that the general Muslim attitude is well-reflected in the above quotes of Vaknin? What other proof is required to show that Muslims are suffering from a mass personality disorder, and their personality had been occupied by Muhammad? The final outcome of this is that the Muslims have not been able to develop healthy means of self-expression and self-directedness. They are fully immersed in their own affairs with the total exclusion of others. They are unable to empathize with other's experience and insist that their opinions and values are "right", and they have a tendency to be easily offended and take things personally. Vaknin has some advice for the inverted Narcissists, which are equally applicable to the Muslims, *"Finally, and most important of all for the Inverted Narcissist: get to know yourself. What are you getting from the relationship? Are you actually a masochist? Why is this relationship attractive and interesting? Define for yourself what good and beneficial things you believe you are receiving in this relationship. Define the things that you find harmful to you. Develop strategies to minimize the harm to yourself"*.

["Masochism" means; the deriving of sexual gratification, or the tendency to derive sexual gratification, from being physically or emotionally abused, the deriving of pleasure, or the tendency to derive pleasure, from being humiliated or mistreated, by another or, a willingness or tendency to subject oneself to unpleasant or trying experiences – Author]

When there is a lack of logical thinking, it is difficult to distinguish between falsehood and truth. Since truth cannot be changed, Muslims have to change their mindset to remain in the "logic-tight" compartment of Islam. Thus lying becomes a second nature, and a false self soon takes over. Muslims make themselves what they want to be and not what they actually are. The typical Muslim mindset is, *"I do not seek to understand in order to believe. I believe in order to understand. We should not aim to understand what we have believed after we are confirmed of our Islamic faith."* (Durant, 1950, p. 932, quote modified by present Author). With this mindset, a Muslim cannot think anything beyond Allah, Qur'an and Muhammad. He lives in a constant dream-like state. Smith (1981, p. 291) commented,

Muslims do not read the Qur'an to understand whether it is divine; rather, they believe it to be divine, and then they read it. This makes a great deal of difference, and I urge upon Christian and secular students of the Qur'an that if they wish to understand it as a religious document, they must approach it in this spirit. If an outsider picks up the book and goes through it even asking himself, 'What is there here that has led Muslims to suppose this from God?' he will miss the reverberating impact. If, on the other hand, he picks up the book and asks himself, what would these sentences convey to me if I believe them to be God's word? Then he can much more effectively understand what has been happening these many centuries in the Muslim world.

Hasan Al-Banna, founder of Muslim Brotherhood, wrote in *The Message of the Teachings* (cited Husain, 2007, p. 52),

Allah is our goal.
The Prophet Muhammad is our leader.
The Qur'an is our constitution.
Jihad is our way.
And death in the way of Allah is our promised end.

In this situation, even if he spends his entire life studying Qur'an, ahadith and Muhammad's biography, he will never detect a single error in the Qur'an though he will easily find similar type of errors in other scriptures. He will never notice that Muhammad was a criminal, a liar, a pedophile, a shameless womanizer, a mass-murderer and a ruthless tyrant, though minor character flaws of some Catholic priests and their sex-scandals will never go unnoticed.

Even if the contradictions of the Qur'an, or Muhammad's flawed character is pointed out, his sick mind will try to camouflage them. All the contradictions and errors will appear as clear proofs of its divinity. He will deceive himself into believing that non-Muslims either know that Islam is the truth and reject it out of pure unreasonableness or else are simply ignorant of it (Schuon, 1980, p. 56). This is how Muslim minds are groomed to become lifelong zombies that they cannot apply minimum logic and reason to discover the true nature of Islam. Their definitions of good and bad, right and wrong, and logical and illogical are reversed.

In extreme cases, Islam sucks away the brain of the Muslims. Two best examples are the well-known "flat earth" and "earth is motionless and sun revolves around the earth" fatwas from Ibn Baz, a noted Islamic scholar from Arabia. Also, another one is "Muslim woman to breast-feed her male colleague" fatwa by Izzat Attya from Al-Azhar. In 1993, Ibn Baaz declared *"The earth is flat. Whoever claims it is round is an atheist deserving of punishment."* (Reyes, 2010, p. 564). Ibn Baz disbelieved the news of the landing on the moon, and even suspected conspiracies behind the propagation of such falsehoods (AbuKhalil, 2002, p. 64). Previously, in 1966, this cleric wrote another quirky fatwa, *"Sun goes around the earth and earth is motionless".* (Weston, 2008, p. 329). According to Izzat Attya (Olson, 2009, p. 97), it is legitimate for a working Muslim woman to breast-feed her male colleague to avoid the sin of *khulwa* (staying with a stranger in one room). We have seen the crippled thought patterns of Muslims in several other instances as well.

Muslim Ummah is such a sick society where parents celebrate publicly if their child had killed himself in a suicide mission along with many innocents. Often the death celebration is like a wedding ceremony where many friends and neighbors flock to the home. The parents of the deceased child distribute sweets with broad smile on their faces. The guests congratulate the joyful parents on the death of their child. Often the mother would ululate in joy over the death of her child (Hassan, 2001, p. 8; Farmer, 2007, p. 56). Parents and siblings often speak of their pride and honored by the society. As example, Umm Nidal, a Muslim mother whose only claim to fame was that she proudly sent three of her sons to die for Allah in terrorist attacks against Israeli targets. Umm is reported to have said (Spencer, 2005, p. 102), *"Because I love my son, I encouraged him to die a martyr's death for the sake of Allah ... jihad is a religious obligation incumbent upon us, and we must carry it out."* And elsewhere, *"I prayed from the depths of my heart that Allah would cause the success of his operation... I encouraged all my sons to die a martyr's death, and I wish this even for myself".* When the operation was over, the media broadcast the news and Umm Nidal was informed of her son's death, she began to cry. Tears of joy rolled down from her eyes on her son's death (MEMRI, 2002). In non-Muslim society, death celebration of own children is even reprehensible to think, because our society consists of highly protective child-centered households.

In Islam we see a totally different kind of guardianship that upsets us. A TV clip repeatedly calls on children, *"Drop your toys, pick up rocks."* In a children's club, a child singer sings *"When I wonder into Jerusalem, I will become a suicide bomber".* In one Islamic school, the words to a children's song go (Pipes, 2004, p. 86), *"How pleasant is the smell of martyrs, how pleasant is the smell of land, the land enriched by the blood, the blood pouring out of a fresh body".*

To find the root cause of Muslim's death worshiping we must look at Hurd's and Durkheim's sociological theory. Hurd (1986, p. 202) agreed that there is a wide variety of ways of treating children in a society, ranging from neglect and selective infanticide in some societies, to the highly protective, child-centered households of modern Western societies. Though there is a physical dependence between a mother and her offspring, according to Hurd, maternal behavior is largely learnt from the customs, values and beliefs of the society. As this differs, the relations between mother and child also changes. It means; the customs, beliefs and ethical values of the Muslim society have a deep impact on how they treat their children.

Now let us look at Durkheim's theory of "social integration" for further analysis of the matter. Social integration is the nature of social links which attach individuals to social groups outside themselves. As social animals, we cannot survive without social integration. According to Durkheim (1897, p. 209), the three groups that have the qualities of social integration are the family group, the religious group, and the political or national group. Out of these three groups, family is the basic unit of society and the most important primary group to humankind (Jayaram & Saberwal, 1996, p. 29). It is also the strongest one amongst all. The second is religious group. Durkheim's take on religion and its origins was social, rather than divine. He explained religion as a structure that served the needs of society and thus the needs of people (cited Slutzky, 2006, p. 21). According to Durkheim, religious practices reinforce societal values. Religion serves as parts of an integrated whole to support each other, thereby strengthening the structure of society.

Though the word "family" has its origin in a Latin word which could be roughly equated a domestic group, for sociological purposes, family and domestic groups are sharply distinguished. A domestic group may be made of individuals between whom no kinship ties exist; but in a family, the members are either related by biological or legal kinship, or lawful sexual intercourse (Seals, 1968, p. 302). In a family, each member is expected to play a certain role which might change according to age. Here each member has some expectations from other members and from the family as a whole. Also the family itself has some expectations from each member. When everyone is playing their roles and all these expectations are fulfilled to a reasonable extent, the members are happy and this is what we call a happy family which is basic minimum requirement for a healthy society. Such a society is generally free from any religious fanaticism.

Now, let us look at Muslim societies. Throughout the history of Islam, Muslim families are often unhealthy and unhappy due to various reasons. Lack of education, poor work ethics, polygamy, concubinage, lack of finance, domestic violence, large families, slavery of women folks, child marriage, etc, make the families backward, unproductive and unhealthy. Since a family is the basic unit of society, conflict within the family has far reaching consequences for the wider social fabric.

A Muslim family is dominated by the male authority as prescribed and supported by Sharia law. It really develops a device where a family is under the private ownership of property of a male member. Even a modern individual Muslim family is founded on the open or concealed domestic slavery of the wife. An educated Muslim wife is nothing but a "darling little slave" and the married status permits the man to benefit from the fruits of woman's work. Often coercion and domestic violence (psychological and physical) remain a method of resolving husband-wife differences (Jayaram & Saberwal, 1996, p. 101). Domestic violence is always directed towards women, sadly, not only by the husband (as prescribed in Qur'an 4.34) but by the son also. As example, in the poor Bangladeshi families, the wife is not allowed to eat unless her husband and son had full stomach food. If there is no food left, the wife does not eat. If there is not enough food, the woman is beaten up by her husband and even by her son (Allen & Thomas, 2000, p. 69). A report (Goodwin, 1994, p. 44) regarding the status of women in Pakistan concluded, *"The average women is born into near slavery, leads a life of drudgery, and dies invariably in oblivion."* The wife and mother definitely deserve a better respect.

Since the family group is at complete chaos, Muslims tend to be over-absorbed into the web of religious society. By this way they come within the strong grip of Islam. The Sharia law is the only guidance for them from cradle to grave. Through this unhealthy Sharia law Muhammad commands them from his grave in Allah's name. It is like a mental slavery; the life of a Muslim is same as that of a prisoner. Islam had made Muslims' lives so wretched that sometimes death becomes a blessed escape from Allah's prison.

Under Sharia law, the individual Muslim ego is overwhelmed by the religious ego; own individual expression is not permitted. Muslims live in such a close proximity that their social customs and beliefs tend to be unified. When there is an over indulgence in religious beliefs (of any religion), the individual either becomes a saint or a Satan. Since Muhammad was a criminal and terrorist; incidents related to crime and terrorism are more common in Islamic society than any other society.

Pilon (cited Copi & Cohen, 1994, p. v) concluded, "*Civilized life depends upon the success of reason in social intercourse, the prevalence of logic over violence in interpersonal conflict*". We cannot see much success of reason in Muslim societies. Had we seen any success of reason in Muhammad and his early companions? They had resorted to violence even for a small conflict resolution. A Narcissist must appear flawless and always correct. To appear to have a fault would be unacceptable to his self-image. At any cost he cannot exhibit any weakness. For Muhammad any healthy criticism was highly upsetting.

For Muslims, everything is about this "grandiose self-image". Muslim Ummah is a shame-based society whereas Western societies are guilt-based. In a guilt-based society children are taught to act rightly but in shame-based society children are taught to act honorably, and if they do not, feelings of shame are the proper response. There is no guilt in Muslims but a huge amount of shame. Shame and honor are positions in society, just as being right (and justified) is a position in the Western culture. Muslims live in a worldview where the predominant paradigm is shame versus honor. If the young people of Muslim society act shamefully, then the family or tribe will react against them. Shameful deeds are either covered up, and if they cannot be covered up, they are revenged.

In shame-based cultures it is only self-image that matters. Hence, sometimes it becomes necessary to misrepresent the "reality" in order to protect the self-image. In Islamic society, a girl who does not want to enter into an arranged marriage, or wants divorce from an abusive husband, or merely talks to a person who is not her relative, etc, is sometimes killed in the name of removing the imputed stain on the family. These allegations do not need to have any legal basis; rather they are based on rumors and gossips. Similarly, a rape victim brings "shame" to the family. The only way to remove this shame is to kill her. Islamic logic is very simple; the honor is restored only when there is absence of shame. Hence it is the rape victim who is to be blamed and punished, not the rapist.

But these are the rules of the jungle. There is no law in the civilized society which prohibits a woman to enter into a marriage of her own choice, or to get a divorce from an abusive husband. It is not illegal for a woman if she communicates with a man who is not her relative. Most importantly, there is no law in a civilized society which criminalizes and gives death sentence to a rape victim. But all these obligations are imposed by the Muslim society and are being rigidly followed by them. What is moral according to the law of the civilization is made punishable in

Islam by the name of Allah. The God of Islam does not recognize that every individual has an integral right to life, a life of worthy living which is something more than a life of mere animal existence. In these days of scientific enlightenment, the integrity and status of an individual cannot be diminished.

It would be wrong to think that all shame-based societies behave in this way. Japan and Thailand have shame-based culture, but their societies do not support honor-killing or women oppression. How do we explain this?

Muslims suffer from huge abnormal shame which is so intolerable that they have to bypass it at any cost. If necessary, they will twist the facts to preserve their narcissistic self-image. The Muslim society has developed a protective barrier of emotionless narcissistic denial. This sick society has convinced the members that it is the rape victim who is to be blamed rather than the rapist. From behind this narcissistic protective barrier, brothers can kill sisters, cousins can kill cousins, fathers can kill daughters, mother can kill sons, and even a son can kill his mother without any remorse. So, instead of saying honor-killing is a sick practice; we rather say the whole society is sick. This will address the problem better.

In Muslim countries women have to hide behind closed doors and black veils. The shame-based society leaves them no option. In Islam, women have no mind, only the "meat" of her body is "Halal" for man to enjoy. As Nasrin (2007, p. 62) lamented, "*My mother used 'purdah'. She wore a 'burqa' [the black veil] with a net cover in front of the face. It reminded me of the meat-safes in my grandmother's house. One had a net door made of cloth, the other of metal. But the objective was same – keeping the meat safe*". Burqa system is completely a religious matter. In no other shame-based society black veils are used, and the guilt-based societies cannot even think of it. Darkness around covering the head means covering her brain. The idea of burqa originated from Muhammad's sick mind. Qur'an (33.59) prescribes veils for women.

In Urdu, women are called "aurat", which came from the Arabic word "awrah", which refers to the genitals of a woman's body. It means, the entire body of a Muslim woman is a huge sexual organ (Warraq, 1995, p. 316). "Nikah" (Muslim marriage) is an Arabic word whose literal meaning is penetration (Kaleeby, 2002). It can be pronounced as "Nokh", which again means the "awrah" – the female genital, i.e., the entire body of a Muslim woman. When the word "Nikah" is used to mean marriage, the actual meaning is not marriage but literally sexual penetration. In sum; according to Islam women are "sex objects". Muslim's attitude towards sex is almost same as that of an animal. Marriage is never a sacrament with him; it is openly a commercial transaction. It never occurs to him to be ashamed that he treats women as prostitutes or animals; he would rather be ashamed of the opposite. Muhammad was guilty of every sex crime known to man, so are the Muslims.

In Islam, there is nothing called marital rape. The wife is a legal sex-slave (often next to three other equally helpless wives). In prostitution, a customer does not need to bother about the sexual gratification of the prostitute. Similarly, the sexual desires and preferences of the women are not recognized in Islam. Marital rape incidents are too high in Bangladesh, as Azad (1995, pp. 240, 248) lamented,

For a woman, the first night after marriage is the night of forcible sex. In Bangladesh, the number of marital rape incidents is several times higher than any other rapes.

Here [Bangladesh], there are single rapes and multiple rapes. Here; father rapes daughter, son-in-law rapes mother-in-law ... top executive rapes sweeper of his office, teacher rapes girl student, Imam rapes the kindergarten girl, brother-in-law rapes the sister-in-law, father-in-law rapes daughter-in-law...
[Original in Bengali, translated by the present Author].

Muslims show a disturbing lack of conscience while treating women. The cruel activities against women allow the Muslim to express his narcissism through the "conquered" women and to transform them into instruments at the service of his narcissism. In Muslim society, there cannot be a meaningful family life. The whole society hates women virulently, passionately and uncompromisingly. It is original and inherent. Also, polygamy is widely practiced. Mirza Aziz (Eraly, 1997, p. 666) had a brilliant explanation as to why a man needed four wives, "*A man must marry one woman of Hindustan to rear up children, one wife from Khurasan to do the household work, one woman from Iran to keep company and talk*". And the fourth? "*Why? One woman from Transoxiana to whip the other three and keep peace*".

The laxity in the number of wives and concubines, freedom of men to marry and remarry, marriage within close relatives, etc, often make Muslim families to proliferate confusingly. So, when little Munawwar Ali goes to Madrassah for Islamic education, his best identity is; he is one of the twenty children by one of the thirteen wives of Sheikh Abdullah Ali! Large family is one of the reasons for which bulk of the Muslims are poor.

In Islam, even the breast-milk of a woman does not belong to her and the husband has the lawful right on it. If the adult husband drinks the milk of his wife under Sharia law, the milk is treated as a food and not as foster milk. According to Malik's Muwatta (30.1.11), "*Suckling ... after the first two years, little or much, it does not make anything haram. It is like food*". Another Hadith (Malik's Muwatta: 30.2.14) says that a Muslim man can drink his wife's milk regularly and still can remain her sex-partner. Any sane person will die in shame, but for Muslims it makes no difference. A society which cannot value women is a sick society. Some progressive Muslims try to fool the civilized world saying that "In Islam, women are treated like queens", but nothing could be further from the truth. Muslims will never recognize that a woman is also a human being; she has her right to life, right to make her own choice.

The whole Muslim society is overly handicapped by superstition which generates fear and subdues logical thinking. Fear is a great motivating force in Islam. Every Muslim lives in a constant fear of Allah's wrath, something like a supernatural alien world and the Big Brother Allah is always watching them. In this supernatural world jinns and angels roam freely and devils constantly in look out for victims. In this situation, the clerics thrive in power. Muslims are anxious not to commit any sin in their journey to a promised paradise and the clerics grab these opportunities. After Rushdie incident, issuing fatwa became a very popular topic amongst these clerics. In the kangaroo court of Islam, many funny fatwas are issued. Some examples (Bhaumik, 2005, pp. 18-22) are as below,

Q. What is the punishment for a man who tells his wife that having sex with her is like having sex with his mother?
A. There is no punishment for what a man says in private to his wife.

Q. If while breaking wind it does not smell or sound, does it still break the wazu (cleaning before prayers)?
A. If you are sure you broke wind and you are not under a false illusion and are not physically challenged, then you should do the wazu again.

Q. If a chicken defecates in my well, has it become impure? How do I purify my well?
A. Throw out 110 buckets of water from your well. Then it will be purified and the water can be used for wazu.

Q. Will Allah accept my prayers if I pass wind while doing my namaz? Should I do the namaz again?
A. Only if you have kept the wind within you and restrained from releasing it are your prayers valid. If not, you should say your prayers again.

This is how the Islamic clerics promote superstition for their own benefit. A Muslim can live his whole life without meeting an alternative view because, literally, Qur'an had been pounded in his brain from birth. In 1979, when Mullahs and ayatollahs drove out Shah and established Islamic Republic of Iran, Ayatollah Khomeini dusted down a number of Qur'anic verses, in particular the verses concerning sexual behavior of the Shiaa Muslims. On their basis, he compiled a set of rules and named it blue book. Parts of the blue book were published by an Italian magazine under the playful title *The Ten Khomeindments*. Some gems and jewels of this book (cited Fallaci, 2006, pp. 211-3) are described below.

1. Marriage with one's own sister, one's own mother or one's own mother-in-law is a sin.
2. If a woman has carnal relations with her future husband, after marrying her the husband has right to demand the annulment of the marriage.
3. A man who has had sexual relations with his own aunt cannot marry her daughter, i.e., his cousin.
4. If a father has three daughters and wants to give one of them in marriage, at the wedding ceremony he must specify which daughter he is giving.
5. If a man marries a minor who has reached the age of nine and if during the defloration he immediately breaks the hymen he cannot enjoy her any longer.
6. If a widowed or repudiated wife has not reached the age of nine, she may remarry soon after the widowhood or the repudiation without waiting for prescribed four months and ten days.
7. If a wife does not obey her husband and is not always available for his pleasure, if under some pretext she does not give him joy, the husband must not give her food or clothing or lodging.
8. The mother and the daughter and the sister of a man who has had anal relations with another man may not marry the latter. But if the latter has had or is having anal relations with an acquired relative, the marriage remains valid.

What kind of sick society is this, where a man should be specifically told that he should not marry his own sister, or own mother, or own mother-in-law? Do these clerics have nothing better work to do? Is there no ethics in Muslim society as such restrictions are needed to be imposed by law? What type of filthy society Muslims live in, where a girl can be widowed or repudiated at the age of nine and before?

These are all descriptive of a very sick society. There is no such thing as democracy or civil liberties. Factors like justice, equal opportunity, rejuvenation, education and enlightenment, which determine the conditions of human societies are miserably lacking. At the same time religious fanaticism and terrorism are fast increasing. Cultural, racial, religious and other prejudices are rapidly creeping into the Muslim Ummah as factors and forces for its disintegration and deterioration. The whole society is stagnated and rotten, and completely apathetic to any kind of positive development. Fearful of change which might be the antidote to their illness, the Muslims march ever more rigidly into the past. Today the whole Muslim society is stinking like a gutter. This society is completely devoid of spirituality. The real God of Humankind is too great and the Almighty God has nothing to do with Allah, Qur'an, Muhammad and Islam altogether. Muslim Ummah can neither be reformed nor rescued from the doldrums of slumber, bondage and decadence. Its collapse is eminent and not far away. It is dying like a rabid dog. In its last days it can only inflict death to everyone and everything that comes within biting range.

8.5: The Causes of Decadence of Muslim "Ummah"

The mass narcissism of Muslim Ummah is solely responsible for its decadence. This society is very unproductive and uncreative; the more Islamic a nation is, the more is its backwardness. There is no democracy, no scientific development, no encouragement of free thinking, no technology – only great emphasis had been given upon memorizing the Qur'an, obeying Allah's Sharia law and following the holy Prophet Muhammad. This is what makes Muslim society a past-oriented and conservative culture, whereas the non-Muslim world is future-oriented, developing, open and creative.

Creativity is the most important human resource of all because it removes stagnation. Without creativity, there would be no progress, and society would be forever repeating the same patterns. A creative mind discovers new ideas or concepts, or new associations of the existing ideas or concepts. From a social and scientific point of view, the products of creative thought (also called divergent thought) are usually considered to have both originality and appropriateness. It is creativity and talent which can transform every blade of grass into a wonder of life. A creative society focuses on; human's ability to grow and learn, human resources and values, originality and learning ability. It looks at other societies as a valuable source of ideas and encourages its individuals to use technology to do totally new things, and to build a knowledge economy based on new ideas.

But in Islam everything is *Insha'Allah* – If it pleases Allah. The Arabs write on every letter *Insha'Allah* for only then the letter will arrive (Jung, 1993, p. 131). Except few, Muslims have no consciousness either individually or collectively. They remain passive in the face of the challenges, and deny the real mess they have made of their lives. They simply put the blame on the infidel world for their low state in every field of human endeavor and hopes that one day Allah will give them success and they will rule over the entire world.

A problem does not disappear just by ignoring it; Allah is not a magic rescuer who will come to solve it. Muslims have tremendous hate for the Western world, but oddly, they cannot avoid contact with them. Saudi children, generation after generation, have grown up being told at the school by Wahhabi-inspired teachers that the West is the source of all evil, but at the same time they also have been forced to accept, without question, that the very existence of the kingdom's ruling elite and the development of its infrastructure is entirely dependent on the intimate cooperation with the West (Bradely, 2005, p. 90). Muslims are, in every respect, dependent on West for technology, modern education, industry, medicine, even for military equipment for jihadi terrorism. The rich Mullahs curse venomously the Western culture, and the way the Muslim world is being corrupted by the Western civilization and lifestyle; but send their children to study at Western universities. As example; Al-Banna, founder of the Muslim Brotherhood encouraged martyrdom in the name of Allah, but his son lived in the comfort of Switzerland (Husain, 2007, p. 52). Kalim Saddiqui, the main Iranian fundamentalist and polemicist in the West, deemed Western civilization "*not a civilization but a sickness*", and not just a small sickness but "*a plague and a pestilence*" but lived comfortably in London till his death in 1996 (Pipes, 2003, p. 43). Muslims can live very comfortably in deception. Ever since the birth of Islam, Muslims are living in deception. Today it had become a second nature to them.

Creativity is a skill that should be developed. Any creative endeavor; e.g., writing a book or play, or, any constructive project brings anxiety. This may lead to various symptoms such as sleeplessness, irritability, or inability to concentrate. Such symptoms are normal reactions to our fear of embarking to the unknown (Masterson, 1990, p. 229). The normal healthy person knows that these syndromes would vanish by the very act of completing the project and hence he persists through the anxieties. But for a person with a false self, these anxieties lead to defensive patterns. As Masterson (1990, p. 17) wrote, "*A false self will neither test nor experiment. It is a defense against experimenting*".

The Narcissist's fear from being successful makes him nervous. At any cost he should prove that he is flawless. He is totally rigid; he will never admit his ignorance in any field (Vaknin, 1999, p. 190). Reality is, naturally, quite different from his fantasies. How such a person can be creative? In any creative endeavor, there is always a chance of failure. We learn from our mistakes and progress further based on that learning because we know that we are not flawless. Anyone, who studies science, does not become a scientist like Einstein at the end. But it does not mean that we should not study science. This is what the false self of a Narcissist cannot understand. As Masterson (1990, pp. 229-30) wrote, "*It is in creative acts – from artistic masterpieces to everyday innovation and problem solving - that the real self is most active. It is the real self that enables us to experiment at work*". So unless the Muslims activate their real selves, we will not see any progress.

Creativity is a natural potential energy in humans. It is incompatible with external and internal rewards or punishments because it is its own reward. It is not only an inherent characteristic of humans but also an essential need. Therefore when creativity is blocked, it has disastrous consequences. As Shapiro & Purpel (2008, p. 430) wrote, "*Whenever this creativity is impeded, the ultimate result is not simply the absence of creativity, but an actual positive presence of destructiveness*".

Since creativity is impeded, its denial brings about a pervasive state of dissatisfaction and boredom. This leads to intense frustration that is conductive to a search for exciting "outlets", which can readily involve a degree of force that is destructive. However, it would be wrong to think that Muslims' destructive tendency is completely a result of subdued creativity. Another important factor is abnormal hate which we cannot see in any other culture. USA had nuked Japan in 1945 causing large numbers of deaths and occupied their land for a long time. British occupied India causing great suffering. During Nazi regime, the Germans had caused much destruction to other nations; but, today hatred towards USA is not found in Japan, Hindus no more cherish any malice against the British and Germans are not hated by those nations whom Nazis had attacked. Every culture had forgotten the past and now works together for a better future. Muslims are different because the deep hatred originated from Muhammad.

Since the members of Jewish faith are the most vulnerable amongst all, we take the Jews as example to find out the actual reason of Muslims' hate towards Jews today, and how it originated. When the Jews declined Muhammad he was furious, and this is the starting point of his enmity towards them. His false self felt deflected and his narcissistic balloon got punctured. So he strengthened his self-image by humiliating and degrading the Jews. Today, Jews-bashing is a political game played by many Muslim nations who have got nothing to do with Israel. Many state controlled newspapers are full of anti-Jews propaganda. A writer on British Muslim forum declared (cited Spencer, 2006, p. 190), *"I am fed up with these dirty filthy Israeli dogs. May Allah curse them and destroy them all, and may they face the same fate as Banu Quraiza". Didn't Muhammad say, "Kill any Jews that fall into your hands?"* But, by hating the Jews today, what Muslims are achieving?

Islam had paralyzed the true selves of the Muslims. This evil Prophet is still living through the lives of his followers. By occupying the Muslim minds, Muhammad made them compatible with his own disorder and secured their submission. After this he made them do what he always dreamt of doing, what he often desired, what he constantly feared of. He compelled them into collaborating in the expression of the repressed side of his personality. The whole Muslim Ummah is a narcissistic supply machine of Muhammad and every individual Muslim is an essential part of it. Every Muslim, even today, is trying to re-inflate Muhammad's false ego, his narcissistic balloon which was punctured by those early Jews. With every hateful activity directed towards the Jews, Muslims are still securing narcissistic supply sources to their Prophet. Muhammad is still consuming the narcissistic supply flowing through these human conduits of his own making.

Muhammad is seen as the personification of the qualities Muslims are trying to copy. In the runner of 2004 American Presidential Election, a Muslim preacher invoked Muhammad to denounce democracy (cited Spencer, 2006, p. 188), *"Our Prophet did not run for office in any election ... he did not win any political debate. [Instead] he won the war against the infidel."*

Subdued creativity and inverted narcissism are the two factors that make the Muslims so destructive and bloodthirsty. And the final result is the backwardness of Ummah. Today, Muslims must understand the root causes of the problem and face the reality. They have to separate this Narcissist's seed which is germinating inside them and recapture their impaired true self from the grip of Muhammad. Unless they can do it, they will never be able to deal with the problems and challenges of life. The alien growth in the human mind, the mental cancer that is the result of following Muhammad, should be uprooted. It is high time the trauma and abuse inflicted upon the Muslims by a ruthless malignant Narcissist should be stopped. Muhammad is still present amongst Muslims in spirit long after he had gone to his grave. By willingly cremating themselves in the narcissistic flame of Muhammad, Muslims will get nothing but misery and misfortune. They suffer in the same way the early companions of Muhammad had suffered. If Muslims want to preserve their mental health, they have no other alternate but to abandon their Narcissist Prophet. No doubt this "waking up" is traumatic but only truth can set them free. It is only the true self that can accept and modulate the various, even conflicting, self-images and resolve any apparent, temporary confusion.

8.6: Unshackling the Victims of Muhammad

Where the mind is without fear and the head is held high

Where knowledge is free

Where the world has not been broken up into fragments
By narrow domestic walls

Where words come out from the depth of truth

Where tireless striving stretches its arms towards perfection

Where the clear stream of reason has not lost its way
Into the dreary desert sand of dead habit

Where the mind is led forward by thee
Into ever-widening thought and action

Into that heaven of freedom, my Father, let my country awake.

Noble-Laureate, Poet Rabindra Nath Tagore (1861 – 1941)

[Note: I read the above poetry in Bengali when I was a school student. It was really mind blowing. When I grew up I understood the deeper meaning of it. I am amazed every time I recite this poem by its sheer simplicity in conveying such deep thoughts with such elegance. To date it still remains one of my favorite poems. While writing this part suddenly I wished to recite it once more. – Author]

For common Muslims, apostasy is an unthinkable act. It is not only a crime punishable by death, but a sin. The apostate is damned both in this world and the next. In spite of this, there was large scale apostasy during Muhammad's lifetime and after his death. Those early Arabs, who took him as a Prophet, could not remain quiet by seeing the irrationalities of his supposed to be revealed doctrine and the contradictions in his behavior. Many of them had no inclination towards Islam, its dogma and ritual. It is estimated that at the time of Muhammad's death, the total number of people who really believed in Muhammad did not exceed a thousand (Warraq, 2003, p. 41). The early rulers had mercilessly criticized Muhammad, Qur'an and Allah. As example, a Muslim leader of the early days is reputed to have said (cited Warraq, 2003, p. 42), "*If there were a God, I would swear by his name that I did not believe in him*". Caliph al-Walid II (ruled 783) is said to have stuck the Qur'an onto a lance and shot it to pieces with arrows. He wrote poem, a similar type of Qur'anic verses and mocked the Qur'an mercilessly as follows,

You hurl threats against the stubborn opponents,
Well than I am a stubborn opponent myself.

When you appear before God at the day of resurrection,
Just say, 'My Lord, al-Walid has torn me up.'

Walid II certainly did not abide by the Allah's instructions. An intensively cultivated man, he surrounded himself with poets, dancing girls and musicians, and lived the merry life of a libertine, with no interest in Allah, Muhammad and Islam altogether (Warraq, 2003, 42).

From history, we can learn countless examples of those who have struggled free from the all-encompassing and suffocating embrace of Islam to breathe the fresh air of freedom. One of them was Ubaydallah b. Jahsh. He joined Islam but afterwards along with three friends left Islam, embraced Christianity and died as Christian in Abyssinia during the lifetime of Muhammad. These freethinkers, who secretly opposed the stubborn dogma of Islam and acknowledged only the moral law while publicly professed Islam, are called "Zindiq" (Warraq, 2003, p. 43). A Zindiq is a guilty of "zandaqa". The first person who was executed on the charge of a zandaqa was Djad Ibn Dirham by the order of Umayyad Caliph in 742 or 743. He denied the divine attributes of Qur'an and accused Muhammad of lying and denied resurrection. Around 760, another famous Zindiq named Ibn al-Muqaffa was executed. He died in the most horrible manner – his limbs were cut off one by one and fed into a blazing fire. From 786, the repression, persecution and execution of the freethinkers were carried out with greater ferocity. Special Magistrates were appointed to pursue the Zindiqs. Often these freethinkers were arrested *en masse*, imprisoned and beheaded or crucified. A short description (Warraq, 2003, pp. 43-54) of some of the early apostates of Islam is as below.

Abu Nuwas, a great classical Arabic and Persian poet, was accused of zandaqa. He was fond of wine. Once he entered a mosque drunk as ever and when the Imam recited the first verse from Surah 109, "*Say! O you unbelievers...*", Abu Nuwas is said to have cried out "*Here I am*". He was handed over to religious police and imprisoned. He was imprisoned on other occasions as well for insulting Islam.

Zindaqa even penetrated the Hashemite family (The Hashemites trace their ancestry from the great-grandfather of Muhammad, although the definition today mainly refers to the descendants of Muhammad's daughter, Fatima). Several members of this family were executed or died in prison. Ibn Abi-l-Awja (executed 772) cast doubt on the justice of some of the punishments described in the Qur'an. He also disbelieved that Islamic pilgrimage was ordered by God.

Bashshar Ibn Burd (714-784), another freethinker, came from a noble Persian family. He was tortured for glorifying the ancient memories of Iran. He was also disrespectful toward the institution of pilgrimage. On one occasion, he left for the pilgrimage but stopped on the way and spent his time in drinking. As the pilgrims were returning, he joined them and pretended on arrival home to have completed the entire pilgrimage. He also ridiculed the Qur'an many times with his satires and denied resurrection. Another skeptic, Hammad Ajrad (executed 777) wrote some verses, which were parody of the Qur'an and preferred those verses over Qur'anic verses during the prayer. Another great poet in Arabic language was Al-Mutanabi (in Arabic, one pretends to be a Prophet). He rejected Muslim religious dogmas regarding it as spiritual instruments of oppression. He also began revolutionary propaganda and claimed to be a Prophet with a new Qur'an. He was imprisoned.

Ibn al-Rawandi (827-911) was a skeptic of Islam and a critic of religion in general. He was a Mutazilite scholar but later rejected Islam completely and became an atheist. According to him, the Qur'an, far from being a miracle and inimitable, is an inferior work from literary point of view, since it is neither comprehensible nor of any practical value and certainly not a revealed book.

Perhaps the greatest freethinker in the world of Islam was Muhammad Ibn Zakariya al-Razi (865 – 925). He had studied mathematics, astronomy, philosophy and literature. He challenged tradition and authority in every field to which he turned his attention. His general philosophical attitude was that no authority was beyond criticism. He was a true humanist and had boundless faith in human reason. Al-Razi argued (cited Hecht, 2004, pp. 227-30),

On what ground do you deem it necessary that God should single out certain individuals [by giving them prophecy], that he should set them up above other people, that he should appoint them to be the people's guides, and make people dependent upon them?

If the people of this religion are asked about the proof for the soundness of their religion, they flare up, get angry and spill the blood of whoever confronts them with this question. They forbid rational speculation, and strive to kill their adversaries. This is why truth became thoroughly silenced and concealed.

Al-Razi maintained the view that reason is superior to revelation and salvation is only possible through philosophy. The Prophets, the Billy goats with long beards, as Al-Razi disdainfully described them, cannot claim any intellectual and spiritual superiority. These Billy goats pretend to come with a message from God, all the while exhausting themselves spouting their lies and imposing on the masses blind obedience to the "words of the master". As for the Qur'an, it is but an associated mixture of "absurd and inconsistent fables". Al-Razi commented,

You claim that the evidentiary miracle is present and available, namely, the Koran. You say: 'Whoever denies it, let him produce a similar one'. Indeed, we shall produce a thousand similar, from the works of rhetoricians, eloquent speakers and valiant poets, which are more appropriately phrased and state the issues more succinctly. They convey the meaning better and their rhymed prose is in better meter. ... By God what you say astonishes us! You are talking about a work which recounts ancient myths, and which at the same time is full of contradictions and does not contain any useful information or explanation. Then you say: 'Produce something like it'?! (cited Stroumsa, 1999, p. 103).

It is clear from the above accounts that Islam never had shortage of apostates. These enlightened people hold philosophical viewpoints that formed on the basis of science, logic, and reason instead of authority, tradition, or any other dogma. Though their field of criticism varied, one point was very common amongst them. None of them either accepted or rejected ideas proposed as truth without judging them under the searchlight of knowledge and reason. They understood the utter hollowness of life under Islam; hence they did not merely react like robots.

Muslims unknowingly sabotage their real happiness. Many people are excited when they ask a question to themselves – "how to find 'meaning' in life?" But Muslims are terrified asking something like this. For others, all of life is a period of experimenting, testing, growing and developing; but for Muslims, experimenting and testing are wasted efforts because they have Allah's divine guidelines to follow. Islam had entered their lives in such a way that a Muslim can spend his whole life in this delusion without even thinking once. They can bury their heads in sand and pretend as if nothing has happened. In this life, everything is *Insha'Allah* and Muhammad will take care of afterlife. What they cannot see is that the entire religion of Islam is based on the truth claim of one man who was a pathological liar and had shown all the symptoms of his lunacy.

If Muslims want to come out of their mental disability, first they have to come out of this "Muhammad-sycophancy" or "Muhammad-slavery" – by whatever name we can call it, and only then they will be able to develop and activate their real self. They have to assert themselves instead of complying. Self-deception leads nowhere; only the real self has the capacity to function successfully in the real world. When they will hear the genuine urges of the real self, they will find a new meaning in their lives.

Those therapists who treat the NPD patients often find it very difficult because of the defensive tactics of the Narcissist on which his grandiose false self relies (Benjamin, 1996, p. 142). The Narcissist uses aggression to coerce others including the therapist. He may often walks out from the therapy saying the therapist "*means nothing to him*" (Masterson, 1990, pp. 174-5). We see the same attitude in Muslims. We all know how die-hard the Islamic belief of a Muslim is. When the truth about Muhammad, Allah and Islam is brought to his notice, he denies it overwhelmingly. Denial is the way Muslims handle what they cannot handle logically. He argues, rejects the facts and sometimes even tries to twist the facts. If he cannot manage with this, he gives threat. If he cannot win or silence the critic by threat, he says that the criticisms have no impression on him. He may even say that his faith in Islam has grown after hearing all the criticisms. He may also walk away. Muhammad had a standing instruction in the Qur'an on this.

When you hear His verses being disbelieved or mocked, do not sit with them until they engage in other talk, or else you will surely be like them. Allah will surely gather the hypocrites and unbelievers altogether in Hell. (Q: 4.140).

What an appropriate advice from one Narcissist to the co-dependent. Now, the most dramatic point in the therapy of a Narcissist! Underneath this aggressive refusal what looks like a failed therapy, there lies an extreme vulnerability. As Masterson commented (1990, p. 175), *"Even when they are not in a session, they cannot get the therapist out of their minds"*.

What actually happens in his mind? When the Muslim says that his faith in Islam has strengthened after facing the critics, it is not an act of faith; rather this "returning to religion" is in order to escape an intolerable doubt. He makes this decision not out of devotion but in search of security (Fromm, 1978, p. 4). A trained psychoanalyst who is not at all concerned with religion considers this step as a symptom of failure of nerve. By the demands of treatment, when the Narcissist is forced to venture out of his narcissistic cocoon and compelled to activate his real self, after a certain time "the denial of reality" fails to protect him. He struggles with himself but at one yield point he gives up. Slowly, the realization that it was my entire fault, that I was sick and needed help penetrates the decades old defenses that he erected around himself. Masterson continued, *"Up to a point, the Narcissist's denial of reality helps him to maintain his psychic equilibrium; but if the denial is too great, it will cause conflict"*. The time frame for this conflict to take place is different for different NPD patients.

When Islam is criticized and exposed, Muslims strongly oppose it sometimes even with violence, but they cannot show a complete apathy to all these criticisms. Like children, though very scared of ghosts, cannot restrain themselves from reading ghost stories; the Muslims, in spite of their dislike, cannot show a complete lack of concern to the critics; something like, *"they cannot get the therapist out of their minds"*. This forces them to look into themselves and their cherished belief, or in other words, to come out of their air-tight cocoon of narcissistic enjoyment and to activate their real self. A conflict takes place and on one day when he regains his self-esteem, he takes baby steps towards recovery. The harsh words of the critics are like "time bombs" waiting to explode. Sooner or later he is on another spiritual journey from Islamic bondage to the "heaven of freedom" as Poet Tagore had envisioned. And yes, this heaven of freedom is much more pleasant than Allah's brothel that Muhammad had envisioned.

Change of Islamic faith can reform a murderer; e.g., the strange case of Anwar Shaikh. During the partition of India / Pakistan (1947) he was a young man, and was so filled with hate against non-Muslims that he went out with a knife and killed three innocent Sikhs, two of them were father and a son. He did not know anyone of them but he killed them because they were the first non-Muslims he saw on the streets (Warraq, 2003, p. 286). This gruesome memory of his crime under the influence of Islamic "drug" pained him so much that he renounced Islam. He argued with himself – how God can command us to kill? Only the strength of reason can set the Muslims free. Renan (cited Warraq, 1995, p. ii) wrote, *"Muslims are the first victims of Islam. Many times I have observed in my travels in the orient that fanaticism comes from a small number of dangerous men who maintain the others in the practice of religion by terror. To liberate the Muslim from his religion is the best service that one can render him"*.

Poet Tagore dreamed of such a society which would be based on truth and knowledge. He inspired people through his poetry to create a free-thinking, united and dynamic nation. Today not only many common Muslims, but preachers, mullahs, imams, scholars, missionaries and even terrorists have apostatized. All of them say that there is better life after apostasy. Many have taken it upon themselves to oppose the Islamic ideology and have become celebrities in their own right. They know the true nature and spiritual bankruptcy of Islam. These former Muslims from all parts of the Islamic world become a torch of guidance to their fellow brethren and give a courageous signal to other Muslims to speak out.

When non-Muslims speak their minds out about the fundamental questions of Islam, their influence on Muslim audiences will always be much more limited than the ex-Muslims because the Muslims spontaneously will bring up the subject of the relative superiority of one religion vis-à-vis another. But this scope is not there when ex-Muslims criticize Islam. Finally, these enlightened ex-Muslims will do the job of opening the exit gate from Islam for their Muslim-born brothers and sisters.

8.7: Conclusion

"Sometimes doubts can do good in us. It can purify false beliefs that have crept into our faith. It can humble our arrogance. It can give us patience and compassion with other doubters. It can remind us how much truth matters".

John Ortberg (2008, p. 122)

"There is a difference between yearning to find the truth and yearning to believe. The first is objective. You empty your mind from all preconceived ideas and prepare yourself to find things that may be contrary to your belief. The other is when you try desperately to validate what you already believe".

Ali Sina

Islam is an extremely defenseless religion and hence vulnerable to collapse. "Defenseless" in the sense, there is not a single atom of truth in it to support. This failed religion, originated from the grand delusion of a malignant Narcissist, is the biggest hoax humanity has ever seen. It is like a house of cards – looks tall, big, mighty and gigantic but the base is very weak. Sina (2008, pp. iv, 260) wrote,

Islam stands on a very shaky ground. It rests on nothing but lies. All we have to do to demolish it is to expose those lies and this gigantic edifice of terror and deception will collapse.

Islam is like a house of cards, sustained by lies. All it takes to demolish is to challenge one of those lies holding it together. It is a tall building, erected on quicksand; once you expose its foundation, the sand will wash away and this mighty edifice will fall under its own weight.

As Vaknin (1999, p. 316) wrote, *"Narcissism is an eggshell, apparently solid, really very fragile. It is fragile because it bases itself on falsehoods"*. The day when criticism will have dismantled piece by piece this enormous falsehood of Islam, the whole edifice will come crumbling down. Then the Muslims will ask themselves how this enormous falsehood could have forced acceptance for such a long time. I can already see some cracks in this gigantic structure.

This is not a wishful thinking. If we look at the history we will find that Communist empire collapsed when the truths about the Bolsheviks were exposed. Bolsheviks first came to power in 1917. After the defeat of Nazism in 1945, the

Soviet Union extended its reaches into Eastern Europe. Its revolutionary message appealed to China, and Mao led the Chinese Communist Party to victory in 1949. Communism spread rapidly to Vietnam, Cambodia, Cuba and Ethiopia, and was also predicted to engulf Iran (Tudeh Party is an Iranian Communist Party) and India (Communist principles were institutionalized into Indian government and adopted in government policy). At one stage, say around 1960, communism looked like the future of the world as Islam looks today. The Soviet empire already ruled over the Eastern half of Europe and its friends ruled the largest country in Asia.

But in spite of such a promising growth, the unnoticing fall of communism started soon after 1956, when Nikita Khrushchev who had inherited Stalin's post as general secretary of the Communist Party told the world how cruel and arbitrary Stalin's rule had been, and how many people had perished. Most of the victims of Stalin were loyal citizens of the Soviet Union and many of them were Bolsheviks (Desai, 2007, p. 15). The destruction of the Berlin wall signaled the end, at least in Europe. In 1989, the Communist empire in Eastern Europe and in 1991, the USSR itself, collapsed.

Islam maintained itself for over fourteen centuries because the basic tenets of Islam were not critically analyzed. Whoever tried had lost his life or imprisoned. But the recent developments in communications technology, particularly satellite television and the Internet in even the remotest harems of Islamic Nations, is profoundly altering the mental climate in the Muslim world. These criticisms are working and will continue to work as therapy for them. Islam is going to face the same fate like communism unless there is a Third World War. In this case Islam will be wiped out like Hitler and his Nazi party. But it is a mathematical certainty that Islam will collapse. Its days are numbered.

Chapter 9: Final Assessment of Muhammad

"Half the harm that is done in this world is due to people who want to feel important."

T. S. Eliot (1888 - 1965)

"The way [in order] to see by faith, one has to shut the eye of reason."

Benjamin Franklin (1706 - 1790)

Every society produces evil people who look for opportunities in religious sentiments of the mass by posing as god-man or so-called Prophets. These god-men use religion to control men's lives so that they can attain power and prosper. For this, they create perverse and deceitful doctrines to force their authority on others in the name of a God suitable to their purpose. These Prophets are the real devils, who use religion to deceive humankind. They separate us from the real God of human race, our real Creator. The deception, death, and damnation of men are these devils' life ambition. Muhammad was such a vulgar imposter in a divine robe.

Muhammad had a totally upside down worldview. He equated love with weakness and feared intimacy. In fact, narcissism and intimacy problems are practically synonymous (Masterson, 1990, p. 122). He inflicted pain and abuse on others as his second nature. He was unable to give his followers a reason to live, so he gave them enough reasons to die – die in Allah's name to enter paradise. He could not convince the Arabs to choose his religion based upon its merits, so he threatened them with damnation. And the religion he preached was more about fantasy less about proof. Any person who, among other atrocities, orders and watches 800 innocent people beheaded and beds the wife of a man whom he had tortured to death that very night cannot be considered psychologically normal. Common sense alone tells us that a fifty-one years old man, who marries a six year old girl, is abnormal. The notion that a godly revelation would focus on the sexual desires of a lecherous man is really disgusting. No religion in the world has ever destroyed family ties as Muhammad has done in Islam. Since the leader was a fake, his promises were also not genuine. If we remove all the immoral, illogical, hateful, and violent verses from the Qur'an, we will be left with an odd collection of plagiarized and twisted Bible stories and meaningless gibberish of a mentally deranged person.

Religion was just a cause for Muhammad. Like Narcissus of Greek mythology, Muhammad actually worshipped his own image – not God. He created a God in his own image and attributed to that God the qualities of his own self. Allah was a plastic entity that Muhammad shaped to meet his needs. That is why Allah seems a multidimensional entity in the Qur'an, an obedient servant that Muhammad used for any occasion from managing the harem affairs of his wives to swearing to punish mercilessly whosoever disagrees with His beloved messenger. For a Narcissist, the cause of God is not really that important. It is an excuse, a tool for domination to extract narcissistic supplies. For Stalin the excuse was communism, for Mussolini it was fascism, for Hitler National Socialism and for Muhammad it was religion. The more they glorify these causes, the more they get power for themselves. In his religious endeavor, Muhammad made mistakes and was defeated many times, but he did not give up. He corrected himself and moved ahead by abrogating verses with suitable additions. No one can deny that on several occasions he intentionally did harm knowing perfectly well that he was obeying his own will and not an inspiration from God. He talked much about paradise, hell, virtue and sin; but his actions did not show that he had really believed whatever he was saying. He lied on several occasions and encouraged lying to propagate his religion. No doubt, Muhammad had mastered the art of deception. He never gave a second thought to compromise morality for political gain. In his mind there was no other determinant. So he raged when confronted with disagreement or opposition, or, anything that threatened his worldview.

He valued people when he found that they could advance his religion but devalued them at the next moment if they did not comply with his whims and wishes. He treated people around him as lifeless objects, and manipulated his followers so cunningly as if he had conquered them, "chained" them, conditioned them and moulded them. He exploited people as if he "knew" that he could do anything he wanted them to do. This magical thinking made him extremely reckless, violent and adventurous. He was so convinced of his mission that he was genuinely surprised and devastated when he failed. When he failed he felt empty and worthless. And every minor success in his cause elevated him from the low of misery to the heights of extreme joy. Throughout his prophetic endeavor, he derived his self-worth from people around him, as if he would collapse and self-annihilate without them.

Muhammad obsessively believed in his own infallibility, brilliance, heroism, and perfection. He gave the Qur'an as the only evidence of his prophethood. At the same time deep inside in his mind he knew that unlike the Biblical Prophets he could not perform miracles. He knew that his Qur'an could not stand criticism. He knew that his religion could not be morally and spiritually at par with other established religions of Arabia, like, Christianity and Judaism; but he did not dare confront the truth. In fact he even could not admit the truth to himself. He only imagined that he was on a divine mission, a messenger of Allah. This is how he failed the "reality test" – he was simply unable to distinguish the actual (external world) from the imagined (the internal world of thoughts and feelings) by making logical analysis of the religion he was preaching or allowing others to do this. For him the reality became shadow and the shadow became reality.

Muhammad was not capable of introspection, i.e., he was not capable to judge his actions from the outside. His critics made him realize that there was a "grandiosity gap" (between his self-image and reality) which made him helpless. Since he could not win in a scholarly debate with the critics, he deceitfully got them assassinated. This was his only way to deal with all his intellectual opponents.

Muhammad considered himself entitled to special amenities and benefits. Though he was the founder of Islam, he exempted himself from the rules that he himself established; he felt that he was above any kind of law. His sense of entitlement coupled with the incredible belief of his own superiority lead him to believe in his invincibility, invulnerability, immunity, and divinity. He dared to hold human edicts, rules, and regulations and human penalties in disdain, and regarded human needs and emotions as weaknesses to be predatorily exploited.

Critics often ask one question; was Muhammad a knowing fraud or he genuinely believed that the revelations were coming from a God? No matter whatever is the truth, it simply does not make much sense. Even if he was sincere, it does not relieve him from the criminal charges that are put on him. If a racially prejudiced white man "sincerely" believes that blacks should not get equal rights in the civilized society, his "sincerity" does not affect our moral condemnation of his belief. For the same reason we condemn those Hindus who still believe in untouchability. In the same way, Muhammad cannot get away in any case. If he was not a knowing fraud, then we can say that he was capable of self-deception. He used to bring messages freely from his God to justify political murders, assassinations, raid, booty, pedophilia, abundant sex even to solve his domestic problems which are clear evidences that he was an absolute fake; his sincerity means nothing. Secondly, he was perfectly capable of distinguishing right from wrong and anticipating the results of his actions and their influence on the society. Though he caused great misery to others, he hardly felt responsible for them. Therefore, he should be held liable for his deeds and exploits. As Vaknin (1999, p. 67) commented, "*A person suffering from NPD must be subjected to the same moral treatment and judgment as the rest of us, the less privileged, are. The courts do not recognize NPD to be a mitigating circumstance – why should we?*"

Muhammad never asked anyone to compile Allah's revelations in a book. Literally, thousand times he said "fear me, obey me, fear Allah, obey Allah", but there was not one "write for me" or "write for Allah". He knew if revelations were written down, it would be a bit difficult to abrogate them in the future, if required. Secondly, Qur'an was revealed to serve his selfish interests and that it would be of no value once he is no more.

Muhammad's actions and commands in Allah's name are immortalized in Qur'an and Hadith collections. These are not only shocking in the standard of our time, but many Meccans during those days were equally shocked by seeing his brutal performance in the name of God. Muhammad succeeded in his prophetic mission because there was no powerful Government to stop him. If Muhammad had been living under Roman rule, surely his mission would have resulted in losing his life and his religion would have been stamped out by strong military action.

A short before the coming of Muhammad, Arabia had become permeated with new ideas of religion, both from Jewish and Christian sources, but mostly from the Christian sources. Paganism was slowly decaying out. A group of people rejected paganism and to fulfill their spiritual needs they looked for an alternative religion. They were known as Hanifites or simply as Hanifs. So Arabia was a fertile ground for a new religion to born. Muhammad was deeply influenced by these Hanifs. If Muhammad had never been born or never had been successful to establish his religion, then perhaps a different Prophet would have taken his place. Probably the new Prophet might have consolidated the Byzantine kingdom and would have fought off the desert Arab tribes successfully. In that case Arabia would have been converted to Christianity.

Probably, the most terrible legacy of Muhammad was his rigid firmness that the Qur'anic revelations were the literal word of God and the significance of these verses are eternal. The irony is that in the entire history of Islam, Qur'an fails to give one solid argument at its favor that cannot be successfully refuted. A nation might read the Qur'an and explain minutely every word for centuries without advancing one step on the road to progress. In the tiresome repetition of the mindless blabbering of a mentally deranged illiterate person; the human mind loses its elasticity, its sagacity, its constructivism and its curiosity. Through Freudian analysis, it can be shown that the prohibition of critical thinking at one point leads to an impoverishment of a person's critical ability in other spheres of thought and thereby obstructs the power of reason (Fromm, 1978, p. 12). Consequently, the intellect becomes atrophied and incapable of an original effort. This is the cause of intellectual bankruptcy of the Muslim nations. As O'Brien (cited Armstrong, 2006, p. 43) concluded, "*Muslim society looks profoundly repulsive ... It looks repulsive because it is repulsive ... A Westerner who claims to admire Muslim society, while still adhering to Western values, is either a hypocrite or an ignoramus or a bit of both ... Arab society is sick, and has been sick for a long time. In the last century, the Arab thinker Jamal al-Afghani wrote, 'Every Muslim is sick, and his only remedy is the Koran'. Unfortunately, the sickness gets worse the more the remedy is taken.*" Also, Muhammad declared that he was the last Prophet of God. This way, Muhammad not only closed all the possibilities of new intellectual thoughts and freedom of ideas, but practically eliminated any chance of reformation of Islam.

The self-serving messages of an illiterate seventh century malignant Narcissist passed down to the Muslims generation after generation as unquestionable word of Allah, and as time passed, men were found to take up these words and make them into weapons to cause injustice, oppression, domination, and for conversion by force. Islam is a bankrupt ideology from the standpoint of humanism. The early Arab invaders were no way better than controlled mass-murderers. They were hard-wired to cheat, kill and loot, and had transformed Islam from a religion into an organized crime. In general, they were brainwashed by Muhammad's teaching to inflict great suffering on other humans without feeling any remorse. The formula of the spread of Islam is simple,

1. Use lies and brainwashing to create an army of controlled, highly motivated mass-murderers.
2. Use that army to enslave large numbers of people (i.e., seize control of their labor power and its fruits).
3. Use that slave labor power to improve the brainwashing process (by using the economic surplus to employ scribes, preachers and missionaries). Then go back to step one and repeat the process.

By the year 750, Arabs subdued many fortified cities and took control from sea to sea, and from east to west – Egypt, and from Crete to Cappadocia, from Yemen to the Gates of Alan (in the Caucasus), Armenians, Byzantines, Egyptians, Persians, Syrians and all the areas in between (Kennedy, 2008, p. 1). However the prodigious success of the Arab conquest proves nothing. Attila the Hun, Genseric the Vandal king, Gengis Khan and Alexander the Great brought many nations into subjection; yet civilization owes them absolutely nothing. A conquering people only exercise a civilizing influence when it itself is more civilized than the people conquered.

Muhammad had isolated the Muslims from the rest of the human society by dividing the humankind into two perpetually hostile groups dar-ul-Islam (the house of Islam), and dar-ul-harb (the house of war), i.e., Muslims and Kafirs. It is not that a Muslim merely thinks that he is superior to the infidels. This unhealthy perception of his superiority is embedded in him which is a part of his every mental cell. He feels that he is entitled to special treatment and to outstanding consideration because he is such a unique specimen. Deprived of contact with others and starved for human interactions, the Muslims bond with their predator. The more helpless a Muslim is, the more he is dependent on Muhammad. The more backward a Muslim nation is, the more it clings to Islam. Today, in this era of scientific development, Muslims must educate themselves to face the reality. If a man knows that he has nothing to rely on except his own powers, he will learn to use them properly. Only a free Muslim, who has ejected Muhammad from his life and liberated himself from Allah's authority – authority that punishes, entices, threatens and demands – can make use of his power of reason.

Muslim's backwardness, envy, disappointment, unhappiness and many other such painful realities are well reflected in Iqbal's poetry *Shikwa* where he complained to Allah about the prosperity, power and education of the non-Muslims in contrast to Muslim's poor condition. After one year of reciting *Shikwa*, Iqbal presented *Jawab-i Shikwa*, where Allah gave a reply to Iqbal's complaint. Last three lines are as follows.

> *Too Musalman ho to taqdir hai tadbir teri*
> *Ki Muhammad se wafa toonay to ham teray hain*
> *Ye jahan cheez hai kiya lauho qalam tere hain.*

(If you are Muslim your prudence is your destiny. If you are loyal to Prophet we are yours. This universe is nothing; the tablet and the pen are yours.)

This poetic composition of Iqbal is based on Qur'anic teaching. According to Iqbal; Muslims' proven loyalty with Muhammad can own Allah. Since being loyal to Muhammad is same as following orthodox Islam; Muslims should practice Islam more rigorously to prosper. If Iqbal is true, then how the infidels have prospered? We, the non-Muslims, do not practice Islam at all. In fact some of us even oppose Islam. In that case how the infidel countries are better than Muslim countries that at least practice a little? If the Qur'an is full of science why the Islamic countries are most backwards? The Muslims do not know the answer because they have even forgotten to ask the question.

There is a lesson to learn in this. The Creator of the Universe has no master-plot or mega-plan to deprive anyone of happiness, prosperity or power. Nor He has any intention to be unfair to the Muslim world. The only reason of the misery of the Muslims is Islam itself. Prophet Muhammad is not the savoir, but an abuser and exploiter of the Muslims. He is like a "black hole" at the centre of the Muslims' incredible dream-like galaxy. Muslims are like objects for Muhammad. He is continuously dragging the Muslims towards him and sucking their blood. Abuse is the eventual act of perverted intimacy. Muhammad used Islam to pervade Muslim psyche, and possessed their mind. Qur'an is the weapon what he had used to achieve his narcissistic goal. He was a predator. As Iqbal said, "*If you are loyal to Muhammad we are yours*". It is of course a tragic event. But it is more than of a tragedy that Muslims do not want to face the root cause of the problem.

Muslims are unable to see the truth because they have ceased to believe that reason is the most valuable and the most specific human power that can establish the validity for norms and the ideas for human conduct. *Homo sapiens*, is a Latin term meaning for "wise man" or "knowing man". But in actuality many times we simply ignore our innate wisdom, believe in superstitions and easily become the victims of imposters. Reason is the only means for discovering the truth. Unlike other religions, Islam is not seen by Muslims from different angles. For this reason all the religions prosper but Islam got stuck in a seventh century mentality. When Muslims begin with the Qur'an, first they conclude that it is Allah's word. Hence they are unable to judge the book with a critical mind. If they change their viewpoint a little they will notice its obvious falsehood.

Religion is supposed to instill ethical behavior, promote human values, fraternity, respect, integrity, and the moral guidelines required for the construction of a better human society regardless of whatever God or Gods are worshipped. But from the beginning, Islam was based on terrorist activities and today, after 1400 years, Westerners have finally realized the term "terrorism" describes their code of behavior. We are living in a world that is becoming smaller and smaller day by day. Human beings; regardless of religion, race, skin color, language, culture or nationality, should unite and cooperate with each other to make life more enjoyable and fulfilling for all. The Qur'anic injunction is viewed as obscene by all who believe in a peaceful, nonracist united world. Is it really possible to imagine a human society where all the people should believe in a collection of superstitious absurdities and in the event that some of them do not, those nonbelievers should be ostracized or slain by the other members of the society? The preposterous content of the Muslim's Qur'an is echoing the power-hungry, lascivious thoughts of Muhammad who presented himself as a Prophet of God. When the contents of the Qur'an are read out of curiosity and not through the eyes of faith, the words speak for themselves. The dispassionate reader cannot help but conclude that the Qur'an is a preposterous fabrication by an ignorant person. Muhammad, the author of the Qur'an, was a licentious Arab. How could such an ignoble person dictate human values to others? Those foolish people of the seventh century Arabia who decided to follow Muhammad can be forgiven, but how the educated people today can be forgiven who still want to be fooled? Who knows better; the almighty, omniscient, omnipotent, merciful, etc., etc Allah who has created heaven and earth in six days and His beloved seal of Prophets, mercy to mankind etc., etc messenger, or a bunch of infidels such as, Darwin, Aryabhata, Galileo, Copernicus, Aristotle, Edward Hubble, Gandhi, Einstein, Meghnad Saha, Stephen Hawking, Amartya Sen and so on? It is the new age of enlightenment and every day new truths are being revealed. I feel sick when I see, today, more than a billion Muslims are unable to see the ploys of one mentally deranged man. Muslims should give way to logical thinking and that is all what is required; the truth will take its own course in time.

References

Theses and Dissertations

1. Arimbi, Diah Ariani (2006); *Reading the Writings of Contemporary Indonesian Muslim Women Writers: Representation, Identity and Religion of Muslim Women in Indonesian Fictions.* Ph.D thesis submitted in September 2006, Women's and Gender Studies, Faculty of Arts and Social Sciences. University of New South Wales.
2. Hazen, Rebecca Ann (2005); *Parental Rejection, Temperament and Internalizing Problems.* Ph.D thesis submitted at The Ohio State University during 2005.
3. Hook, Tarah Lynn (2007); *The Role of Self-concept and Narcissism in Aggression.* Ph.D thesis. Department of Psychology. University of Saskatchewan. Saskatoon.
4. Kotb, Heba (2004); *Sexuality in Islam.* Ph.D Thesis submitted in December 2004 on Clinical Sexology. Maimonides University. Egypt.
5. Lyon, Peter D.S (2006); *A Solution for Ethnic Conflict: Democratic Governance in Afghanistan, A Case Study.* Thesis submitted to the Faculty of Graduate Studies for the Degree of Master of Arts in August, 2006. Department of Political Studies, Faculty of Arts. University of Manitoba. Canada.
6. Shepley, Robin P. (2001); *Children Diagnosed with Attachment disorder: A Qualitative study of the Parental Experience.* Thesis submitted to the Faculty of the Virginia Polytechnic Institute and State University for M. Sc degree in Human Development on July 26, 2001.
7. Slutzky, Shana (2006); *'Reversion' to Islam: A study of racial and spiritual empowerment among African-American Muslims.* Thesis submitted for B.A degree in Anthropology at Haverford College, April 2006.
8. Talvitie, Vesa (2006); *The Freudian Unconscious in the Context of the Cognitive Orientation.* Ph.D thesis submitted and publicly discussed on September 15. 2006. Faculty of Behavioral studies, University of Helsinki. Finland.
9. Wesner, Bradley S. (2007); *Responding to the Workplace Narcissist.* Thesis submitted for M.A degree in Communication Studies during July 2007. Indiana University. US.

Reports

1. Hudson, Rex A. (2009); *The Sociology and Psychology of Terrorism: Who Becomes a Terrorist and Why?* A Report Prepared under an Interagency Agreement by the Federal Research Division. Library of Congress. Washington, D.C.
2. Borum, R. (2004); *Psychology of terrorism.* University of South Florida. Tampa.

Newspaper and Journals

1. Abbott, Alison (2007); *Scanning Psychopaths. News Feature.* NATURE, Vol. 450.13 December 2007.
2. Akhtar, S (1999); *The Psychodynamic Dimension of Terrorism.* Psychiatric Annals. 29(6) June 1999.

3. Bhaumik, Saba, Naqvi (2005); *Ayatollahs All.* Outlook magazine, December 12, 2005 issue. Vol. XLV, No. 49.

4. Dreibholz, Ursula (1983); *A treasure of early Islamic manuscripts on parchment. Significance of the find and its conservation treatment.* AIC Preprints of papers presented at the 11th annual meeting in Baltimore, Maryland, 25-29 May 1983. Washington, DC.

5. Dreibholz, Ursula (1996); *The Treatment of Early Islamic Manuscript Fragments on Parchment in The Conservation and Preservation of Islamic Manuscripts*, Al-Furqan Islamic Heritage Foundation, London.

6. Dreibholz, Ursula (1999); *Preserving a treasure: the Sana'a manuscripts.* Museum International. Islamic collections. Vol. LI, No. 3, July 1999 issue. Blackwell Publishers. Oxford.

7. (Dr.) Mitra, Rajat (2007); *Devil in the Flesh.* Outlook magazine. January 22, 2007 issue. Vol. XLVII, No. 4.

8. Goldner-Vukov, Mila and Moore, Laurie Jo (2010); *Malignant Narcissism: From Fairy Tales to Harsh Reality.* Psychiatria Danubina; Vol. 22, No. 3. Faculty of Medical and Health Sciences. University of Auckland.

9. Hassan, Nasra (2001); *An Arsenal of Believers: Talking to the Human Bombs.* Published on November 19, 2001. The New Yorker Magazine. Condé Nast Publications.

10. Lengua, L.J., Wolchik, S.A., Sandler, I.N. and West, S.G. (2000). *The additive and interactive effects of parenting and temperament in predicting adjustment problems of children of divorce.* Journal of Clinical Child Psychology. Vol. 29, May 2 2000 issue.

11. McCormick, G. H. (2003). *Terrorist Decision Making.* Published in June 2003. Volume 6. Annual Review of Political Science.

12. Nasrin, Taslima (2007); *Let's Burn the Burqa.* Outlook magazine, January 22, 2007 issue. Vol. XLVII, No. 4.

13. Ram Swarup (1992); *Swords to sell a god.* An article published on June 16, 1992. The Telegraph. Calcutta. India.

14. Vazire, Simine; Naumann, Laura P; Rentfrow, Peter J and Gosling Samuel D (2008); *Portrait of a Narcissist: Manifestations of Narcissism in Physical Appearance.* Journal of Research in Personality. Issue 42.

15. Whelan, Estelle (1998); *Forgotten Witness: Evidence for the Early Codification of the Qur'an.* The Journal of America Oriental Society. January to March Issue, 1998. University of Michigan. USA.

16. Willis, John Ralph (1967); *Jihad fi Sabil Allah- Its Doctrinal Basis in Islam and Some Aspects of Evolution in Nineteenth-Century West Africa.* The Journal of African History. Volume 8, no. 3.

Books

1. (Brig.) Malik, S. K (2008); *The Qur'anic Concept of War.* Adam Publishers and Distributors. New Delhi. India.

2. (Dr.) Brahmachari, Radheshyam (1999); *Islami Dharmattva – Ebar Ghare Ferar Pala* (Original in Bengali). Save India Mission. Kolkata. India.

3. (Dr.) Ambedkar, B. R (1940); *Pakistan or the Partition of India.* Govt. of Maharashtra publication. India.

4. (Dr.) Razzaque, Russell (2008); *Human Being to Human Bomb*. Icon Books Ltd. Cambridge.

5. (Dr.) Shrikhande, Mehra (2009); *Paranormal Experiences: Beyond the Realms of Reason*. Unicorn Books. New Delhi. India.

6. (Ed.) Allen, Tim and Thomas, Alan, *(2000); Poverty and Development into 21st Century*. OUP. UK.

7. (Ed.) Bjorgo, Tore (2005); *Root Causes of Terrorism; Myths, Reality and Ways Forward*. Routledge. Taylor and Francis Group. Abingdon. UK.

8. (Ed.) Bostom, Andrew G (2008); *The Legacy of Islamic Antisemitism – From Sacred Texts to Solemn History*. Prometheus Books. NY.

9. (Ed.) Costello, Charles G. (1996): *Personality Characteristics of the Personality Disordered*. A Wiley-interscience Publication. NY.

10. (Ed.) Faith, Wendy and McCallum, Pamela (2005*); Linked histories: postcolonial studies in a globalized world*. University of Calgary Press. Alberta. Canada.

11. (Ed.) Krizeck, James (1964); *Anthology of Islamic Literature: From the Rise of Islam to Modern Times*. Penguin Books, Harmondsworth.

12. (Ed.) Livesley W. John (1995); *The DSM-IV personality disorders*. The Guilford Press. A division of the Guilford publications Inc. NY.

13. (Eds) Shienbaum Kim and Hasan Jamal (2006); *Beyond Jihad, Critical Voices from the Inside*. Academica Press, LLC. Bethesda.

14. (Ed.) Spencer, Robert (2005); *The Myth of Islamic Tolerance. How Islamic Law Treats Non-Muslims*. Prometheus Books. NY.

15. (Eds) Svi Shapiro and David E. Purpel (2008); *Critical Social Issues in American Education: Democracy and Meaning in a Globalizing World*. Lawrence Erlbaum Associates, Inc. Publishers. New Jersey.

16. (Ed.) Warraq, Ibn (2002); *What the Koran really says – Language, Text and Commentary*. Prometheus books. NY.

17. (Eds) Jayaram, N and Saberwal, Satish (1996); *Social conflict*. OUP, New Delhi, India.

18. (Prof.) Hasan, Ahmad (2001); *Al-Sunaan, a collection of Hadith, Vol. - 1 (Abu Dawud, Sulayman b. al-Ash'ath)*. Kitab Bhavan. New Delhi. India.

19. (Sir) Muir William (1992); *The Life of Muhammad* (first published in London in 1894). Reprinted by Voice of India. Delhi. India.

20. (Sir) Sarkar, Jadunath (1972); *The History of Aurangazeb*. Vol. 3. Orient Longman. India.

21. (Trans) Wolf, Kenneth B. (1978); *Conversion and Continuity: Indigenous Christian Communities in Islamic Lands, eighth to eighteenth Centuries*. Pontifical Institute of Mediaeval Studies. Toronto.

22. (Trans.) Seale, M. S (1978); *Qur'an and Bible: Studies in Interpretation and Dialogue*. Croom Helm Ltd. London.

23. (Trans.) Sheridan, Alan (1999); *The Fabric of Affect in the Psycho-analytic Disclose*. Originally published as 'Le Discours Vivant' in France and authored by Andre Green in 1973. Hartnolls Ltd. Bodmin, Cornwall.

24. Abelard, Peter (1836); *Sic et non (yes and no) in Ouvrages inedits*, (ed. V). Cousin. Paris.

25. Abhedananda, Swami (2005); *Life Beyond Death – A Critical Study of Spiritualism*. Ramakrishna Vedanta Math. Kolkata. India.

26. AbuKhalil, As'ad (2002); *Bin Laden, Islam, and America's new "war on terrorism"*. Seven Stories Press. NY.

27. Adil, Hajjah Amina (2002); *Muhammad, the messenger of Islam: his life & prophecy*. Islamic Supreme Council of America. Washington DC.

28. Ahmed, A. A (2006); *The Hidden Life of The Prophet Muhammad*. AuthorHouse. Indiana.

29. Al-Ghazali, Abu Hamid al-Tulsi (1993); *Ihya' Ulum al-Din (Revival of Religious Learnings)*. Translated in English in four volumes by Fazl-ul-Karim. Darul Ishat, Urdu Bazar, Karachi, Pakistan.

30. Ali, Ayaan Hirsi (2007); *Infidel*. Free Press. NY.

31. Al-Kindy, Farahat (2005); *The Comprehensive Guide For Da'wah In Mosques (Masjids)*. Ahmad Al-Fateh Islamic Center. Bassam Bokhowa Publishers. Bahrain.

32. Amarasingam, Amarnath (2010); *Religion and the New Atheism: A Critical Appraisal*. Koninklijke Brill N V, Leiden.

33. Andrae, Tor (1955); *Mohammed, the Man and His Faith*. (trans.) Theophil Menzel. Harper & Row Publishers. NY.

34. Archer, John Clark (1924); *Mystical Elements in Mohammed*. Yale University Press. USA.

35. Armstrong, Karen (2006); *Muhammad: A Biography of the Prophet*. Phoenix Press. A division of the Orion Publishing Group Ltd. London.

36. Armstrong, Karen (2006); *Islam: A Short History*. Phoenix Press. A division of the Orion Publishing Group Ltd. London.

37. Aslan, Reza (2006); *No God but God*. Arrow books. The Random House Group Ltd. London.

38. Azad, Humayun (1995); *Nari* (woman), originally in Bengali. Revised third edition. September 1995. Agami Prakasani. Dhaka, Bangladesh.

39. Badlani, Hiro G. (2008); *Hinduism: Path of the Ancient Wisdom*. iUniverse. Bloomington.

40. Barkey, Henri J., and Graham E. Fuller (1998); *Turkey's Kurdish Question. Carnegie Commission on Preventing Deadly Conflict Series*. Rowman and Littlefield Publishers. USA.

41. Bart, Simon (2002); *Undead science: science studies and the afterlife of cold fusion*. Rutgers University Press. New Jersey.

42. Barthelemy, Jean-Dominique and Ryan, Stephen D. (1963); *God and His Image: An Outline of Biblical Theology*. Continuum International Book Publishing. London.

43. Beck, Aaron T. and Freeman, Arthur (1990); *Cognitive Therapy of Personality Disorders*. The Guilford Press. NY.

44. Becker, Carl Heinrich (1909); *Islam and Christianity*. Bibliolife. London.

45. Beckerlegge, Gwilym (1998); *World religions reader*. Routledge. NY.

46. Bell R. and Watt W. M. (1977); *Introduction to the Quran*. Edinburgh University Press. UK.

47. Benjamin, Lorna Smith (1996); *Interpersonal diagnosis and treatment of personality disorders*. The Guilford Press. A division of the Guilford publications Inc. NY.

48. Bhattacharyya, S.K (1987); *Genocide in East Pakistan / Bangladesh*. Published by A. Ghosh. Houston.

49. Blunt E and Blunt G.W (1830); *The American Annual Register for the year 1827-28-29.* NY.

50. Bowie, Bob and Bowie, Robert A. (2004); *Ethical Studies.* Nelson Thornes Ltd. Cheltenham. UK.

51. Bradely, John R (2005); *Saudi Arabia exposed.* Palgrave Macmillan. NY.

52. Britton, Ronald (2003); *Sex, death, and the super-ego: experiences in psychoanalysis.* H. Carnac (Books) Ltd. London.

53. Caird, John (1956); *An introduction to the philosophy of religion.* Chakravarti and Chatterjee Publishers. Calcutta. India.

54. Caner, Ergun Mehmet and Caner Emir Fethi (2002); *Unveiling Islam.* Kregel Publications. USA.

55. Cappi, Michael (2007); *A Never Ending War.* Trafford Publishing. Victoria. Canada.

56. Carlyle, T (1973); *Sartor Resartus: On Heroes and Hero Worship.* Everyman's library. London.

57. Charles R. H. (1999); *The Book of the Secrets of Enoch.* Book Tree. USA.

58. Chase Frederic H (1958); *Saint John of Damascus: writings.* "Fathers of the Church" series. NY.

59. Checkley, Hervey (1976); *The Mask of Sanity.* St. Louis, MO, Mosby. USA.

60. Claxton, G (2002); *The Wayward Mind: An Intimate History of the Unconscious.* Little Brown. London.

61. Clayton, C. J., Barlow S. H., and Ballif-Spanvill B. (1998); *Principles of group violence with a focus on terrorism.* In *Collective violence*, edited by H. V. Hall and L. C. Whitaker. Boca Raton, FL: CRC Press.

62. Clifford W.K (1897); *The ethics of belief, in Lectures and Essays.* Macmillan. London.

63. Cohen, Jared (2007); *Children of Jihad.* Gotham Books. Penguin Group (USA). NY.

64. Compton, Michael T. and Kotwicki, Raymond J. (2007); *Responding to individuals with mental illnesses.* Jones and Bartlett Publishers. Sudbury, Massachusetts.

65. Cook, David (2005); *Understanding Jihad.* University of California Press. USA.

66. Cook, David (2007); *Martyrdom in Islam.* Cambridge University Press. USA.

67. Cook, Michael and Crone, Patricia (1977); *Hagarism: The making of the Islamic world.* Cambridge.

68. Copi, Irving and Cohen, Carl (1994); *Introduction to logic*, Ninth Edition (January, 2000). Prentice-Hall (India), New Delhi. India.

69. Coughlin, Kathryn M. (2006); *Muslim cultures today: a reference guide.* Greenwood Press. Westport.

70. Crayton, J. W. (1983); *Terrorism and Psychology of the Self.* L. Z. Freedman, and Y. Alexander (Eds), Perspectives on Terrorism. Scholarly Resources. Wilmington, Delaware.

71. Crenshaw, M. (1986); *The psychology of political terrorism.* In M.G. Hermann (Ed.) Political psychology: contemporary problems and issues. Jossey-Bass. London.

72. Crone, Patricia (1987);*Roman, Provincial and Islamic Law: The Origins of the Islamic Patronate.* Cambridge.

73. Dagher, Hamdun (1995); *The Position of Women in Islam.* Light of Life. Villach. Austria.

74. Dasti, Ali (1985); *Twenty Three Years.* George Allen & Unwin. London.

75. Dawkins, Richard (2006); *The God Delusion.* Bantam Press. GB.

76. Desai, Meghnad (2007); *Rethinking Islamism – The Ideology of the New Terror*. T.J International Ltd. Padstow. Cornwall. GB.

77. Donaldson-Pressman Stephanie and Pressman Robert M. (1997); *The Narcissistic Family: Diagnosis and Treatment*. Jossey-Bass. A Wiley Company. San Francisco.

78. Downing, Terry Reese (2009); *Martyrs in Paradise: Woman of Mass Destruction*. Author House Publication. Bloomington. USA.

79. Durant, Will and Durant, Ariel (1961); *The story of civilization – The age of reason begins*. Simon and Schuster. NY.

80. Durant, Will (1950); *The story of civilization – The age of faith*. Simon and Schuster. NY.

81. Durant, Will (2006); *The Story of Philosophy*. Pocket Books, a division of Simon & Schuster. NY.

82. Durkheim, Emile (1897); *Suicide,* 1951 Edition, The Free Press. NY.

83. Engler, Barbara (2009); *Personality Theories*. Eighth edition. Houghton Miffin Harcourt Publishing Company. Boston.

84. Eraly, Abraham (1997); *The Last Springs -- The Lives and Times of Great Mughals*. First edition. Penguin books. New Delhi, India.

85. Ernst W. Carl (2005); *Following Muhammad: Rethinking Islam in the Contemporary World*. Yoda Press. New Delhi, India.

86. Etheredge, Cole (2005); *The Price of Ignorance*. iUniverse. Lincoln. USA.

87. Evans, Joseph Claude (1984); *The metaphysics of transcendental subjectivity: Descartes, Kant, and W. Sellars*. B. R Grunter Publishing Company. The Netherlands.

88. Fallaci, Oriana (2006); *The Force of Reason*. Rizzoli International Publication Inc. NY.

89. Farmer, Brian R. (2007); *Understanding Radical Islam: Medieval Ideology in the Twenty-first Century*. Peter Lang Publishing Inc. NY.

90. Feuer, L. (1969); *The Conflict of Generations: The Character and Significance of Student Movements*. Basic Books Inc. Publishers. NY.

91. Fletcher, Richard (2003); *The Cross and the Crescent*. Penguin Books. London.

92. Flores, Philip J. (2004); *Addiction as an attachment disorder*. Rowman & Littlefield Publishers Inc. USA.

93. Fowler, Samuel Whittemore (2010); *Afoot and Delighthearted*. XULON Press. USA.

94. Foxe, John (1827); *Foxe's Book of martyrs: being a complete history of the lives, sufferings and Deaths of the Christian Martyrs*. Charles Gaylord, Boston.

95. Freud, Sigmund (1979); *On Psychopathology: Inhibitions, Symptoms and Anxiety and other Disorders*. Penguin Books. NY.

96. Freud, Sigmund (1989); *Civilization and Its Discontent*. W. W Norton & Company Inc. NY.

97. Fried, R. (1982); *The psychology of the terrorist*. In *Terrorism and beyond: An international conference on terrorism and low-level conflict*, edited by B. M. Jenkins. Santa Monica.

98. Frieling, Rudolf (1978); *Christianity and Islam*. Floris Books, Edinburgh.

99. Fromm, Erich (1978); *Psychoanalysis and Religion*. Yale University Press. London.

100. Fromm, Erich (1964); *The Heart of Man: Its Genius For Good and Evil*. Harper and Row, NY.

101. Gandhi. M. K (1961); *My philosophy of life*. Pearl publications, Mumbai, India.

102. Gay, P. (1987); *A Godless Jew*. Yale University Press. New Haven.

103. Geiler, N. L and Saleeb, Abdul (2002); *Answering Islam – the Crescent in the light of Cross.* 2nd edition. BakerBooks. Michigan. USA.

104. Gibb, H.A.R (1969); *Mohammedanism: A Historical Survey.* Oxford University Press. UK.

105. Gibbon, E (1941); *Decline and fall of Roman Empire.* Vol. 5. Everyman's Library. London.

106. Goel, Sita Ram (1987); *The Calcutta Quran Petition.* Voice of India.

107. Goldziher, Ignaz (1971); *Muslim Studies.* Edited by S. M Stern. Allen and Unwin. London.

108. Goodwin, Jan (1994); *Price of Honour.* 2006 Edition. Sphere. London.

109. Guillaume, A (1955); *The Life of Muhammad*: A translation of Ibn Ishaq's Sirat Rasul Allah (Ibn Hisham's notes). OUP, Oxford.

110. Guillaume, A (1978); *Islam.* Harmondsworth. UK.

111. Gunny A (1996); *Images of Islam in Eighteenth Century Writing.* Grey Seal, London.

112. Hagee, John (2007); *Jerusalem Countdown.* Front Line. Lake Mary. Florida.

113. Hare, Robert D. (1993); *Without Conscience: The Disturbing World of the Psychopaths Among Us.* The Guilford Press. A Division of Guilford Publications. Inc. NY.

114. Hassan, Steven (1990); *Combatting Cult Mind Control.* Park Street Press. Rochester. USA

115. Haykal, Muhammad Husayn (1976); *The Life of Muhammad,* translated by Isma'il Razi A. al-Faruqi (from eighth edition). Chapter 5: From the beginning of Revelation to the Conversion of Umar; Chapter 8: From the Violation of the Boycott to al Isra'. American Trust Publications. Plainfield. USA.

116. Hecht, Jennifer Michael (2004); *Doubt: A History: The Great Doubters and Their Legacy of Innovation from Socrates and Jesus to Thomas Jefferson and Emily Dickinson.* HarperSanFrancisco.

117. Hick, John. H. (1993); *Philosophy of Religion.* Prentice-Hall of India, Mumbai, India.

118. Hitchens, Christopher (2007); *The Portable Atheist: Essential Readings for the Non-believer.* Da Capo Press. Perseus Books. Philadelphia.

119. Hitti, Philip K (2002); *History of the Arabs,* First published in 1937, revised tenth edition, Palgrave Macmillion, Basingstoke, UK.

120. Hotchkiss, Sandy (2003); *Why is It always About You? The Seven Deadly Sins of Narcissism.* Free Press. NY

121. Hume, David (1992); *An Enquiry Concerning Human Understanding.* Progressive publishers. Calcutta. India.

122. Huntington, Samuel (1996); *The Clash of Civilizations and the Remaking of World Order.* Viking. Penguin books. New Delhi. India.

123. Hunsicker, A. (2006); *Understanding International Counter Terrorism: A Professional's Guide to the Operational Art.* Universal Publishers. Florida.

124. Hurd, Geoffrey and associates (1986); *Human societies – An introduction to sociology.* Routledge & Kegan Paul. GB.

125. Husain, Ed (2007); *The Islamist.* Penguin Books. London.

126. Ignatieff, M. (1998). *The Warrior's Honour. Ethnic War and the Modern Conscience.* Penguin Books. Toronto.

127. Iyengar, B.K S (1976); *Light on Yoga.* Schochen Books, NY.

128. Jeffery, Arthur (1937); *Materials for the History of the Text of the Qur'an*. Leiden. Netherlands.

129. Jung, C.G (1933); *Modern Man in Search of A Soul*. A Harvest Book. Houghton Mifflin Harcourt Publishing Company. NY.

130. Kaleeby (2002); *Dictionary of the Qur'anic Phrases and its Meaning*. Compiled by Sheik Mousa Ben Mohammed Al Kaleeby, Maktabat Al Adab, Cairo. Egypt.

131. Keller, Nuh Ha Mim (1999); *Reliance of the Traveller*, A Classic Manual of Islamic Sacred Law. Amana Publications. Beltsville, Maryland.

132. Kennedy, Hugh (2008); *The Great Arab Conquests: How the Spread of Islam changed the World we live in*. Phoenix. Orion Books Ltd. London.

133. Kernberg, Otto (1985); *Hysterical and Histrionic Personality Disorders*, in Psychiatry vol. 1, edited by R. Michels and J.O Cavenar. Philadelphia; Lippincott.

134. Khalid Muhammad Khalid (2005); *Successors of the Messenger* (English Translation of al Khulafa al Rasool: Biographies of the Five Rightly Guided Caliphs of Islam). Dar Al-Kotob Al-Ilmiyah Publishing House. Beirut. Lebanon.

135. Khan, M.A (2009); *Islamic Jihad: A Legacy of Forced Conversion, Imperialism, and Slavery*. iUniverse, Inc. NY.

136. Kline. P (1972); *Fact and Fantasy in Freudian Theory*, Methuen & Co Ltd, London.

137. Knap, Stephen (2009); *Crimes Against India, and the Need to Protect Its Ancient Vedic Tradition*. iUniverse. Bloomington.

138. Kohut, Heinz (1977); *The Restoration of the self*. International Universities Press. NY.

139. Lachkar, Joan (2008); *How to Talk to a Narcissist*. Routledge. Taylor and Francis Group. USA.

140. Leaman, Oliver (2006); *The Qur'an: an encyclopedia*. Routledge. Abingdon.

141. Lewis, Bernard (2003); *The Assassins*. Phoenix. London.

142. Lewis, H. D (1961); *Philosophy of Religion*. The English Universities Press. London.

143. Maberry, Jonathan (2008); *Bad Moon Rising*. Kensington Publishing Corp. NY.

144. Mahmoud, Omar (2008); *Muhammad: An Evolution of God*. AuthorHouse. Bloomington.

145. Mahmud, Abdel Haleem (1978); *The Creed of Islam*. World of Islam Festival Trust.

146. Manji, Irshad (2004); *The Trouble with Islam Today. A Wake up Call for Honesty and Challenge*. Mainstream Publishing Company (Edinburg) Ltd.

147. Marcuse, Herbert (1972); *Eros and Civilization: A Philosophical Inquiry into Freud*. Abacus Books. USA.

148. Margoliouth, David Samuel (1914); *The Early Development of Mohammedanism*. Charles Scribner's Sons. NY.

149. Margoliouth, David Samuel (2010); *Mohammed and the Rise of Islam*. Cosimo Classics. NY

150. Martin, Gus (2010); *Understanding Terrorism: Challenges, Perspectives, and Issues*. SAGE Publications Inc. California.

151. Marvasti, Jamshid A. (2004); *Psychiatric treatment of sexual offenders: treating the past traumas in Traumatizers: A Bio-Psycho Social Perspective*. Charles C. Thomas Publisher Ltd. Illinois.

152. Masterson, J.F (1981); *The Narcissistic and Borderline Disorders. An Integrated Developmental approach*. Brunner-Routhe. NY.

153. Masterson, J. F (1990); *The Search for the Real Self.* The Free Press (A division of the Simon & Schuster Inc.). NY.

154. Matos, Julio (2009); *Welcome to the End Times.* Holy Fire Publishing. Summerville.

155. McAuliffe, Jane Dammen (2006); *The Cambridge companion to the Qur'an.* Cambridge University Press. UK.

156. McCarthy, Andrew C. (2010); *The Grand Jihad: How Islam and the Left Sabotage America.* Encounter Books. NY.

157. McCloud, Sean (2004); *Making the American religious fringe: exotics, subversives, and journalists (1955 - 1993).* The University of North Carolina Press. USA.

158. McGinniss, Joe (1989); *Fatal Vision.* New American Library. NY.

159. Merz-Perez, Linda and Heide, Kathleen M (2004); *Animal cruelty: pathway to violence against people.* AltaMira Press. A division of Rowman. Littlefield Publishers, Inc. Lanham, UK.

160. Miller, Judith (1997); *God Has Ninety-nine Names: Reporting From a Militant Middle East.* Touchstone. Simon & Schuster. USA.

161. Monte, C.F. (1995); *Beneath the Mask: An Introduction to Theories of Personality.* Harcourt Brace College Publishers. NY.

162. Morf, G. (1970); *Terror in Quebec – Case Studies of the FLQ.* Clark, Irwin. Toronto.

163. Morse, Chuck (2010); *The Nazi connection to Islamic Terrorism: Adolf Hitler and Amin al-Husseini.* WorldNetDaily. Washington DC.

164. Naipaul, V. S (1998); *Beyond Belief: Islamic Excursions among the Converted People.* Abacus. London.

165. Nasr, Vali (2007); *The Shia Revival: How Conflicts within Islam will shape the Future.* W. W Norton. NY

166. Nicholson, Reynold (1969); *A Literary History of the Arabs.* Oxford University Press.

167. O'Brien, Darcy (1985); *Two of a kind, the Hillside Stranglers.* New American Library. NY.

168. Oak, P.N (1996); *Islamic Havoc in Indian History.* Published by A. Ghosh. Houston.

169. Olson, Dean T. (2009); *Perfect enemy: the law enforcement manual of Islamist terrorism.* Charles C Thomas Pub Ltd. Springfield.

170. Ortberg, John (2008); *Faith and Doubt.* Zondervan. Michigan. USA.

171. Pafumi G. R. (2010); *Is Our Vision of God Obsolete?* Xlibris Corporation. USA.

172. Payeur, Bernard (2006); *Canada: The Fractured Nation Interviews. An Enquiry into the Breakup.* Trafford Publishing. Victoria, Canada.

173. Pearl, Mariane (2003); *A Mighty Heart: The Brave Life of My Husband Daniel Pearl.* Virago Press. GB.

174. Pearlstein, Richard M. (1991); *The Mind of the Political Terrorist.* Scholarly Resources, Wilmington, Delaware.

175. Peter, Anthony St (2010); *The Greatest Quotations of All-Time.* Xlibris Corporation. USA.

176. Peters, F.E (1986); *Jerusalem and Mecca: The topology of the Holy City in the near east.* New York University Press.

177. Peterson, Scott (2002); *Me Against My Brother: At War in Somalia, Sudan and Rwanda.* Routledge. London.

178. Phares, Walid (2005); *Future Jihad: Terrorist Strategies against the West.* Palgrave Macmillan. NY.

179. Pipes, Daniel (1983); *In the Path of God*. Transaction Publishers. New Brunswick. USA.

180. Pipes, Daniel (2003); *Militant Islam Reaches America*. Norton Paperback. USA.

181. Pipes, Daniel (2004); *Miniatures: views of Islamic and Middle Eastern politics*. Transaction Publishers. New Brunswick. USA.

182. Puckett, Newbell Niles; Hand, Wayland Debs; Casetta, Anna; Thiederman, Sondra B. (1981); *Popular beliefs and superstitions: a compendium of American folklore* (Volume 1). Ohio collection of Newbell Niles Puckett. Published by G.K. Hall & Co., Boston.

183. Radhakrishnan. S (1970); *The Present Crisis of Faith*. Orient Paperbacks. New Delhi, India.

184. Ralhan O.P (1998); *Encyclopedia of Political Parties, Volumes 33-50*. Anmol Publications Pvt Ltd. Daryaganj. New Delhi. India.

185. Ram Swarup (1984); *Understanding Islam through Hadis*. Voice of India.

186. Rao, K.L. Seshagiri (1990); *Mahatma Gandhi and Comparative Religion*. Motilal Banarsidass Publishers. Delhi. India.

187. Reich,W. (1998); *Understanding terrorist behavior: The limits and opportunities of psychological inquiry*. In *Origins of terrorism: Psychologies, ideologies, theologies, states of mind*, edited by W. Reich, Woodrow Wilson Center Press. Washington, DC.

188. Reyes, Christopher (2010); *In His Name*. AuthorHouse. Bloomington.

189. Richardson, Joel (2006a); *Antichrist: Islam's Awaited Messiah*. Pleasant Word. A division of WinePress Publishing. Enumclaw.

190. Richardson, Louise (2006); *What Terrorists Want – Understanding the Terrorist Threat*. John Murray publications. London.

191. Rippin, Andrew (1991); *Muslims: Their religious beliefs and practices. Volume 1*, Routledge. London.

192. Riviere Joan, Strachey James and Gay Peter (1960); *Sigmund Freud: The Ego and the Id*. W.W Norton & Company. NY.

193. Rodinson, Maxime (1980); *Muhammad* (Original in French, translated to English by Anne Carter). The New Press. NY.

194. Rodinson, Maxime (1981); *A Critical Survey of Modern Studies on Muhammad* in Studies on Islam ed. M. Swartz. NY.

195. Roy, Tathagata (2007); *A Suppressed Chapter in History – The Exodus of Hindus from East Pakistan and Bangladesh 1947 -2006*. Bookwell. New Delhi. India.

196. Russell, Bertrand (1950): *Unpopular Essays*, Chapter. X (Ideas that have harmed mankind), Simon and Schuster. NY.

197. Russell, Bertrand (1996); *Why I am Not a Christian and other Essays on Religion and related Subjects*. Routledge. Taylor and Francis Group. Abingdon. UK.

198. Russell, Bertrand (2009); *Marriage and Morals*. Routledge. NY.

199. Sagan, Carl (1997); *The Demon Haunted World: Science as a Candle in the Dark*. Ballantine Books. Random House Inc. USA.

200. Salovey, Peter (1991); *The Psychology of Jealousy and Envy*. The Guilford Press. NY.

201. Sarat Rachanabali' (A complete work of Sarat Chandra Chattopadhyay) published by Sarat Samity, Calcutta. The quotations are taken from his essay 'Bartaman Hindu-Mussalman Samasya' which literally means, Contemporary Hindu- Muslim Problem. Chattopadhyay wrote this essay during 1926.

202. Savarkar, Veer (1985); *Six Glorious Epochs of Indian History*. Savarkar Prakashan, Bombay, India.

203. Scheff, T. J. (1990); *Microsociology: Discourse, emotion, and social structure*. The University of Chicago Press. Chicago.

204. Schimmel, Annemarie (1985); *And Muhammad is His messenger – The Veneration of the Prophet in Islamic Piety*. Chapel Hill. University of North Carolina Press.

205. Schmid, Alex P. (2011); *The Routledge Handbook of Terrorism Research*. Routledge. NY.

206. Schuon, Frithjof (1980); *Stations of Wisdom*. Perennial Books, London.

207. Seals, David L. (1968); *International Encyclopedia of the social sciences, Vol. 5*. The Macmillan Company and the Free Press. NY.

208. Shaikh, Anwar (1995); *Islam: The Arab National Movement*. The Principality Publisher. Cardiff. UK.

209. Shaikh, Anwar (1998); *Islam and Human Rights and Other Essays*, Published by A. Ghosh, Houston, USA.

210. Shaikh, Anwar (1999); *Islam: Sex and Violence*. Published by A. Ghosh. Houston.

211. Shaikh, Anwar (1999); *This is Jihad*, Published by A. Ghosh, Houston.

212. Sherif, Faruq (1995); *A Guide to the Contents of the Qur'an*. Garnet Publishing. UK.

213. Shourie, Arun (2002); *The World of Fatwas*. Rupa & Co. New Delhi. India.

214. Shourie, Arun (2008); *Indian Controversies, Essays on Religion in Politics*. Rupa & Co. New Delhi. India

215. Sina, Ali (2008); *Understanding Muhammad, a Psychobiography of Allah's Prophet*. Felibri.com. USA.

216. Smith, Jane Idleman and Haddas Yvonne. Y (2002); *The Islamic Understanding of Death and Resurrection*. OUP. NY.

217. Smith, Wilfred Cantwell (1981); *On understanding Islam: selected studies*. Mouton publishers. The Hague. The Netherlands.

218. Snow, Robert L. (2003); *Deadly Cults: The Crimes of True Believers*. Praeger Publishers. CT. USA.

219. Spencer, Robert (2002); *Islam Unveiled: Disturbing Questions about the World's Fastest-growing Faith*. Encounter Books. San Francisco.

220. Spencer, Robert (2003); *Onward Muslim Soldiers: How Jihad still threatens America and the West*. Regnery Publishing. Washington DC.

221. Spencer, Robert (2005); *The politically incorrect guide to Islam (and the crusades)*. Regnery Publishing. Washington DC.

222. Spencer, Robert (2006); *The Truth about Muhammad*. Regnery Publishing. Washington DC.

223. Spencer, Robert (2007); *Religion of Peace? Why Christianity is and Islam isn't*. Regnery Publishing. Washington DC.

224. Spencer, Robert (2009); *The Complete Infidel's Guide to the Koran*. Regnery Publishing Washington DC.

225. Sproul R. C and Saleeb, Abdul (2003); *The Dark Side of Islam*. Crossway Books (a division of Good News Publishers). Wheaton. Illinois.

226. Stevenson. L and Haberman. D.L (2004); *Ten Theories of Human Nature*, Oxford University Press. London.

227. Stout, Martha (2005); *The Sociopath Next Door*. Broadway Books (a division of Random House. Inc). NY.

228. Strachey, James and Gay, Peter (1961); *Sigmund Freud: The Future of an Illusion*. W.W Norton & Company. NY.

229. Strachey, James and Gay, Peter (1966); *Sigmund Freud: Introductory Lectures on Psycho-analysis*. W.W Norton & Company. NY.

230. Stroumsa, Sarah (1999); *Freethinkers of medieval Islam: Ibn al-Rawāndī, Abū Bakr al-Rāzī and their Impact on Islamic Thought*. Koninkaijke Brill NV. Leiden. Netherlands.

231. Syed M. H. (2004); *History of Delhi sultanate*. Anmol Publications Pvt. Ltd. New Delhi. India.

232. Tallis, F (2002); *Hidden Minds: A History of the Unconscious*. Areade Publishing. NY.

233. Taylor, Maxwell, and Ethel Quayle (1994); *Terrorist Lives*. Brassey's, London.

234. Tisdall, W. St. C. (1894); *The Religion of the Crescent or, Islam: Its Strength, Its Weakness, Its Origin, Its Influence*. 4th edition published in 1916. SPCK London.

235. Tomkins, Silvan (1995); *Shame and Its Sisters*. Duke University Press, Durham. North Carolina.

236. Toynbee, Arnold (1935); *A Study of History* (Volume - III). OUP. GB.

237. Trifkovic, Serge (2002); *The Sword of the Prophet*. Regina Orthodox Press. Boston.

238. Trifkovic, Serge (2006); *Defeating Jihad: How the War on Terror may yet be own, in spite of ourselves*. Regina Orthodox Press. Boston.

239. Twenge Jean M and Campbell W. Keith (2010); *The Narcissism Epidemic*. Free Press. A Division of Simon and Schuster Inc. NY.

240. Vaknin, Sam (1999); *Malignant Self Love. Narcissism Revisited*. Narcissus Publications. Skopje. Prague. Czech Republic.

241. Vivekananda, Swami (1947); *Complete Works of Swami Vivekananda, Volume 1*. Vedanta Press & Bookshop. Los Angeles.

242. Voltaire (Francois-Marie Arouet) (1745); *Letter to Benedict XIV* (written in Paris on August 17, 1745).

243. Vygotskii, Lev Semenovich and Rieber, Robert W (1998); *The Collected Works of L.S. Vygotsky: Child psychology Vol. 5 (Child Psychology)*. Plenum Press. NY.

244. Walker, Benjamin (2002); *Foundation of Islam, the Making of a World Faith*. Rupa & Co. New Delhi. India.

245. Warraq, Ibn (1995); *Why I am Not a Muslim*. Prometheus Books. NY.

246. Warraq, Ibn (1998); *The Origins of the Koran, Classic Essays on Islam's Holy Book*. Prometheus Books. NY.

247. Warraq, Ibn (2000); *The Quest for the Historical Muhammad*. Prometheus Books. NY.

248. Warraq, Ibn (2003); *Leaving Islam, Apostates Speak Out*. Prometheus Books. NY.

249. Weston, Mark (2008); *Prophets and Princes: Saudi Arabia from Muhammad to the Present*. John Wiley and Sons. USA and Canada.

250. Winn, Craig (2004); *Prophet of Doom. Islam's terrorist Dogma in Muhammad's own Words*. Cricketsong books. A division of Virginia publishers. Canada.

251. Winnicott, D. W. (1960); *Ego Distortion in Terms of True and False Self*, in 'The Maturational Process and the Facilitating Environment: Studies in the Theory of Emotional Development'. International UP Inc. NY.

252. Wolman, Benjamin (1999); *Antisocial Behavior, Personality Disorders from Hostility to Homicide*. Prometheus books. NY.

253. Zarctsky, E (2004); *Secrets of the Soul: A Social and Cultural History of the Psychoanalysis*. Vintage Books. NY.

254. Zayn Cynthia and Dibble Kevin (2007); *Narcissistic Lovers – How to Cope, Recover and Move On*. New Horizon Press. New Jersey.

255. Zell-Ravenheart, Oberon (2004); *Grimoire for the Apprentice Wizard*. The Career Press. Franklin Lakes. New Jersey.

Internet

1. Admin (2010); *Hallucination – Causes of Hallucination*. URL: http://cure4migraine.net/2010/02/hallucination-causes-of-hallucination/ (Last accessed October 02, 2011)

2. Ghamidi J. A, Zaheer K., Sina, A (2007); *Probing Islam*. Faith Freedom International. URL: http://www.news.faithfreedom.org/downloads/probing-islam.pdf (Last accessed October 07, 2010).

3. Glazov, Jamie and Warner, Bill (2007); *The Study of Political Islam*. An interview of Bill Warner published on February 05, 2007. FrontPageMagazine.com. URL: http://97.74.65.51/readArticle.aspx?ARTID=297 (Last accessed November 19, 2011)

4. Haleem, M A S Abdel (1992); *Grammatical Shift For The Rhetorical Purposes: Iltifat And Related Features In The Qur'an*. Bulletin of the School of Oriental and African Studies, 1992, Volume LV, Part 3 at Islamic Awareness. URL: http://www.islamic-awareness.org/Quran/Text/Grammar/iltifaat.html (Last accessed July 03, 2011).

5. Islam-Watch (2007); *Twenty Three Years: A Study of the Prophetic Career of Mohammad*. Published on February 18, 2007. URL: http://www.islam-watch.org/Ali_Dasti/Twenty-Three-Years-of-Muhammad1.htm (Last accessed November 02, 2011)

6. Kasem, Abul (2007); *Activities of Allah*. Published on Islam-Watch on January 06, 2007. URL: http://www.islam-watch.org/AbulKasem/BismiAllah/9a.htm (Last accessed November 02, 2011)

7. Lester, Toby (1999); *What Is the Koran?* Atlantic Monthly January 1999 issue. URL: http://www.theatlantic.com/doc/199901/koran (Last accessed August 03, 2011).

8. MEMRI (2002); *An Interview with the Mother of a Suicide Bomber*. Published by the Middle East Media Research Institute on September 19, 2002. URL: http://memri.org/bin/articles.cgi?Page=archives&Area=sd&ID=SP39102 (Last accessed April 21, 2011)

9. Noor Allah Marqadah, (2010); *New Page 4 - Official Website of Silsila-i-Aalia Owaisia Qadria.* Maintained by Owaisi Qalander Foundation. URL: http://www.chiefqalander.org/English/Frames/Main.htm (Last accessed August 19, 2011).

10. Rappoport, Alan (2009); *Co-Narcissism: How We Accommodate to Narcissistic Parents*. URL: http://www.alanrappoport.com/Co-Narcissism%20Article.pdf (Last accessed December 10, 2011)

11. Salih, Mumin (2009); *It is Official: Muslims Reinterpret the Quran!* Published on Islam-Watch. URL: http://www.islam-watch.org/MuminSalih/Muslims-Reinterpret-Quran.htm (Last accessed November 27, 2011)

12. Shaikh, Anwar (1998a); *ISLAM: The Arab Imperialism*. (Unpublished in print, but available as an e-book on Islam-watch). URL: http://www.islam-watch.org/AnwarSheikh/Islam-Arab-Imperialism.htm (Last accessed August 02, 2011).

13. Smith, Saleem (2009); *Considerations of a Canadian Ex-Muslim*. URL: http://www.considerationsofacanadianex-muslim.org/conclusions.html (Last accessed September 02, 2010)

14. Taher, Abul (2000); *Querying the Koran.* The Guardian. Guardian News and Media Limited. Published on August 08, 2000. URL: http://www.guardian.co.uk/Archive/Article/0,4273,4048586,00.html (Last accessed November 03, 2011)

15. Vaknin, Sam (2003); *The Inverted Narcissist*. URL: http://www.9types.com/movieboard/messages/13677.html (Last accessed August 19, 2011)

16. Vaknin, Sam (2004); *Narcissistic Leaders.* Knowledgerush. URL: http://www.gorgelink.org/freebooks/vaknin/branded/Politics_19753.pdf (Last accessed December 11, 2011)

17. Vaknin, Sam (2006); *The Developmental Psychology of Psychopathology* (PDF, 2nd edition). A Narcissus Publications Imprint, Skopje 2006. URL: http://www.narcissistic-abuse.com/development.pdf (Last accessed November 03, 2011)

Acknowledgement

If I were a malignant Narcissist myself like the Prophet Muhammad, I would write my acknowledgement something like this,

These acknowledgements will be very short, because I have nothing much to acknowledge. I did all the work in this book. No one else did much because they were hardly competent. Sometimes they did suggest changes but I did not pay much attention, because I knew that they were always wrong even before they said anything. But I allowed them to speak only when they praised my work. If you do not like the book blame them. But if you like the stuff, then do not forget, it was me, and me only, who authored the book.

Of course I am kidding.

I could fill another book of equal size, describing the work of the people who have improved this one. This book would not exist without the help and excellent advising of many people who assisted me throughout the process of writing this one. My special thanks go to Ali Sina who had "shaped" this book from an unformed idea about Muhammad's narcissism to a full-fledged systematic research you just read. In addition there are many other people whom I owe thanks for various suggestions and constructive criticisms. I am grateful to all of them more than words can tell.

There are many unsung heroes, who are working, either openly or hiding, for a peaceful collapse of Islam and to liberate the Muslims from the evil grip of their Narcissist Prophet. They give their time and talent to awaken the world but ask nothing in return. To all these soldiers of truth and defenders of civilization against the Islamic barbarism, I would like to say few words – wherever you are, and however you are contributing to this struggle, my gratitude and thanks.